MW00812703

The Impossible Community
Realizing Communitarian Anarchism

John P. Clark

The Impossible Community: Realizing Communitarian Anarchism
John P. Clark
This edition © PM Press 2022
All rights reserved. No part of this book may be transmitted by any means without permission in writing from the publisher

ISBN: 978-1-62963-714-3 (paperback)
ISBN: 978-1-62963-778-5 (ebook)
Library of Congress Control Number: 2019933025

Cover design John Yates / www.stealworks.com
Interior design by briandesign

10 9 8 7 6 5 4 3 2 1

PM Press
PO Box 23912
Oakland, CA 94623
www.pmpress.org

Printed in the USA

Contents

Preface

This book is about the quest for the free community, the community of liberation and solidarity. It seeks to convey the message that we need to think more deeply and carefully about the meaning of free community, and about the obstacles that stand in the way of its realization. Above all, it seeks to convey the message: "Create it now."

Underlying this work is a sense of horror and a sense of hope. The horror arises from the fact that humanity is in the process of inflicting on the planet the sixth great mass extinction in the history of life on Earth, while at the same time we have the means to flourish without devastating the biosphere. The horror arises from the fact that over a billion human beings live in absolute poverty, suffering from chronic malnutrition and other ills, while we have much more than an adequate material basis for a good life for all. A question underlying everything here is why we continue to live in a state of denial and disavowal, and how we might emerge from that state.

The hope comes from the fact that we have long had an answer to these questions, and some have begun to make that answer a reality. The effective response to such an extreme denial of reality was discovered thousands of years ago. This response is that, first, we must do whatever is necessary to awaken ourselves from our deadened state, and to open ourselves up to reality, to others, to nature, to the things themselves. Second, we must dedicate ourselves to a path of liberation and solidarity. And third, we must find, here and now, a community of others who have taken the risk of awakening, and who are following the same path, for this the only way that the path can be sustained.

Acknowledgments

This work is inspired above all by the experience of community and solidarity. I would like to express my deep gratitude for the knowledge, support, and inspiration I have received from the many small groups, communities, cooperatives, publishing projects, research groups, and collectives in which I have participated, or to which I been close personally, over the years, and which have in various ways helped shape my thoughts and feelings about community.

Among these are the AMMA Center, *A Rivista Anarchica*, Black Pearl Mutual Aid and Pleasure Club, Blue Iris Sangha, Borsodi's Coffeehouse, Broadway Food Co-op, *Capitalism Nature Socialism*, Centro Studi Libertari, Common Ground Collective, Community Co-op, Creating Communities of Liberation and Solidarity Group, Crescent City Anti-Authoritarians, Delta Greens, *Divergences*, Earth First!, Ecosocialist Horizons, Family Farm Defenders, *Fifth Estate*, Freeport Watch, Free University of New Orleans, Frontyard Cooperative Preschool, Glad Day Books, Harvest Moon Co-op, Industrial Workers of the World, Innovative Education Coalition, Institute for Social Ecology, Iron Rail Bookstore & Library, Lha Charitable Trust, *Libertaria*, Louisiana Himalaya Association, Loyola Greens, *Mesechabe*, New Orleans Food Co-op, New Orleans Food Not Bombs, New Orleans Free School Network, New Orleans Friends Meeting, New Orleans Libertarian Alliance, New Orleans Philocafé, New Orleans Social Ecology Group, NOLA Anarchists, North American Anarchist Studies Network, Pax Christi New Orleans, Occupy NOLA, Oystershell Alliance, Planet Drum Foundation, *Psychic Swamp*, *Research on Anarchism*, Seventh Ward Soul Patrol, Solidarity Economy Group, "Street Named Desire" Collective, University Cooperative Preschool, and the ZigZag Study Group.

Portions of this book were published previously. We are grateful to the following publications and presses for their generous permission to reprint the text.

To *Situations: Project of the Radical Imagination*, a publication of The CUNY Graduate Center, for portions of Chapter 2: Critique of the Gotham Program.

To Manchester University Press for portions of Chapter 5: Anarchy and the Dialectic of Utopia.

To *Capitalism Nature Socialism* for portions of Chapter 6: The Microecology of Community, Chapter 8: Disaster Anarchism, and Chapter 9: The Common Good.

To *Perspectives in Anarchist Theory* for portions of Chapter 7: Bridging the Unbridgeable Chasm.

To Guilford Press for portions of Chapter 10: Beyond the Limits of the City.

To the *Journal of Environmental Thought and Education* and *Sougou Ningengaku (Synthetic Anthropology)* for portions of Chapter 3: The Third Concept of Liberty.

To *Truthout* for the original version of "Postscript: On Grassroots Revolution".

■ 1

Introduction: In Search of the Impossible Community

In contemporary political theory, libertarianism and communitarianism are usually looked upon as occupying opposite ends of the political spectrum. Thus, this work, which is in large part the elaboration of a libertarian communitarianism, might be met with a certain skepticism and, indeed, might even be dismissed as entirely self-contradictory. But such reactions would reveal more than anything the unfortunate limits of contemporary political discourse and, more particularly, those of its dominant Anglo-American forms of expression. The actual existence of a phenomenon is a powerful argument in favor of its possibility. And there is, in fact, a long tradition of libertarian communitarian thought, a tradition that possesses considerable coherence and consistency. There exists, moreover, a vast range of historical phenomena that have inspired this tradition, and which instantiate many of its claims concerning social possibilities. The goal here is not only to continue this tradition and defend it, but also to explore what it would mean to realize its most radical implications. It is to show how a radically anarchistic conception of freedom and a radically communitarian conception of solidarity complement and fulfill one another. It is to show, to paraphrase Bakunin, that liberty without solidarity is privilege and injustice, while solidarity without liberty is slavery and despotism. It is to defend the thesis that it is to the degree that these values are synthesized in the free community that both injustice and despotism can be avoided.

It might, moreover, seem paradoxical that the free community that is our object of concern is described as "impossible." In a variation on a popular theoretical parlor game, we might compare the "possibilities" and "impossibilities" that are relevant here to the famous "knowns" and "unknowns" identified by former defense secretary Donald Rumsfeld. His goal was to direct the public's attention to certain "unknown unknowns" (specifically, certain unknown and ultimately nonexistent weapons of mass destruction) about which it should be appropriately terrified. In the present discussion, our approach is ontological rather than epistemological, replacing "knowns" and "unknowns" with "possibilities" and "impossibilities." In particular, we will focus on certain "Possible Impossibilities" about which we should be appropriately inspired (though they might be terrifying to some). "Possibility" will be used here in two senses. In the first sense, it will mean that which is *actually* possible, given the nature of things. In the second sense, it will mean that which is *ideologically* possible, that is, defined as possible according to the existing system of social determination.

Accordingly, there are four kinds of ideological possibilities: actually possible ideological possibilities, actually impossible ideological possibilities, actually possible ideological impossibilities, and actually impossible ideological impossibilities. Possible Possibilities include everything from supplying everyone in the world with one or more cell phones with increasingly bad reception to putting the proverbial "man" on the proverbial "moon." Impossible Possibilities include all the "false promises" of the dominant system, from infinitely expanding abundance based on devastation of the biosphere to harmonious social order based on egoistic competition for wealth and status. Possible Impossibilities include things that are possible only in "another world" beyond the present system of social determination and social domination. One such thing is the Impossible Community discussed here. Finally, Impossible Impossibilities include objects of fantasy that might be quite marvelous to dream about, but which it is pointless to "demand," and which should never be "taken for realities."

Free Community as the Concrete Universal

This work is an inquiry into the possibilities for the emergence of free community "in and for itself." At times, such a problematic will be expressed in terms of the Hegelian conception of ethical substance and the related distinction between a mere abstract moral ideal and a concrete social sphere in which the ethical—the immanently realized good—is embodied. It will be shown that, from this perspective, the moment of community "in itself" exists to the extent that (to mention the five spheres that are a central focus here) the social institutional structure, the social ethos, the social ideology, the social imaginary, and the social materiality form an effective material basis for free community—that is, for both historically realized freedom and historically grounded solidarity. The concrete universal (the community as universal particular) is expressed not in the mere externality of an institutional form, but through the embodiment of ethical substance in the form of life of the communal subject (an ethos that is in dialectical relationship with the *imaginary, ideological, institutional,* and *material* moments of communal being). The moment of community "for itself" exists to the extent that all these spheres have developed to the point that effective communal agency emerges.

For the free community, this means that universality expresses itself through particularity as that community creatively shapes its form of life through an open, attentive, and caring relationship to the concrete human and natural realities it encounters within and around itself. The word that Hegel generally uses for "universal" is *Allgemein*, which connotes that which is "common to all." The term he uses for "particular," *besonder*, has its origin in the idea of being separated, and is related to *sondern*, meaning "to sunder." These terms convey the idea that the concrete universal realizes the common through the particular, and brings together that which was separated. Accordingly, our concern will be, as it was for Debord and the Situationists, who inherited much of the same legacy, the "critique of separation." Beyond this critique, it will be to seek the real possibilities for solving the problem of separation, a problem that is identical with the problems of social domination, social alienation, and social antagonism. Our concern will be the problem of the world, that which situates all situations.

As part of this project, we will investigate what we might call the question of social ontological difference. This question addresses the difference between communal being and communal beings. We will explore the ways in which the latter beings presuppose the former way of being, which is close to what both Hegel and the communitarian anarchist philosopher Gustav Landauer called *Geist*.[1] Communal being is the irreducible, wholly gratuitous activity of free communal self-creation. It has nothing to do with *essence*, in the sense of a common quality that can be abstracted from beings or instantiated in them. It is, in fact, the very antithesis of the concept of an abstract universality (whether ethnic, racial, cultural, religious, or political) that infects essentialist communitarianism.

The most prominent, and certainly the most prolific, philosophical defender of dialectical thought today, Slavoj Žižek, draws a sharp distinction between the quest for the concrete universal and what he sees as the regressive project of communitarianism. The former, he says, "has nothing whatsoever to do with any kind of aesthetic organic totality, since it reflexively 'includes out' the very excess and/or gap that forever spoils such a totality—the irreducible and ultimately unaccountable gap between a series and its excess, between the Whole and the One of its exception, is the very terrain of 'concrete universality.'"[2] He concludes that "the true politico-philosophical heirs of Hegel," the true defenders of concrete universality, are not those "who endeavor to rectify the excesses of modernity via the return to some new form of organic substantial Order (like the communitarians)," but rather those "who fully endorse the political logic of the excess constitutive of every established Order."[3] More recently he has suggested that we should take from Hegel the idea that "the ultimate goal of every substantial ethical unity is to dissolve itself by giving rise to individuals who will assert their full autonomy against the substantial unity which gave birth to them."[4] The echoes of the Freudian Oedipal problematic are obvious. The failure to achieve autonomy results in, at best, a failure to come to terms with paternal authority and achieve full subjectivity, at worst, in bondage to the suffocating maternal, "organic" realm. As Žižek also states: "The direct choice of the 'concrete universality' of a particular ethical life world can only end in a regression to premodern organic society that denies the infinite right of subjectivity as the fundamental feature of modernity."[5]

Žižek is obviously right about the implications of typical defenses of "organic, substantial Order" (particularly the kind with an essentializing, disturbingly ouroboric, upper-case "O"). The concrete universal cannot, as he phrases it so aptly, be "the organic articulation of a whole in which each element plays its unique, particular but irreplaceable part."[6] The quest for such a totality has been one of the most disastrous illusions of civilization. Though in some ways it sounds like a kind of innocuous New Age romanticism, it also evokes the entire history of organicist authoritarian ideology from Plato (or a certain "Plato") through twentieth-century fascism. However, there is more than one variety of communitarianism, and more than one particular kind of "particular ethical life world." The communitarianism defended here does not espouse any "totality," aesthetic or otherwise, that is alleged to be full, complete, and "without remainder." Such closure is anathema to the anarchist communitarian vision. Perceptive exponents of anarchism have always accepted its paradoxical nature as both the party of plenitude and the party of excess. The question is not *whether* but rather *where* we can find that "excess-rectifying excess" that inevitably brings to ruin any project of totalization.

There are many ways in which the communitarian anarchist project differs from any totalizing project. Perhaps the most radical difference lies in the self-transformative, antiessentialist dimension, what might be called the Castoriadian moment of the communitarian anarchism (or anarchist communism) defended here.[7] This crucial moment of free, self-determining community lies in its quality of being the activity of the creative collective subject exercising the powers of the social imaginary, and demonstrating that it has no underlying substrate of communal essentiality, but rather always is what it is not and is not what it is. The free community is dynamic, self-disclosing *ethical substantiality* devoid of any underlying *metaphysical substance*. At the heart of free community lies a dialectic of social determination and creative self-negation and self-transformation. As in any case of authentic creativity, there is content that emerges ex nihilo. The creative process cannot be reduced entirely to the conditions out of which it arose, or there would be no moment of creativity. But, at the same time, the process cannot *create itself out of nothing*. It would be absurd to imagine that the creative matrix, the context that nurtures creativity, could itself be created ex nihilo.[8] There is a need for some positive grounding, and thus there is the possibility of a project, the possibility of evoking negative capability. The free community is a becoming-whole that presupposes that as *members of a community* the participants always "count themselves in," but *as members of a free association* they always also "count themselves out," since they and their community itself are in a constant process of going beyond any given communal bounds.

This is the experience of community that some have seen in struggles such as the Bolivian indigenous social movements. In their "Epilogue" to Raúl Zibechi's *Dispersing Power*, the Colectivo Situaciones conclude that "the common" that these movements seek to actualize "is not absolutely realizable—it is an open universality, unable to be grasped in its totality," so that community is not an already given reality, but "a coming about, an intent, a step forward."[9] The living community is never an object with complete being in itself, "organic" in Žižek's sense, with a fixed identity with which the members can simply identify. It is an "open universality" in that it is the terrain on which the dialectic between universality and particularity endlessly works itself out. For Situaciones, "the communitarian . . . activates by way of permanent differentiation," and the community "evades the crystallization initiatives or the freezing up of groups into institutional or state forms and at the same time electrifies popular energies. Dispersion, as a way of returning to the common, insists on combating its alienation into fixed and closed forms, including the closing up of the collective into pure communities."[10] The awakened, liberatory community, as the site of the emergence of universal particularity, is a self-negating and self-transcending whole. There is nothing "pure" about it other than the excessiveness of pure life.

In the Midst of Crisis

One of the crucial projects for contemporary critical social theory is the exploration of the significance of the constitutive exception. The dialectical analysis of such exceptionality constitutes one of the most revealing forms of immanent critique of historical social formations that are fraught with negativity and contradiction. One of the chapters to follow analyzes how the meaning of constitutive exceptionality, of being "the part of no part," can be disclosed in a moment of extreme crisis, in this case, the Hurricane Katrina disaster. But one must look to the conditions of life of more than a billion human beings who inhabit the great Third World megalopolises (a landscape of social disaster that Mike Davis analyzes so brilliantly in *Planet of Slums*[11]) to find the most significant realm of constitutive exceptionality within the global capitalist order. If, for many, New York, or perhaps London, is still "the City," for everyone, whether they know it or not, such places as Mumbai, Lagos, Mexico City, and Sao Paulo are the Truth of the City.

Yet it would be a mistake to look too hastily to this radical exceptionality as the royal road to some new revolutionary subjectivity. We might say that it is but one of many roads that lead in the general direction of such a subjectivity, for the reigning abstract universality is riddled with constitutive exceptionality. It is a highly self-contradictory, ideologically distorted universality, containing moments of both truth and falsehood. The system is indeed in the process of producing its own gravediggers, but it unfortunately never generates a convenient, readymade gravedigger identity, as it simultaneously produces class, racial, sexual, and other hierarchical identities. The way to concrete universality requires a painstaking exploration of often not very well-delineated regions of historical truth and falsehood, an experimentalist exploration that proceeds not merely through theory, but through transformative practice.[12]

The connection between the Impossible Community and this constitutive exceptionality is crucial. The historic role of the "part of no part" might be compared in some ways to that of the slave in Hegel's master–slave dialectic. The slave, by facing the reality of his or her own contingency (by facing mortality), goes through a crisis of selfhood that opens the way for a development of a higher critical and spiritual consciousness. This idea will be echoed at various points in the present discussion, particularly regarding the theme of crisis and how an awakening of empathy and of communal consciousness can arise out of it. Those who are thrown—either through permanent marginalization or immediate disaster—into the condition of being "the part of no part" experience such a crisis and the possibilities inherent in it. Zibechi says regarding the "formation of non-state powers" that "collective energies reappear in an infinity of instances, especially in disaster situations or those in which an individual alone cannot solve the problem."[13] What some experience when disaster strikes is what multitudes experience through the ongoing disaster of living on the periphery of a brutal world system. However, what emerges out of traumatic marginalization and exclusion is liberatory communitarian potentiality, not an automatic historical necessity. Much of the present work is an exploration of what kind of theory and practice might be needed in order to realize this potentiality, whether among the oppressed masses of the squalid megalopolises and immiserated countrysides of the global periphery, among the alienated and disaffected subcultures of a disintegrating global center, or elsewhere.

The methodology of redeeming and radicalizing trauma aims at what Paulo Freire classically calls conscientization, the kind of realization that, rather than remaining on the level of self-consuming abstraction, inspires and impels collective transformative practice (thus demanding "the impossible"). In a sense, this methodology moves from, as Marx stated it, "the ruthless critique of all things existing," to something analogous to Artaud's "theater of cruelty," to what we might call "the theory of cruelty." As Artaud described the theater of cruelty, it aimed at "a passionate and convulsive conception of life," releasing a process in which "great social upheavals, conflicts between peoples and races, natural forces, interventions of chance, and the magnetism of fatality will manifest themselves."[14] A "politics of cruelty," a ruthlessly compassionate confrontation with social reality, would do something similar. It would actuate an awakening to previously ignored social (and social ecological) problems and crises and could lead to an engaged response to them. The "convulsive," a crucial term for the surrealists with whom Artaud was for a time closely associated, refers to that which evokes a sudden, violent coming to awareness or awakening.

As will be shown, we can learn much about such awakening and engagement from communities that have arisen out of trauma and crisis. One of the greatest inspirations for this work has been the Common Ground Collective, a project with strong anarchist inspiration that was created in the wake of Hurricane Katrina, whose motto was "Solidarity Not Charity." This idea is, however, much more than a motto, and the example of the tens of thousands who put solidarity into practice has had an enormous influence on the hopes expressed here (as will be explained in the discussion below of "Disaster Anarchism"). One of the central questions underlying that discussion is the extent to which there is a potentiality for solidarity to emerge from crisis, whether local, regional, or global, whether temporary or ongoing. Rebecca Solnit states provocatively in her inspiring work *A Paradise Built in Hell* that what she calls "disaster communities" "suggest that, just as many machines reset themselves to their original settings after a power outage, so human beings reset themselves to something altruistic, communitarian, resourceful, and imaginative after a disaster, that we revert to something we already know how to do. The possibility of paradise is already within us as a default setting."[15]

Grounds for Hope

We must explore diligently the nature of this "something" that is already present. This book assumes the necessity of a moment of materiality that gives support to the practice of solidarity. In this, it differs significantly from postanarchist positions that begin with a valid critique of naïve, static, and dogmatic concepts of human nature, but end at the point of a denial of the material realities of natural and social history. Biology, anthropology, and ecology are not "destiny," but any social theory that fails to take each of these realms seriously is destined to fail.[16] Social determination (including the totality of the five spheres of determination discussed here) is not in itself a self-enclosed system, but exists in dialectical interaction with other determinations that reflect the nature of existing society as an inseparable part of larger processes of natural and social development. In recognizing such realities and determinations, this project constitutes an effort not merely to supersede, and certainly not merely to negate, but rather to continue and fulfill the work of classical anarchist thinkers such as Reclus and Kropotkin, who explored in great detail the intersection between what can only provisionally be divided into the natural and the social.[17]

Even if this undeniable realm of materiality is not quite so clearly delimited as a literal "default setting," it constitutes a reservoir of objective possibility upon which we can draw in the quest to create a world of solidarity and mutual aid. We have good reason to believe that, contrary to Hobbesian mythology, cooperative behavior is not the product of a contrived antisocial contract (an egoistic agreement between clashing antisocial competitors) enforced by a coercive power, but rather is something that is quite natural for human beings. As David Graeber points out, the anthropological evidence reveals that contract, rather than arising from ruthless self-interest, emerges within a context of social cooperation. He cites the pioneering anthropologist Marcel Mauss (the nephew of Durkheim), who showed in his classic work *The Gift* that "the origin of all contracts lies in communism, an unconditional commitment to another's needs, and that . . . there has never been an economy based on barter: that actually-existing societies which do not employ money have instead been gift economies in which the distinctions we now make between interest and altruism, person and property, freedom and obligation, simply did not exist."[18]

Hobbesian ideological common sense holds that altruism is at most a precarious social artifact, if it is not entirely illusory. However, Tomasello has shown that altruistic behavior appears spontaneously very early in life. He reports: "Infants of fourteen and eighteen months of age confront an unrelated adult they have met just moments previously. The adult has a trivial problem, and the infants help him solve it."[19] Experimental evidence shows that Hobbesian ideology, despite all its loud claims of realism, in fact turns reality on its head, as is typical of ideology in general. In experiments with young children, the addition of positive contingencies serves to make cooperative behavior conditional and to erode spontaneous cooperative tendencies. In these experiments, children who were rewarded for previously spontaneous altruistic behavior "actually helped *less* than those who had not been rewarded."[20] Tomasello's findings help validate the communitarian anarchist hope that there are deep-seated aspects of human nature that can be revived and regenerated when the opportunity for cooperation arises, and especially when extraordinary or extreme conditions cry out for mutual aid and solidarity.

In his discussion of cooperation on the social level, Tomasello concludes that the key factor in such cooperation is mutualism, a quality much beloved by anarchists in general, and by communitarian anarchists in particular. He contends that "human cooperation in the larger sense of humans' tendency and ability to live and operate together in institution-based cultural groups" is dependent above all on "mutualism, in which we all benefit from our cooperation but only if we work together, what we may call collaboration."[21] He argues that although the motivation is not competitively egoistic, in such activity the resulting benefits of cooperation to each participant are evident and further encourage mutual aid. In mutualism, "each of our efforts is required for success, and shirking is immediately apparent," and ultimately "my altruism toward you . . . actually helps me as well, as you doing your job helps us toward our common goal."[22] This aspect of Tomasello's argument helps ground the communitarian anarchist hope that when mutual aid and solidarity occur, they will be experienced not only as intrinsically satisfying, but also as practically beneficial to the participants.

This hope has also been given support by the work of Elinor Ostrom, winner of the Nobel Prize for economics. Ostrom, in a large body of experimentally based work, has shown that "management of resources" (which really means "care for the Earth") through participatory decision-making by those who use them results on the whole in better care for them than is the case with either private or state management. As Ostrom and Nagendra summarize these findings: "When users are genuinely engaged in decisions regarding rules that affect their use, the likelihood of users following the rules and monitoring others is much greater than when an authority simply imposes rules on users."[23] This reinforces and brings up to date what social anthropologists who have studied the relation between communal peoples and the natural world have always known. Mark Plotkin summarizes their findings in his fascinating and highly instructive book on ethnobotany and tribal medicine: "Where you have forests, you have Indians—but more importantly, where you have Indians, you have forests."[24] Michael Tomasello and Elinor Ostrom, among many others, reinforce the communitarian anarchist contention, going back to Reclus and Kropotkin, that that there are grounds, in human evolution, in human nature, in the history of human community, and in the structure of cooperative activity itself, for the creation of a world consisting of a community of free communities.

Anarchy, Solidarity, and Legitimacy

One of our key questions will be that of the nature of social solidarity. In perhaps the best-known analysis of the concept of solidarity in classical social theory, Durkheim distinguishes between two forms, which he identifies as mechanical solidarity and organic solidarity. He explains that members of "primitive" societies were united by what he calls the "mechanical" type, in which "the individual" is "tied directly" to the society "without any intermediary," and by means of "a more or less closely organized totality of beliefs and sentiments common to all members of the group," so that "the individuals are like 'social molecules'" that "can act together in so far as they have no action of their own, as with the molecules of inorganic bodies."[25] He holds that modern societies are united through the "organic" form of solidarity. In this type, each individual is dependent on society by means of his or her complex dependence on the parts of that society. The whole constitutes a "system of specialized and differentiated functions," which has a unity analogous to that of "a living body."[26] Under this form, with its increasing division of labor, "the activity of each individual becomes more personalized to the degree that it is more specialized," and "the individuality of all grows at the same time as that of its parts."[27]

Durkheim's account contains an element of truth to the degree that it focuses on the difference between a society in which there is a consensus concerning certain traditional values ("beliefs and sentiments") and a society in which there is a diversity of fundamental values. It correctly points out that there are areas in which the person becomes increasingly individualized as the society becomes in some ways more complex and diversified. But this depiction goes badly astray, on the one hand, by overlooking in many traditional societies the areas of greater social complexity and greater acceptance of certain kinds of social diversity, and, on the other, in ignoring the strong tendency toward standardization of values and practice in modern societies. It also misses the fact that solidarity that is based on factors such as traditional narrative, communal ritual, and complex kinship relationships results in a consonance of elements within the whole that has much in common with the "organic." It can be compared to "the body's seemingly intuitive integration of its diverse faculties" that

Nuland sees as the basis for the metaphor of "the wisdom of the body."[28] In contrast, modern organization based on large-scale political and economic apparatuses operates very much on a "mechanical" or "mechanistic" model of external force imposed on resistant material. Indeed, it becomes increasingly clear, even to many ordinary participant-observers in contemporary society, that the modern techno-bureaucratic state and the equally techno-bureaucratic corporate economic order function to an ever-increasing degree as massive machines that act upon the whole of society.

Amending the classic analysis to take account of these realities, we will see the emergence of free community as the culmination of a development from traditional organic solidarity, passing through coercive mechanistic administration (which works to dissolve true solidarity), and culminating in free communitarian solidarity. This development is a dialectical one in which there are moments of negation, preservation, and transcendence of previous social forms. As the discussion of "the third concept of liberty" below will show, the free community, though in no way a regression to any previous social form, recapitulates in many ways the organic, cultural basis for solidarity that was lost with the decline and dissolution of traditional societies. In addition, it develops the liberatory potential of forms of individuality that emerged over the history of civilization. Finally, it posits a kind of collective agency that develops potentialities implicit in the long history of participatory democracy and communal freedom that spans the ages from indigenous societies to contemporary liberation and solidarity movements.

Closely related to the question of communal solidarity is that of communal legitimation. It is important to understand the specific ways in which the free community establishes its legitimacy, and the manner in which its legitimation processes differ from those of previous social forms. Max Weber famously traced the legitimacy of any social order (defined by the degree to which there is "voluntary submission" to that order) to one of three kinds of authority. The first is called *rational authority*, and is identified with "belief in the 'legality' of patterns of normative rules," and "the right of those elevated to authority under such rules to issue commands." The second is labeled *traditional authority*, and is defined as that which is based on "the sanctity of immemorial traditions and the legitimacy of the status of those exercising authority under them." And the third is identified as *charismatic authority*, and is said to be derived from "devotion to the specific and exceptional sanctity, heroism or exemplary character of an individual person, and of the normative patterns or order revealed or ordained by him."[29]

It is argued here that the free community that is the goal of communitarian anarchism possesses three parallel bases of legitimation. As anarchistic concepts, these bases might be conceived of as forms of solidarity, rather than forms of authority, in view of the conventional hierarchical and authoritarian connotations of the term "authority." Yet it should be recognized there is a long history of anarchist theories of legitimate authority, which has focused in particular on the "authority of competence" as a legitimate form. Thus, these forms of legitimation may validly be seen as forms of nonauthoritarian authority, in addition to being forms of solidarity. In the free community, the function of Weber's *rational authority* is performed by solidarity based on the libertarian communitarian *counterideology*. The function of Weber's *traditional authority* is carried out through the solidarity that is embodied in the community's practice, that is, in the libertarian communitarian ethos. And the function of Weber's *charismatic authority* is exercised through the solidarity that is inspired by the libertarian communitarian *imaginary*.

The Universal Particular and the Dialectic of Modernity

If in modern Western social theory it is Hegel who poses most trenchantly the problem of the universal particular, it is Georg Simmel who within classical social theory signals the centrality of this problematic. Simmel describes history as the record of a project of dividing society into two opposed spheres of universality and singularity, carried out through the negation and annihilation of developed particularity. If one purges his account of its ideological elements, one finds that he reveals strikingly the roots of this dualistic project in the quest for political and economic domination. In his analysis of the evolution of law, for example, Simmel shows that the origins of this project lie far back in the history of ancient empire. He explains that "the idea of total power that was contained in the Roman concept of the state had its correlate in the notion that next to the *jus publicum*, there was a *jus privatum*. . . . On the one side, there was only the community in the broadest sense; on the other side, there were only single persons."[30] Note that "the community in the broadest sense" is the "community" in its most abstract and artificial sense, *the state*, which is at the same time the absolute negation of community in its most real, concrete, and historically grounded sense. The entire future history of civilization is encapsulated in this opposition between an abstract universality and an abstract singularity.

The imperial project expressed in this formulation ("total power") has continued for two millennia and is now reaching perfection in late modernity. Indeed, one of the strongest reasons for conceptualizing our age as "late modern" rather than "postmodern" is that the latter term obscures the manner in which the contemporary period is so precisely the realization and fulfillment of the logic of modernity as the final stage of the logic of civilization. The modern period, as Simmel notes, has continued the imperial project of dualistic polarization through the creation of "an all-embracing public realm" that was first established in the form of "princely absolutism."[31] As we now know, the completion of this process has required the coordinated efforts of the global state system and the global market economy. The engine of universalization has been this corporate-state apparatus, the impersonal, mechanistic Modern Prince that long ago began to displace obsolete "princely absolutism." The ensuing world historical project has progressively reduced society to a polarity between a realm of abstract universality and a realm of abstracted singularity, the multitude of increasingly atomized individuals.

As Simmel describes the developing history of this process, "it was fundamentally a matter of destroying the narrow, internally homogeneous 'intermediate' associations whose hegemony had characterized the earlier condition in order to conduct development upward toward the state and downward toward the unprejudiced freedom of the individual."[32] Thus, central to the project of modernity has been the destruction of the particular in the form of communal mediations (the process that Marx epitomized in his famous judgment that as capitalism advances triumphantly, "all that is solid melts into air"), leaving a stark dualistic opposition between the abstractly universal sphere of the "free" state and the "free" market, and the abstractly individual sphere of the "free" citizen/subject and the "free" producer/consumer.

Simmel notes that this reductive polarization process is a function of political scale and could be seen as emergent even in the medieval period, as urbanization and concentration of power began to accelerate.

> As early as the Middle Ages, English cities exhibit a pattern in which the larger municipalities were ruled by single corporations

or magnates, whereas in the smaller cities, the people as a whole held dominion. Corresponding to the smaller circle, there is a homogeneity of elements that underlies the unvarying rate of their political participation; but in the larger circles, this homogeneity is fragmented, allowing only for the mass of private individuals on one side, and for the single ruling personality on the other.[33]

This historical development continued into the modern period as the nation-state and market economy emerged, imposing their distinctive forms of universality and singularity. Simmel observes: "Eighteenth-century individualism wanted only freedom, only the removal of the 'intermediate' circles and middle levels that separated men from mankind, that is, that inhibited the development of pure humanity that supposedly constituted the value and core of each individual's existence, but which was hidden and truncated by particularistic historical groupings and bonds."[34] Thus, according to the dominant ideologies of the Enlightenment and of much of the subsequent Age of Revolution, communal ties are seen as an obstacle to liberation. Community itself, to the extent that it is not reformulated as nationality and citizenship in the nation-state, is seen as the antithesis of freedom.

Yet, over the two centuries that followed, it became clear that the individual being was torn away from communal ties, not primarily to accede to some abstract "pure humanity" but rather to become a more disciplined and obedient subject of the modern nation-state and a more productive and profitable producer and consumer within the modern capitalist economy. Simmel was far from oblivious to these tendencies, and for this reason he is a key figure in the development of critical social theory. For example, he recognizes, no less than Marx did, that "the cash economy and its associated liberalistic tendencies" have not only "loosened or dissolved narrower confederations" and "inaugurated a world economy," but have indeed "encouraged economic egoism to every degree of remorselessness."[35] As power became more and more centralized over the modern period, "the people" saw their "dominion" vanish entirely while "the single ruling personality" merged increasingly into the massive impersonal bureaucratic state and the vast impersonal market economy.[36]

However, despite Simmel's insights, his analysis lapses into progressivist ideology when he assumes that social "homogeneity" would be eliminated as part of modern society's inexorable movement toward a better future of greater individuality and diversity. In reality, while communal homogeneity has certainly declined, the state and the market have increasingly imposed a new homogeneity in spheres of thought, activity, and valuation.[37] According to the ideology of social progress espoused by Simmel (and modern social thought in general), the developing moment of universality would "pull" the singular individual "toward all that is human, suggesting to him the notion of an ideal unity of mankind."[38] But we now know that this is no more than a modernist illusion, the fantasizing of an abstract idealist "union" that serves to disguise continuing division and domination. As Rancière has pointed out concerning the fate of abstract university in a world dominated by the state and capital, "The universal is incessantly privatized by police logic, incessantly reduced to a power-share between birth, wealth and 'competence,' which is at work in the State as well as in society."[39] To the extent that this illusion has not been dissolved by late modern (alias "postmodern") disillusionment, it has been reduced to a shadowy existence in liberal and "progressive" rhetoric. It is now clear that the moment of universality can only be redeemed through the project of realizing concrete universality, as opposed to regression to the ideological illusion of universality, and that concrete universality can only be achieved if the abstract singular and the abstract universal are negated, transcended, and concretized through the universal particular.

Contemporary Anarchist Theory: Bridging the Gap

In recent anarchist theory, Bookchin and other programmatic thinkers have strayed into abstract universality and an accompanying dogmatism, while many egoists, post-anarchists, and post-structuralist anarchists have fallen into a one-sided focus on singularity and particularity, often failing to show clearly how they can avoid the risk of relativism. The truth of universality defended on one side and the truth of singularity defended on the other must both be recognized, but each must be radicalized and developed further through dialectical engagement. The argument here for recognition of the crucial moment of the universal particular and concrete universality constitutes a response to these two divergent tendencies in contemporary anarchist thought.

The present work focuses specifically on correcting the antidialectical errors of these two tendencies. It seeks to rectify, on the one hand, the post-anarchist misrepresentation of dialectical thought, and, on the other, Bookchin's misguided "dialectical naturalist" attempts to turn dialectical thought into something rather close to that misrepresentation. There is no need at this point to go into great detail concerning Bookchin, whose thought is the topic of detailed discussion below.[40] Yet it will be useful to mention an example of the kind of problems that emerge in his work.

Through most of the 1980s, I espoused a politics of social ecology that adhered closely to Bookchin's formulations of municipalism and decentralized democracy, rooted explicitly in the historical anarchist tradition and in European and North American radical history. Beginning in the early 1990s, I became heavily involved in the struggle against a major transnational mining corporation that was a dominant political force in my local community, and which also was undertaking vast projects of mineral exploitation, including the world's largest gold mine and third-largest copper mine, in West Papua (the western half of the island of New Guinea). This project involved enormous ecological destruction, social oppression, and cultural genocide against the Papuan people.

The more deeply I became engaged in this struggle, the more I discovered the very specific ways in which the particularities of local ("municipal") issues and struggles (whether in Timika and Tembagapura on the island of Papua, or in New Orleans and Austin on the island of North America), have universal dimensions. This does not mean merely that there are abstract "human rights" that are violated here and violated there, so that "we are all in this together" as human beings, or even that there is some generalized neocolonial relationship between the First and Third Worlds. What it means is that by immersing oneself in the particularities of local issues and struggles, one discovers how they are related in very specific ways to the global capitalist economy, the global nation-state system, the global system of industrial technology, neocolonialism, various forms of racism and ethnic domination, patriarchal values and institutions, the global ecological crisis, and, indeed, every significant dimension of the world system, as well as the complex ways that all these elements interact at various levels, including the national, regional, bioregional, ecosystemic, local, and even personal ones.[41] One discovers that the more deeply one immerses oneself in the particular, the more the universal appears in its greatest concreteness and specificity.

Over a decade of engaged inquiry into this dialectic of particularity and universality, I increasingly found Bookchin's municipalism, despite its localist dimensions, to be in some ways a form of abstract universalism, inadequately grounded in world history, disconnected from the realities of contemporary global society, and based on a highly Eurocentric theoretical problematic. It is revealing that as we moved into the twenty-first century, Bookchin could publish a book on the city with no references to places such as Kolkata, Beijing, Jakarta, Rio, Nairobi, or, indeed, any of the great Third World megalopolises. In fact, at the close of a century that saw the rise of neocolonialism and its sprawling urban slums that are the true dystopian future of the city, the contemporary Global South and its cities appear nowhere in Bookchin's work.[42] It must be admitted that such a gap has not been atypical in Western anarchist thought. These harsh global realities, and, indeed, the entire world beyond the industrialized West, are only now beginning to take their proper place at the center of anarchist theory.

Post-anarchism has tended to stray in a quite different direction from Bookchin's kind of abstract universalism. It has, in fact, criticized the anarchist tradition for such universalism, among other shortcomings. However, one of the major weaknesses of post-anarchism is its often simplistic and inaccurate representation of the anarchist tradition to which it claims to be "post." Nathan Jun, in *Anarchism and Political Modernity*, has perceptively criticized these shortcomings, concluding that the works of the post-anarchists "have been characterized by remarkably limited engagement with actual anarchist texts coupled with problematical exegesis."[43] Through careful analysis of both classical anarchist and poststructuralist texts he makes a convincing case for certain strong connections between the two, notably in the cases of Deleuze, and perhaps most strikingly, of Derrida.

Interestingly, the Derridean ideas that seem most anarchistic to Jun are those that echo (though perhaps they echo a bit too faintly) the radical dialectical tradition that is defended here. Thus, Jun sees great merit in Derrida's rejection of "binary logic," that "operates within the limits of an exclusive disjunction," rather than accepting the possibility that "something is both A and ~A simultaneously."[44] Such a rejection is precisely what has distinguished dialectical logic, beginning millennia before the advent of Derrida and poststructuralism. Deconstruction, Jun says, fights against "the multiplicity of totalized binary oppositions which are constantly and variously manifesting themselves within multiple sites of oppression" by "'overturning,' 'displacing,' 'resisting,' 'disorganizing,' and 'transgressing' these oppositions wherever they arise," and it should certainly be commended for doing this.[45] Yet it would be difficult to see how these concepts are in any way an advance over dialectical concepts (all of which are connotations of *Aufheben*) such as "negation," "abolition," "superses-sion," "annulment," "cancellation," "suspension," "sublation," "preservation," and "transcendence."

For a typical example of more recent representations of the clas-sical anarchist tradition, we might look at a critique of the tradition by Todd May. May's analysis is particularly instructive because he has done excellent work on anarchism and is clearly one of the most capable and sophisticated contemporary anarchist theorists. Though he identifies his position as post-structuralist, rather than post-anarchist, his critique is similar to that of the post-anarchists. He asserts that "almost all anar-chists rely on a unitary concept of human essence: the human essence is good; therefore, there is no need for the exercise of power."[46] He adds that anarchists are "suspicious of all power," because "the image of power with which power operates is that of a weight pressing down—and at times destroying—the actions, events, and desires with which it comes in contact."[47] The problem is not that this description is entirely wrong. It is true that an important part of the anarchist project has been to investi-gate the degree to which "goodness," or a grounding for "goodness," can be found in human nature. Both this question and that of the nature of power have been central concerns to classical anarchists. It is also true that some have said naïve, simplistic, and one-sided things about both of these topics. However, the problem with this generalization is that it nevertheless ignores a large part of what that tradition has said about these issues and, indeed, overlooks the most challenging and sophisticated insights found in the tradition.

For example, the account overlooks the deterministic aspects of many classical anarchist theories, including those of such major figures as Godwin and Bakunin.[48] Even though Godwin had a belief in the gradual "perfectibility" of humanity, his deterministic position led him to conclude that actual human nature could exhibit a great range of good and evil qualities. Indeed, he judges in his magnum opus, *Political Justice*, that "the whole history of the human species, taken in one point of view, appears a vast abortion. Man seems adapted for wisdom and fortitude and benev-olence. But he has always, through a vast majority of countries, been a victim of ignorance and superstition."[49]

It is also quite clear that Godwin had a very complex conception of power and its relation to human action, and, we might say, to his conception of a kind of deterministic autonomy. In *Political Justice*, he writes of many meanings and types of power, including, for example, the power of desire, of prejudice, of reason, of truth, of understanding, of conscience, of will, of imagination, of education, of resistance, of coercion, of government, of parties, of legislatures, of judiciaries, of executives, of multitudes, of the people, of physical objects, and of physical causes.

Bakunin also had a deterministic, and radically dialectical view of human nature. The human being, he says,

> enters life without a soul, without a conscience, without the shadow of an idea or any feeling, but with a human organism whose individual nature is determined by an infinite number of circumstances and conditions preceding his will, and which in turn determines his greater or smaller capacity to acquire and assimilate the feelings, ideas, and associations worked out by centuries of development and transmitted to everyone as *a social heritage* by the education which he receives. Good or bad, this education is imposed upon man—and he is in no way responsible for it.[50]

Whether we accept Bakunin's socially deterministic account of the shaping of the self, passages such as this, which are very common in his works, debunk the myth that classical anarchism had an extreme, ahistorical "natural goodness" view of human nature.

Regarding the issue of power, it is true that Bakunin made sweeping statements about "opposing all power," but he also wisely contradicted such simplistic statements and revealed that his considered view of the matter was more complex. Thus, in *Federalism, Socialism and Anti-Theologism*, he states that in revolutionary struggle, "power is diffused in the collective and becomes the sincere expression of the liberty of everyone."[51] In *God and the State* he discusses a "social power" that is not at all repressive.[52] In fact, not only does he not see it as necessarily repressive; he sees power in the nonrepressive sense as basic to the functioning of the revolutionary movement and the good society. Granted, the classical anarchists were not proto-Foucauldians, and many tended to see hierarchical power as predominantly repressive, but as the example from Godwin also shows, even on this issue, the story is much more complex.

To mention a problem that is particularly relevant to the present analysis, post-anarchism's depiction of dialectical thought, whether within or outside of anarchist theory, is an area in which the misrepresentation has been most extreme. To take one of a multitude of pertinent examples, Lewis Call claims in an article on Ursula K. Le Guin that those who attempt "to describe Le Guin as a dialectical thinker must find a way to account for the sustained assault on binary thinking that is such a fundamental feature of her work."[53] That such a statement is even possible shows the extent to which false stereotypes of dialectical thought post-anarchism and the post-modernist milieu in general. In reality, dialectical thought is itself the most sustained attack in the history of philosophy on binary thinking. It is rather well-known for (and often attacked for) its rejection of the principle of contradiction, one of the pillars of binary thinking. Dialectical thought goes to great pains to show that binary oppositions are *never* an adequate depiction of reality and that they *always* self-destruct. As in the case of Ursula K. Le Guin, dialectical thinkers do not ignore the existence of binary oppositions, but rather take them up and subject them to something that can quite accurately be depicted as a "sustained assault."[54]

In Defense of Dialectic

This is not the place to present a detailed exposition of the nature of dialectical philosophy.[55] However, since it is the basis for the present work, and since it has been so systematically misrepresented in contemporary thought, it might be helpful to add a few words about what dialectic is and what it is not.

Radical dialectic sees the world (including the social world, the natural world, and the world of ideas) as the site of constant change and transformation that takes place through processes of mutual interaction, negation, and contradiction. It asserts that a dynamic, self-transforming reality is always a step, or several steps, ahead of our processes of conceptualization. Things are in a state of becoming and therefore always are not what they are, and always are what they are not. We must recognize that negation is determination. Things are what they are not, in the sense that everything to which they are related is internal to the nature of their being. All phenomena are conditioned by the wholes (which are, in fact, only relative wholes) of which they are a part (and also not a part). The objects of dialectical analysis must always be understood as being in motion. In the process of dialectical inquiry, which is itself a process of transformative interaction with those objects, the analyst and the categories of analysis are themselves transformed. Dialectical analysis rejects the idea of simple teleological unfolding of potentiality. In their processes of development, phenomena generate a supplementary otherness that refutes any idea of their self-contained identity and completeness. Adorno states this idea thus: "The name of dialectics says no more, to begin with, than that objects do not go into their concepts without leaving a remainder, that they come to contradict the traditional norm of adequacy. Contradiction . . . indicates the untruth of identity, the fact that the concept does not exhaust the thing conceived."[56] This statement illustrates the fact noted above that the limitations of the principle of contradiction was hardly a discovery of poststructuralism, and that anyone who represents dialectical thinking as a fetishization of binary oppositions needs to rethink the problem of representation.

An important work on psychoanalysis once made the crucial distinction between "psychoanalytic method" and "the doctrine of Freud."[57] The author's hope was that the reader would avoid identifying with psychoanalysis any absurdity or prejudice that Freud happened to espouse. It is equally important to understand that dialectic should not be identified with "the doctrine of Hegel" or "the doctrine of Marx," but only with the ideas of these thinkers when they are at their most critical and dialectical. Hegel's dialectic has nothing to do with an inevitable development of World History toward Absolute Spirit. Marx's dialectic has nothing to do with an inevitable succession of historical modes of production culminating in Communism. Above all, it is important to realize that when one is told that dialectic means "thesis-antithesis-synthesis," one can be certain that the source of such a view, whether attacking dialectic, defending it, or giving a supposedly neutral definition of it, has never really investigated the phenomenon. It is true that there are some cases of such a triadic dialectical movement (including very important ones, such as in Hegel's account of Being, Nothing, and Becoming in the *Science of Logic*). But there are, in fact, very few such cases, and defining dialectic according to such a mechanical model is a prime example of nondialectical thinking.

Žižek notes the ironic fact that among critics of Hegel and dialectic it is "fashionable to insist how there is always a remainder of contingency, of particularity, which cannot be *aufgehoben*, which insists and resists its conceptual (dis)integration."[58] The irony is in that this supposedly embarrassing remainder is precisely what any authentic dialectical analysis is meant to reveal. Žižek notes further irony in the fact that *Aufhebung*, "the very term Hegel uses to designate this operation is marked by the irreducible contingency of an idiosyncrasy of the German,"[59] which consists in the fact that the same concept can have at the same time seemingly contradictory significations such as "to negate," "to cancel," "to preserve," "to suspend," and "to transcend." The hostile stereotype of dialectic as teleological dogmatism would have it aiming at a final result "without remainder," as all is merged into some grand mystical synthesis. However, one of the primary meanings of *Aufheben* is "to preserve," and what is preserved includes various loose ends, further contradictions, and radical negativity. If one takes a dialectical approach, one always pays the most careful attention to "what remains," realizing that forgotten remainders always come back to haunt.

It can only be concluded that radical dialectic manages to be at least as antiessentialist, antisubstantialist, and antidogmatic as is any form of postmodernism, without succumbing in any way to the postmodernist tendency to collapse into relativism, nihilism, cynicism, or late capitalist ideology. It should also be recognized that nonradical pseudodialectic, the utilization of rigid, stereotyped formulas of development mislabeled "dialectical," is itself mere ideology, and can collapse into almost anything. The goal of the present work is to be fully and consistently dialectical. The achievement of this goal is, of course, impossible, but this impossibility fortunately opens up new possibilities for others to carry out the task more adequately.

The Structure of This Work

The chapters that follow focus in various ways on the two main themes of this book: the inquiry into the ways in which social transformation is possible, and the analysis of the goal of such transformation, which is the free community proposed by the communitarian anarchist tradition. The next chapter, "Critique of the Gotham Program" takes the form of a sympathetic critique of one of the most advanced statements of the American radical Left today, the *Manifesto for a Left Turn*. However, as in the case of the work of Marx that inspired its title, the primary aim is not so much the critique of a given text as the critique of social reality, the sort of critique that is capable of opening up new possibilities for radical social transformation. In pursuit of this end, a theory of social determination is outlined that encompasses an analysis of the spheres of the social institutional structure, social ideology, the social imaginary, the social ethos, and the social materiality. It is argued that a successful transformative political movement must constitute a comprehensive and deeply rooted *form of life*.

Modern political thought has been the site of a continual struggle for appropriation of the concept of liberty or freedom. Chapter 3, "The Third Concept of Liberty," argues that the most advanced conception of freedom is offered by a communitarian anarchist theory that synthesizes "negative freedom" as noncoercion and nondomination, "positive freedom" as self-realization or flourishing, and "absolute freedom" as authentic agency realized through active participation in the collective self-determination of a free community. It is shown that the roots of such a concept are found in their most highly developed (albeit ideologically distorted) form in Hegel's social thought, and that the eminently practical and experimental communitarian anarchism formulated by Gustav Landauer helps us understand how such an ideal might become a powerful concrete social reality today.

Chapter 4, "Against Principalities and Powers," explores the converse of the theory of freedom, the anarchist theory of domination. The first part of the chapter investigates the major elements of the radical critique of domination, as developed in anarchist thought and in the history of critical and dialectical social theory. It is shown that this critique has established that social domination constitutes a comprehensive system containing distinct forms of domination that interact dialectically and that operate pervasively through the various spheres of social determination. It has also revealed the historical movement in the direction of social domination through impersonal mechanisms that are largely unconscious, automatic, and systemic. The second part of the chapter is an application of this critique of domination, in the form of a critical analysis of the major contemporary liberal theory of domination. It is shown that this theory is reductive, ahistorical, and ideological, that it renders much of social domination invisible, and that, in the end, the position destroys itself if carried to its own logical conclusion.

A social theory focused on the ideal of free community and the elimination of all forms of domination is inevitably characterized as "utopian." Chapter 5, "Anarchy and the Dialectic of Utopia," analyzes the crucial importance of utopian ideas and practice to the communitarian anarchist project, in addition to exposing the perils of many forms of utopianism. This analysis is inspired by a long tradition of libertarian communitarian thought and practice that shows the extent to which the impossible community has its roots in historical realities. This includes the communist and communitarian anarchist theoretical tradition, as developed by Reclus, Kropotkin, and Landauer, in addition to the rich history of utopian socialism and radical intentional community, ranging from the Fourierist and Owenite communal experiments of the nineteenth century through the Gandhian ashrams and radical kibbutzim of the twentieth. It is argued that there is a need for a deeply *topian* utopianism that synthesizes the utopian quest for a good that lies beyond the limits of conventional possibility and the topian sense of place, of embodied reality, and of the emergence of the good here and now.

Chapter 6, "The Microecology of Community," marks a transition from the general theoretical discussion of the opening chapters to a more specific analysis of existing possibilities for social transformation. It explores the need for a politics rooted in primary communities such as affinity groups, base communities, and small intentional communities. It argues that liberatory social transformation requires a material basis in a political culture consisting of a dense network of grassroots institutions that address the most fundamental spheres of our social being. It is argued that many of the ideals of this tradition are realized in contemporary forms of small group organization and that such phenomena offer hope for the emergence of a larger movement for social regeneration.

Chapter 7, "Bridging the Unbridgeable Chasm," defends the thesis that the contemporary anarchist movement in North America has made important advances in the development of the needed liberatory political culture. It refutes various contentions in Murray Bookchin's well-known polemic, *Social Anarchism or Lifestyle Anarchism*, in which he argues that the contemporary anarchist movement has retreated from meaningful social engagement, is engaged in ineffectual self-indulgent gestures, and has lost its emancipatory potential.[60] Such arguments are also representative of negative stereotypes of contemporary anarchism in current popular culture and political discourse. It is argued that, in reality, contemporary anarchist practice continues a long history of successfully synthesizing personal and communal liberation and has much to offer to the project of reaffirming and revitalizing the libertarian communitarian tradition.

Using the Hurricane Katrina disaster as a case study, Chapter 8, "Disaster Anarchism," shows how a moment of crisis and catastrophe can help reveal the nature of the system of domination and give rise to new forms of liberatory struggle and grassroots community organization. In such moments, in which the established institutional structure fails, or even collapses, the dominant ideology, imaginary, and ethos are challenged by the force of events and space is opened for the emergence of what had long seemed impossible. In an analysis inspired by the communist anarchist perspective of philosopher and social geographer Reclus, it is argued that the grassroots response to the Katrina catastrophe and the forms of organization and cooperation that came out of it offer inspiration for a larger libertarian and communitarian movement for social transformation.

In Chapter 9, "The Common Good," inspiration for renewed communitarian anarchism is found in the Gandhian Sarvodaya movement in India, the largest significantly anarchist-inspired movement to appear between the Spanish Revolution and the present moment. It is shown that Gandhi and the Gandhian movement put into practice such anarchist values as radical decentralism, antistatism, local participatory democracy, economic self-management, and focus on the central place of personal transformation and base organization in the process of social revolution. The chapter also shows how this Gandhian heritage is carried on in the Sarvodaya Shramadana movement of Sri Lanka. It follows a decentralist, participatory model of collective action based on a concept of personal and social awakening that moves from the level of the person to the family, to the local community, and then to successively larger spheres of social interaction. The Gandhian tradition, while giving no blueprint for social transformation, is shown to be in many ways exemplary in addressing the interconnected spheres of institutions, ideology, imaginary, ethos, and materiality.

The final chapter consists of a detailed communitarian anarchist critique of the theory and practice of libertarian municipalism as developed in the thought of Murray Bookchin. Though this tendency currently has relatively little political influence in the Western world that inspired it, it is still quite significant for several reasons. First, it remains the most elaborately developed political perspective in the previous generation of anarchist social thought. Second, much of the critique of libertarian municipalism applies to programmatic theory in general and can be helpful in understanding a problematical tendency that is recurrent in anarchist thought. Third, a major goal of the present work is to defend dialectical social theory, and the critique shows the distinction between nominally dialectical analysis and a truly radical dialectic.[61] Fourth, it is important to recognize that there is an important core of truth in libertarian municipalism, which, purged of rigid and dogmatic elements, has much to contribute to communitarian anarchist and social ecological theory. And finally, it is important because some of the positive potential has been realized through its influence on the Rojava Revolution, which has been one of the most hopeful developments in recent history.[62] Whatever the limitations of Bookchin's formulation may be, decentralized participatory democracy promises to be of crucial importance in future communal struggles against empire and for the liberation of humanity and nature.

2

Critique of the Gotham Program: From Libertarian Socialism to Communitarian Anarchism

"It has always been the impossible that has created humanity's new realities."

—Landauer[1]

"Be realistic, demand the impossible."

—May 1968 slogan

Today, any true manifesto of radical politics would necessarily seem like a thoroughly impossible document. It would demand the impossible, and allow the impossible to make certain demands upon us. It would make manifest the impossible. That is, as one read it, one would be lured by the reality of the impossible and begin to be transformed into an impossible person. As many read it, they would begin to be transformed into an impossible community.

As the *Manifesto for a Left Turn* notes, we have passed through a period in which demands for the impossible have been heard less and less.[2] We have lived through the era of "There is no alternative." However, it is becoming increasingly clear that despite all attempts at repression and denial, we are in the midst of unprecedented historical crisis in which reality itself demands the impossible, whether one likes it or not. The *Manifesto* draws our attention to important aspects of this crisis.

Yet, though the crisis is unavoidable, the mechanisms of denial persist. For ordinary consciousness, the crisis presents the specter of traumatic impossibility. When we confront such impossibility, our very anxiety attests to its reality, but, far from demanding it, we force it back into the realm of the utterly unthinkable. The cost of such denial is that as this traumatic impossibility is repressed, so are all the possibilities that might prevent its emergence. In the end, the crucial question is whether we are capable of creating an alternative possibility, rather than merely falling victim to a repressed one.

So we might say that "a specter is haunting the Left." It is the Phantom of Possibility. It is the Ghost of a Chance.

The Chance is, of course, the chance that revolutionary, liberatory social transformation is still possible. This is the Possible Impossibility that the famous slogan asks us to demand. However, the problematic of "demanding" the necessary impossible has always been a bit misleading. The impossible that we have in mind is hardly lying around somewhere waiting to be delivered to us on demand. (By whom—the State? the Party? History? Technology? Experts? God? Amazon?) Rather, the realization of this impossible requires an act. Or to put it another way, without the act (or, more precisely, many acts that replace the myth of the one heroic Act), everything becomes simply impossible.

The problem of the act has become a major preoccupation in radical Left thought. Perhaps it would be more accurate to say that the true preoccupation has been the problem of the nonact. This agonizing problem is posed most strikingly by our collective failure to create a powerful movement to prevent global ecological catastrophe, even though we are in the midst of epochal climate change and the sixth great mass extinction in the history of life on Earth, even though the causes of these problems and the necessary preconditions for their solution are increasingly clear. Even the political ideologists who are most absurdly pessimistic about human nature proclaim that the first law of nature is self-preservation. Nevertheless, the mass of humanity manages to refrain from acting boldly in its own self-interest, and those who profess a disinterested regard for the good of humanity and a belief in the need for social change follow suit.

The *Manifesto* points out the ways in which the American Left in particular has shown itself to be incapable of such transformative actions. It states, for example, that "many Leftists and left-liberals . . . were convinced they could eventually push the [Democratic Party] to more progressive positions on economic and foreign policy issues, so they shunned third party and radical alternatives, refusing to raise anti-capitalist demands." The question is how, after repeated failures, and even when that party continually moved in a direction precisely opposite to the direction of their "pushing," they could persevere in their illusions, and "push on." How could they see the same phenomenon repeated over and over and still act as if this repetition was not occurring? How could they see the social and ecological crisis continually intensifying and yet exert their concerted efforts by supporting (critically, and with reservations, of course) an institution that plays a central and indispensable role in creating that very crisis?

The *Manifesto* offers a partial explanation in the fact that "many intellectuals and electoralists and some institutions such as organized labor, civil rights organizations, and women's groups have been integrated into the party machinery and hold berths at the Democratic Party's ostensible governing bodies." As true as this is, it explains the motivation of only a small segment of the Left as a whole. The minority who have become part of the party machinery have not really encountered mass resistance at the grassroots level to this co-optation of their movements, so more systemic forces that produce the nonact have to be delineated.

We can understand certain dimensions of the nonact if we shift our focus from the mechanism of denial to the Lacanian concept of fetishistic disavowal. In fetishistic disavowal, one has certain crucial knowledge but acts as if one lacks it. As Žižek has noted in his many examples of this mechanism, it is encapsulated in the phrase, "Je sais bien, mais quand même," that is, "I know very well, but nevertheless."

A generation ago, many on the Left thought that, if only "the Movement" (the Great Floating Signifier) could get certain truths across to the people, then everything was bound to change. Both major parties are controlled by big business! The mass media are run by a few big corporations! Our tax money is used to support tyrants and oppress people around the world! Each year, ordinary working people produce more, but their real wages decline! Et cetera. But now all this, and much more, is common knowledge. Unfortunately, the prevailing attitude is: "I know I should be as mad as hell, and I know I shouldn't take this anymore!" I know very well, but nevertheless. Of course, we find an entire fetishistic Left that succumbs to such disavowal and rallies under the banner of "Vive le Quand-Même-isme!"

Part of the problem is the ease with which malaise can be co-opted when people are offered ineffectual substitute gestures. As mentioned, the now-classic case is ecological crisis. Huge numbers of people now know that climate change is leading us toward global ecological catastrophe. Yet their response remains on the gestural level of increasing their recycling, consuming more organic food, or buying "green" clothing and other fashionable ecocommodities. In other words, they act in ways that are most consistent with the prevailing institutional structure, the dominant consumptionist imaginary, the dominant economistic ideology, and, most immediately, the dominant ethos—that is, they act (perhaps we should say with the Skinnerians, they "emit behavior") in ways that are most continuous with the ways that they and everyone else are accustomed to acting. It's an old story. As Brecht put it: "Wir wären gut [grün, rot] anstatt so roh / Doch die Verhältnisse, sie sind nicht so!"[3]

The Left has largely lapsed into a mode of permanent protest. It has become obsessed with reactive negation almost to the exclusion of the creative negation of the negation. Consequently, there is a tendency to hope that if the evils that are the target of protest only get worse, it will shock the public into recognition. This is the trap of "So-bad-it's-goodism." In fact, the Left has no monopoly on this perspective, which goes back deeply in the Judeo-Christian tradition: "O felix culpa!" Even the Fall from Paradise turned out to be a good thing! Modern philosophy has carried on the tradition, as when Hegel observes (as *we know very well*) that world history is "the slaughter-bench at which the happiness of people, the wisdom of States, and the virtue of individuals have been victimized." But he contends that all these evils (*nevertheless*) must be accepted as "the means for realizing" the ultimate good, "the essential destiny" and "absolute aim" of World History.[4] And Marx, in this case a faithful student of Hegel, pointed out (correctly) that history "progresses by its bad side."[5]

In one sense, such philosophizing merely reinforces the folk psychology of civilization, which has always held that the infliction of punishment "teaches a lesson" to the victim. In addition, it expresses the deeply teleological, progressivist (and antidialectical) view of history that has been the dominant myth of modernity. The problem is that the "bad side" of history, while undoubtedly moving it along, often takes it in a *bad* direction and teaches the *wrong* lessons. It is not only the inadequate development of productive forces that brings back, as Marx ironically labeled it, "die ganze alte Scheiße."[6] Not unless we are willing to admit that institutional structures, structures of the social imaginary, ideological structures, and even shared character structures are productive forces in a larger sense, since their inadequate development, or more accurately, their maldevelopment, also generate that Slime of History that mires us in domination.

Late capitalism hardly lacks contradictions, and it would not be surprising if the masses would decide to junk rampant neoliberalism for the promise of job security, good housing, adequate medical care, and perhaps protection from the most conspicuous forms of poisoning their air, water, and food supply. If a tough war on crime, rigid economic protectionism, and a harsh crackdown on illegal immigrants were thrown in, they might clamor with even more enthusiasm for an interventionist state. The disquieting but inescapable conclusion is that the transformative contradictions might very well transform in a rightist, authoritarian, or even fascistic direction. Contradictions do not lead anywhere in particular when taken in abstraction from the institutional structure and political culture within which they emerge. When social contradictions are looked at with a degree of abstraction (e.g., as contradictions within an economic system), left turns and right turns might seem equally plausible. When looked at concretely, in the context of the totality of social relations, they can be expected to lead in a direction determined largely by the prevailing institutional structure and the dominant political culture.

If one were to predict on this basis what kind of future world is most likely (barring our success in the urgently needed project of discovering the secret of how to "turn" the direction of history), one might be forced to conclude that, sadly, it is a spectrum of possible ecofascisms, ranging from the relatively friendly and constitutional to the relatively brutal and genocidal, as a desperate response to social and ecological crisis. A second possible scenario would result from a continuing failure to respond either desperately and brutally or wisely and humanely to these crises: global collapse, population crash, and barbarism. A third possibility (the one we need to manifest for) is, of course, a "turning"—of the wheel of nature, of the wheel of the law, of the wheel of history.

If we hope to make this turning possible, we must pose the question of what conditions exist that could offer the basis for a liberatory response to contradictions or, to put it another way, a response that would infuse brute contradictions with reason, passion, and imagination, and transform *automatistic contradiction* into *creative contradiction*. We must conclude that on this topic Hegel and Alcoholics Anonymous are right. Acts of will, good intentions, "oughts," "shoulds," and "musts" are not enough. As the former puts it, we reach an impasse if we remain on the level of *Moralität*, of abstract moral ideals and moralistic encouragement. Morality attains its fulfillment in *Sittlichkeit*, in which the right and the good are given ethical substance through their embodiment in history and in social reality. When this occurs, "oughts" and other normative terms take on new life, as they serve as links between imagined social possibilities and concrete social forms in which those possibilities can be realized.

But the prior question remains of why movements for change have remained on the level of the gesture and the ought. In considering the problematic of developing transformative social praxis and understanding the barriers to such praxis, the concept of overdetermination is relevant. This theoretical concept was introduced by Freud and then developed by Althusser and other thinkers. Freud applied the term to the processes of condensation or displacement in the dreamwork. In the first case, the dream image represents many ideas in the unconscious. In the latter case, a seemingly unimportant image represents a reality that is highly invested with libidinal energy.

Overdetermination is often taken to mean multiple causation, perhaps taking the case of condensation as the paradigm, or following the apparent meaning of the word itself. However, multicausality is only the most obvious dimension of the process, for there is always an implicit logic behind the appearance of multiple, reinforcing causes. On a deeper level, overdetermination means structural or systemic determination. The power of the determination can only be understood by grasping how the multiple determinants are expressions of the structure of a whole (whether a highly integrated, stable whole, a whole riddled with contradictions and in a process of decomposition, or something between these extremes). Althusser applies such concepts to the analysis of society, but he focuses overwhelmingly on the moment of contradiction within the social structure. He directs his attention to the ways in which contradictions can "merge into a ruptural unity."[7]

An illuminating exercise would be to reexamine his paradigm case (the Russian Revolution), considering the ways in which the phenomena he examined exhibit moments of both rupture and nonrupture, including in the latter case pseudorupture, or the ideological illusion of rupture, in which elements of character-structure, social hierarchy, et cetera are reproduced in a new guise. However, the question posed here is another one. It is the question of what we can discover about the overdetermination of action (or nonaction) by the social system in its moments of noncontradiction, and how conscious social practice can effectively counter this determination and create new determinants in the relevant spheres.

There are (at least) five spheres that are essential to the analysis of how social reality is generated, how it is maintained, and how it might be transformed. These spheres are the social institutional structure, the social ideology, the social imaginary, the social ethos, and the social materiality. The complex dialectic between these five spheres and various dimensions of these spheres must be explored in specific detail to make sense out of the senseless folly of the nonact. Since there is a dialectical relationship between the spheres, they should not be thought of as discrete realms. They are analytically distinguishable but at the same time dialectically identical with one another. The detailed analysis of this dialectic and the possibilities for transcending it cannot be undertaken here, but a brief sketch of the project might be useful.

The present analysis is in a strange way prefigured by Pascal's famous wager concerning the existence of God. The core of Pascal's analysis in the *Pensées* focuses on how one is socialized into becoming a believer, while the present concern is how the individual is socialized into the dominant social system—and how one might be socialized out of it.[8] However, in both cases the subject is conversion. The word "conversion" derives from the Latin *vertere*, to turn, and *com* or *con*, meaning completely. A conversion is a radical turn. The question is how one can make a radical turn.

Pascal's wager is often dismissed with disdain, for after all, how could it possibly work? One is asked to balance the rewards in the after-life (eternal bliss) that one might gain from belief if one is right, against the posthumous cost of believing (nothing happens) if one is wrong, and then to bet on belief. One can only conclude that it is quite implausible that this balancing act could ever lead to real conviction. This objection is obviously valid. However, it overlooks all that is brilliant in Pascal's analysis and in fact misrepresents his position by taking one point in abstraction.

In Pensée 245, Pascal says that "there are three sources of belief," which he specifies as "reason," "custom," and "inspiration." Each of his "sources" is paralleled by a sphere of determination in the present scheme of explanation. The role of Pascal's "reason," which offers arguments for the existence of God or for the value of belief, is performed here by *the social ideology*. The role of "custom," which for Pascal means religious rituals, is performed here by *the social ethos*, and the role of "inspiration," which refers to appeals to feelings and emotions tied to certain images, is performed in the present analysis by *the social imaginary*. A fourth sphere to be discussed here, the *social institutional structure*, also appears implicitly, since it was, of course, for Pascal the structure of the Church that was the framework for the ideology, the ethos, and the imaginary, while here it is either the dominant social order or the socially and personally transformative community of liberation that challenges that order.

Pascal's analysis also parallels the present one in the very heavy emphasis he places on the power of ethos. In Pensée 233, he emphasizes the crucial role of habitual practice. He advises us as follows:

> You would like to cure yourself of unbelief and ask the remedy for it. Learn of those who have been bound like you, and who now stake all their possessions. These are people who know the way which you would follow, and who are cured of an ill of which you would be cured. Follow the way by which they began; by acting as if they believed, taking the holy water, having masses said, etc. Even this will naturally make you believe, and deaden your acuteness.

Pascal's insight is that even if one *does not believe*, if one nevertheless *acts as if one believes* (i.e., enters into the ethos of the believer), one will *come to believe*, or, to state it more critically, one will achieve a level of bad faith that is a reasonable facsimile of belief. In effect, "je ne sais pas, mais quand même." Two corollaries of this insight are important here. One is that even if *one believes*, if one in fact *acts as if one does not believe* (enters into the ethos of the nonbeliever), one will come *not to believe*, or, more precisely, one will achieve a level of bad faith that is a reasonable facsimile of nonbelief. Politically, this usually means today a lapse into "liberal" or "progressive" politics, the politics of gestures and representation. Finally, if one *believes and acts as if one believes* (enters into the ethos of belief), then one can believe in good faith, accepting the practical consequences of and undertaking the project of one's belief. Politically, this means that one becomes capable of the Act. (In honor of the philosopher, we might call it the "Pascalage à l'Acte.") Pascal's insight is that if you really want to be a *croyant*, then become a *pratiquant*. But there is a deeper implicit truth behind this. If you want to be a *pratiquant*, then become a *pratiquant*!

With this in mind, let us look briefly at the five spheres of social determination that have been mentioned. The first, the social institutional sphere is the most obvious determinant and constituent of social reality. It is the moment of externality, the material and substantial expression, of social reality. It is the sphere that is usually given the most attention in Left social critique. It includes the structure of capital and its various sectors, the state apparatus, and the technological system. It includes the formal structure of social reality, including institutional systems of domination and oppression based on sex, gender, race, sexual orientation, culture, and ethnicity. As a formal structure, it includes the determining rules of the system. Yet it obviously intersects with the sphere of social materiality, since institutions consist not merely of structural principles but also of the actual structuration of material constituents in accord with such structural principles.

Although the institutional sphere is the most conspicuous sphere of social determination and the one analyzed most extensively, there remains a need for a deeper and more complex dialectical investigation of the interrelationship between its constituent elements and its interaction with the other spheres of social determination. For example, there are important dialectical interactions (ranging from mutual reinforcement to highly antagonistic contradiction) between productionist and consumptionist institutions, and also between these institutions and both consumptionist and productionist forms of social ideology, forms of the social imaginary, and forms of practice (ethos).

The second sphere consists of the social ethos, habitus, or structure and content of practice in everyday life. In so far as it includes the content of social practice, it intersects with the institutional structure, but it also constitutes part of the collective subjective dimension of the dominant system. Ethos encompasses the prevailing cultural climate of a community or society, its habits, its linguistic expression, its gestures, its rituals. Ethos is the sphere of certain satisfactions and gratifications that accompany practices, either within the confines of the system of domination or beyond it. Ethos is the sphere of social psychological reality. It can only be understood through a very specific analysis of everyday life and all the habits, practices, gestures, and rituals that it entails. This is the area that is neglected most in Left social analysis, but as the discussion of Pascal's wager indicates, it is perhaps the most crucial area for the establishment or transformation of patterns of behavior and forms of consciousness.

The third sphere is the social imaginary. This is the sphere of a society's or community's collective fantasy life. It includes socially conditioned self-images, commodity images, and images of the other. It includes the prevailing myths and paradigmatic narratives in contemporary society. It is a sphere in which the elements of a productionist imaginary, a consumptionist imaginary, a patriarchal imaginary, a nationalist-statist imaginary, and a technological imaginary interact dialectically. It is related to certain preeminent institutions of the imaginary, such as advertising, marketing, mass media, the arts, and mass culture in general. It includes many of the phenomena that the Frankfurt School investigated as part of the culture industry and that Situationism uncovered in the society of the spectacle.

The social imaginary includes, in Lacanian terms, both the symbolic and the imaginary (and might be reconceptualized as two spheres on this basis). The study of the social imaginary explores the social dimensions of desire, need, and demand. The Lacanian Big Other exists within the social imaginary. Žižek has often pointed out that there has been a historical shift in the primary superego injunction from "Thou Shalt Not!" to "Thou Shalt—Enjoy!" However, this shift has been far from complete, and superego mechanisms vary widely depending on one's location within the global capitalist system. In late capitalism, the Big Other has undergone its own identity crisis so that now it takes the form of both the productionist/authoritarian Big Brother who makes infinite demands on us and the consumptionist/ pseudolibertarian Big Mother who offers infinite satisfactions. (The late capitalist imaginary can be summarized in one phrase: "The Big Tit backed up by The Big Stick.")[9]

Fourth, there is the sphere of social ideology. After the institutional sphere, this is the sphere that has received the most attention from the Left and in radical critique. The sense in which the term "ideology" is used here follows generally the traditional usage in critical theory.[10] An ideology is a system of ideas that purports to be an objective depiction of reality but in fact constitutes a systematic distortion of reality on behalf of some particularistic interest or some system of differential power. Though such a system of ideas may contain certain elements of truth to varying degrees, it nevertheless qualifies as ideology because it is also a systemic expression of false consciousness. The more specific subsystems of ideology within the dominant system parallel the various realms of the social imaginary. Thus, there are economic, political, racial, sexual, nationalist-statist, technical-scientific, and other subsystems of ideology that interact dialectically (conditioning one another in ways that may be mutually reinforcing or contradictory) within the larger ideological system. The quasi-hegemonic ideological sector in the present era is that of economistic ideology, and there is a dialectic between the productionist and consumptionist dimensions of this sector. Thus, the system of production is lauded for satisfying the needs of the consumer better than any other possible system; yet the ideology of self-satisfaction through commodity consumption (in addition to being internally self-contradictory) contradicts and, in fact, significantly erodes the contending productionist ideology, with its more traditionalist values of "the work ethic," "the productive citizen," "the job well done," "pride in one's work," et cetera. Ideology is propagated especially through a range of ideological institutions, including discursive media, newspapers, magazines, news programs, talk radio, advertising, marketing, schools, churches, and conventional wisdom as expressed in public opinion. We should not overlook, of course, "the discourse of the university," systems of knowledge that are ultimately at the service of power, whether in formally academic or nonacademic expressions. The discourse of the little masters is at the service of the Master.

We have seen an ever-increasing dominance of economism, and, in particular, of its consumptionist dimension, on a global level, especially in the advanced industrial societies. This has been carried out above all through consumptionist institutions, the consumptionist imaginary, consumptionist ideology, and a consumptionist ethos. This is not to say that the productionist dimension of economism is not also crucial, as is nationalism/statism. Strongly productionist or disciplinary institutions such as the prison, the school, the office, the factory, and the military rely more heavily on productionist ideology, the productionist imaginary, and a productionist ethos for support and legitimacy. Yet there are always multiple interactions. Thus, schools and the military, for example, are legitimated not only by productionism but by the consumptionist image of personal success and upward mobility. Economic enterprises are legitimated not only by the various moments of economism, but also by nationalism/statism, through concepts such as the national interest and national power. It is important to understand the complex dialectic between these various moments if we are to comprehend the power of the system of domination to resist transformation. But though we need to understand all the moments in themselves, the relative significance of these moments must also be considered. Such a consideration will show, for example, that the consumptionist ethos, embedded in a consumptionist institutional structure, and reinforced by the consumptionist imaginary and ideology, is much more powerful than is usually recognized (because of ideological lag, many of our clichés and stereotypes remain productionist, even as the society becomes institutionally, imaginarily, and ethotically much more consumptionist).

The fifth sphere of social determination is the sphere of social materiality. This sphere might be described as the physical, chemical, and biological milieu with which we interact as persons and communities, a milieu that we help determine through our activity and which also helps determine us through its activity. On a deeper, more dialectical level, we must see ourselves as integral parts of the sphere of social materiality and as co-constituting, with other parts, the social ecological whole (or process of becoming-whole). It might be helpful to conceive this sphere not in terms of opposed interiority and exteriority but rather in terms of nonexclusive "extimacy," to use this Lacanian concept in a dialectical and naturalistic sense. We cannot really understand the flourishing of persons and communities or the obstacles to that flourishing (that is, the vicissitudes of freedom and domination) without an understanding of the physical, chemical, and biological conditions of social materiality. If this seems a bit abstract, consider the materiality and material exchanges involved in the petrochemical industry and the geosocial reality called "Cancer Alley" in a bioregion such as southeast Louisiana. This sphere, touched on at various points here, will be explored in much greater detail in future inquiry into the theory of dialectical social ecology.

The point of this analysis of social determination is not only to understand how the various spheres determine and reinforce the existing patterns of thought and action, or to comprehend the nature of their current processes of evolution and transformation. It is also to understand what must be done if patterns of thought and action are to emerge that truly challenge and begin to overturn the system of social domination. It points to the conclusion that an effective movement for social transformation must consist of a growing community whose members are in the process of creating for themselves a different institutional framework for their everyday lives, a different social ethos that emerges in the actual living of those lives, and a different social imaginary and nonideological social (counter-)ideology expressed in their ideas, ideals, aspirations, beliefs, desires, passions, and fantasies.

We must ask what kind of (nonprogrammatic) program and transformative vision might appeal to those who believe in a world that is free, just, democratic, cooperative, and ecological, and more importantly, that might actually lead to the creation of communities of liberation and solidarity that break decisively with the dominant institutional structure, social imaginary, social ideology, and social ethos. Such a transformative program would envision the creation of personal relationships and primary groups (families, affinity groups, base communities) in which caring, cooperation, freedom, justice, and democracy are part of the practice of everyday life. It would foresee the creation of new liberatory communities, democratic ecovillages and towns, and democratically self-managed enterprises. It would imagine the creation of democratic participatory media, arts, music, film, and video. It would look forward to the creation of mutualistic associations to fulfill cooperatively our needs for childcare, health care, education, celebration, expressions of social solidarity, spirituality, and experience of nature.

Many of these ideas were prefigured, for example, in Martin Buber's vision (following his friend Gustav Landauer) of a socialism that was both libertarian and communitarian, and which was aimed at the creation of "an organic commonwealth" that would consist of "a community of communities." Buber proposed what he called a "full cooperative" that would combine cooperative living, production, and consumption.[11] His ideas helped inspire the development of the early socialist kibbutzim. The experience of these communities demonstrates the enormous potential of the cooperative community when it achieves developed institutional expression, though it also shows how this potential can be undermined when the community fails to maintain its distinctive character through its ideology, imaginary, and ethos, and instead conforms increasingly to a larger society with conflicting values (such as capitalist economic values, group privilege, and colonialist oppression).

It is unfortunate that in the United States, at least since the decline of the classical workers' movement, the Right has been so much more skilled at creating and sustaining highly participatory (albeit rigid and hierarchical) institutions, while the Left has specialized in demonstrating, protesting, publishing in its print media, and hoping to have an effect on institutions that are simply not designed to respond to its demands. Accordingly, the best examples of successful organization in (at least partial) opposition to the dominant American late capitalist consumptionist society come from the Right. The rapid growth and internal strength of many right-wing movements can be attributed in large part to their success in grassroots organization, and in creating institutions and practices that fulfill primary social needs and address diverse aspects of the lives of their members. This is particularly true of the religious Right, which includes in the United States tens of millions of active participants who find support for their beliefs and ideals in the everyday practice of their local church, which is in effect a highly participatory grassroots community.

Such a small primary community offers to its members a distinctive ethos, a form of life that synthesizes ideas, beliefs, images, symbols, rituals, practices, habits, and organizational forms. The members of the group find in the community a comprehensive social environment that structures much of their everyday lives. In the most developed of these communities it includes classes, study groups, and other educational activities, a range of social groups based on age, sex, marital status, or interests, recreational activities, camps and retreats, counseling and consolation in times of difficulty, and beyond the local group, an extensive system of external ideological support, including magazines, books, CDs, DVDs, and complete radio and television networks with diverse programming, all of which reinforce the values and practices of the primary group. To this must be added, of course, the core of more formalized ritualistic behavior that is central to religious practice.

The *Manifesto* points out a highly significant development when it notes that since they are "no longer rooted in neighborhoods, the [Left] social movements, in general, seem uninterested in mounting popular mobilizations against foreclosures and other evictions, repossessions and rent gouging, and lack a language with which to discuss the relation of rising food prices with the zooming prices of oil and speculation in commodities markets."[12] The words "no longer" are significant, since they impel us to think back to the time in which radical social movements in the United States were rooted in such communities—most notably during the heroic periods of the classical workers' movement and the civil rights movement. A social movement that aspires to fundamental social transformation must once again be rooted in primary and grass-roots communities—in neighborhoods, in workplaces, in personal and family life, and in all of people's everyday social interactions. It will then be able to mobilize the base because it will in a strong sense *have* a base.

Though primary or base community organization is almost entirely alien to the current mainstream American Left, on the global scale it has been important to major radical and revolutionary movements. One of the most instructive examples of the socially transformative small community is the history of the Christian base communities of Latin America that were inspired by liberation theology. These communities began to flourish in the 1960s and 1970s and developed into an international movement of perhaps several hundred thousand groups (one study estimates that there were as many as eighty thousand in Brazil alone in the mid-1980s), and many millions of participants. Individual base communities range in size from a few dozen to over one hundred members. Members meet frequently for religious celebrations, Bible study with an emphasis on the social justice message of the Hebrew prophets and the Gospels, and political activism centering on the ideas of social liberation and "the preferential option for the poor." These communities have had an enormous influence on social justice and revolutionary struggles in South and Central America and can certainly be given some credit for the degree of success that the Left has had in a number of countries that long suffered under right-wing authoritarian regimes.

Another important historical example that is at least as instructive is the Gandhian Sarvodaya (Welfare of All) movement in India, which inspired many millions and was a central force in overthrowing the British raj. This movement will be discussed in detail below,[13] but it will be useful to summarize its contribution briefly at this point. The movement had certain shortcomings from which we can also learn (e.g., a naïve faith that exploiters would be moved to voluntarily redistribute their wealth), but its enormous accomplishments are instructive and inspiring. One of Gandhi's goals was that small groups of committed activists would form an *ashram* in each village throughout India. In Sarvodaya's usage, the term *ashram* meant a political and spiritual base community in which the members lived communally. It was seen as a step toward the establishment of Sarvodaya villages, in which the cooperative principles of the movement could be practiced in a more comprehensive manner. In addition, it was hoped that eventually every village in India would have a *gram sevak*, a well-trained and self-disciplined full-time Sarvodaya community organizer. The larger goal was a system of village *swaraj*, meaning democratic self-rule and economic self-management in the local community. Self-rule would be carried out through the *gramsabha*, or village assembly, and the *panchayat*, or five-person village council. The spinning wheel became the symbol of the movement, in part for its functional role in decentralized, self-managed production, but also because spinning was seen as an edifying meditative activity, and a communal one that promotes solidarity. *Khadi*, or homespun fabric, was also emblematic of the movement, for it was seen as an expression of all of its aesthetic, ethical, political, economic, and spiritual values. The concept that is perhaps most closely associated with the Gandhian movement is satyagraha, the Force of Truth. It expresses the idea that injustice and oppression can be most successfully overturned through the participatory political act, through massive direct action or civil disobedience directed at the very structures of injustice. The movement also developed the idea of *bhoodan*, or gift of land, in which land was donated for cooperative village farming projects. Though it never succeeded in making cooperative production the norm in Indian agriculture, five million acres of land were put into cooperative projects.

Many of the principles of the Gandhian movement have been carried on by the Sarvodaya Shramadana movement in Sri Lanka, which will also be discussed in more detail later.[14] The movement interprets *sarvodaya* as a "unity of awakening" on every level from the person and family, through the village to the larger society. *Shramadana* means a "gift of labor." The movement has created a "Five Stage Development Process." It begins with the members of a village community perceiving a problem and then discussing it with Sarvodaya field workers. A shramadana camp is then organized to plan the project and begin the village awakening process. Local groups, training programs, and planning meetings are then organized to prepare for the work. A formal Sarvodaya Shramadana Society is then formed to help finance the projects. Microcredit programs are often established and the movement has created several thousand village community banks and savings societies. Finally, the work is undertaken and completed, after which the participants reach out to other communities with similar needs to offer their labor, skills, experience, technical abilities, and material aid. Millions of Sri Lankans have participated in Sarvodaya projects for well over half a century, and projects have been carried out in about half of the country's twenty-three thousand villages. It has perhaps been the most far-reaching grassroots development movement in the world, though it remains almost unknown to the American Left.

It should be noted that the base communities of Latin America, the Gandhian movement, and the Sarvodaya Shramadana movement have all been developments in the global South. The American Left might be less dispirited and lacking in direction were it willing to find inspiration in movements and experiments that are outside the framework of Western modernity (or Western postmodernity for that matter). It is telling that the *Manifesto* can conclude that changes such as "the collapse of the Soviet Union" and the transformation of other Leninist regimes "have all but removed the traditional sources of radical imagination from the political landscape." However, if the "radical imagination" of the Left was reduced to getting its inspiration from Leninist bureaucratic state capitalist regimes, then the problem was much deeper than collapse or mutation on the part of these regimes. The *Manifesto* contends that "despite all of its warts, the ideological anti-capitalism, anti-imperialism, the military power of the Soviet Union, and its promise of liberation filled the hearts of millions of oppressed people in the West as well as the global South with hope." However, by the time of its demise, the appeal of the USSR had dwindled all over the West, and many in the global South who strategically allied themselves to varying degrees with the Soviet Union in an era of Cold War polarization had no such illusions. They ("they" meaning especially the masses of people engaged in grassroots struggles) often had their own ideas of freedom, socialism, and self-determination and did not look to the USSR for the "promise of liberation."

It is unfortunate that radicals in advanced capitalist societies have not in general looked to the global South (apart from tendencies there that are strongly influenced by European political movements) for the reinvigoration of the radical imagination. The South has had and still has today an enormous amount to teach them, as shown by the movements just mentioned. There are many other examples, and, more importantly, a larger cultural context that generates them. As radical ecofeminists such as Vandana Shiva, Ariel Salleh, and Maria Mies have pointed out, there are around the world age-old traditions of caring labor and mutual aid by women, peasants, and indigenous peoples that challenge not only the economistic, acquisitive values of capitalism, but the instrumentalist, dominating values that have plagued humanity since the origins of civilization in patriarchy and ancient despotism. The reaffirmation of these liberatory traditions is becoming particularly powerful in indigenous movements of Latin America that challenge the traditional Left and the ideology of postcolonialism on behalf of a radical decolonialism founded on traditional communal values and modes of social interaction and interaction with nature.

As inspiring and instructive as these developments may be, one should not however conclude that Western and specifically American radical and revolutionary traditions do not contain the resources for a new direction for the Left. Indeed, the *Manifesto* itself points out some of these possibilities. In particular, it mentions ideas concerning radical democratic politics, cooperative economics, cooperative housing, radical media, transformation of personal life, and a new relationship to nature, ideas that all have roots in American radical politics since the New Left of the 1960s. Some of these ideas are discussed in concrete detail in the *Manifesto*, while others are mentioned only briefly and need clarification and elaboration. We should look more carefully at some of these important themes.

The *Manifesto* expresses strong support for "radical democratic institutions . . . in communities" (37). It states, for example, that "the Right to the City would invest authority for issues regarding the allocation of space to community democratic decision-making" (57). This would indeed be a very important advance. Presumably, if this important authority could be democratically controlled by the local community, many other powers could also devolve to that grassroots level. However, the meaning of the "community" that has control is crucial. A deep and authentic commitment to radical participatory democracy would require placing decisions about space and many other key questions in the hands of institutions such as assemblies, councils, and citizens' committees, at the most basic levels, such as the neighborhood or town. In fact, some decisions could be even more decentralized if some responsibilities were allocated to (or perhaps better, appropriated by) assemblies and committees at the level of the block or section of the neighborhood. The degree to which abstract, formal democracy can be transformed into direct democracy will determine the degree to which a democratic ethos and a democratic practice can become integral to each citizen's life activities.

Another point in the *Manifesto* that is relevant to democracy in the community is what it calls "fights for socialized medicine and for the expansion of mass public transportation" (37). Both of these demands, as stated, are typical elements of liberal and social democratic programs. So we might ask how medicine and transportation might not only be more "socialized," but also how they might be fundamentally transformed in a radically democratic and participatory manner. To what degree could there be a radical decentralization of preventive health care to the neighborhood level through situating health care workers and medical clinics in each neighborhood (though obviously some technologies will require central locations)? In addition to fulfilling the present need for *mass* transportation, we need to think about *demassifying* planning. To what degree can the siting and scale of housing, workplaces, shops, parks, recreational spaces, and civic centers be planned to minimize the need for individual or mass transportation and maximize the level of interaction and participation in the local neighborhood community? A crucial radical democratic project is to combat the New Urbanist co-optation of ideas such as walkability, low energy consumption, social and ethnic diversity, and the rich intermixture in the neighborhood or town of homes, workplaces, shops, play areas, and arenas for cultural activities. We must show in practice how these goals can most authentically be realized, not through ecoapartheid, but rather through creatively diverse, humane, just, and democratic communities.

The nature of its housing is obviously one of the key determinants of the overall nature of the community. The *Manifesto* takes a strong position in favor of "housing as a non-commodified public utility, that is, either publicly owned or organized as limited equity cooperatives (no tenant can sell her apartment privately, only back to the co-op)" (57). This general goal is a highly desirable one and such explicit support for socially owned or cooperative housing is essential. However, certain issues about how to achieve it need to be faced. Is this a proposal that even single-family homes be publicly or cooperatively owned? If so, how would such a system be structured? What would be the advantage of public ownership as opposed to cooperative ownership? Participatory democratic decision-making is a central goal of the *Manifesto*, but would this not be achieved much more successfully through cooperative rather than "public" ownership, if the latter is defined as *state* ownership? Would community land trusts fit into the *Manifesto*'s picture of noncommodified housing? Under such a structure, land is owned collectively, while a house or apartment is owned individually, but can only be sold to a new land trust member, and only for the equivalent of the original cost plus improvements. Through such cooperative housing, speculation is eliminated and improvements to the community through the "collective force" of the citizens accrue to the community as a whole.

The *Manifesto* expresses a strong commitment to cooperative economics. It advocates "the founding of radical democratic institutions at the workplace," efforts to "decommodify essential services," and "new forms of collective ownership and control over the natural and productive resources" (37). Such concepts could be developed into a wide-ranging program for a democratic system of production based on worker self-management. The United States has a rich history of radical labor movements (most notably the Industrial Workers of the World) that have fought for democratic control of the economy, in addition to valuable experience of self-managed worker cooperatives, from the important self-managed sector of the plywood industry from the 1930s through the 1950s, to the contemporary worker cooperative movement spearheaded by the US Federation of Worker Cooperatives. Few people today in the United States have ever heard the case for self-managed production, but when it is presented it often finds a highly receptive audience.

There remain many questions that have to be faced in proposals for a self-managed economy. The Mondragon cooperatives in Spain, the largest system of worker cooperatives in the world (with eighty-four thousand workers, a cooperative bank, cooperative housing, a workers' university with four thousand students, and a health care system) found that democratic decision-making becomes difficult if units grow to much more than five hundred members. For this reason, efforts were made to create a federation in which the constituent cooperatives would not exceed this scale greatly (the average for individual cooperatives is now about eight hundred). A challenge will be to create economic democracy in which cooperation can take place on a very large scale, in effect creating a larger federation of federations, while democratic control remains effectively at the base. It must also be assured that there are no second-class workers (as emerged in the Mondragon system) and that all units and participants within the federation have a position of relative equality. Another challenge arises from the fact that even a large expansion of the cooperative, economically democratic sector would not in itself mean a thoroughgoing decommodification of economics, in so far as it would occur within a market system of exchange. For this reason, it is important to investigate alternative systems of exchange that could be put into effect on a much larger scale than the systems of labor exchange and local currencies that presently exist, even while vastly expanding these existing alternatives.

The *Manifesto* rightly points out the importance of immigrants to the economies of many of our communities, stresses the issue of immigrant rights, and notes that immigrants have made important contributions to revitalizing labor struggles in certain areas. We might ask further whether some immigrant groups, whose members have much stronger communal ties and feelings of solidarity than does the general populace, and which are not as well integrated into the dominant consumptionist culture, might be capable of forms of cooperative and community-based organization that could be a model for other segments of the population. For example, we might reflect on the fact that perhaps one-third, if not more, of the population of El Salvador now lives in the United States. There are other significant, if perhaps less statistically striking, examples. Of course, the problem of "illegality" is an enormous one, and the Right would react viciously to greater militancy on the part of any foreign-born workers. But then, class struggle has been called "struggle" for a reason. As "America" globalizes itself into the world, the world globalizes itself into "America"— whether "America" likes it or not. Perhaps "America" will finally be dragged kicking and screaming into the world, and the American Left along with it.

The *Manifesto* also confronts the key issue of media and communication (central to questions of the social imaginary and the social ideology) when it states that the Left has lacked "a truly national presence, a public press that regularly reports and comments on the economic, political, and cultural situations and a network of major educational institutions that constitute counterhegemonies to the prevailing capitalist 'common sense'" (7). This observation points to crucial dimensions of a more general problem, which is the relative monopolization of the means of communication and the existence of a prevailing ideological and imaginary hegemony. One of the two practical proposals that are emphasized in bold type in the *Manifesto* is "starting a newsweekly in both hard copy and internet" (60). In doing so, it points out one of the many crucial gaps in Left political culture in this country. If we consider the enormous contribution that has been made to the Left by a single radio and television news program *Democracy Now!*, we can begin to imagine what a comprehensive system of radical Left media might accomplish.

However, we should keep in mind that as undeniably essential as the radical press may be, the existence of one or more national newspapers on the Left is not likely to be a major catalyst for social transformation. A number of countries have long had important Left dailies. France, for example, has had the Communist daily *L'Humanité* (founded in 1904), and *Libération* (founded in 1973), which was established as an extreme Left publication and was generally Left for much of its history, not to mention other important papers with more center-Left sympathies. It must be recognized that movement newspapers play a significant role in social movements and that they have contributed to the relatively greater importance and endurance of the European Left, as compared to its highly marginalized American counterpart. It is also important to realize, however, that newspapers are more an expression of the power and vitality of a social movement than they are the overriding force that creates and develops the movement (or else Trotskyists and Maoists would be a hundred times stronger than they actually are, and *Libé* would have converted the French bobotariat, rather than succumbing to it). Nevertheless, they are an important element of a larger system of communication that helps generate an alternative social imaginary and alternative social counterideology, and, not least of all, that helps create an ethos of liberated communication that is part of the everyday lives of a growing community.

Above all, it is crucial to create media that flow out of and support transformations at the personal, small group, and grassroots community levels. The electronic mass media are, much more than the print media, central to the shaping of consciousness today. But even beyond creating alternative mass print and electronic media, we need to think about a goal of creating democratic participatory media that are not merely marginal to people's lives. Can we see a flourishing of diverse media in the neighborhood? Can we create a movement for micropower radio that would demonstrate that every neighborhood can create a community radio station? Can we show the feasibility of a community video project in every neighborhood? Can we demonstrate the possibility of a community newspaper in every neighborhood? Can "seizure of the means of communication" be seen as an immediate, concrete project with real prospects for significant successes?

The *Manifesto* confronts some of the most crucial questions concerning social transformation, those related to subjectivity and the personal dimension, when it asserts that radical democracy should be extended to "everyday social interactions, including the home," and that we should "rethink personal relationships within the framework of class and innovative and creative psychic economies" (37, 3) However, this is also one of the areas on which the text is most vague. For example, it is not made clear *how* class is to be used as a basis for this rethinking, why considerations other than class (gender, ethnicity, sexual orientation, etc.) do not demand such rethinking at least as exigently, or precisely what the intriguing concept of "innovative and creative psychic economies" might imply.

The idea of radically democratizing the home calls for some discussion of how patriarchal values still intrude into family and personal life, how the society of mass consumption is revolutionizing these areas, how the insights of feminism, radical psychology and psychoanalysis are relevant to the project, and what democratized forms of personal and family life might look like, at least in general terms. Under late capitalism, there has been a disintegration of the traditional productionist ego and a weakening of traditional forms of personal life. How, specifically, do these developments offer new opportunities for social creation and how do they create new obstacles to collective action?

It is important to recognize that psychological conditions are material social forces that demand careful and specific analysis. It has become increasingly clear that to celebrate uncritically the disorganization of the classic productionist ego and the disintegration of the traditional authoritarian character structure and to hope that forms of liberatory nomadism and rhizomatics will emerge automatically from their decline is to lapse into the most ungrounded abstract idealism. In an earlier era, Wilhelm Reich could write astutely of the emotional plague that was expressed in the rigid, authoritarian character structure. But today we are faced with new forms of emotional plague that are characterized by widespread depression and anxiety, and the proliferation of narcissistic states and the so-called borderline personality.

Confronting these social psychological realities is essential when we ponder the question of the grounds for the existence of fetishistic disavowal even within aspiring communities of liberation. Why do we see repeatedly in this context the phenomenon of "I know very well" (I have a good critique of domination and concept of a liberatory society), but "nevertheless" (I can't act in a way that moves effectively from one to the other)? Why, instead of regenerative social creation do we so often see forms of leftist repetition compulsion: either an automatistic reversion to the politics of permanent protest or an automatistic reiteration of abstract idealism through escapist utopian theorizing.

It is obvious that the issue of the personal being the political must be explored in much greater theoretical depth and with much greater practical diligence than has been customary. And it is impossible to confront issues of personal and psychological transformation in a serious manner without considering how primary groups shape selfhood and personality. It is here that the transformative potential of small groups such as affinity groups and base communities seems so obvious. Could we use our radical imagination to envision a political movement in which *every participant* is a member of a primary group or microcommunity of a dozen or more members who are collectively at work on embodying in their personal and communal lives values of love and compassion, solidarity and mutual aid, peace and justice, freedom and creativity?

And what is true of human nature is also true of nature. Thus, the *Manifesto* states wisely that we must "rethink the relationship between Nature and production" (3). However, it says little about where this rethinking might lead us, or what other areas might have to be reconsidered if we take seriously our place in the natural world. Indeed, it is in general rather vague on questions of ecology and the natural world. From the formulation just cited, one would expect a discussion of the far-reaching implications of the fact that the dominant system of production has led us into the sixth great mass extinction in the entire history of life on Earth, and into catastrophically disruptive climate change. There is also a need for a consideration of why the society at large and the mainstream of the Left in particular have been unable, even when having some recognition of the gravity of the crisis, to act accordingly (lapsing once more into fetishistic disavowal). The developing ecological catastrophe should be looked upon as more than another argument that capitalism functions rather badly. Instead, it should be seen as the ultimate intrusion of the traumatic real, something like a collective death sentence for humanity and much of life on Earth. We might begin to think seriously about what the conditions might be for a reprieve to be granted.

Consider an example that shows with striking irony the degree of inaction that has been exhibited by the Left. The Emirate of Abu Dhabi and private enterprise together are building a carbon-neutral, waste-free city for fifty thousand inhabitants. The project, Masdar, has to a large degree languished over the past decade, yet it does exist and has a few thousand inhabitants. Its primary function will be to serve as greenwashing for those who play a crucial role in global ecological destruction (in 2006, the United Arab Emirates had the second-highest per capita level of CO_2 emissions in the world). Nevertheless, it poses the question of why, among the tens of millions of activists of the Left around the planet, not even a relative few have been able to come together to plan and create an ecocommunity that even remotely approaches the proposed scale of Masdar, and that would offer a real-world embodiment of not only ecological soundness but also social justice and radical democracy.

More fundamentally, there is a general failure to consider the profound challenge that ecological crisis poses for all of our dominant institutions and ways of thinking and perceiving. We need to ask what a truly ecological culture and system of production might look like, with some degree of specificity—as if we are actually planning to create them on some scale or another. We might try to imagine how radically such a social order must differ from the social world in which we live, which, if we are to speak honestly, must be called a culture of extinction, a culture of extermination, an ecocidal culture. We might ask whether today's ecocidal industrial and technological system can continue to exist, and if it cannot, what kind of just and humane system could possibly replace it. We might also ask what changes in culture, institutions, and personal relations might follow from the insights of ecofeminism concerning the connections between the quest to dominate nature and the system of patriarchy. We might ask how bioregional values and the idea of reinhabitation might fit into radical politics. We might ask how the radical imagination can be directed toward the question of what forms an ecological selfhood, a radically ecological politics, and a future culture of nature might take. According to Thoreau's famous dictum, "in wildness is the preservation of the world."[15] Is it possible that "in wildness is the preservation of the Left"? Or even beyond its preservation, its regeneration?

Another important subject addressed by the *Manifesto* is the future of the nation-state. It asks: "Will nation-states reassert their autonomy, or are new political arrangements needed to insure a world of growing equality and democracy? If so, what would they look like, within the current system of global power? If not, what are the arguments, under present conditions, for the possibility of state autonomy" (43). These are important questions, and given the de facto concentration of power in the nation-state system and the system of transnational capital, we will have to judge in various cases whether a shift in the balance of power away from the nation-state or back toward it will be preferable (i.e., less disastrous). It should be added that it is not clear what "state autonomy" can possibly mean in a global corporate capitalist world order. We must recognize that both the nation-state and transnational bodies necessarily reflect their positions within the larger global system of power that has both statist and corporate dimensions.

In this connection, it must be noted that the *Manifesto* does not clearly face the problem of the centralized, hierarchical, bureaucratic state. Nor is the problematical nature of representation, the current ideological foundation of that institution, confronted forthrightly. A manifesto for radical democracy should, one would think, consider the degree to which authentic democracy can exist at various scales, within both political and economic institutions, and the degree to which popular power is necessarily alienated in large-scale and centralized units of decision-making. It would seem that such considerations would point to the conclusion that the "new political arrangements" that are needed are ones that allow communities to reappropriate the powers that are now alienated to corporations, to nation-states, and to a lesser degree, to transnational political entities. In this sense, the challenge for radical democracy is to transform the base communities, the popular base, into the effective material base of social organization.

Many of the ideas expressed here have long been part of the anarchist tradition (in addition to being part of a larger libertarian socialist tradition) and that tradition still has much to offer to radical politics. It is rather disconcerting to read in the *Manifesto* that "even the anarchists have few ideas beyond protest and resistance" (24). It is true that the general public, absorbing their political education from the corporate media, identifies anarchism with a certain dimension of anarchist youth culture. As a result, it seems to be no more than a postadolescent conspiracy with the single guiding principle that "you have to break a few windows to make an omelet." But there is more to it than this, and critical political thought needs to be a bit more perceptive.

There has existed in recent times a broad spectrum of anarchist ideas concerning social organization, even if we limit the list to those that are more detailed than those expressed in the *Manifesto* itself. Although some of these ideas are deeply flawed, as a whole they constitute a theoretically rich and highly suggestive body of theory. Castoriadis's ideas of a self-managed economy were basically anarchist. Bookchin's libertarian municipalism and confederalism were originally elaborated within an anarchist theoretical framework. Fotopoulos's "inclusive democracy" presents an anarchist economic and political model. Some anarchists have been inspired by Parecon or Participatory Economics, as developed by Albert and Hahnel. Many still adhere to and attempt to update anarcho-syndicalism and revolutionary unionism. Many others carry on the tradition of cooperativism or mutualism. Karatani's associationism, as discussed in his book *Transcritique*,[16] is a synthesis of Marxist theory and anarchist (mutualist) practice. Even the least systematic tendency within anarchism, the anarchist youth culture, while focusing on anticapitalist and anticorporate globalist struggles has developed ideas of affinity group organization, association for mutual aid, and networking that go significantly "beyond protest and resistance."

Furthermore, It is significant that the most provocative political document in recent times, *The Coming Insurrection*, emerged out of (as the French police phrased it) the "anarcho-autonomist" milieu .[17] As Julien Coupat points out in an interview in *Le Monde*, "One hasn't seen power become fearful of a book for a very long time."[18] The work is noteworthy for confronting the modes of colonization of the subject, the need for effective and immediate radical transformation of everyday life, and the emancipatory dimensions of actual social struggles. It faces both the impending catastrophe and the actually existing one, identifies the central place of the affinity group and base communities in a communal future, and reflects critically on the meaning of popular assemblies. While completely rejecting all illusions about the forms of bureaucratic and terroristic state capitalism that have masqueraded as "communism," it also helps divulge the well-kept secret that the senility and death throes of various forms of statist despotism and (anti)social (un)democratic (non)reformism have masked the continual birth and rebirth of communist practice.

The work is not without serious limitations. Its greatest strength, its expression of radical opposition and marginality, is at the same time its greatest weakness. The modes of invisibility and social insurrection that it proposes are forms of both self-expression and self-limitation of social revolutionary power. It leaves underdeveloped the most crucial modes of radical transformation that must be expressed through intensified social *visibility*, *audibility*, and we might even say *tangibility*, and it says little about the socially and ecologically regenerative action that is desperately needed. But what is significant is not the work's limitation (limitations are easy to find everywhere) but the astounding fact that out of a moribund contemporary Left can come such energy, creativity, and transformative vision. It is, in fact, evidence that there is still a Left in the West, that there are still living seeds of liberation in the global rotten core.

And perhaps a few more words should be added about that notorious anarchist youth culture. Those who lived through the aftermath of Hurricane Katrina saw many hundreds of young anarchists (and even thousands from the larger anarchistic *mouvance*) come to New Orleans and the surrounding region to help desperately needy communities that their state and corporate masters abandoned cruelly and murderously. They came with ideas such as organization based on nonhierarchical solidarity, self-determination on the level of the local neighborhood community, and the creation of lasting grassroots cooperative institutions. Some of these young people were willing to devote months or even years of their lives—living in makeshift dormitories or tents, sometimes sleeping on floors, working long hours in unhealthy conditions, receiving no financial remuneration, using up their own savings, putting aside other plans for their lives—to put these ideas into practice. Some describe their experience, despite all the tragedy, frustration, and *betrayal* that they endured, as the most fulfilling time of their lives. Yes, they also protested and sometimes got arrested, and they deserve recognition for their resistance. However, they deserve even more credit for the positive dimensions of both their vision and their action to save and restore communities.

In conclusion, the *Manifesto* is valuable for its analysis of the roots of the current social crisis. It shows that there are aspects (particularly economic ones) of this crisis that few have begun to comprehend adequately, and that need to be understood clearly. However, we know that awareness of crisis and even of its causes does not in itself lead to liberatory forms of social transformation. In a culture of denial, fetishistic disavowal, and co-optation, such knowledge is fairly easily assimilated into the dominant system of thought and practice. Its existence can even function as a form of legitimation of that very system and its illusions of freedom and openness to dissent. No manifesto can in itself create all the conditions for social (or personal) transformation, and needless to say, neither can any critique of a manifesto do so. But if a text is to function as a manifesto of radical politics, a manifesto that proclaims the need for a radical turning, it will offer to the reader, or perhaps even impose on the reader, something that will remain with and, indeed, haunt that reader. It will inspire specific, immediate, transformational action, the beginning of such a turning. I would suggest that it would perhaps offer something like this injunction: "Create your own community of liberation. From this moment on, direct your most concerted efforts, your best work, and your greatest feats of imagination toward creating the impossible community, and do so first of all precisely where you are, with those around you."

Doing so would not mean, as some might hastily conclude, a fetishism of the local and bare particularity. It would mean, after fully recognizing and passing through whatever singularity, the creation of a community that expresses the universal particular. It would mean regenerating, in the creation of forms of life embodying communal individuality, the particular, concrete universality on which the great commons, that larger concrete universality, can finally be founded.

The tradition of communism, in its most meaningful and histori-cally grounded sense (the most libertarian and participatory communism), is the tradition of the commons, the practice of humanity through 99 percent of its history. It is also, as Peter Linebaugh shows so beautifully in *The Magna Carta Manifesto*, a deeply rooted tradition that lived on even in Europe into the medieval and modern periods and has only been suppressed in both the West and globally through the most concerted efforts of the centralist and imperialist nation-state, and the ruthlessly colonizing market economy.[19] Communism, not as an ideology or abstract political program, but as communal practice, as the activity of "common-ing," may be the only possible transition to any liberatory form of socialism, at the same time that it already supersedes any future socialism that it may help create.

In our present predicament, we seem to be faced with a coming community that is capable of almost anything except coming, and a coming insurrection whose destructive powers are much more evident than are its creative ones. We must retrieve the history of commons, the commune, and communism, and resituate our creative communal prac-tice within that history. In doing so, we will help destroy the identification of communism and the common with certain ideological constructs that have been used to legitimate forms of state capitalism, bureaucratic centralism, and political vanguardism that have inevitably worked to dissolve ruthlessly the authentic communal sphere. In doing so, we will give a definitive answer to the paradoxical question, "Why is communism so good in practice, though it never seems to work in theory?" That answer lies in the creation of forms of life that challenge, materially and expe-rientially, the dualistic split between critical theoretical reflection and concrete communal practice. We might debate ad infinitum the question of whether another world is possible. But we will only find a convincing answer by demonstrating that if something is actual, then it is undeniably possible. The answer lies in the realization of the impossible community.

3

The Third Concept of Liberty: Theorizing the Free Community

> "From nature I come to the work of man. The idea of mankind being premised—I shall prove that it gives us no idea of the state, since the state is a mechanical thing, any more than it gives us an idea of a machine. Only something that is an object of freedom is called an idea. So we must go even beyond the state!—For every state must treat free men as cogs in a machine; and this it ought not to do; so it must stop."
>
> —G.W.F. Hegel[1]

The Senses of Freedom

Isaiah Berlin, in a famous essay, popularized the idea that there are in modern political thought two main conceptions of freedom, which he called "negative" and "positive."[2] Ever since, debate has raged about the validity of his classification. There seems to be little doubt that he described a certain concept of negative freedom accurately. However problematic this concept may be, it has the merit of being a rather clear and distinct idea. It is what has generally been meant by "freedom" in the classical liberal tradition associated with theorists such as Hobbes, Locke, Mill, and Spencer. And it has been shared by their successors, including Hayek, Friedman, and Nozick, in what most Anglo-American observers call "libertarian" thought today.

According to Berlin, the negative concept of freedom poses the question, "What is the area within which the subject—a person or group of persons—is or should be left to do or be what he is able to do or be, without interference by other persons?"[3] Thus, negative freedom means freedom from coercion and the threat of coercion. From this standpoint, "if I am prevented by others from doing what I could otherwise do, I am to that degree unfree; and if this area is contracted by other men beyond a certain minimum, I can be described as being coerced, or, it may be, enslaved."[4] Negative freedom focuses on one's ability to "do what one wants to do" without being prevented from doing so by force and coercion or by the threat of force and coercion. Whether one is unable to do so for other reasons, or whether it is advisable for one to do so, are not seen as relevant to this issue.

Berlin holds that the positive concept of freedom focuses on the question "What, or who, is the source of control or interference that can determine someone to do, or be, this rather than that?"[5] He says that it "derives from the wish on the part of the individual to be his own master. I wish my life and decisions to depend on myself, not on external forces of whatever kind. I wish to be the instrument of my own, not of other men's, acts of will. I wish to be a subject, not an object; to be moved by reasons, by conscious purposes, which are my own, not by causes which affect me, as it were, from outside."[6] The emphasis is thus not on noncoercion, but rather on self-determination, often interpreted as the ability to carry out one's true will or to act in a truly rational manner (though whether one actually succeeds in these endeavors is not part of this definition of freedom).

It has often been pointed out that both conceptions of freedom, as formulated by Berlin, are in a sense both negative and positive. In each case, there are certain obstacles to freedom that might stand in the way of its attainment, and there are some desired or desirable actions (following one's own desires or choices, whether de facto, or in some ideal sense) or states of being (becoming a rational agent, becoming autonomous) that are goals of free activity. The negative conception focuses on the absence of obstacles, in the form of coercive action, to the pursuit of one's goals. The positive conception focuses on the quest to achieve those goals.

In delineating the nature of positive freedom, Berlin directs attention almost exclusively to one particular version of that concept. He calls this "the positive doctrine of liberation by reason," and warns that it has been a pernicious force in history to the degree that it has led to the imposition of coercive force by some for the alleged good of others. He claims that various forms of this doctrine "are at the heart of many of the nationalist, communist, authoritarian, and totalitarian creeds of our day."[7] This is undoubtedly true; these "creeds" have in fact appealed to such a doctrine for justification. Where Berlin's analysis fails, however, is his invalid identification of the class of positive concepts of freedom with one subcategory of such concepts. He commits the fallacy of hastily generalizing from *certain* positive concepts of liberty to "*the* positive concept of liberty." However, not all positive conceptions of freedom can be reduced to the concept of "liberation by reason," and not all of those that have espoused "liberation by reason" have gone in the authoritarian direction repeatedly described and predicted by Berlin. These conceptions have concerned not only *self-determination*, but also, more broadly, *self-realization*.

The tradition of positive freedom as self-realization is much more far-reaching than one would suspect from Berlin's discussion, and has a rich history in Western political thought. It has deep roots in the Aristotelian tradition, in the vision of human flourishing or *eudaimonia* as the actualization of a wide spectrum of human potentialities. This theme has been carried on and developed more critically in dialectical thought, and has been central to Hegel and German idealism, and to Marxism and neo-Marxist philosophies. However, developed theories of positive freedom have also existed in Anglo-American thought, and Berlin's generalizations fail even to take even these into account.

T.H. Green, one of the foremost liberal theorists of the nineteenth century, developed a very sophisticated conception of positive freedom as self-realization. According to Green, there is a negative moment of "freedom from" in the emergence of positive freedom, in that certain constraints must be overcome for it to be achieved. These include, on the one hand, the constraint of excessive coercion, and, on the other, the constraint of deprivation of the means for one's personal and social development. Addressing the issue of coercion, he asserts that "there can be no freedom among men who act not willingly but under compulsion," but he adds that noncoercion "is in itself no contribution to true freedom."[8] What he means is that noncoercion contributes to true freedom as a precondition for the latter, but it does not contribute as a constituent of such freedom. The other sort of constraints that must be eliminated as a precondition for "true freedom" are a spectrum of social evils. Green mentions such social ills as overcrowding, bad health conditions, widespread addiction, and poverty.[9]

In the absence of these constraints, or, stated affirmatively, if the necessary preconditions for the emergence of true freedom are present, human beings can go on to develop their highest potentialities as social beings. Green cites St. Paul on behalf of the concept that this true freedom requires self-determination or agency. It is a "freedom from the law, from ordinances, from the fear which these inspire" that is achieved when one is "conscious of himself as the author of the law that he obeys."[10] Such freedom results from one's making "the fulfillment of the law of one's being" into the "object of one's will."[11] It consists, moreover, of the attainment of a good that is not merely one's own, but is a common good. It is "a positive power or capacity of doing or enjoying something worth doing or enjoying," and is achieved "in common with others."[12] More specifically, it is a form of social self-realization that includes such constituents as good health, proper education, sound housing, economic security, moral responsibility, shared social values, and active participation in the political community.

L.H. Hobhouse carried on the development of this modern liberal concept of positive freedom. In his book *Liberalism*, he presents an analysis of liberty as a multidimensional phenomenon that includes civil, fiscal, personal, social, economic, domestic, local, racial, national, and international liberties as its constituents. If one examines what he means by these various elements, one finds that they include the rule of law, equality under the law, governmental fiscal responsibility, freedom of thought and expression, equality of opportunity, nondiscrimination, freedom of association (including labor organization), sexual equality, child welfare programs, public health and education programs, national and racial independence, and freedom from militarism, and aggression.[13]

The British liberal positive conception of freedom was carried over in post–New Deal American liberalism, notably through the influence of its most important political philosopher John Dewey, who was influenced by Hobhouse. In *Liberalism and Social Action*, Dewey traces the evolution of liberalism from a laissez-faire, economistic ideology with a negative concept of liberty to a philosophy of social engagement with a broad, positive conception of freedom. He explains that the liberal concept of freedom has evolved in relation to the movement of history and changing human needs and aspirations:

> During the late seventeenth and early eighteenth centuries it meant liberation from despotic dynastic rule. A century later it meant release of industrialists from inherited legal customs that hampered the rise of new forces of production. Today, it signifies liberation

from material insecurity and from the coercions and repressions that prevent multitudes from participation in the vast cultural resources that are at hand.[14]

When he explains the core of the "renascent liberalism" that he defends, he does so entirely in terms of positive freedom as self-realization. The "end" of liberalism, he says, is "the liberation of individuals so that realization of their capacities may be the law of their life," and the means that it utilizes to pursue that end is "freed intelligence as the method of directing change."[15] Dewey concludes by defining the "cause for which liberalism enduringly stands" as "the cause of the liberty of the human spirit, the cause of opportunity of human beings for full development of their powers."[16] This commitment to human freedom as self-realization has been the great strength of modern liberalism and the basis for much of its appeal. In fact, the decline in influence of modern liberal ideology has resulted in part from the fact that liberal discourse, in both its practical political and its theoretical forms, has shifted to a narrower focus on the defense of specific, often economistic, rights and entitlements, and the larger vision of freedom as social self-realization, rather than evolving further, has receded to the background.

The self-realization tradition is carried on today within the modern liberal tradition notably in the human capabilities approach developed by Amartya Sen and Martha Nussbaum. It is obvious that the realization of human capacities can reasonably be formulated as the attainment of a kind of positive freedom, and this is, in fact, what Sen does in his book *Development as Freedom*, in which he discusses development in relation to a many-dimensional "substantive freedom."[17] If the human capabilities approach is interpreted in this way, it encompasses both positive and negative aspects of freedom, but constitutes as a whole a positive self-realization conception. Nussbaum elaborates on the nature of this self-realization in her Central Human Functional Capabilities Approach, in which she specifies ten areas of capability that are significant. These include: (1) "life"; (2) "bodily health"; (3) "bodily integrity" (including freedom of movement, freedom from aggression, and sexual and reproductive freedom); (4) the "senses, imagination, and thought" (including educational and cultural opportunities, freedom of expression, and religious freedom); (5) the "emotions" (including freedom of personal development and freedom from fear); (6) "practical reason" (including freedom to plan one's own life and freedom of conscience); (7) "affiliation" (including the ability to develop social feelings and relationships, freedom of speech and assembly, dignity, and freedom from arbitrary discrimination; (8) relationships to "other species" (development of an engaged relationship to the natural world); (9) "play" (access to various forms of enjoyment); and (10) "control over one's environment" (including freedom of political participation, the right to hold property, freedom from arbitrary interference, and the right to rewarding and dignified work).[18]

Nussbaum's approach, which is an important contemporary example of a theory of positive freedom, is not easily subject to the extreme abuses against which Berlin constantly warns. Its larger focus is on freedom in the positive sense of opportunity to attain certain states of being that are identified with the human good, but it also includes a strong dimension of negative freedom (since this is also a precondition for such opportunity to exist). Nevertheless, there are grounds on which such a theoretical framework might justify a level of social coercion that is far beyond what would be acceptable to classical liberals and to many antiauthoritarians and libertarians, both Right and Left. A major shortcoming is that it touches on the issue of self-determination (in point four), but it does not make this a central area of concern or critical analysis.[19]

Despite such limitations, it must be recognized that the modern liberal positive concept of freedom developed over the past century and a half includes, in some form, all the elements of the anarchist conception of freedom defended here: the absence of coercion, the attainment of personal and social self-realization, and the existence of agency or self-determination. Though this conception ultimately lacks critical understanding of the system of domination, and lapses in some ways into ideology and abstract idealism, it is vastly superior to the concepts of freedom developed in classical liberalism, neorepublicanism, and the more economistic versions of welfare liberalism. Though lacking a strong critical-dialectical dimension, it is a significant theoretical step in the direction of the conception of freedom that is defended here.

Berlin's attempts to discredit such positive conceptions of freedom are a complete failure. This is true of his claim that "the fundamental sense of freedom" is "freedom from chains, from imprisonment, from enslavement by others" and that other senses are only "an extension of this sense, or else metaphor."[20] He does not defend this claim through careful analysis of etymology, through an examination of the history of usage and connotation in various relevant language communities, or even through a consideration of the theoretical issues involved in determining what might be considered a "fundamental sense." Instead, he merely asserts his position repeatedly. In reality, Berlin's privileged sense of the term is "fundamental" only for justifying his own political ideology and that of the political tendencies (classical liberal, neoliberal, or right-wing libertarian) that share his ideological commitments. In fact, the term is used meaningfully and coherently not only in his "fundamental sense," but also in a range of other senses that are grounded in historical and contemporary usage. If one considers the etymology of the term, one finds that it is derived from roots that connote "not in bondage," "noble," "joyful," "dear," and "beloved," and which thus have both negative and positive connotations. If one looks at the history of the usage of the term, one finds that it has been used in both popular and theoretical contexts in both negative and positive senses. Some of the important chapters in the history of the positive usage have just been mentioned.

Nevertheless, Berlin objects that advocates of positive freedom (and this would apply even more to advocates of the more complex conception of freedom developed here) confuse freedom with other social values. According to this objection, the concept of freedom simply "cannot do all the work" conceptually that the theorists of positive freedom demand of it.[21] One should not, the argument goes, confuse a free society with one in which people achieve self-realization, or one that has various other qualities that one might consider desirable, but which should not be equated with freedom. However, as an examination of etymology and usage shows, this objection fails. One simply cannot establish the superiority of one's favorite conception of freedom by claiming one's inalienable right to rewrite the dictionary. Just as Berlin and his allies can say that their opponents confuse the free society with one that promotes self-realization or some other value, one could with equal justice (or injustice) say that Berlin and his followers confuse a free society with a noncoercive one.

A.J. Liebling stated famously, and quite astutely, that "freedom of the press is guaranteed only to those who own one."[22] One might accordingly say that advocates of negative freedom "confuse" freedom of the press with the absence of laws against censoring the press. One might go one step further and claim that "the fundamental *meaning* of freedom of the press is the ability to have access to a press and to use it to express one's ideas." Such a claim would be nonsense, but it would be no more nonsensical than are Berlin's contentions. In fact, *both* freedom as the ability to publish *and* freedom as the absence of coercive restrictions on publishing are meaningful and coherent senses of freedom. In the face of differing uses of the term, the question of which concept can best "do the work" theoretically and whether it should have more or less work to do depends on the more philosophically fundamental question of the nature of the work that a conception of freedom ought to be called on to do. Linguistic fundamentalism offers no adequate answers to any of these questions. It is hoped that those more adequate answers can be found in a broader and more complex conception of freedom that brings into dialectical relationship the dimensions that have been uncovered in the various contending conceptions. I call this broader conception "the third concept of liberty."

The present proposal for an alternative to Berlin's two senses of liberty is not the only one that has been suggested. Quentin Skinner contends that he has "isolated a third concept of liberty," based on the assumption that separate concepts exist if a "descriptive term" (such as "liberty") "can be coherently used with more than one range of reference."[23] One can, in fact, validly claim to "isolate" such a concept using this assumption; however, unfortunately for advocates of Skinner's approach, this claim turns out to be an entirely trivial one. According to such a standard, a vast multitude of distinct concepts of liberty already exist, since every variation in definition results in a different "range of reference," and many of these variations, no matter how minute, irrelevant, or misguided, will be susceptible to the minimal demand of "coherent use." So the real question is whether Skinner's proposed third concept is worthy of any more attention than the multitude of actual or possible "isolatable" concepts. Skinner thinks so, based on his contention that, contrary to Berlin, we can "speak about negative liberty," without necessarily speaking "about absence of interference."[24] In such cases, what "we speak about" is "the predicament of those who recognize that they are living in subjection to the will of others," a situation in which "freedom can be restricted and constrained in the absence of any element or interference or even any threat of it."[25]

However, this position does not in the end diverge substantively from the classical liberal position, inasmuch as classical liberals long ago gave up any hopes for benevolent despots acting noncoercively and have overwhelmingly supported the idea of limited government, or even minimal government, without despots, benevolent or otherwise. Thus,

Skinner does not pose any significant challenge to the classical liberal position when he states that "knowing that we are free to do or forbear only because someone else has chosen not to stop us is what reduces us to servitude."[26] This concept does not add anything substantive to the classical liberal idea that "coercion or the threat of coercion" (or, we might say, interference or the threat of interference) is a limitation of freedom. Republicans will reply that they are pointing out the significant fact that the "servitude" exists even if those with power are benevolent and do not have any intention of "interfering." However, in such cases the servitude does not stem from the benevolence or lack of desire to interfere. It comes, as in any other case, from the fact that there exists the power to coerce, that is, that the threat of coercion remains, whether or not coercion is used in any particular case, and classical liberals would agree on this.[27]

This takes us to the more distinctive "third concept of liberty" that is defended here. This defense looks above all to Hegel for inspiration, but seeks to overcome the ideological limitations of that philosopher's position. It proposes a concept of freedom based on communal personhood, social self-realization, self-determination, strong agency, and recognition. It is an attempt to synthesize, develop further, and reconcile (without denying necessary tensions) the dimensions of freedom that are central to the negative conception of freedom as noncoercion, the positive conception of freedom as self-realization, and the positive conception of freedom as self-determination. While only a sketch of a dialectical conception of freedom will be presented here, a fully developed dialectical theory requires a detailed exploration of the ways in which these three dimensions are mutually reinforcing, the ways in which they are in tension with one another, and the ways in which they might come into partial or radical contradiction with one another. The underlying thesis of this discussion is that this project of synthesizing these three dimensions of freedom can be seen to be viable, based not on any mere abstract thought experiment but rather on critical reflection on real historical experience and existing social possibilities.

Abstract Freedom

Hegel engages in a sustained critique of what he sees as abstract ideas of freedom. The goal of his analysis of such concepts is to show that they are one-sided and nondialectical, and that their limitations and contradictions point in the direction of a more consistent, comprehensive, and fully developed conception. Though they contain a moment of truth that can and ought to be developed, they fail to recognize the complexity of phenomena, including those most fundamentally related to the self and one's experience, and fail to conceptualize phenomena within the context of a larger matrix of determination. Hegel explains that an "abstract and formal freedom of subjectivity" finds its content, or more accurately, fails to find adequate content, "only in its natural, subjective embodiment, i.e., in needs, inclinations, passions, opinions, fancies, &c."[28]

According to this analysis, Berlin's negative freedom would be the paradigm case of abstract freedom, in seeing "liberty" merely as the absence of forces that hinder, through force or the threat of force, the expressions of one's will and desires. Hegel does not deny that the existence of a significant sphere of noncoerced choice is an important dimension of freedom, or that it is, indeed, a necessary condition for developed freedom. However, he contends that, in itself, it does not constitute meaningful freedom, and is compatible with merely instinctual, manipulated, or mechanistic action.

The negative concept of freedom captures a certain moment of the relationship to the other, that is, the other as resistant force and obstacle that must be overcome. However, it becomes fixated at that stage and fails to see the possibility of passing over beyond that moment. Hegel explains that "in all impulses I begin from an other, from something which is for me external," while "freedom is only there where there is no other for me which I myself am not." Consequently, "the natural man, who is determined only by his desires" (and thus trapped at the level of mere negative freedom) "is not at home with himself: however self-willed he is, the *content* of his willing and opining is yet not his own, and his freedom is *only formal*."[29] The key issue is what it would mean to have *substantive* rather than merely *formal* freedom. Hegel explains that minimally this would mean that: (1) what is willed is in a meaningful sense *one's own*; and (2) what is willed must have developed or realized content. Negative freedom satisfies neither of these requirements.

It should be noted that although Hegel's critique of abstract freedom would seem to be aimed primarily at theories of negative freedom, it is in fact more far-reaching in its implications. He also raises questions about *positive* conceptions of freedom that focus exclusively on freedom as the satisfaction of needs or as the mere teleological unfolding of potentiality. Such theories usually entail an inadequately critical theory of need, overlook ways in which the concrete development of freedom requires much more than the simple fulfillment of needs, and fail to grasp the aspects of human agency and social self-determination that go beyond the limits of any mere positive actualization of inherent potentialities.[30] Such theories typically overlook processes of mutual determination between phenomena, the dynamic and historical nature of phenomena, the determination of phenomena within larger contexts, and the open and creative aspects of dialectical development. A positive concept of freedom is an abstract concept if it fails to be adequately critical and dialectical in any of these ways.

Freedom as Self-Determination

Hegel's concept of freedom is in many ways a classic example of what Berlin depicts as freedom as self-determination. His position is in some ways a development of Kant's view that in order to be authentic moral beings we must be "self-legislators." However, Hegel moves this requirement from the level of abstract moralism to that of concrete social reality. What remains is the idea that for us to be full moral agents or ethical beings, our activity cannot be something imposed upon us by an arbitrary, alien authority or by brute force, but rather must be the product of our own deliberation, affirmation, and autonomous choice.

He contends that for authentic, developed freedom to exist, the will must be "related to nothing except itself and so is released from every tie of dependence on anything else." If this is achieved, it will then be "true, or rather truth itself, because its self-determination consists in a correspondence between what it is in its existence (i.e., what it is as objective to itself), and its concept; or in other words, that the pure concept of the will has the intuition of itself for its goal and its reality."[31] In Hegel's terminology, the correspondence between the will's existence and its concept means that it has gone through a process of development and unfolding and has attained the limits of its realization (though its "realization" includes the fuller realization of its quality of constantly going beyond itself).

In an undeveloped form, the will is under the control of mere impulse, whim, or desire. The world (including objects, persons, and even society in general) is looked upon as an obstacle to the self-assertion of such a will. The achievement of freedom requires a condition in which the other is no longer experienced as an alien force resisting the will. There is, rather, a process of reconciliation between self and other. "Freedom and reason consist in my raising myself to the form of I = I, in my knowing everything as mine, as *I*, in my grasping each object as a term in the system of what I myself am, in short in my having my *ego* and the *world* in *one and the same* consciousness, finding myself again in the world and, conversely, having in my consciousness what *is*, what has *objectivity*."[32]

A passage such as this one can easily give the impression that Hegel's position is a form of abstract idealism, in which the needed reconciliation is achieved merely through a change in thought processes. But this is exactly what he rejects. Instead, he shows "how finding myself again in the world" is based not on mere thinking, but rather on changes in the material conditions in the world, in social institutions, and in social practices. One is able to find oneself in the world because through one's action one has left the trace of one's activity in that world. One has consciousness of objectivity not merely because one has imagined objectivity, but because one has engaged in practical activity, thus engaging objectivity. When Hegel lapses into abstract idealism, it is not on the superficial level of recommending that contradictions be overcome through positive thinking or a retreat into a world of abstract ideals. It is rather on a deeper ideological level.

Hegel's conception of freedom is based on a theory of strong agency, in which a community can only be said to be free if its members actually participate in processes of self-determination. The existence of strong agency implies that the community has passed, in Marx's terminology, from the era of prehistory into the period of real history. No longer do conditions from which human beings are alienated constitute the major social determinants. In other words, no longer do things make things the way they are. Instead, the members of the community have developed a critical awareness of the processes of social determination (and the necessary limitations of those processes), and they take these processes into their own hands. They use things to make themselves what they are (though as culturally situated, communal beings they do not create themselves ex nihilo). Moreover, they engage in this self-creative activity as a community, and do not allow this process to fall into the hands of any particularistic interest. Strong agency implies not only that the community is the collective agent of social determination, but that, in a meaningful sense, the individual members of the community exercise such agency.

A carefully argued and convincing case for the existence of a theory of strong agency in Hegel's social philosophy is presented by Robert Pippin in *Hegel's Practical Philosophy*.[33] There, Pippin discusses a number of conditions that must be fulfilled for authentic agency and social freedom to exist, according to Hegel's account. First, in true agency, the activity of the agent must be understood and endorsed by that agent. In Pippin's words, "it must make a certain kind of sense to the agent, and that means it must fit in intelligibly within a whole complex of practices and institutions within which doing this now could have a coherent meaning."[34] The implication is that the members of the community must have a common understanding of the action within the context of the community's life, and must will the action in a collectively meaningful sense. Second, the actions must not be coerced and must instead flow from the agent's own deliberative processes. One will have "reflectively endorsed the action as, all things considered, what I ought to be doing," so that it is done "voluntarily" and is "non-coerced."[35] Here, the truth of the claims of negative freedom is recognized. One cannot in a strong sense be said to be a "free agent" when one's actions, however admirable they might seem in abstraction, are concretely determined by force or the threat of force, so that what one would will according to one's considered judgment is overruled. Third, the action must not only be understood and endorsed in a narrowly rational sense, but it must also be felt and experienced as a form of free self-expression. As Pippin puts it, there is "an actual and experienced identification with one's deeds and practices and social roles,"[36] so that they are experienced as one's own actions. Elsewhere, he explains that what one determines to occur "shouldn't seem or be alien, as if belonging to or produced by someone or something else or as if fated or coerced or practically unavoidable, and so forth."[37] As in Marx's famous depiction of nonalienated labor, one "feels at home" (*fühlt sich zu Hause*) in one's free social activity. Finally, as the reference to reflective endorsement implies, the actions must not merely be minimally "endorsed" but must rather be a product of one's own reason in the relevant sense. A true agent would act out of consideration of "moral, ethical, and political normative constraints" that "are not experienced as 'external,'" but are rather "internal." This means that they are a product not of any hypothetical or collective reason, but of "the subject's own reason."[38] The nature of moral and political reason is, of course, a crucial question, and there is no reason to think that Hegel correctly understood all its dimensions. However, the relevant point here is his contention that if social freedom is to exist, the social agents must be capable of reasoned deliberation concerning the moral and political good, and of endorsing actions based on a conception of that good.

Needless to say, this last criterion has far-reaching implications for ethics. It means that social norms are not preexisting realities to be discovered, or particular modes of instantiation of preexisting realities, as in some forms of Platonism, natural law theory, or Kantian deontology. Rather, social norms (and obviously, for Hegel, this does not mean merely descriptive norms but morally prescriptive ones) are creative products of processes of participatory social determination. "It is by being instituted and held to that [norms] function as norms at all, are actual. Their normative authority is not an expression of nature, but they function as independent forms of self-regulation."[39] In a sense, this is the Hegelian version of the Lacanian dictum that "the Big Other does not exist." There is no purely transcendent source of moral authority that can be separated from human creative activity, imagination, and volition.

Agency and Critical Reason

The implications of Hegel's requirement of rational reflection are much more radical than Hegel himself recognized, and more so than Pippin implies in his sympathetic presentation of the Hegelian position. Pippin notes the important point that "what can look like a purely rational reflection on the limitations of some normative institution is in reality the pull of another unavoidable, already-in-place institutional commitment."[40] He gives as examples of such contending commitments the appeal to contractual obligation, conscience, professional standards, status in the family, and national loyalty. If the goal is strong agency, all of these standards for decision-making must be subject to fundamental critique. It is true that, as Pippin notes of the paradigmatic example of Antigone and Creon, "each is trying to argue for what, respectively, any sister or any ruler must do."[41] However, the very ultimacy of the conflict between duties in this case, its disruptive and traumatic nature, opens the way to a reconsideration of the grounds for any delivered views of what family members and rulers must do.

Pippin points out that while the Hegelian position emphasizes duties that result from the "station" that one occupies in society, based on "the sort of critical reflection available at the time," it is quite plausible to claim that in many cases the "station" itself "does not in itself conform to the demands of reason."[42] Moreover, the "critical reflection available" should not be identified with a de facto prevailing level of critical reflection, much as arguments in obscenity cases have appealed to *l'homme moyen sensuel*.

No one can literally step outside of his or her epoch, but one can make use to a greater or lesser degree of the historical, scientific, and philosophical resources that are available to that epoch. One can, in effect, often overrule "the ruling ideas of one's age," and this is, indeed, a fundamental project of dialectical critique.

One of the obvious strengths of Hegel's position is his critique of abstract, ungrounded views of society and social change, and his withering attack on proposals for reconstructing society (or realizing "freedom") based on *Moralität*, and appealing to abstract moral idealism, when what is needed is an ethical analysis that is grounded in *Sittlichkeit*, and that exhibits a deep understanding of historical realities and complex social conditions and possibilities. Pippin notes accordingly that in moral reasoning "requesting, providing, accepting, or rejecting practical reasons, in other words, are all better viewed as elements in a rule-governed social practice."[43] It should be added, however, that they are also part of a much larger social (and natural) world that encompasses the practice and contains many other elements that may ultimately challenge or even demolish it.

Pippin states that "the practical issue of adequacy must be answerable only within such a practice, all given the way a practice or institution has come to embody the crises, breakdowns, and changes that have made it what it is."[44] But this addresses only one dialectical moment of determination, the way in which a phenomenon is a product of its own history, and contains within itself that history, with all the possibilities and contradictions that it entails. However, other relevant moments reflect the ways in which a phenomenon is determined by what it is not, and the way in which it is determined by its place in larger wholes of which it is a part. "Given" all this, what is "within such a practice" is identical with that which is outside the practice, and that which exceeds the bounds of the practice. A line between the various spheres can only be drawn provisionally, or else dogmatically and ideologically.

Pippin vacillates between unusually acute insights into the radical implications of Hegel's position and certain innocuous illustrative commonplaces that work to limit that radicality. Thus, he observes that "the trust and solidarity without which cooperative action is impossible, and which cannot be justified on egoistic premises, or on the basis of 'self-interest rightly understood' is, if it exists and if Hegel is right, best understood as the product of a collective historical experience of its absence and only partial presence."[45] This points directly to the overwhelming majority of human history that was lived in communities of solidarity based on kinship (a history only recently ended for much of the world), and to the long subsequent history of the commons, caring labor, and cooperative endeavor during an age in which such solidarity has been only "partly present." But Pippin's valid observation on historical experience leads him to comment that "for us, now, 'because families should try to foster independence in their children' might count as a perfectly fine and conclusive reason in such a practice, with no more needing to be said, for the agent."[46]

It may be true, as Pippin contends, that the agent does not have to appeal to a comprehensive philosophy of history to justify practices; however, it is necessary that the agent should possess the degree of consciousness of social processes that is necessary for agency. Not only does the conclusion ("So . . .") mentioned not follow from the premise, but what is more, it is a recipe for disaster in a world in which "independence" is ("for us, now") an ideologically charged concept that means anything but true "independence." Indeed, the adoption of such a concept requires the systematic forgetting (by the "agent") of precisely that "collective historical experience" that might point to a path of reconciliation between the freedom and independence of the person and a mutual solidarity with and dependence on the community.

Recognition and Nondomination

For Hegel, true freedom can exist only in a community of mutual recognition. An essential moment of freedom is the recognition by each person of the personhood of each other person, which implies that they are not mere objective beings-in-themselves, but also subjective beings capable of being beings-for-themselves, that is, self-conscious, self-creating, self-determining beings. As Hegel states in the *Encyclopedia*: "It is necessary that the two selves standing over and against one another in their determinate being for others, posit and recognize what they implicitly are, or are according to their concept, namely they are not merely natural [things] but are rather free."[47]

Hegel describes this mutual recognition as a form of reciprocity. He says: "universal self-consciousness is affirmative self-knowledge in another self" in which "each self as a free individual retains its absolute independence,"[48] providing that it fulfills the criteria for agency. At the same time, "by negating its immediacy or desire [*Begierde*], it no longer distinguishes itself from the other."[49] In other words, it overcomes bondage to the uncritical, heteronymous willing that forms the basis for abstract negative freedom. Consequently, "each has real universality in the shape of reciprocity. Each knows itself to be recognized in the other free person, and knows this insofar as it recognizes the other and knows him to be free."[50]

A precondition for knowing that the other is free, and for recognizing the other as free, is, of course, that the other is, in fact, free. This theme in Hegel's works is best known through the master–slave dialectic, though it is a persistent undercurrent in his thought. He states in the *Encyclopedia* version of the master–slave dialectic that "it is only with the release and liberation [*Freiwerden*] of the slave that the master also becomes fully free. In this condition of universal freedom, in being reflected into myself, I am immediately reflected in the other person, and conversely, in relating myself to the other I am immediately related to myself."[51] It is only within the context of a certain kind of equality that true recognition can possibly exist. Recognition cannot exist between a person who has the status of personhood and another person who is assigned the status of a thing, or that of a mere means. The implications of this principle are obviously very far-reaching.

Hegel's position is far from the abstract idealist one in which freedom could result from a pure mental act of recognition, or even from collective acts of mutual recognition, so that the act of recognition would in itself confer freedom. This would be a deeply ideological position, which would posit that by some miracle of pure thought the slave could become free even while enslaved, the exploited worker could be accorded dignity even while being forced into dehumanizing labor, one's neighbor could achieve equality even while being subjected to racist oppression, and women could gain their rights, even while suffering under the yoke of patriarchal domination. Contrary to all such illusions, freedom requires, as Hegel says, the "release and liberation" of the oppressed and enslaved. Recognition is not a sufficient condition for liberation, whereas liberation is a necessary precondition for full recognition.

Williams notes that one of the most important elements of freedom for Hegel is what he called *Freigabe*.[52] This concept means, negatively, "the renunciation of attempts to dominate and control the other," and more positively, "allowing the other to be, being open to the other, and affirming the other as she determines herself to be," and thus implies an obligation "to accept and respect the other as an end in herself such that controlling, dominating, and manipulating behaviors are inappropriate."[53] Hegelian freedom can thus be significantly realized only in a community in which all systematic forms of domination are eliminated. It is only thus that it can be called a free community, that is, a community of self-realizing beings who are agents in their own development.

A corollary to this principle of nondomination is that mutual recognition requires the abolition of a social order based on coercive force. Williams, in his carefully argued analysis of Hegel's theory of recognition, draws this logical conclusion. He explains: "Coercion is a negation that must itself be negated; coerced recognition ends in failure. Genuine reciprocal recognition requires that the other be allowed to be, and this implies that coercion, force, and violence must be renounced as the basis of human relationships."[54] In the end, Hegel's politics of recognition requires him to posit a state that will negate its own nature as the supreme coercive institution in society. The free state can only be a state that is not a state.

Reconciling Universality and Particularity

A question that is of crucial importance to Hegel's view of the realization of freedom in history, and, indeed, to his entire social philosophy, is that of how the universal is to be reconciled with the particular. One of his criticisms of abstract conceptions of freedom is that they are based on a contradiction between the individual on the one hand and society, and indeed reality as a whole, on the other. As long as this contradiction is not overcome, the "finding oneself in the other" that he sees as basic to self-determination cannot be achieved. It is important, therefore, to explore the ideological nature of Hegel's defense of the state as the universal mediator that resolves all contradictions, and the ways in which the failure of his defense of the state, far from leading merely to a theoretical dead end, in fact points toward an authentic, nonideological solution to the problem that he faced.

For Hegel, the state is the historical institution that performs the function of mediating between the singular, the particular, and the universal. The state, he says, "is the actuality of concrete freedom" in which "personal individuality and its particular interests . . . pass over of their own accord into the interest of the universal," so that "they know and will the universal," they "recognize it as their own substantive mind," and they "take it as their end and aim and are active in its pursuit."[55] Thus, through the state, the individual and general interests are reconciled, and the individual consciously wills the universal. For Hegel, it is not only in some future state whose existence is fully one with its concept that the universal and particular will be thus reconciled. Rather, he asserts that "the principle of modern states has prodigious strength and depth because it allows the principle of subjectivity to progress to its culmination in the extreme of self-subsistent personal particularity, and yet at the same time brings it back to substantive unity, and so maintains this unity in the principle of subjectivity itself."[56] He sees this reconciliation as a tendency that is inherent in existing modern states.

Hegel is forced to make such a historically unfounded claim, for otherwise it would be impossible for him to defend the legitimacy of the state. The legitimate state would be nothing more than an abstract, ungrounded ideal of the sort that he so often subjects to devastating critique. But how can one look at the history of the modern nation state, either up to Hegel's own time, or during the period since (in which the practical, historical implications of its "principle" have become increasingly apparent), and conclude that what has taken place has been such a reconciliation, rather than the precise opposite? Only seventeen years after Hegel's death, Marx could write with great perceptiveness and even more prescience that if one observes the dominant course of modernity, one finds not a growing substantial unity, but rather that "all that is solid melts into air." It is now clear that he was describing the corrosive effects not only of economic rationality and commodification under the market economy, but also of the techno-bureaucratic and administrative rationality of the modern state.

According to Hegel's analysis, "in dealing with ethical life," we either "start from the substantiality of the ethical order, or else we proceed atomistically and build on the basis of single individuals."[57] His contention is valid, but it undermines his own position if applied consistently and nonideologically. According to his argument, one must start from real substantiality, not the hypothetical substantiality of some idealized entity. But Hegel's state is precisely such an idealized entity. Ethical substantiality (in Hegel's time and ever since) has been embodied not primarily in nation-states but rather in the histories, values, and practices of evolving communities and cultures. This substantiality developed through most of its history entirely outside the bounds of the state, and since then has existed in contradiction to the state, which has acted as an alien, *atomizing* force in society, reshaping communal beings into *single individuals* organized externally through the proliferation of the complex legal systems, the vast bureaucracies, and the powerful punitive and coercive mechanisms that constitute the state apparatus.

The State and the Problem of Agency

Hegel is unwilling to accept the radical implications of his own theory of agency. Thus, he states that "the right of giving recognition to what my insight sees as rational is the highest right of the subject," but he immediately adds that "owing to its subjective character it remains a formal right; against it the right which reason *qua* the objective possesses over the subject remains firmly established."[58] This formulation has questionable implications. It can imply a hierarchy of the objective over the subjective that reduces a necessary condition of agency to a formal condition that can be negated. Hegel recognizes elsewhere, however, that such a formal condition is capable of being developed and given content so that its most salient element, action in accord with one's own "insight," can be preserved. A fully dialectical approach would reject the hierarchizing of the objective over the subjective and explore the possibilities for achieving an actualization of the subjective in a realm of objectivity, through a community and ethical order in which there is a dynamic tension between individual insight and social institution, in which the dialectic between communal solidarity and various elements of freedom is at the heart of the social order.

In the end, Hegel leaves us with a theory of strong agency but with no hint of where we might find a strong agent. Redding points out that Hegel attacks republican politics for producing "a 'general will' without a willing subject," and thus failing to express "the experience of *subjects* at all."[59] But the same issue arises concerning Hegel's own conception of statist politics, which shows him to be in some ways a good neo-Rousseauian. His proposed political order lacks the institutions and practices that would permit agency and expression of will in the strong sense that his theory requires. As Pelczynski comments, "after the breath-taking conceptualization of the modern state in §260 [of the *Philosophy of Right*], Hegel's description of its political organization comes rather as an anti-climax."[60] The section in question, which was cited above, expresses his extravagant claims for the overcoming of the opposition between universal and particular through the state. However, when one examines his description of the structure of the state, it is difficult to imagine such an institution as a form of individual and collective self-determination.

Consider the constituents of Hegel's proposed political order. We find that the major constituents of such a system are: first, a constitutional monarch who is to symbolize the unity of the society; second, an executive that consists of a "universal class" of civil servants; third, a legislature, that consists of estates based on the de facto class structure (and in which the aristocrats representing the agricultural class gain positions by birth, the business representatives are elected not by the public but by their professional associations, and civil servants are sent as advisors on behalf of Universality); and, finally, the force of "public opinion." It is obvious that such a system fails to take into account the most distinctive aspects of personal experience, interpersonal relationships, and, in short, *social particularity and social singularity*. These, as a matter of historical fact, relate not primarily to that vast abstraction called the state (whether in its various empirical forms or in Hegel's idealized version), but rather to the true loci of cultural specificity: the locale, the place, the basic community of embodied practice. These social realities simply have no place in Hegel's system of determination.

Hegel contends (in Kolb's formulation) "that to be free we need customs, ways of life that are not our own arbitrary construction or imposed on us immediately but conform to the nature of our freedom."[61] This means that we need a more participatory, localized, and regionalized ethos. The great enemies of such an ethos have been, in addition to traditional hierarchical forms of domination (patriarchy, authoritarian religion, racism), the reductionist, atomizing, deracinating forces of capitalism and the state. The issue of sensitive, responsive, caring *communal life* is crucial to the problematic of freedom. But, largely as a result of his statism, the mature Hegel has little to say about the art of living in community.

A Noncoercive State?

Hegel is unusual among classical political theorists in already having a clear recognition of what political anthropology has since his time told us in great detail about the state: that it arose out of force, coercion, and conquest. He says that "the struggle for recognition and subjection to a master constitute the phenomenal shape out of which the common life of human beings has arisen—the origin of the state." However, he argues that while coercion is "the ground of this phenomenon," it is not "the ground or basis of right."[62] Rather, "coercion is a necessary and relatively justified moment in the transition from the condition of self-consciousness sunk in desire and particularity to the condition of the universal self-conscious-ness [ethical life]. Coercion is the external or phenomenal origin of the state, but not its substantial principle or basis."[63] In effect, the state's whole bloody history of conquest, imperialism, war, mass murder, oppression, and enslavement is justified as part of its fulfillment of its destiny, which is precisely to move beyond the uncivilized brutality of coercion.

It was not Marx but Hegel who first presented a fully elaborated theory of the withering away of the state *as a coercive apparatus*. He should be recognized, therefore, not so much for his contributions to the ideolog-ical legitimation of state power, but for his presentation of one of the most devastating (though largely implicit) immanent critiques of state power. His message is, in effect, that the state can only realize its true destiny, and justify itself, by doing precisely that which it cannot possibly do, given its nature as the state. In short, the task it is conferred constitutes an "Impossible Impossibility." The point at which Hegel lapses into ideology is usually rather obvious, because it is the point at which he begins to say things that he would never have said if he had read Hegel carefully. The true concept of the state, its real historical destiny, can only be understood through reflection on the content and context of the real historical state. It can be nothing other than what its actual determinants dictate. Hegel could have told him this.

Williams expresses Hegel's predicament vis-à-vis the historical state very clearly in his explication of the implications of the theory of recogni-tion. According to Hegel's own analysis "coercion is a negation that must itself be negated; coerced recognition ends in failure. Genuine reciprocal recognition requires that the other be allowed to be, and this implies that coercion, force, and violence must be renounced as the basis of human relationships."[64] Thus, a social order based on recognition requires the abolition of the state. Hegel was, of course, quite aware of the implica-tions of his own ideas. His solution to his dilemma—either he must give up the possibility of freedom in history or he must give up the state—was to give up the state. But fortunately, from his ideological point of view, it was only in giving it up that he would truly find it. This meant proposing an impossible development of the historical state in which the realization of its concept would mean the abolition of its character as a coercive mechanism, which is taken as a nonessential moment in the unfolding of its historic destiny. He substitutes for the real negation of coercion the ideological illusion of its negation. For all his rationalism, it is at this point that reason succumbs, and we might say succumbs "absolutely," to imagination. For not only does he dream of the "mature state," the object of his fantasies, it is also when he gazes on the actually existing state that he sees instead this sublime object of desire.

Nevertheless, Hegel must offer some rational account of how the state will in practice reconcile the universal and particular. Quite appropriately, the *ideological* answer to this question is that it will do it through *ideology*. What is it that assures in Hegel's state that citizens exercise their all-important agency by willing the universal, thus achieving the reconciliation between the individual and the universal, so that no massive coercive mechanism will be required to enforce social order? As Kolb points out, it is such eminently ideological forces as organized religion and institutionalized patriotism.[65] We might describe it more generally as statist ideology, whether religious or political. For Hegel, "the guarantee of the constitution" depends first on "the spirit of the whole people, namely in the determinate way . . . in which it has the self-consciousness of its reason. Religion is this consciousness in its absolute substantiality."[66]

Beyond this identification is the recognition that self and society both achieve their realization through the state. Such recognition depends on patriotism, which is "trust (which may pass over into a greater or lesser degree of educated insight), or the consciousness that my interest, both substantive and particular, is contained and preserved in another's (i.e., in the state's) interest and end, i.e., in the other's relation to me as an individual."[67] This is not, in fact, a bad definition of the psychology of patriotism. It relies on a kind of faith that one's interest is identical to that of the state, and it therefore depends on one's ability to attain a greater or lesser degree of insight—greater when reality seems to confirm one's faith, lesser when it does not.

Hegel fails to appeal to the third major sphere of statist ideology, its economistic form. He has very good reasons for neglecting this mode of legitimation, even though it is in reality the one most closely tied to the real historical destiny of the modern state and its realization of its concept. A recognition of the state's claim to legitimacy based on its service to economic self-interest, and its guarantee of a higher standard of living conflicts with his view that the state takes humanity beyond the realm of mere satisfaction of need. Moreover, it is in this mode of legitimation that the ideological mechanism becomes most transparent to reasonably perceptive beings. Thus, Hegel's appeal must of necessity be limited to the religious and nationalist forms of statist ideology.

By this point, the requirement of real agency has retreated far into the background. Acts of consciousness are substituted for effective political action, and the real course of history is systematically fantasized away. Kolb points out that Hegel hoped that an ideological force such as nationalism could function as "a check on the unbridled expansion of civil society's self-interested psychology."[68] But what Hegel failed to recognize is how the state and capitalism could both propagate forms of technical and instrumental rationality that would reinforce one another (even as the various forms also contended with and contradicted one another), and ultimately create the illusion that there is no alternative to such rationality, while at the same time mystifying it through such ideological concepts as loyalty to one's country, and later, the happiness, freedom of choice, and self-actualization of each person. Hegel could hardly imagine what "an expansion of self-interested psychology" might ultimately mean in an age in which a *bürgerliche Gesellschaft* that had become far less "civil" than "bourgeois" had turned us all into *très petits bourgeois*, members of the final universal class of the society of mass consumption.

The Kingdom of God Was within Hegel

There was in Hegel's thought from the beginning a tendency that pointed in a direction quite contrary to his later statism. In his early theological manuscripts (*Theologische Jugendschriften*), Hegel saw in the idea of the "Kingdom of God" a vision of a free community of mutual self-realization based on love and solidarity. This idea should be looked upon as part of the Joachimite tradition (inspired by twelfth-century mystic Joachim of Fiori), which divides history into three stages, the Age of the Father, in which obedience to law is central, the Age of the Son, in which faith becomes all-important, and the Age of the Holy Spirit, in which love becomes the animating and organizing force in society. From this perspective, history achieves fulfillment through the triumph of a social order based on love (mutual aid, solidarity, voluntary cooperation), while the imposition of order based on force and coercion (law), or ideology (faith), is a regression.

In his early works, Hegel describes the community of love, the Kingdom of God, as "the living harmony of men" through which human beings "enter through being filled with the Holy Spirit," that is, by "living in the harmony of their developed many-sidedness and their entire being and character."[69] Such a community is thus one that attains the unity and nonalienation, and also the self-realization that are identified with freedom in Hegel's mature work. He says of the unity that is achieved in such a community that "the same living spirit animates the different beings, who therefore are no longer merely similar but one; they make up not a collection but a communion, since they are unified not in a universal, a concept (e.g., as believers), but through life and through love."[70]

What Hegel means is that they are not united through an abstract universal, in which the idea of unity is a substitute for the substance of unity. Rather, they are unified through the concrete universal of an embodied form of life. He explains that in such a community founded in love, "the separate does still remain, but as something united and no longer as something separate."[71] There is a unity-in-diversity, the reconciliation between universal and particular that he will later describe as the basis for the ethical order. Hegel's crucial concept of recognition based on equality was also present in these early texts. "True union, or love proper," he says, "exists only between living beings who are alike in power and thus in one another's eyes living beings from every point of view; in no respect is either dead for the other. This genuine love excludes all oppositions."[72]

This concept of the community of love recedes into the background of Hegel's later thought, but does not disappear. For example, in the *Science of Logic*, he identifies the concrete universal with love. He states that the universal can "be called free love and boundless blessedness, for it bears itself towards its other as towards *its own self*; in it, it has returned to itself."[73] And as late as in the *Philosophy of Right*, he states that the content of concrete freedom is already present "in the form of feeling—in friendship and love, for instance. Here we are not inherently one-sided; we restrict ourselves gladly in relating ourselves to another, but in this restriction we know ourselves as ourselves. In this determinacy a man should not feel himself determined; on the contrary, since he treats the other as other, it is there that he first arrives at the feeling of his own selfhood."[74]

Of course, all this is to be sublated, or sublimated, into its statist forms, in which there is much more negation than preservation. Nevertheless, such passages remain an implicit critique of statism. For in statist relationships (including in a social order of the sort Hegel depicts in the *Philosophy of Right*), one cannot truly "feel oneself to be oneself" and "feel undetermined." Rather, suffering under the burdens of the society of division and alienation, one can only struggle, perhaps with the soothing aid of ideology, to convince oneself that one has such feelings.

Moreover, in such passages, Hegel continues to point to the fact that relations of affinity, love, and solidarity, the most immediate free relationships of one to another, can be the basis for a larger free community. It is in such relationships that we discover the self in the other, that is, as a subject who shares our own internality, our own wealth of personhood, while still recognizing the other as other, as a being whose unique mode of being must be respected, who must not be coerced of manipulated. We do this first through our most immediate affinities, and then extend them out from the smaller to larger communities of recognition and care. This implicit libertarian and communitarian moment never disappears entirely from Hegel's thought. Throughout his works, there is always this other Hegel, perhaps haunted by his own Joachimite roots, haunted by the Free Spirit, pointing toward another solution.

The Free Community

In recent times, some of the most important strains of communitarian social thought have looked to Hegel as a major source of inspiration. This is not entirely without reason. His emphasis on the inescapable context of social meanings in which any decision-making processes take place is a healthy corrective to the dominant abstract, acultural tendencies in modern and contemporary political thought. His focus on the community of mutual recognition offers a strong, and indeed inspiring, basis for revitalized communitarian thinking. Nevertheless, one does not find in his thought any detailed investigation of the actual history of community, or any developed inquiry into the intersubjective dimensions of communal experience. It is not surprising that the social theories of the liberal tradition that Hegel rightly attacks as abstract, ungrounded, and ahistorical should neglect such historical realities. Within a theoretical framework such as Hegel's, which emphasizes so heavily the importance of concrete historical development, however, it is more striking. This cannot, of course, be a mere oversight.

Despite its strong libertarian and communitarian dimensions, Hegel's philosophy is deeply infected with an ideology that demands the denial, the negation, and ultimately, even the annihilation of the actuality of free community. Just as this ideology compels him to systemically ignore most of the history of embodied freedom in his analysis of freedom in history, it requires him to render invisible most of the history of communal solidarity in his history of social formations and institutions. Thus, he minimizes, as mere transitional stages to something much more real and rational, or completely dismisses, as primitive social forms entirely outside the course of world history, the ethical substantiality of women's caring labor, most of the forms of cooperation within families (especially extended kinship groups), mutual aid in villages and small communities, tribal and traditional institutions of solidarity, and various forms of the commons, to mention a few of the gaping holes in Hegelian World History. In reality, the products of this enormous neglected history of communal solidarity constitute the true ethical substantiality that is the primary material base, present here and now, for the emergence of the free, nonalienated, nondominating society of the future.

These serious flaws and limitations in Hegel's problematic must be recognized; but nevertheless, the Hegelian concept of freedom, if it is subjected to dialectical critique and purged of various ideological elements, offers a powerful basis for theorizing this other path toward free community. One of the thinkers who contributes most to this project is the German communitarian philosopher Gustav Landauer, who was a major anarchist and cooperativist political theorist of the early twentieth century. Landauer, whose importance is only now beginning to be recognized, was a leader of the libertarian wing of the European socialist movement, participated in the Bavarian Council Republic, and was martyred in the crushing of that historic experiment in 1919.

Landauer's concept of freedom has much in common with Hegel's, above all in his analysis of spirit (Geist) as the force that expresses and sustains freedom in history. Spirit, according to Landauer, is something "communal," the "One and Universal Idea" that creates "coexistence, community, agreement and interiority."[75] He adds that spirit is another name for solidarity, though for him this term has a much deeper and richer social-ontological meaning than it does for most political theorists.[76] He explains that "spirit is a grasping of the whole in a living universal" and "a unity of separate things, concepts and men."[77] This concept of spirit as "a living universal" is very much in the tradition of Hegel's idea of concrete universality. For Landauer, universality finds reality in the particular, as objectivity is embodied in living and developing subjectivity, that is, in the spirit-filled community that is aware of its own destiny and capable of self-determination. In short, the free community is the realization of the universal particular.

Landauer's radically libertarian politics includes a strong commitment to the actuality of participatory deliberation and decision-making at the most basic level. He envisions the establishment of democratic, self-managed cooperatives for production, consumption, and, above all, life in common. The free community would, through many-sided cooperative endeavors, pursue an ideal of voluntary agreement to the greatest extent possible. Thus, the actualization of his libertarian socialism would result in a concrete, practical realization of the idea of agency through self-determination that is only developed in theoretical abstraction, based on an idealized depiction of history, in Hegel's own political vision.

In Landauer's view, the unity of the community would not result exclusively, or even primarily, from the rational deliberation processes of democratic self-management, but would flow from diverse forms of collective self–expression. Spirit operates through all of the most dynamic and creative dimensions of communal life. Landauer says that "in our most secret dream and desire, in the figures of art, our strongest will, deep contemplative insight, purposeful action, love, despair and courage, psychic distress and joy, in revolution and unity, there life, power and glory dwell."[78] There would thus be two poles of the communal self-expression; on one hand, the fulfilling and gratifying work of free, voluntary cooperation, and, on the other, the joyful and exhilarating play of free cultural creativity.

Unlike Hegel, who was under the sway of progressivist and Eurocentric ideology, Landauer recognizes the value of humanity's traditional communal institutions, the magnitude of the losses inflicted by a destructive civilization, and the importance of dissident historical tendencies that have carried on the traditions of free community. Breaking rather radically with the conventional wisdom of his time, he contends that "we have to shed our fixation on some linear development according to which all previous periods were nothing more than precursors to our own."[79] In primordial human society, individuals were "held together by a common spirit," but this was destroyed and replaced by what he calls "external organization." As history progresses, "the church and the secular organizations of external coercion gain strength and grow continually worse," as society is subjected to "serfdom, feudalism, the various departments and authorities," and ultimately, "the state." The result is "an eventual decline of spirit" and "of the immediacy that flows from the individuals and leads them to unity."[80] The state plays a crucial role in the tragedy of history because at the same time that it dissolves spirit, it also increasingly expands its own domain and comes to function as a substitute for spirit. "Where there is no spirit and no inner compulsion, there is external force, regimentation, the state. Where spirit is, there is society. Where unspirit is, there is the state. The state is the surrogate for spirit."[81]

Nevertheless, spirit produces its historical legacy and lives on. For Landauer, it is crucial that we focus all our efforts on rediscovering all the submerged and neglected expressions of spirit and make them the basis for larger processes of social regeneration. Within a social order that is on the whole spiritually moribund, spirit expresses itself in part through "isolated thinkers, poets, and artists without a social context, without external roots."[82] But it also continues to survive in social practices and institutions. Landauer criticizes Marx for rejecting the significance of the history of communal freedom (in effect, for being more Hegelian than Hegel in this respect). Thus, he overlooks the significance of "a medieval republic of cities or a village *mark* or a Russian *mir* or a Swiss *Allmend* or a communist colony."[83] Landauer disputes Marx's contention that free, stateless communism must, or even can, be reached through a transition through a highly centralized state. In his view, such a state, far from creating a transition to the free community, acts to "kill the forms of living community" that form our priceless communitarian heritage and "contain the seeds and living crystals of the coming of socialist culture."[84] He laments the fact that most socialists of his time had no interest in "farm cooperatives, credit unions, or worker cooperatives" but rather found inspiration for their future socialism in "capitalist department stores."[85]

The Community of Communities

Landauer's thesis, taken up and communicated to a larger audience by his close friend, the Jewish mystical philosopher Martin Buber,[86] is that society can only become a free community if it is made up of smaller communities in which freedom and solidarity are practiced in all aspects of life. "Society is a society of societies of societies; a league [*Bund*, or union] of leagues of leagues; a commonwealth of commonwealths of commonwealths; a republic of republics of republics."[87] The essential point of this series of formulations is that the free society is a "community of communities of communities." The reiteration here should not, of course, be taken to mean literally that there are precisely three levels of social organization. Rather, it signifies that at each of the federative levels of society there must be a concrete realization of freedom and solidarity, embodied in personalities, sensibilities, practices, and institutions, that makes possible its reality at the next level. It is only in this way that freedom as agency and self-determination can have substantial social reality.

Thus, according to Landauer's libertarian socialism, free community must be created from the bottom up. It must attain fulfillment at each level, and then express itself at each subsequent level, from the individual person, to the family, to the workplace, to the "autonomous local community," to "the county or group of communities" and to "more comprehensive groups that have an ever smaller number of duties."[88] If citizens are to be effective social agents, as many responsibilities as possible must be retained at the more primary levels, where democracy and participation can be actualized most fully. It is only when some function cannot be carried out at a more basic social level that it should be delegated to a higher level. Landauer calls a society organized through such free federation "le contr'État," which he describes as "the state that is no state," but rather "a community of people outside the state; not as a sum of isolated atoms, but as an organic unity, a web of many groups."[89]

According to Landauer, a necessary condition for the development of such free community on a scale that is sufficient to challenge the existing social order is the powerful exemplary force that can be offered only through realized commun.al practice. In his view, "only example can do it."[90] The primary reason why Landauer is such a crucial figure in transformative social theory is the fact that he grasped with passionate intensity a simple and obvious truth that has been generally neglected by radical social theorists: a movement for freedom cannot possibly succeed when the *ethos*, the all-important ethical substantiality emphasized by Hegel, is overwhelmingly on the side of unfreedom. The title of Landauer's book is *Aufruf zum Sozialismus*. It is an *Aufruf*, a "call" to socialism, and has the ethical, religious, and spiritual connotations of a *Berufung*, a "calling" or "vocation." Landauer calls upon lovers of freedom to put their greatest efforts into the practical undertaking of creating communities of liberation, of immersing themselves in the realm of ethical substantiality that actually exists, and, from within it, fostering organically the expansion of this realm of embodied freedom.

It might seem surprising that Landauer identifies as one of the most powerful forces at the service of such liberatory transformation as that of "envy." However, this is an acute insight into the nature of social movements. Landauer points to something that is, in fact, grasped widely, at least on an intuitive or visceral level. Many on the Left may deny and repress the significance of this phenomenon, because of its association either with egoistic self-interest, which is morally problematical, or with the *ressentiment* for which the Left is regularly indicted, not entirely without cause. But we might distinguish between vicious envy, which was rightly classed as one of the deadly sins, and virtuous envy, which spurs one on toward the good. The latter is an expression of the ancient truth that it is inherent in human beings to desire the good, and that they are moved to action when there is some good end in view. According to Landauer, "once socialist colonies with their own colonies are scattered everywhere on the land," everyone will observe "their joy in life, in its inexpressible though quiet manner," so that "envy will become greater and greater" and "people will begin to see, to know, to be certain."[91] One problem that this analysis poses for members of the traditional Left is that it puts them in a painfully precarious position. It requires them to do something that would actually cause others to envy them.

Landauer, drawing on his deep knowledge of the history of free community, is quite confident (unlike the current reactive and demoralized Left) that this is possible. This is in no way an acceptance of the currently prevailing form of envy as a desideratum of the good society. In fact, the free community will begin to move beyond the psychology of egoistic calculation and life as a game of zero-sum competition (alias phallocentrism). However, those who are not yet part of such a liberatory culture can obviously not be expected to respond as if they are. Landauer suggests that it would not be a bad thing if they feel intense feelings of envy for (less provocatively, we might say a certain *desire* for) a community whose members no longer suffer under the heavy burden of enviousness.[92] They may even feel compelled to join such a community. In Landauer's view, this peaceful propaganda of the deed, carried out through the force of example, is the most powerful force for liberatory social transformation. Through it, "hope" will cease being a mere slogan or cliché in a society of resignation, and will become a lived sensibility.

Landauer correctly sees that the only real, material basis for the abolition of the state is the growing reality of such a free, self-realizing community. He outlines, in his 1908 work *Revolution*, the nature of the only problematic of "dual power" that truly promises an end to the system of domination:

> On the one side, we have the power of the state and the powerlessness of the masses, which are divided into helpless individuals—on the other side, we have socialist organization, a society of societies, an alliance of alliances, in other words: a people. The struggle between the two sides must become real. The power of the states, the principle of government and those who represent the old order will become weaker and weaker. The entire system would vanish without a trace if the people began *to constitute themselves as a people apart from the state.*[93]

A revolutionary project cannot have as its primary goal the development of forces capable of seizing state power and using that power as an instrument for social transformation. Instead, the overriding goal must be the achievement of widespread, pervasive social transformation (communization), so that a transformed (not merely *prefigurative* but *transfigured*) community can challenge state power. Landauer concludes *Revolution* with his most famous statement, which is in effect his final judgment on the fateful issue of "state and revolution":

> The state is a social relationship; a certain way of people relating to one another. It can be destroyed by creating new social relationships; i.e., by people relating to one another differently. . . . We, who have imprisoned ourselves in the absolute state, must realize the truth: *we* are the state! And we will be the state as long as we are nothing different; as long as we have not yet created the institutions.[94]

Without the emergence of communal organization as a realized, substantial counterforce to the concentrated power of the state and the class interest that is inseparable from it, the resurgence of domination is inevitable. As Landauer states, "the revolutions of today . . . no longer focus on the absolute king, but do not yet turn against the new form of totalitarian power: the absolute state."[95] It matters little whether there is a determinate or an empty "place of power" in a system, if its "place of power" is a place of concentrated or centralized power. In such a case, it will quickly become a site of domination.

One of the great merits of Žižek's Hegelian-Marxist political analysis is his unwavering critique of forms of superficial radicalism that ultimately reduce to ungrounded, abstract negation. He justifiably attacks the contemporary Left and pseudo-Left for abandoning the classical Hegelian-Marxist idea of determinate negation, in which "the New will emerge from the very contradictions of the present society, through its immanent self-overcoming," and he warns against vain hopes for deliverance through some "unmediated Outside."[96] A crucial issue is just how determinate this determinate negation must be. Landauer, though at best impressionistic in his analysis of the nature of social contradictions, is highly suggestive concerning an issue that is seldom confronted directly: the manner in which structural social contradictions can take on material expression in the embodied activity of social contradiction, the very activity of "immanent self-overcoming."

This is certainly something that was a powerful reality in the classical workers movement, and has been expressed most memorably in the Industrial Workers of the World slogan "building the new society within the shell of the old." And it is also something that seems quite alien to most of today's Left, particularly in the global North. Žižek himself seems to limit severely the radical implications of determinate negation when at one point he equates it with having a "concrete program of changes or idea of the new order to be installed."[97] True, the contemporary Left has in general abandoned even this programmatic dimension of negation, but social reality cannot ultimately be negated through programs of change, even concrete ones, or ideas, even of a new order. The great virtue of Landauer is his insistence that the dominant order, including state power on which it rests, must be negated through the immediate creation of a counterpower consisting of real, communal "ethical substance," the living, embodied contradiction of the present society of domination.

Thus, one moment of the struggle against domination is this seemingly immediate negation of state power and other forms of domination. Yet everything, whatever moments of immediacy it might possess, is at the same time the product of complex mediations.[98] It is necessary to consider the ways in which the struggle against domination might be successfully mediated, not abstractly or in general, but in various determinate historical contexts. Accordingly, Landauer considers the possible role for the state in the transition from the system of domination to a system of free community of communities, under certain historical conditions. He describes a socialist (meaning "libertarian socialist") position that holds that after "free and diverse forces of multiplicity" are achieved, "the state is left with only one task: to prepare for its own abolition and to make way for the endless ordered multiplicity of federations, organizations, and societies that aspire to take its place and the place of economic individualism."[99] What Landauer proposes is the antithesis of the self-defeating authoritarian socialist strategy of centralizing power in the state, with its vain hope that the state can itself enforce the resolution of social contradictions, after which it could innocuously begin withering away. In Landauer's analysis, the state, after having been subordinated to the power of the free community of communities, would be forced to progressively dismantle itself and redirect resources into the hands of these communities.[100] According to such a problematic of transition, the process of destatification would be proportional to that of the extent of communization.

Politics and Spirit

Some of today's most acute political philosophers have traced the roots of the present impasse of the Left to the fact that it has succumbed to an ethos of reactivity and adopted a politics of permanent protest. They point out the crucial need to discover the preconditions for the possibility of the world historical act and the socially transformative event. Landauer's libertarian socialism, as theoretically limited as it may be in some ways, offers inspiration and guidance for such a project. It is a politics that is centered on the creation of the preconditions for transformative social action. Its act is not, however, "the Act" depicted in the heroic masculinist myth of "le Grand Soir," the cataclysmic revolution in which all is overturned. There is no authentic revolution that "ne s'autorise que d'elle même," that is its own justification, though one can always find revolutionaries who "ne s'autorisent que d'eux mêmes," who are quite content to be their own justification. As heroic as this standpoint claims to be, it is far from clear that it has been driven by courage more often than by fear and anxiety. Creative revolutionary activity is a definitive break with all Promethean revolutionary mythology and all heroic will to power (including counterpower). Landauer notes very perceptively that "a true change in humanity requires a supplement to revolution."[101] The problem with revolution has generally been that as an event it has been much too *auto-autorisant*.

Typically, there is a strong "common spirit" that arises during a revolution, but once the revolution is over, it disappears. The problem has been that while the revolution *generates* spirit, it is not deeply *grounded* in spirit. The necessary supplement to revolution is all the evolutionary activity that is embodied in what Landauer calls "spirit."[102] The fetishism of the heroic Act represses awareness of the need for that careful and caring moment-to-moment action.[103]

The creative act is a paradoxical synthesis between the act of creation of being ex nihilo and the act of nurturing that which is becoming. Both of these are species of acting that require negative capability, that "doing without doing" that allows being to emerge out of the depths. Such an approach avoids what Hegel criticized so aptly and incisively in radicalism and revolution, the tendency not merely to "get to the roots" of things, but to pull things up by their roots, to succumb to the illusion of the blank slate, to seek to force transformation on the basis of abstract ideals. Landauer recognized—in fact, far more acutely than Hegel did—the importance of concrete ethos, of basing a many-sided vision of freedom on socially embodied practice and actualized forms of life. This is expressed well when Landauer epitomizes "socialism's solution" to the social question as "land and spirit."[104] The community must be animated by a creative spirit of solidarity and freedom. But it must also be grounded in a place, in the physical, bioregional, psychological, cultural, historical, and spiritual *topos*.

At this point, it might be useful to return to Berlin's critique of positive conceptions of freedom, for some might see Landauer's "politics of spirit" as exhibiting exactly the dangers that Berlin warned about in such conceptions.[105] At the end of "Two Concepts of Liberty" Berlin attacks what he sees as the "monism" entailed by positive concepts of freedom and defends the "pluralistic" nature of the negative concept. Such monism, he contends, arises from "the belief that some single formula can in principle be found whereby all the diverse ends of men can be harmoniously realized."[106] Such a belief has, he thinks, authoritarian implications, while "pluralism, with the measure of 'negative' liberty that it entails" is "a truer and more humane ideal."[107] However, Berlin is wrong on two counts. First, the negative concept of freedom does not in fact imply authentic value pluralism. And second, a more encompassing conception of freedom such as Landauer's, that includes its positive dimension is, in reality, most congruent with value pluralism.

Laurence Davis defines value pluralism as "the view that there are various forms and styles of life which exemplify different and incompatible virtues which are neither ranked by some impersonal criteria of moral worth nor derive from common ultimate principles." Interestingly, he states that he once proposed this definition to Isaiah Berlin and that Berlin accepted it.[108] Though it is understandable that Berlin would have liked to think that the classical liberal negative view of freedom promotes this kind of pluralism, there is nothing in the concept of negative freedom that implies it, nor does the ideology of negative freedom actually function to promote it. A society that is committed to negative freedom in the sense of minimizing overt coercion or the threat of overt coercion can quite "freely" adhere to a dominant system of values that is nonpluralistic, and it can impose this system both formally and informally by incorporating it into the institutional structure and the structure of social practice. Such a society can "freely" reward conformity to the dominant system of values, since rewards are not coercive. As everyone knows, there is a difference between an offer and a threat. What many do not wish to recognize is that offers, particularly when institutionalized and allied with systems of power, can interfere with the free development of persons and communities, and can be a mechanism for the enforcement of value conformity.

While Berlin's concept of freedom has nothing specific to do with value pluralism, the anarchist concept, with its emphasis on self-realization and self-determination, makes such value pluralism an inherent part of freedom. A basic dimension of freedom, according to anarchism, is the free development of the personality according to the diverse potentialities and inclinations of persons. The anarchist conception of freedom is based in part on the thesis that the elimination of forms of domination will liberate the potentialities for diversity on the levels of the person, the community, and the natural world. Anarchists observe that the actually existing system of domination has moved historically in the direction of social and ecological monoculture. One dimension of this systemic tendency is the movement toward value monism. Anarchism contends that only by dismantling the system of domination can this epochal tendency that has spanned the history of civilization be reversed.

Berlin's position is based on a certain illusion of pluralism or what we might call at best a *weak pluralism*. Negative freedom, as he conceives of it, is not only compatible with the continued existence of concentrations of power and forms of domination, but also, in fact, functions de facto as an ideology legitimating the system of domination. A plurality of values is permitted within that system to the degree that such plurality can coexist with the structures of domination. However, those structures (institutional, ideological, imaginary, and ethotic) are not themselves value neutral or value free. They function through the imposition of social values. To the extent that members of a society participate in these structures, they internalize the dominant values embedded in the structures (whether they affirm these values explicitly or not, as they usually do not). What is at least as significant is that they enact those values through their social practice. Thus, they reproduce the dominant values both through their acts of mind and through their social acts. By means of their very ubiquity (pervading social institutions, the social ideology, the social imaginary, and the social ethos) the dominant values take on a powerful moral force, achieve a high degree of self-evidence, and thus constitute *ethical reality* for the members of the society. Another way of saying this is simply that social value is systemic in nature and there exists a dominant system of values. Thus, Berlin's ideological version of value pluralism exists within a value-monistic context. The pluralistic moment functions ideologically to legitimate the dominant monistic moment of the system.

The fetishism of commodities (which will be discussed further in Chapter 4) illustrates the functioning of such ideological mechanisms perhaps most strikingly. A social agent may assert that the highest good for him or her is, for example, religious faith, moral integrity, family values, the sanctity of life, individual freedom, or some other values. Yet, at the same time, this agent may devote the vast majority of his or her waking life to producing and consuming commodities, may invest more psychical energy into the commodity than in any supposedly higher good, and may regularly decide conflicts between other values and commodity values in favor of the commodity. This is, in fact, what occurs regularly in liberal capitalist societies. Liberal value pluralism thus has an abstract idealist character, and acts ideologically to disguise the larger context of an overriding value monism. This monistic value system is not an absolute and undifferentiated totality, something that is approximated only in the most pathological forms of obsessive compulsive disorder.[109] It is, rather, an unstable, self-contradictory unity-in-plurality, given both the mutually reinforcing, and mutually contradictory character of various elements of the system of domination. However, the monistic moment remains dominant. The system of domination rests on a relatively coherent system of values that continues to perform its legitimating function with relative success, despite recent signs of increasing vulnerability.[110]

Landauer's communitarian anarchism contends that authentic plurality and diversity emerge not out of the consumer choices and negative freedom of a capitalist system with a night-watchman state, but rather from the creative activity of persons and communities bound together through ties of respect and recognition, and free from forms of domination and social hierarchy. This philosophy of freedom and spirit has had few echoes in contemporary social philosophy and political theory. A notable exception is Kovel's *History and Spirit* (notably subtitled *An Inquiry into the Philosophy of Liberation*), in which a strikingly similar conception is developed with considerable philosophical and psychological sophistication. For Kovel, spirit concerns "what happens as the boundaries of the self give way."[111] Drawing on the Hegelian-Marxist dialectical tradition, psychoanalytic thought, and existential and phenomenological philosophy (among other sources), Kovel shows that the history of the human species and the history of civilization have produced a mode of consciousness in which the *differentiation* of beings within the context of an encompassing unity is transformed into forms of *alienation* and radical *separation* that not only distort reality but create the preconditions for forms of social domination based on the objectification and instrumentalization of the other.

For Kovel, like the early Hegel, love and solidarity are the forces that can reverse this alienation and objectification, and for him, as for Landauer, they are the forces that are at the core of revolutionary political transformation. He explains that love is a condition that exists "when, through the union with another being, subject and object are rejoined within the individual,"[112] and as Hegel explained, only such reconciliation can make possible a social order based on freedom. Kovel's analysis takes seriously the moments of both unity and difference and preserves the dialectical relationship between parts and wholes and between identity and difference in intersubjective relationships and in the relationships between humans and nature. His thought suggests the direction that radical politics might take if it were to fulfill the promise, hinted at in the early Hegel, and in Landauer, of becoming "the Party of Eros" and creating an "Erosocialism" that is also an "Ecosocialism." The connections cannot be explored here, but it is clear that the concepts of spirit and love that underlie the relationship between humans in Landauer's vision of socialism imply a similar transformed relationship of reconciliation between human beings and the ecological communities of which they are a part. It is noteworthy that exactly ten years after *History and Spirit* appeared, Kovel coauthored "An Ecosocialist Manifesto," in 2001, at the beginning of a century in which a crucial question will clearly be "ecosocialism or ecobarbarism?"[113]

Neither Hegel nor Landauer, nor both taken together, answer fully the question of how freedom, in its third and most meaningful sense, can be achieved in a living community's institutions and practices. However, they contribute enormously to our understanding of what this question might mean in the most radical and concrete sense. In doing so, they reveal one aspect of this question that requires the most intense investigation. They challenge us to inquire into how the moment of explicitly deliberative and participatory self-determination, that is, a liberatory politics, can be related to, and placed in a condition of mutual determination with, the moment of nondeliberative, historically situated, organically developing cultural creativity, that is, a liberatory ethos.

The most intense investigation in matters of practice requires, as both Hegel and Landauer understood, a search for truth in which essential dimensions of what one seeks can be discovered only through a creative process in which the idea finds concrete, determinate fulfillment in the act. This moment of actualization is at the same time the moment in which the third concept of liberty is realized, and the third great epoch of history emerges. This is the epoch in which humanity finally frees itself and the Earth from the yoke of domination.

4

Against Principalities and Powers: Critique of Domination versus Liberalization of Domination

The System of Domination

The Greek word that is famously translated as "principality" is *arche*, which connotes not only "power," "domination," and "commandment" but also "principle," "origin," and "beginning." *Arche* refers both to the originating principles of domination and also to the actually existing systems of rule and domination that those principles justify. The idea of *arche* as "origin" denotes its claim to primacy and priority, in the senses of both metaphysical ultimacy and historic precedence. The Greek word traditionally translated as "power" is *exousia*. "Powers" are those rulers and authorities who command and control others. Their ability to rule and their legitimacy are based, in the last instance, on *arche*, as it is expressed both through the system of domination, and through the spheres of social determination through which *arche* operates: the social institutional structure, the social ideology, the social imaginary, the social ethos, and the social materiality.

The anarchist critique of domination is a critique of both principalities and powers. It is not only a *phenomenology* of power, in the sense that it theorizes the modes of exercise of power, its appearances, but it is an *archaeology* of power, in the sense that it investigates the origins, history, and nature of the underlying forms of domination that constitute the system of domination. Much of the present work concerns this anarchist critique of domination, the free community as the means of escape from that system, and ultimately, the means toward the abolition of that system.

In this chapter, the elements of the anarchist critique of domination are briefly outlined, and the theory of domination that has recently emerged within liberal political theory is subjected to critical analysis. The term "liberal theory," as it is discussed here, refers to a tradition of political theory characterized by an ideological defense of individual freedom and rights within the context of the global capitalist economy and global nation-state system.[1] Liberal theory is significant, inasmuch as it functions as the conventional wisdom, the default position, in contemporary Anglo-American political theory. It is the primary mode of theoretical legitimation of the system of domination. We will see that the liberal analysis of domination fails because it is both insufficiently archeological and inadequately anarchical. It fails to comprehend adequately the relation of the phenomena of domination to the system of domination. And it fails to uncover and move beyond its own complicity in defending elements of that system.

Foundations of the Critique of Social Domination

The anarchist concept of domination is the correlate of the "third concept of liberty" as it is developed here. According to this analysis, domination has three major elements: the systematic use of coercion, the threat of coercion, and overt interference with lives and well-being of persons and communities; the systematic denial to persons and communities of real agency in the shaping of their destinies; and the systematic imposition of constraints on the self-realization and flourishing of persons, communities, and the natural world.

There are two major sources of the critique of domination that is defended here. The first is classical anarchist theory, especially as expressed in the thought of communitarian anarchist philosopher and social geographer Elisée Reclus. Important dimensions of this critique were already highly developed in Reclus's works, in which one finds a penetrating and comprehensive analysis of a system of domination based on social hierarchy and class rule.[2] Reclus summarizes his findings as follows:

> We find everywhere, in all social relations, positions of superiority and subordination. In short, even in our own time the guiding principle of the state itself and of all the particular states that make it up, is hierarchy, by which is meant "holy" archy or "sacred" authority, for that is the true meaning of the word. This sacrosanct system of domination encompasses a long succession of superimposed classes in which the highest have the right to command and the lowest have the duty to obey.[3]

This statement encapsulates the most important elements of Reclus's account of the nature of domination. He contends (and shows in his extensive analysis of world history and social institutions) that there is a system of domination, that it constitutes a hierarchical order that pervades all social relations, and that it expresses itself through positions of dominance and subordination within the system. However, his analysis goes more deeply than this. He presents an extensive critique of various specific forms of domination, including the state, capitalism, patriarchy, racial domination, authoritarian religion, and the domination of nature. Although he focuses heavily on the state and capitalism, he shows how these and other forms of domination mutually interact to shape the diverse institutions, values, and practices of the society. In many ways, his analysis anticipates the present analysis, in which the *system* of domination is seen as consisting of specific *forms* of domination that function through the dialectical interaction of social institutional structures, the social ideology, the social imaginary, social ethos, and social materiality.

This is illustrated in Reclus's pioneering writings on urbanism. There, he shows how concentrated power and social domination are built into the very landscape of urban society, so that the institutional structure, the material infrastructure, and the ethos of domination become inseparable. He explains how the physical face of the city is in fact ideological, and reflects the city's specific place in the system of domination. Some cities, he says, function merely as centers of production, and exhibit an ethos that is "banal, bourgeois, routine, lacking in originality, and lifeless," while other cities are centers of political and commercial power and "are clearly designed for domination, and overwhelm the surrounding countryside."[4] Reclus also launched a critique of early "urban renewal" programs, showing how putatively reformist or progressive planning schemes function within the system of domination, merely displacing urban problems from one site to another, while the roots of poverty and blight in the normal functioning of the capitalist and statist system itself are not addressed. Domination in these cases does not take the classic form of personal dominance and subordination, but masquerades as public-spirited urban problem-solving. Thus, the changing face of the city and the ideology that guides it hide underlying power-relationships.

Reclus also made a significant contribution to understanding the ways in which the developing technological megamachine and the instrumental rationality that it entails interact with the system of economic domination. He notes how, by the late nineteenth century, economic and technological domination had found expression in the minutest details of the operation of vast commercial operations. He observes that under industrial capitalism, machines, animals, and humans are "viewed as so much force to be quantified numerically," so that they can be "used most profitably for the employer, with the greatest productivity and the least expense possible."[5] In this system, "all of the workers' movements are regulated," and each detail in the production process "is calculated and profits the master."[6] Reclus thus shows that by this point in history technological domination had not only become deeply embedded materially in the institutions of society, but was taking the form of a technological ethos in which the worker him or herself becomes the mechanized object of technique.

These analyses only begin to suggest the scope and depth of Reclus's exploration of a wide spectrum of spheres through which the forces of domination are dispersed throughout society. In addition to his study of the urban landscape and the mechanization of society, his analysis encompasses such topics as the authoritarian family, violence and brutality against women, repressive morality, authoritarian religion, nationalist ideology, racism, the psychology of militarism and war, the repression of the body, authoritarian education, the aesthetics of domination, inhumane treatment of animals, and the commercialization of nature, to mention some of the most important themes. In summary, Reclus's project already, at an early date, showed that there is a system of domination consisting of various forms that constitute not only the underlying systemic structures of power, but also multidimensional forms of life.

The other major contribution to the critique of domination has come from the critical-dialectical tradition that arose out of Hegel's philosophy. While this critique is implicit in Hegel's own thought, Marx's social theory is the crucial turning point at which critical and dialectical theory becomes a self-conscious philosophy of liberation. Marx made three major contributions to the critique of domination. The first is the most general one from which the others follow, that is, his demonstration of the meaning of a radically dialectical social theory. The second consists of his specific findings concerning the systemic and impersonal nature of social domination, as uncovered in his critique of political economy, the central focus of his life's work. And the third involves an even more specific dimension of this critique, his prophetic analysis of the fetishism of commodities.

Dialectical theory and practice implies giving oneself up absolutely to the course of the dialectic, that is, to the movement of reality, to the things themselves. It is a process of kenosis, in which the subject is willing to give up any claim to particular content as its own, to become nothing in order to become all. This is the most anarchistic practico-theoretical position possible. Those who mistake for dialectic the elements of dogma and contrived teleology in Hegel and Marx miss entirely the subversive, antidogmatic, nonessentialist essence of dialectic. They miss the core of dialectic that Marx called "the ruthless critique of all things existing." Dialectical social theory shows that all "things," including all social phenomena, are deceptive in their usual mode of appearance, inasmuch as they appear to be static, self-identical, and independent, that is, to be merely what they are.[7] However, they are not in fact static, but in a process of constant transformation and development. They are not self-identical but rather are pervaded by self-negating contradiction. As this was later expressed succinctly, "objects do not go into their concepts without leaving a remainder."[8] There is always a supplement. And finally, these objects and phenomena are not independent, but can only be understood in relation to other realities that constitute them. These realities include larger wholes of which they are parts (which are themselves dynamic, developing phenomena, and thus relative wholes, not closed or completed totalities), and the other elements of these larger wholes. Dialectical social theory is thus a many-sided critique of the objectification or reification of any aspect of reality.

It might seem confusing when dialectical theorists such as Hegel and Marx state that one phenomenon is "identical" with another (e.g., that production and consumption are identical). However, this has nothing to do with any "identity theory" in which particularity and difference are explained away, but quite the opposite. It is an expression of the doctrine of internal relations, the view that the "outside" is "inside" and that there is no way of insulating a reality from that outside. It expresses the fundamental truth that "negation is determination" and "determination is negation." It means that we must look both at systemic determination and at the repressed side of any relationship of mutual determination. This is the message of Hegel's master–slave dialectic, in which he shows that domination produces not only the master's freedom to consume the product of the slave's labor, but also the master's dependence on that labor. This is also the message of Marx's dialectical analysis of labor, in which he shows that the answer to the question "what do we produce through our labor" is not merely "the product," but also a system of production, a system of distribution, a system of consumption, relations of production, social classes, wealth and poverty, pride and humiliation, solidarity and alienation, and, not least of all, on the most general level, ourselves and our social world.

Another crucial dimension of dialectical social theory is its recognition that the analytical concepts themselves change in the process of dialectical analysis (as does the analyst). One proceeds in social theory, as Hegel does in his logic, with abstract, relatively empty concepts, and through the course of inquiry these concepts become increasingly more concrete and rich in content. The mark of dogmatic theory is that it begins with abstract, unreflective concepts and repeats those same concepts at the same level of abstraction throughout the analysis, while in dialectical theory concepts gain both universality and richness of particularity in the course of the analysis. The fundamental flaw of dogmatic theory is that it is excessively attached to certain conceptions of reality and to the material conditions that create those conceptions, and cannot let go of either.

Marx's application of this kind of dialectical analysis to the historical phenomenon of capitalism resulted in his demonstration of the systemic nature of economic domination. He showed that capital in the most general sense constitutes value reproducing and expanding itself through circulation or exchange. Human activity of very specific kinds was certainly a precondition for the emergence of capitalism, but the modes of functioning of the system were not the product of conscious planning on the part of human agents. The capitalist emerges with and within the system. "The expansion of value, which is the objective basis or mainspring of the circulation M-C-M,[9] becomes his subjective aim, and it is only in so far as the appropriation of ever more and more wealth in the abstract becomes the sole motive of his operations, that he functions as a capitalist, that is, as capital personified and endowed with consciousness and a will."[10] Capitalists as particular individuals may to varying degrees be greedy or generous, ruthless or kindhearted, authoritarian or indulgent, domineering or respectful, unscrupulous or honest. However, capitalism is a system of economic domination not because of the degree to which individual capitalists exhibit undesirable character traits or treat people badly on a personal basis, but because the ever-increasing concentration of wealth and power is built into the system, and the structure of the system dictates that the human good and the natural good are subordinated to the demands of capital. In another striking example of the principle that "the truth is out there," the very name of the system gives away the secret of the system. It is called "capitalism" because under it, capital rules. It is capitalocracy.

Marx applied his idea of the "ruthless critique of all things existing" most momentously to one particular class of existing things: those things called commodities. Marx begins the chapter on "The Fetishism of Commodities" in *Capital* with the observation that "a commodity appears, at first sight, a very trivial thing, and easily understood. Its analysis shows that it is, in reality, a very queer thing, abounding in metaphysical subtleties and theological niceties."[11] Smith's concept of the "invisible hand," and Hegel's "Cunning of Reason," had already expressed the idea that social forces have a certain logic that escapes the intentions of individuals. But never before the "Fetishism" chapter had there been so concise and powerful an expression of the concept that forces of social domination work in unconscious, mystified, and impersonal ways. In a world of commodities, Marx explains, "the mutual relations of the producers, within which the social character of their labor affirms itself, take the form of a social relation between the products," and "the social character of men's labor appears to them as an objective character stamped upon the product of that labor."[12] Individuals go about their daily life, selling their labor for wages, exchanging money for commodities, unaware of the ways in which their own actions are an expression of class domination, unaware of the ways in which the seemingly objective quality of economic value disguises social relations of domination. To the producers, "their own social action takes the form of the action of objects, which rule the producers instead of being ruled by them."[13] Thus, class domination takes on a systematically mediated form that is very different from the old paradigm of socially dominant groups directly and visibly dominating subordinate groups. As domination becomes ever more deeply embedded in the system of things, the possibility opens for the rule of objects to exceed the grasp not only of the producers but even that of the nonproducers.[14]

The Radical Critique of Domination

Reclus's conception of a system of domination consisting of a number of multidimensional forms that pervade everyday life, and Marx's dialectical analysis of the systemic, structural, impersonal operation of the mechanisms of domination, taken together, provide the essentials of the comprehensive critique of domination. The subsequent century of critical and dialectical social theory developed these early insights into a rich theoretical framework.

The tradition of radical urbanism initiated by Reclus is carried on notably in Walter Benjamin's analysis of the *passages* or "arcades" of Paris and Henri Lefebvre's theory of urban space. Benjamin shows that the *passages* were part of the movement toward social domination through the commodity and the capture of desire by the economistic imaginary. Yet they also presented a "dialectical image," since at the same time that they represented the forces of domination by the commodity they also expressed the utopian and liberatory force of a desire that surpasses the limits of economistic domination. Lefebvre points out, and demonstrates through extensive theoretical and empirical analysis, that in late capitalist, urban, technological society, space itself becomes pervasively ideological. It takes on "a sort of reality of its own" similar to the powerful sense of reality "assumed in the same global process by commodities, money and capital," so that "in addition to being a means of production it is also a means of control, and hence of domination, of power."[15]

Thus, space begins to achieve a relative autonomy within the processes of mutual determination. Like technology, it is not a neutral medium, but rather "escapes in part from those who would make use of it," and even "the social and political (state) forces which engendered this space now seek, but fail, to master it completely."[16] Critical urbanism reveals, for example, that in the end Fascist architecture is not merely an *effect* of authoritarian state domination; it is *part* of authoritarian state domination. The mall, the descendent of the *passages*, is not a mere *effect* of capitalist domination it is *part* of capitalist economistic domination. It is not merely the case that the ruling class dominates through the organization of space, but more ultimately, that the system of domination operates through a ruling class and through the organization of space.

Throughout the course of the twentieth century, the theme of the autonomy of the technological system becomes increasingly central to the critique of domination. Major contributions to this development include Jacques Ellul's *The Technological Society*, Lewis Mumford's monumental two-volume critique of the history of technology, *The Myth of the Machine*, Langdon Winner's *Autonomous Technology*, and David Watson's *Against the Megamachine*, to mention a few of the most important works.[17] Mumford encapsulates very well the emergence of the impersonal, systemic dimension of technological domination:

The center of authority in this new system is no longer a visible personality, an all-powerful king: even in totalitarian dictatorships the center now lies in the system itself, invisible but omnipresent: all its human components, even the technical and managerial elite, even the sacred priesthood of science, who alone have access to the secret knowledge by means of which total control is now swiftly being effected, are themselves trapped by the very perfection of the organization they have invented.[18]

Advocates of the view that domination must be personal argue that there can be no domination without agents of domination. Mumford's analysis points out the fallacy of reading too much into such a need for agents. It is obvious that no one would argue absurdly that a system of social domination could exist without the presence of human beings who act socially and thereby make the operation of the system possible. However, the fact that such agents must exist in no way demonstrates that the phenomenon of domination can be reduced to domination by specific agents, nor is it evidence against the existence of domination by systemic forces that do not correlate with specific agents. The actual history of domination shows that the reciprocal interaction and mutual determination between agents and system result in a degree of loss of agency in a strong sense (intentional, purposeful activity) on the part of such agents. To the extent that the system constrains both the dominant and the subordinate, and to the extent that systemic constraints are not the result of intentional acts of the dominant, the simple model of domination as a direct relationship between dominating agents and dominated subjects breaks down.[19]

Some aspects of these themes are developed further in the Frankfurt School's critical theory of society, which synthesizes the Marxian idea of commodity fetishism, Weberian concepts of bureaucracy and technique, and Freudian themes of desire and the unconscious to help explain the evolution of domination in late capitalist society. The resulting critique shows that an understanding of domination today requires recognition of the central role of the culture industry and mass consumption, the growing tendency toward total administration, and the spread of instrumental rationality to all spheres of existence. In *Eros and Civilization*, Marcuse points out how the traditional personal and hierarchical dimensions of economic domination have declined in importance. Obviously, this does not mean that the subjective dimension disappears within this transformed system. Marcuse himself argues that in late capitalism aggressive impulses proliferate within the subjective realm but find few channels for expression. Lacan describes how desire and demand take on new forms in relation to the other/Other, as these are defined and generated by the dominant system, including both the Symbolic Order and the Imaginary Order that is dialectically related to it. De Certeau and Foucault show that an infinite number of more or less personal and creative tactics of power are generated in response to the system, apart from any strategies of power dictated objectively by the logic of that system. However, despite all these transformations of subjectivity, and indeed because of them, the modes of operation of the system of domination itself become more impersonal. "At its peak, the concentration of economic power seems to turn into anonymity: everyone, even at the very top, appears to be powerless before the movements and laws of the apparatus itself."[20]

Marcuse develops this idea in *One-Dimensional Man*, where he argues that late capitalist, industrial society "alters the base of domination by gradually replacing personal dependence (of the slave on the master, the serf on the lord of the manor, the lord on the donor of the fief, etc.) with dependence on the 'objective order of things' (on economic laws, the market etc.)."[21] At the same time that some of the more blatant manifestations of social domination disappear and it becomes more deeply embedded in objective reality, the system also increasingly legitimates itself through consumptionist values based on the fruits of social domination and the domination of nature. The system "sustains its hierarchic structure, while exploiting ever more efficiently the natural and mental resources, and distributing the benefits of this exploitation on an ever-larger scale."[22]

The role of the commodity, as the primary means of allocating such benefits, becomes central to the legitimation process, displacing to a certain degree such classical mechanisms of domination as authoritarian conditioning and formal ideological indoctrination. The claims of classical ideology could to a certain degree be assessed as objectively either true or false. But when ideology is embedded in the objective order of things (as ideology invades and increasingly pervades the fabric of the ethos), it ironically escapes the realm of objectivity. Adorno defines the commodity as "a consumer item in which there is no longer anything that is supposed to remind us how it came into being. It becomes a magical object."[23] In effect, you can't argue with magic. This is the character of advanced forms of domination: they operate in ways that leave few obvious traces of their functioning. Thus, the Frankfurt School shows that we have entered a period in which domination operates increasingly through two divergent but complementary means, through values of mass consumption and the harnessing of desire (repressive sublimation) on the one hand, and through the mechanism of techno-bureaucratic control and instrumental rationality on the other. These are the two poles of the historic tendency away from traditional dominance and subordination and toward impersonal mechanisms of social domination.

A decisive step in the development of the theory of domination is the convergence of many of these themes in the situationist concept of the society of the spectacle. According to the situationist analysis, the "increasing value of the world of things" finally culminates in the spectacle, a vast system of representation with overwhelming power over a generally pacified mass of consumers and spectators. Debord contends that the principle of commodity fetishism is "absolutely fulfilled in the spectacle, where the perceptible world is replaced by a set of images that are superior to that world yet at the same time impose themselves as eminently perceptible."[24] He calls the result "spectacular domination."[25] This analysis is particularly noteworthy for the ways in which elements of the social imaginary, social ethos, and social materiality are fused into a unified yet widely dispersed apparatus of domination that at once intimately pervades everyday life and at the same overawes the masses as a distant and overwhelming power.[26] Domination takes on its most impersonal, systemic, and mystified form, even as the techniques of control increasingly address precisely the realm of subjectivity. *L'Imaginaire* is most certainly *au pouvoir*, as the subject is controlled above all by the hopeless quest for a satisfying identity through identification with an endless stream of commodified images, the fragments of the good life. The ultimate object of desire becomes the *objet petit achat*.

While the critical-dialectical tradition has offered these powerful insights into the role of the capitalist economy and the bureaucratic state in the system of domination, its analysis has sometimes been weaker in other areas, and perhaps most notably regarding patriarchy. This demonstrates the value of the anarchist insistence on the necessity of an intensive exploration of all forms of domination. In fact, there is no better example of the relevance of a dialectical view of domination than in the case of patriarchal domination. Patriarchy is more than a hierarchical system of dominance and subordination. During its long history, it has had a profound effect on all other forms of domination, on all social institutions, and on the psyche. Throughout the history of civilization, it has produced values and practices that express hierarchical dualism, aggressiveness, instrumentalism, possessiveness, and egocentrism. Patriarchy as a historical form of domination encompasses not only formally patriarchal institutions, but also a patriarchal imaginary, a patriarchal ideology, and a patriarchal ethos, all of which mutate in relation to changing historical conditions, and interact with and condition other moments of domination. Even when formal patriarchal social structures are dismantled and social organizations allow participation of larger numbers of women in higher status positions, domination can be perpetuated by the legacy of patriarchal values, sensibilities, and character structures, which are inscribed in the seemingly "post-patriarchal" institutions and practices that have been conditioned by patriarchy over its history. The history of combining greater opportunities for women with the continuing dominance of patriarchal values started with Plato's proposal to open to qualified women positions as "philosopher-kings" who oversee a fundamentally hierarchical, masculinist system of power. That history continues as liberal programs allow more women into high positions in a fundamentally masculinist system of economic, political, and technological domination, a system in which a growing number of poor urban women, peasant women, and indigenous women find themselves in an increasingly immiserated and marginalized position.

There is much more to the critique of domination than can be sketched in this brief introduction. However, we can conclude at this point that any adequate critique must take into account certain basic points that have been established by the anarchist and critical-dialectical analyses. First, it must be recognized that social domination constitutes a *system of domination*, within which there are a number of distinct *forms of domination* (capitalism, the state, patriarchy, etc.) that interact dialectically and condition one another, and which, though sometimes containing mutual contradictions, function on the whole to reinforce one another. Second, adequate attention must be given to the roles of all the major *spheres of social determination*, including the roles played in the system of domination by social institutions, the social ideology, the social imaginary, the social ethos, and social materiality. Third, there must be a comprehensive analysis of the ways in which domination works both through overt processes of dominance and subordination of more or less distinct, identifiable groups, and also through *impersonal mechanisms* that are largely unconscious, automatic, systemic, and structural. Finally, the analysis must reflect a clear understanding of the historical development of the system of domination, and of the fact that in the age of techno-bureaucracy and mass consumption, the system has been moving consistently in the direction of the predominance of such impersonal mechanisms. In a techno-bureaucratic, commodified, and mediatized society, domination takes on increasingly more ideological and mystified forms that give it a quality of *invisibility*. In the end, domination becomes so firmly embedded in the various spheres of social determination that it can tolerate a considerable degree of conscious awareness of some dimensions of domination as domination, without in any way threatening its fundamental legitimacy and efficacy.

Domination in Contemporary Liberal Theory

Until recently, there were few if any attempts within mainstream Anglo-American liberal political thought to theorize the concept of domination.[27] Rawls and most well-known liberal theorists devote little or no attention to this concept. An exception of sorts is Bruce Ackerman, who goes to some length in *Social Justice in the Liberal State* to discuss the issue of "genetic domination," but his analysis has nothing to do with major processes of social domination, and in the end, merely helps prove the rule.[28] The closest thing to an analysis of actual domination is Michael Walzer's discussion of "monopolistic control of a dominant good" in *Spheres of Justice*; however, his analysis remains brief and never really confronts the nature of systemic forms of domination.[29] This situation has changed somewhat in the past fifteen years, primarily as the result of Philip Pettit's influential book *Republicanism*.[30] In this work, Pettit presents the most detailed defense of a concept of freedom as nondomination in liberal (or liberal "republican") political theory. His book has received widespread recognition in academia, and has the distinction of being recognized as a major influence on the policies of the social democratic Zapatero government in Spain (2004–11).

Pettit's work has inspired a number of variations on the republican theory of domination, and it provides the overall parameters of ongoing debate of the issue within contemporary liberal thought. For example, Richard Dagger, in "Autonomy, Domination, and the Republican Challenge to Liberalism"[31] accepts Pettit's view of nondomination as central to the concept of freedom, but argues that it must be related more clearly to the more basic value of autonomy.[32] Paul Gowder also accepts the essentials of Pettit's formulation of the issue, but responds to Pettit from a more mainstream liberal position. He argues that liberal egalitarianism produces a more adequate account of the relationship between domination and other social ills than does the republican alternative.[33] Frank Lovett has done a series of articles developing his variation on the theme of republican freedom as nondomination in the tradition of Pettit, while attempting to take a more systemic approach. This has culminated in a recent book-length analysis of the issue, *A General Theory of Domination and Justice.*[34] And Michael J. Thompson, in his analysis of "Reconstructing Republican Freedom," goes further than most others in the debate on addressing the systemic and structural aspects of domination within the context of a defense of a republican conception.[35] This growing literature deserves detailed critical analysis. However, the focus of the present critique will be Pettit's own theory of domination, since his analysis remains the definitive statement of the liberal position on the issue.

It is useful to begin a critique at the beginning, with first principles, when the position analyzed is of the sort that attempts to establish such principles. According to Pettit: "Every grand approach to politics gives us an axiom or set of axioms from which judgments on more particular institutional matters are meant to flow," and which "claim to be a good starting point for organizing intuitions."[36] Such an approach, he thinks, should be judged on "the attractions of the axiom or axioms, both in themselves and in the organizational role that they are allotted," and "for the plausibility and adequacy of the theorems that are derived from those axioms."[37] Thus, we begin, in effect, with our intuitions and with further intuitions about how to organize our intuitions.

Though intuitions may be taken as a starting point for an argument, they are found in our actual experience, not at some absolute beginning-point, but rather in the midst of things. Thus, one might investigate the degree to which the most "fundamental" intuitions, as fundamental as they may appear, they are less a "starting point" for either organizing other intuitions or organizing institutions, and more a product of the influence of already organized institutions. But we find in Pettit's work little such critical reflection on the genesis of our presuppositions. Rather, he tells us that the merits of his "central axiom" include that it is "traditional and modest," that it will appeal to various factions in contemporary political theory, and above all, that it will produce results that are "attractive."[38] He recommends that in pursuing such results we utilize the method of "reflective equilibrium." Reflection is a good thing, and equilibrium can sometimes be a good thing. And, in fact, a method of *absolute reflective equilibrium* would approach the dialectical method, in that it would seek to reflect all the major contradictions of the world, and the quest for equilibrium, the project of working out the implications of these contradictions, would be an infinite one. However, Pettit's method is instead the familiar liberal one of *relative reflective equilibrium*, in which only *some* contradictions are reflected, the most challenging ones are bracketed, and equilibrium is reached much more easily. Relative reflective equilibrium is the philosophical correlate of the consensus politics and the marketing strategies of mass society. It is the pursuit of the greatest attractiveness for the greatest number.

According to the critical-dialectical perspective, the surer path to significant truth is the precisely opposite one. We should follow the way of truth until it confronts us with results that we find entirely unattractive, and perhaps shocking and traumatic, and leave us, at least for a moment, dazed and confused. Even our old enemy Plato was a good enough friend to give us this advice. But then again, he suffered to a certain degree from a case of painful dialectic. The message of radical dialectic is that the most valuable condition that we can possibly fall into is that of *reflective disequilibrium*, and that above all we should be wary of too quickly lapsing into any state of equilibrium. Reflection may certainly help us "extend" our "intuitions," and a consistency that takes us beyond bias and confusion is a laudable goal, but the biggest favor that reflection can do for us is to take us beyond the *fallacy of hasty equilibration* and help us realize how fallacious, and indeed idiotic, some of our most basic intuitions may be.[39]

We might reflect further on the nature of reflection and the reflective condition. We might ask, for example, what it is that we *reflect* when we *reflect upon* political questions. We find that most notably, we reflect all the contradictions, both social and social ecological, that have shaped us as politicized beings. As Leibniz pointed out, we are the kind of beings who mirror the universe. This includes both the social universe and the natural one. However, we are not monads, but rather communads, universal singularities capable of reflecting our being in common, and of expressing that common being. We are also quite capable of *not* consciously reflecting it. A concept of social domination will be helpful to the extent that it traumatizes us into seeing some important truth about ourselves and the world we reflect. For example, an unattractive concept might help us understand better our own complicity in the processes of domination, while a more attractive (ideologically marketable) concept might lead us to locate all significant responsibility elsewhere. Or the unattractive concept might show us ways in which the struggle against domination is more complex and challenging than we thought, and that it requires more extreme and demanding forms of action than we thought, while the more attractive concept might lead us to believe that a politics of gestures and tokenism is actually effective. We will return to this theme at the conclusion of the analysis, after we have seen where Pettit's intuitions have taken him, and what he reflects. But, to continue this beginning, we need to look at the content of Pettit's central axiom, the republican concept of liberty, or "freedom as nondomination."

Pettit states that by "nondomination," he means "a condition under which a person is more or less immune, and more or less saliently immune, to interference on an arbitrary basis."[40] Domination, the obstacle to such immunity, has three aspects, according to this view. The first two aspects are forms of coercion. There is, first, "coercion of the body, as in restraint or obstruction," and, second, "coercion of the will, as in punishment or the threat of punishment."[41] The third aspect consists of "manipulation," which "is usually covert and may take the form of agenda-fixing, the deceptive or nonrational shaping of people's beliefs or desires, or the rigging of the consequences of people's actions."[42] The recognition of this final dimension would seem to point to the need for a deep, systemic critique of forms of social domination, an undertaking that, it is argued here, demands developed analyses of authoritarian, hierarchical, and exploitative social institutions, and of accompanying forms of social ideology, of the social imaginary, and of the social ethos. However, Pettit quickly precludes the need for any such systemic analysis by limiting the inquiry narrowly, reducing "domination" to a general term covering acts of "arbitrary" interference, either in the form of coercion, or in the more obvious and overt forms of manipulation. Moreover, despite his recognition that domination is often "covert," he later reverts to the view that it is something that is in general openly recognized. Thus, after his initial insight into the covert quality of much of social domination, he seems determined that the most covert should remain as covert as possible.

Domination as Arbitrary Interference

A fateful step in this reductive process is Pettit's decision to include the idea of malevolent intention as an essential element of the core concept of domination. He contends that "all interfering behaviors, coercive or manipulative, are intended by the interferer to worsen the agent's choice situation by changing the range of options available, by altering the expected payoffs assigned to those options, or by assuming control over which outcomes will result from which options and what actual payoffs, therefore, will materialize."[43] Since all instances of domination are by Pettit's definition instances of coercive or manipulative interference, all domination must have such an intention. This definitional strategy is a very effective means of rendering much of social domination invisible,[44] since the social ideology of domination, the dominating social imaginary, and the ethos of domination produce the kind of systemic shaping and distortion of reality that allows all, including the dominant, to participate in structures of domination, not merely without intending such worsening of the condition of the dominated, but even while believing that the system of domination serves the true interest of the dominated. The critical force of the concepts of the covert, the deceptive, and the nonrational is negated.

In one of his most theoretically decisive variations on his depiction of domination, Pettit describes it as "subjection to an arbitrary power of interference on the part of another—a *dominus* or master—even another who chooses not actually to exercise that power."[45] He does not intend that we interpret the term "master" metaphorically, as in the sense of Lacan's "discourse of the master."[46] Pettit is looking for actual, literal masters caught in the act of mastering. To be such a master "involves occupying a position where another can interfere on an arbitrary basis in your life: specifically . . . where another can interfere with greater or lesser ease on a more or less arbitrary basis across a smaller or larger range of choices."[47] This account personalizes domination in the person of such a master. Accordingly, mastery can be either an easier or a more difficult undertaking, and its efficacy will depend in part on the master's personal effort. Furthermore, such a concept of mastery is concerned with processes of domination that go on at a conscious level. It focuses our attention on the master's intentional interference with the subordinate's conscious choice, but at the same time directs our attention away from the ways in which the system shapes the limits of conscious choice, creates the objects of choice, and distorts choice.

Choice is related closely to desire, which Pettit mentions early in his book, referring to the relationship between domination and "the deceptive or nonrational shaping of people's beliefs or desires."[48] It is significant that he largely abandons the analysis of desire in favor of a focus on choice. The topic of choice, is, of course, an obsession of contemporary analytical philosophy, mirroring contemporary market economics, and is conducive to analysis through abstract, ahistorical modeling.[49] The exploration of the phenomenon of desire, on the other hand, takes us into the complexities of ideology, the imaginary, and the systemic shaping of subjectivity. Pettit will have none of this. He takes a small step in the direction of the recognition of the systemic nature of domination when he identifies the mere power to interfere, as opposed to actual interference, as one of its important aspects. But this is a very small and inadequate step, since it still focuses on individual acts of interference that are either actual or possible. Such an account fails to recognize that under an institutionalized system of domination, the ideological effects, the imaginary effects, and the ethotic effects are exercised pervasively, apart from actual or possible acts of overt interference by agents of the system or dominant elites within the system. Within such a system, to be is to be interfered with.

Pettit attempts to clarify the meaning of interference in his theory by stating that "for the record, I think that someone has an arbitrary power of interference in the affairs of another so far as they have a power of interference that is not forced to track the avowed or readily avowable interests of the other: they can interfere according to their own *arbitrium* or decision."[50] This is, however, a dangerous thing to put on the record. In *Republicanism*, Pettit is usually careful to keep open the possibility that the state can legitimately act on behalf of the real interests of individuals and communities, even if the "interested" parties do not agree with the view of their interest enforced by the state through its agents. However, what he commits himself to here is the view that if individuals (or, presumably, groups or communities) have "avowed" that a state policy conflicts with their interest, or if they can "readily avow" this in response to an attempt to impose the policy, the state would engage in domination by overriding their "avowal" and imposing its own will and decision. The state would then, we are told, be "forced" to fall in line and do a better "tracking" job. Of course, real-world nation-states are structured so that they are constitutionally (i.e., by their fundamental nature) incapable of doing this, so the true implication of the argument is not that the state should be *reformed*, but rather that it should be *rejected* as incapable of fulfilling the demands of morality, according to Pettit's own analysis of these demands.

The degree to which Pettit overlooks not only deeply embedded, systemic forms of interference with human freedom and self-development, but also quite overt forms, is quite striking. Thus, he states that "the ideal of targeting all forms of domination, not just those in which there is actual interference, means that we are going to be relatively ill-disposed towards tolerating relations of domination, even relations of domination where the stronger party may usually be expected to stay their hand; we are going to look less fondly on the traditional relationship of husband to wife, for example, or employer to employee."[51] It is very revealing that it does not seem to occur to Pettit that, under actually existing patriarchy, women are subjected to enormous levels of violence and brutality ("actual interference"), and that much of this exists within, or is deeply conditioned by, "the traditional relationship of husband to wife." In many countries today, the proportion of females in the population is reduced significantly by mistreatment of women, in others, murder and maiming of women in "honor" killings, dowry deaths, and revenge attacks is widespread, and in countries like the United States, the most dangerous place for a woman to be is in the home. Neither does it seem to occur to Pettit that employers subject masses of employees to violence and brutality in order to discipline and control them; that they use intimidation, at best, and assassination at worst, to combat labor organizing; and that they regularly call upon the massive coercive powers of the state to defend their claims to a disproportionate share of property and power. One would never guess from Pettit's analysis that we live in a world in which millions of people are literally enslaved and that coerced labor is utilized even in affluent countries such as the United States.[52]

Obviously, when confronted with these realities of institutionalized violence in the world, Pettit would respond that, of course, he laments such conditions, and that his theory covers all cases of "arbitrary interference." But this is entirely beside the fact. One of the most striking aspects of ideology is the manner in which it creates blind spots in its adherents, producing an inability to focus attention on certain aspects of existing social reality. Though Pettit fails to understand the way in which systemic domination goes far beyond the potentiality for specific "acts of interference," he also fails to understand the other pole of domination—that in the real world the "traditional relationship of husband to wife" and "of employer to employee" are pervaded by violence and the threat of violence, rather than one in which power can be expected to "stay the hand." The real world of domination is much more disturbing than the one that exists in Pettit's liberal reformist imagination.

However shocking Pettit's blindness to the extent of actual interference under existing forms of domination may be, the deeper problem in his analysis remains the fact that it renders invisible the widespread systemic domination that cannot be reduced to actual or possible conscious acts of individual volition. It is noteworthy that when Pettit looks for a paradigm case of the phenomenon of "both interference and domination," what enters his mind is "a crime of assault." He thinks that in an assault there is "the assumption and exercise of domination by the criminal."[53] It might seem strange that he chooses such an example, since it conflicts so obviously with the ordinary idea of domination. Even in cases in which individual actions are described as examples of domination, one finds that there is a systemic quality to what takes place. For example, in cases of persistent domestic abuse it is quite fair, in view of the pervasive trauma and terrorization involved, to say that one or more family members are subjected to domination. However, in cases in which, for example, a mugger, a belligerent drunk, a bully, or a bigot assaults another person, it is reasonable to describe what occurs as an attack, an act of aggression, an act of force, a violent act, a violation, a personal injury, or, possibly, an act of coercion. Although such usage is not impossible in English, it would occur to few, if any, in the real world, using ordinary language, to describe it as "an act of domination." Why then, does it occur to Pettit? Obviously, it is because his ideological project requires a shifting of the focus of domination from the systematically social to the incidentally individual.

As we have seen, for Pettit, domination involves the clear imposition of the will of one upon another. Thus, it is likely "to occasion a specific kind of uncertainty" when the victim "is subject to the arbitrary will of another."[54] When domination occurs, it is "a matter of common knowledge" that the dominated person "is exposed to the possibility of arbitrary interference," that the dominated "cannot speak his or her mind without risk of falling out of favor," and that the dominated "cannot be ascribed a voice that claims the attention and respect of others."[55] Yet not only has much of domination never fit this model, the system of domination has, in fact, continually evolved away from such subjective manifestations and, as Marcuse and others have pointed out, toward more systemic, "objective" forms of expression. The relatively rapid mutation of Western racial domination is perhaps the most conspicuous case. This is what Thalberg showed in a well-known article forty years ago, when he observed the decline of what he called "visceral racism," and an evolution toward forms of institutionalized racial domination.[56] This evolution was analyzed in great depth in Joel Kovel's indispensable work *White Racism.*[57] There, Kovel traces the evolution of racial domination from the "dominative racism" typical of the Old South, to the "aversive racism" that long pervaded American mainstream culture, and finally to contemporary postmodern "metaracism," which operates through "economic and technocratic means," and which is quite compatible with tolerance, formal equality, and, indeed, liberal republicanism.[58]

Liberalizing Economic And Political Domination

Many aspects of Pettit's analysis of both economic and political domination demonstrate his failure to address systemic domination, and even to see major forms of domination as involving domination at all. His example of economic domination illustrates the problem very well. He says that, as a general rule, "exploiting someone's urgent needs in order to drive a very hard bargain" constitutes domination as arbitrary interference. He cites as a specific case that of "the pharmacist who agrees to sell an urgently required medicine but not for the standard fee—not even for the fee that is standard in the circumstances of an emergency call—only on extortionate terms," so that the pharmacist "interferes in the patient's choice to the extent of worsening what by the received benchmark are the expected payoffs for the options they face."[59] Pettit's example deals, as he says, with the exploitation of needs. An ethical principle stating that institutions and practices that exploit basic needs for economic gain constitute morally unjust forms of social domination would have far-reaching implications. In fact, it would fundamentally challenge the entire basis of global capitalism. If the standard for just economic transactions were the moral claims of "urgent needs," this would delegitimate not only the existing system of distribution of essential medicines, but also the existing system of distribution of the global food supply. However, Pettit undercuts the radicality of the appeal to needs by stipulating that adherence to the "received benchmark" for prices, rather than the satisfaction of actual needs, should be the norm for transactions. His demand is, in the end, only that the system should abide by its own explicit rules, which is the politically innocuous, ideological position typical of moralistic defenders of any system of distribution or of domination.

Given Pettit's adoption of such limitations on the scope of critique, it is not surprising that he holds that one does not need to oppose the "free market" in order to combat domination. Though he does not clarify adequately what he means by such a "free market," it is nevertheless clear that he assumes that it is compatible with a centralized, interventionist state. He does not see as problematic the fact that such a state invariably creates the framework for property distribution through coercion and the threat of coercion, and that it also invariably acts coercively on behalf of various economic interests. Furthermore, he does not confront the issue of the systemic tendencies internal to a capitalist system toward concentration of wealth and economic power. It should be remembered that, as Marx showed, the essence of capital is the process of value *expanding* through circulation. Pettit's failure to notice this tendency is not surprising, since his analysis does not in any way examine capitalism as a historical phenomenon having a specific (though always evolving) structure, and systemic rules of operation. He states that "short of great differences of bargaining power" such a market "does not mean that anyone is exposed to the possibility of arbitrary interference by any other or any group of others."[60] Yet the crucial question is the degree to which significant differences in bargaining power, and the tendency for those differences to increase, are built into the system itself.

Pettit's only specific analysis of the problem of generalized "arbitrary interference" under capitalism considers the possibility that "one seller may be able to interfere with another by undercutting the other's price."[61] He concludes that this practice is not a threat to freedom, since the second seller is equally free to try to undercut the first.[62] But the issue at stake is certainly not whether enterprises can strive to compete under capitalism, but whether capitalism generates structures of domination that interfere with the realization of the free person and the free community. This is precisely the form of interference that Pettit ignores: that in a system of property based on abstract entitlement and coercive enforcement of unjust property claims, those persons and entities having disproportionate control of means of production, land, and financial capital have enormously greater "bargaining power" than those who rely primarily on the sale of their labor, and that this disparity in power generates economic and other forms of social domination.

Pettit's account of political domination exhibits the same limita-tions as does his analysis of the economic. His political theory is out of touch with the real world of global megastates interacting dialectically with global megacorporations and the global technological megama-chine. None of these structures of power, or the larger system of which they are elements, have much to do with the problem of domination as he conceives of it. For example, he never confronts the seemingly ines-capable question of whether large, bureaucratic states acting through complex systems of law might contain any inherent tendencies toward domination. He contends that law "that answers systematically to people's general interests and ideas" constitutes "a form of interference," but "does not compromise people's liberty; it constitutes a non-mastering inter-ferer."[63] He simply assumes that such "properly constituted law" can exist unproblematically at the level of a modern nation state. Yet loss of respon-siveness to the community's needs and desires, "interests and ideas," is observed to occur even when a much smaller scale is reached. Zibechi notes that, in Bolivia, capital and the state have promoted the merger of small communities into larger political units that are easier to influence and control. He shows that the assemblies and other political organs in self-governing neighborhood communities of two hundred to three hundred families have a radically democratic, self-determining character, but that there is a loss of autonomy and alienation of power when these small communities have been agglomerated into large neighborhoods of ten thousand inhabitants.[64] Studies of self-managed production (e.g., the Mondragon cooperatives) have led some analysts to the conclusion that when self-managed enterprises and workers' assemblies grow larger than a few hundred members they become far less responsive to the workers' "interests and ideas."[65] Pettit makes no attempt to confront the evidence that such questions of scale might pose a challenge to his utopian "repub-lican" assumptions (which are, in effect, profoundly antirepublican in that they help subvert public power).

At one point, Pettit does explicitly consider the issue of "dispersion of power." However, his analysis of the issue remains entirely within the context of the nation-state and its major divisions. Not only does he fail to consider statist versus nonstatist contexts, he fails even to consider how the character of the state has changed fundamentally as we have evolved from the world of classic republicanism to one in which there are now nation-states of over a billion people, in which most people in the world live in nation-states with populations of over 100 million, and in which there are even "constituent states" (i.e., divisions of nation-states) with over 100 million people (200 million, in the case of the Indian state of Uttar Pradesh). Nor does he appear to have the slightest suspicion that technological development might be relevant to the nature of the modern nation-state, that the development of digital technology, communications technologies, surveillance technologies, information-gathering technologies, weapons technologies, nanotechnologies, neurotechnologies, and psychotropic technologies could be in any way relevant to the problem of domination. Robert Michels's "Iron Law of Oligarchy" was not without foundation when he formulated it over a century ago, and considering the vast growth in both scale and technological complexity of organizations and institutions, it is foolhardy to fail to take seriously today their oligarchical and automatizing tendencies.[66] Pettit expresses some sympathy for the positive conception of freedom as "participation in a self-determining polity," but he devotes little or no attention to the most serious political, economic, and technological issues that define the constraints on meaningful self-determination today.[67]

Another telling comment by Pettit on political domination concerns the possibility of a colonialism that operates without significant interference. He notes that republican writers' "condemnation of domination, even where it is not particularly associated with interference, shows up in their hostility to colonialism, even benign colonialism."[68] Though colonial domination has involved various degrees of oppressiveness, one wonders where in history Pettit has discovered a colonialism that has been "benign" and involved little or no interference.[69] Since the classic republican writers were colonialists, it is not surprising that they would have held such an overtly ideological view, but it seems almost inconceivable that Pettit would want to perpetuate such a misconception at this late date in history.[70] The fact that such an interpretation is even possible shows rather clearly the way in which the ideology of domination leads to a contrived and systematically distorted reading of history. This raises the question of the specific role such a reading might play within Pettit's problematic. Of course, it would be absurd to imagine that he contemplates future republican projects of reestablishing "benign colonialism." The main function of his perpetuation of this myth is merely to reinforce his general ideological principle that "interference" should be identified with the reality or possibility of consciously willed and overtly imposed acts, rather than with the systemic effects of power. The real danger is not that Pettit's theory could be used to reinstate old-fashioned colonialism, but that it can and will be used to continue to legitimate "noninterfering" policies that more critical observers might suspect of being forms of economic neocolonialism.

From Real Consent to Possible Contestation

One of the preeminent strategies of radical critique and liberatory politics has always been to take the dominant system at its own word. What would "liberty and justice for all" mean if put strictly into practice? What would "government by consent of the governed" mean if actual consent were required for any governing to take place? Taking such principles seriously would obviously have revolutionary implications. However, Pettit's putative project of combating domination moves in precisely the opposite direction. Rather than radicalizing the idea of consent, and realizing its implications, Pettit proposes replacing legitimacy based on "the consent of the governed" with a much weaker principle of legitimacy.

For Pettit, republicanism can exorcize the specter of systemic domination by building into the system certain procedural mechanisms of "contestation." He contends that nondomination demands "a conception of democracy under which contestability takes the place usually given to consent" and requires "not that government does what the people tells it but, on pain of arbitrariness, that people can always contest whatever it is that government does."[71] Nondomination, according to this analysis, does not require "actual consent" to the exercise of state power," but only "the permanent possibility of effectively contesting it."[72] Rather than recognizing power at the base as a necessary condition for responsiveness and nonarbitrary action, Pettit places the burden on "the people" to "contest" the action of the state in presumably exceptional instances in which there is reason to suspect "arbitrariness."[73] State interference is presumed to be legitimate, so long as it is "guided by certain relevant interests and ideas and those interests and ideas are shared by those affected."[74] It is not necessary for the people to "have actively consented to the arrangements under which the state acts," but only for them to be able "to contest the assumption that the guiding interests and ideas really are shared and, if the challenge proves sustainable, to alter the pattern of state activity."[75]

Such an approach is both idealist and ideological. It is based on a fundamental misrepresentation of how domination, and even power in general, operates in the real world, and it serves to mystify and justify the operations of power and domination. The state, Pettit claims, may act without explicit consent if it represents ideas and interests shared by the people. But this makes the state, and whatever interests and forces act through the state, the major social agents. The people become, in turn, the major social patient, which must either accept the manner in which it is acted upon, or else respond through "contestation." A crucial issue is the meaning of "possibility" in the proposal that there be "the permanent possibility" of effective contestation. One must ask what the actual chances are that the people, given its character as a habitual nonagent, can occasionally assume agency and mount a "sustainable" challenge to the state and the forces that act through it. History overwhelmingly supports Rousseau's judgment of the efficacy of occasional democratic moments in a society that is fundamentally undemocratic: "The people of England regards itself as free; but it is grossly mistaken; it is free only during the election of members of parliament. As soon as they are elected, slavery overtakes it, and it is nothing."[76] Pettit's contestation sessions would encounter the same problems, but one step further removed from real freedom.

When Pettit finally explains the "general preconditions" for contestability, in which the extent of the possibilities for real agency might be clarified, we find that, unsurprisingly, his discussion remains on an abstract, rather than substantive, level. In effect, he presents proposals that presuppose developed ethical substantiality, but when he explains their basis, we find only underdeveloped moral insubstantiality. We discover that, ultimately, the responsiveness of the system must depend on the good intentions of all involved. These intentions will be reinforced by rather diffused processes through which good citizenship will be encouraged. In Pettit's ideal republic, political decision-making and contestation will be "debate-based" and "the considerations relevant will be required to have a characteristically neutral cast: they will be constrained not to favor any one sector of opinion or interest over another."[77] So, neutrality will be "required" and enforced by "constraint." One is tempted to ask how many divisions neutrality has under this system. Unfortunately, these divisions do not seem to materialize anywhere in the discussion. The best Pettit can do is to suggest that "there will be a requirement on the authorities to decide on the basis of suitable considerations and to make clear which considerations are moving them."[78] It is more than likely that they will make it clear that they are moved by the best interests of all. We end up with a government neither "of laws" nor "of men" (to cite classic republican and liberal ideology) but rather something much purer, more ethereal, and equally ideological, "a republic of reasons."[79] What Pettit does not recognize is that under a corporate state system within a technocratic mass society, formalistic mechanisms for "contestation" will have only a marginal influence, and abstract requirements or encouragements of "neutrality" will be ineffectual, given the social context of decidedly nonneutral systems of power and spheres of social determination.[80] The result will be, in more senses than one, "a republic of rationalizations."

Finally, we come to one of Pettit's most revealing discussions, the point at which his argument becomes most clearly its own immanent critique. This is the point at which he poses the question of what will happen in his debate-based system when the debate reaches an ultimate impasse. One must assume that this would occur quite frequently in large, diverse societies that are riddled with internal contradictions (i.e., in all late-capitalist, late-modern societies). In such a situation, dissenters "cannot view the judgment against them as anything other than an exercise of arbitrary power" because either it "is not dictated, at any level, by an interest that they share in common with others," or "it is not directed by procedures which they can accept."[81] Since debate can go no further, the nondominating solution is clear. Dissenters must be allowed to secede. Pettit admits that this solution is in principle correct. He states that "at the limit, the ideal of nondomination may require in relevant cases that the group are allowed to secede from the state, establishing a separate territory or at least a separate jurisdiction; that possibility has to be kept firmly on the horizon."[82] One cannot imagine any large nation-state of the kind advocated by Pettit actually adopting such a policy, and Pettit himself is clearly unhappy with the direction in which the logic of his analysis has taken him. He quickly adds that "secession is not always possible and not always desirable overall, even from the point of view of the seceding parties."[83] He evidently hopes that the truth that he just discovered will conveniently disappear from the horizon.

No doubt it will, within his liberal ideological universe, as normal processes of denial and fetishistic disavowal take their course. However, any critical reader who has followed his argument will realize that the relevant case is not that in which dissenters do not want to secede, but obviously, that in which they would consciously choose secession. We might call this liberalism's "hard case of political consciousness." Pettit suggests that in the former case (the easy case), "measures of conscientious, procedural objection" can be instituted on the model of policies that allow special treatment for groups such as indigenous people, the Amish, or military conscientious objectors. He stipulates that such procedures should not allow the dissenters "to escape the burdens of a system of coercion from which they continue to benefit."[84] However, none of this solves the significant problem of groups desiring to secede when faced with policies that they find intolerable. These are the cases in which dissenters desire precisely to escape unwanted and unjustified burdens, and have no desire for benefits that are the price of a bad, coercive bargain.

At this point, it becomes clear that anarchist confederation (what Proudhon, Bakunin, Reclus, and others call "federalism") is the fulfillment of the moral trajectory of Pettit's position, if it is allowed to break through the fetters of liberal ideology. It should be noted further that anarchist confederation, in which federating groups can opt out of specific policies that they find unacceptable, would actually give these groups far less reason to see complete secession from a larger association as a desirable option than would Pettit's statist system (if made morally self-consistent), in which the costs of remaining within the larger association are far greater for dissenting members. It is not unreasonable to assume that the social expression of a more organic solidarity that arises out of real agency and a strong sense of the common good would have greater stability and legitimacy than a more mechanistic form of association (the sovereign nation-state) based on the vicissitudes of political and economic power.

Failures of the Liberal Theory of Domination

It must be concluded that Pettit's reductive account of domination is a failure in ways that exhibit the typical ideological lapses of liberal political thought. First, its model of domination as involving "acts of arbitrary interference" leads it to ignore the ways in which the centralized nation-state and capitalism function as forms of domination. Second, it misses the deep, systemic qualities of other forms of domination such as patriarchy, racial domination, technological domination, and the systematic domination of nature. Third, it misses completely the dialectic between these various forms of domination and the decisively determining moments of these forms. And it should be added, finally, that the position destroys itself, if carried to its own logical conclusion. In the end, Pettit's reduction of political nondomination to the availability of formalistic mechanisms of contestation, and the reduction of economic nondomination to a matter of "undominated choice" comes close to Rancière's description of the masking of domination by antidemocratic ideology. Such ideology, he says, "den[ies] the forms of domination that structure society" in two ways: first, it "masks the domination of State oligarchies by identifying democracy with a form of society"; second, it "masks that of the economic oligarchies by assimilating their empire to the mere appetites of 'democratic individuals.'"[85] While Rancière's target is what we might call "hard antidemocratic ideology," Pettit shows that precisely the same mechanisms infect what we might call "soft antidemocratic ideology." Pettit claims that when the state imposes formally nonarbitrary laws, those subjected to these laws are only "nonfree," rather than being "unfree." However, one must conclude that such a distinction is eminently unsuccessful in dissolving the issue of state domination. Other forms of systemic domination remain similarly unscathed.

The work of Pettit, and of others who espouse similar ideas, have advanced liberal theory to a certain extent by reintroducing concepts of the political community, of citizenship, of mutual respect and recognition, and of the common good into a tradition that had increasingly reduced the political to the operation of mechanisms for economic redistribution. Some theorists influenced by Pettit have tried to introduce more systemic and structural dimensions to the analysis. Yet for very good ideological reasons, liberal theory, including its republican versions, remains unable to address adequately the ways in which domination takes on impersonal, structural, systemic forms. It is also required to neglect the ideological, imaginary, and ethotic dimensions of domination. Yet these neglected spheres are the very ones (in addition to social materiality) that need most to be reexamined in the age of global capital, the global nation-state system, the global society of mass consumption, and the global technological megamachine.

If we adopt the liberal approach of conceiving of domination solely according to the model of groups and individuals "arbitrarily interfering" with other groups and individuals, we will remain on the level of *exousia*, of powers, and fail to confront and overcome the principles and principalities that are the essence of *arche*. We will miss not only the most crucial systemic dimensions of social domination, but also the entirety of the most fateful form of domination presently existing, the domination of nature that is inseparable from social domination. Domination of nature does not fit the model of arbitrary interference with free choice; however, it does fit the conception here of forms of domination as highly organized, historically evolving systems of power that act through social institutions, the social imaginary, social ethos, and social materiality, to seriously undermine freedom. In this case, the infringement on freedom can be seen as massive use of force and intervention, and the fundamental shaping of major institutional, ideological, imaginary, ethotic, and material social determinants in ways that interfere with or destroy the self-activity of beings (organisms, populations, species, ecosystems, etc.) within the biosphere, and prevent their flourishing, self-realization, and attainment of good.

Despite the "attractiveness" to Pettit and others of the liberal concept of domination, it has the distinct disadvantage of obscuring the most significant forms of social domination today, including global capitalism and the global nation-state system, and the most significant problem presently confronting the planet, the sixth great mass extinction of life on Earth. The most advanced stage of ideology is reached when the forms of everyday activity allowed by the system produce global economic, political, and technological domination, plus global ecocide, but at the same time, this activity can conform to the highest standards of good citizenship and green consumerism. At this point, politics as the "art of the possible" reveals its ultimate limit. The only recourse is impossibility.

The Ideological Collapse of Republicanism

It might be useful to conclude this critique of the republican theory of domination with a more explicit discussion of the rationale for subsuming contemporary republican theory under liberal ideology. Frank Lovett, in an effort at a definitive statement of contemporary republicanism, illustrates very well the failure of republican political theory to establish itself as a distinctive contemporary alternative. Lovett argues that "republicanism does not collapse into liberalism if there is a real and substantial difference between the former's view of liberty as independence from arbitrary power, and the view of negative liberty as non-interference, generally embraced by the latter."[86] If the liberal tradition in fact has said much the same things about "arbitrary power" as republicanism has (as it, in fact, has), and if it has not "generally embraced" the classical liberal concept of negative freedom (as it, in fact, has not), then republicanism collapses into liberalism (as it, in fact, does), and more specifically, into liberal ideology. Lovett contends that "in the main" the issue "comes down to this: on the view of negative liberty as non-interference, any sort of public law or policy intervention counts by definition as an interference and, ergo, a reduction in freedom. Being committed to the received view of negative liberty, liberals thus tend to be overly hostile to government action."[87]

Lovett's depiction of liberalism fails to recognize both that much of the real-world liberalism has moved from a negative to a positive concept of liberty, and also that much of it has changed its view of legitimate intervention. It is simply not true that modern liberalism has seen social legislation as "arbitrary interference." In reality, it has vigorously advocated a broad spectrum of "public law" and "policy intervention" as basic to a free society. Republican theorist Iseult Honohan, in her book *Civic Republicanism*, perpetuates the same misunderstanding of liberalism when she claims that "republican politics promotes the non-domination of all individuals in every aspect of their lives," while liberals "have been more concerned with specific acts and with abuses of state power, and have drawn the public–private distinction in such a way as to make state intervention to prevent other harms problematic."[88] To the contrary, real-world liberals have advocated extensive state action with the goal of protecting the public from harms and expanding its effective freedom. Honohan's inaccurate identification of liberalism with the classical form obscures the extensive overlap between much of the actual liberal tradition and the largely academic artifact of contemporary republicanism.[89]

This overlap can be seen in Quentin Skinner's depiction of the republican tradition. Skinner goes to some lengths to elaborate a "neo-roman understanding of civil liberty"[90] that he sees as the republican alternative to the classical liberal view. He proposes a number of tenets that are basic to republicanism. The citizens possess "specific civil rights." Law is based on "the will of the members of the body politic" and "the consent of all its citizens." "The will of the people" is defined as "the sum of the wills of each individual citizen" and "the will of the majority." Citizens possess "equal right of participation in the making of laws." They are able to "enjoy [their] possessions freely and without any fear," and to "rise by means of their *virtu* to positions of prominence." Lawmaking power is vested in "the people or their accredited representatives," and all citizens are "equally subject" to the laws.[91]

These hallmarks of republicanism will hardly seem unfamiliar to anyone acquainted with modern liberal politics. Its core consists of such fundamental liberal political principles as: (1) supreme law-making authority or sovereignty possessed by the body of citizens; (2) the independent nation-state as the context of this sovereignty; and (3) the rule of law. To these are added the fundamental liberal economic values of (4) security of possessions, upward mobility, and equality of opportunity. All of this is commonplace in modern liberal capitalist ideology.

One can have no quarrel with Skinner's project of investigating the place of republicanism and the "neo-roman" concept of liberty in the history of ideas. However, one must ask what it means for such an early modern ideology to be adopted today by advocates of late capitalism and the massive bureaucratic state. The answer is that such an ideology can only perform a regressive ideological function (much as its counterpart classical liberalism now does). This ideology was "republican" in a strong sense at its origin and for some time thereafter because it was part of a movement to replace the private, arbitrary rule of monarchs with the public, responsible rule of the citizens. Freeing people from monarchy and the remnants of feudalism, so that they could participate in early capitalism and the early modern nation-state, was a substantive gain in freedom during a certain historical epoch.

Thus, in the eighteenth century, the term "republican" could signify radical opposition to the established order of domination, and the demand for popular power. Godwin could write that at the coming of the French Revolution: "My heart beat high with swelling sentiments of liberty. I had been for nine years in principle a republican."[92] Today, however, this ideology is, and has long been, effectively *antirepublican*, since it legitimates massive, irresponsible structures of domination that are incompatible with effective control of the polity by the citizens. Merely to repeat venerable republican and liberal clichés about freedom as popular sovereignty, the rule of law, and so on, without taking account of how the meaning of these concepts has been transformed with the evolution of corporate capitalism and the bureaucratic state, results in the ideological legitimation of the present system of domination, and obscures and mystifies the processes that erode substantive freedom.

Skinner explains that "what the neo-roman writers repudiate *avant la lettre* is the key assumption of classical liberalism to the effect that force or the coercive threat of it constitute the only forms of constraint that interfere with individual liberty" and "insist, by contrast, that to live in a condition of dependence is in itself a source and a form of constraint."[93] This was, no doubt, significant for the relatively brief historical period in which classical liberalism was more or less identical with liberalism. But "modern" or "welfare" liberalism has also argued that freedom is much more than the absence of coercion or the threat of coercion. *Après la lettre*, a long liberal tradition has developed that incorporates all significant tenets that Skinner associates with neo-romanism, and that has, in fact, moved well beyond them in developing its comprehensive concept of positive freedom.

Skinner holds that the great insight of republicanism is to see that not only coercion, but also dependence, is a form of constraint, and that the latter is the more decisive form. However, dependence is a much larger reality than Skinner and other contemporary republicans imagine. The most famous analysis of dependent and independent being in the history of philosophy is Hegel's master–slave dialectic, in which a being moves from a condition of dependence on "the alien being before which it has trembled" to a position in which "he destroys this alien negative moment, posits *himself* as a negative in the permanent order of things, and thereby becomes *for himself* [*für sich selbst*], someone existing on his own account [*ein für sich Seiendes*]."[94] In capitalist and statist society, the masses, including even those who may be exemplary republican citizens, "tremble" in the face of powerful alien forces, the sublime Commodity and the sublime Nation-State. The imaginary domination that arouses their awe is supplemented by an institutional domination that is, in turn, embodied in the structures of social practice, and finally, by ideological domination. The latter transforms dependent being, indeed participation in the very structures of domination, into independence, through the magic of theory.

5

Anarchy and the Dialectic of Utopia: The Place of No Place

The highest aspirations of the imagination are called utopia. But utopia is just as much the *enemy* of the imagination, and it is our nemesis today. We live in the shadow of a terrifying utopia and must search the shadows for those other utopias that have been eclipsed. The dominant utopia is the utopia of endless material progress, based on a fundamental utopian fantasy of infinite powers of production and infinite possibilities for consumption. This utopia inspires the system of superpower that is expanding its global domination and threatening the very future of life on Earth.

The ultimate telos of this dominant utopia is the reduction of the world to the most literally utopian state; to the condition of being an "ou-topos," a "no-where." Yet its everyday reality is presented as an inevitable march of progress that promises everything to everybody everywhere. As Ronald Reagan, the great utopian salesman, once said: "Progress is our most important product!" Through this march, it drives relentlessly toward the destruction of all diversity and complexity—of ecosystems, cultures, personalities, and imaginations. It progressively undermines any sense of place, but more fundamentally, it demolishes and dissolves the actual rich specificity of natural place, the biological diversity upon which that cultural sense rests materially. Beyond its everyday reality is its ultimate triumph and ultimate utopian nightmare. That is its ontological breakthrough: its actual attainment—through both its omnicidal nuclear technologies and its ecocidal industrial machine—of the power to transform our world into its most radically utopian state, into the ultimate nowhere of nonbeing.

Fortunately, there are other utopian possibilities, other utopian spaces, and other utopian times, for us to choose. For every empty space there is a richness of place; for all empty duration there is a fullness of time. In reality, we never live simply in space or place, but rather in *splace*—the locus of a dialectic between abstract, mathematicized, technologized, bureaucratized, commodified space and personal, communal, and ecocommunal place. Splace is the site of struggle for the liberation of utopian possibilities and the defense of topian realities, and against the forces of spatial domination.[1]

The Origins of Utopia

The divergent paths of utopian thinking had already been traveled by the time of the original, paradigmatic utopias of world literature: the *Republic* of Plato and the *Daodejing* of Laozi. Of course, even these "original" utopias have origins deep in history and prehistory. Plato's utopian project is a critical defense of civilization and civilized domination. It is situated at a point in history at which civilization had emerged triumphant and promised a glorious future if only its achievements could be consolidated and brought to perfection.

Thus, it is an effort to legitimate and further develop civilized self-consciousness and the institutional structure of civilized domination. In that sense, it is not only written *in* history, but written *on behalf of* history. In expressing the telos of civilization, it seeks to banish the remnants of the pre-civilized and to exclude that which remains outside of, and resistant to, civilization. Yet it contained all the contradictions of what we might call the project of "civilization in one country."

On the other hand, Laozi's utopia constitutes the first great rebellion of poetic thought against the civilized order. It looks back to pre-civilized personhood and the pre-civilized community (*the Uncarved Block*), and finds there a realm that escapes the order of domination. It looks to those natural and cultural forces that are the devalued and rejected other of civilization, and affirms their reality and worth. In this sense, it is a work written *against* history.[2]

Plato's *Republic* represents the effort of civilized rationality, the logos of domination, to banish the forces of resistance, and to establish itself, once and for all.[3] The forces of resistance are exactly those encountered by Odysseus, the archetypal Hero of Greek civilization: the powers of nature, desire, the unconscious, the primitive, and the feminine. Odysseus, through the exercise of rational self-repression and assertion of will, conquers these forces in their mythical guise—as Circe, Calypso, the Lotus-Eaters, Scylla, Charybdis, and so forth.

Plato's task was to translate this story into philosophy. He presents the same process of conquest in nonmythical form (though he reserves for myth an important place as an arm of theory). He theorizes it as the quest for the ideal state, ruled by the wise. It is a state in which reason itself is said to dominate through their edicts, in which desire and the body are subjected to the control of reason and its rational representatives, and in which knowledge and power are unified in a system of rule.

A truly utopian—and totalitarian—conception of justice is finally attained. For justice (the theme of the work) is discovered to be that harmony in which all contradictions are resolved, all conflict pacified, all resistance broken. Plato's subject matter is how to subject matter (the world of untamed nature) to the rule of reason, so that even the most irrational and unruly forces are brought under control.

It is pertinent that the title of Plato's work is not *Polis* but rather *Politeia*. While he presents us with a depiction of an "ideal state," to do so is not its primary function. Allan Bloom points out that the title can more accurately be translated as "The Regime."[4] Bloom divulges the usually well-kept secret (a philosophical "purloined letter") that the unifying theme of the book is less the abstract idea of justice than the concrete reality of power, its attainment, its exercise, and its systematization.[5] We might call it the original utopia of state power.

The *Daodejing*, on the other hand, is the original utopia of stateless freedom. Ironically, this work has sometimes been interpreted as a manual for the cunning ruler. Literal-minded readers East and West have seen it as a book of advice on how to rule successfully, a do-it-yourself book for the crafty prince who wants to learn how to control his subjects without appearing to dominate them.[6] Granted, the title itself has been aptly translated as the "Book of the Way and Its *Power*."

But this is a subtle work, and it is among the most dialectical and poetic of the classics of world literature. What less would one expect from an author whose name means not only "the Old Sage" but also "the Old Child"? He is one who unites wisdom and spontaneity, experience and innocence, seriousness and play. What the Old Boy tells us is that the Daoist prince is the ruler who rules without ruling, the Empire is the realm beyond force and coercion, and the power is the very negation of domination. This is why the *Daodejing* can appropriately be called "The Anarchist *Prince*," and Laozi the "anti-Machiavelli."

The *Daodejing* depicts an Empire in which all beings are allowed to follow their "natural" course of development, their *Dao*. The result is a world in which humanity and nature are in harmony, in which human beings live together peacefully and cooperatively, and in which universal self-realization is fostered. However, the Daoist harmony is not that of a pacified or homogenized world in which all conflict, opposition, and otherness is dissolved. Rather it is a discordant harmony, in which unity is expressed through multiplicity and difference, and in which beings are mutually determined by and even contain within themselves their other.

The Daoist utopia is achieved through a rejection of domination in all of its forms, whether political, economic, patriarchal, technological, or even epistemological. Through an ontology of unity-in-difference, the other is given authentic recognition. Knowledge becomes sympathetic understanding and participatory consciousness, as opposed to conquest and subjugation. The hierarchies of the utopia of domination (reason over desire, form over matter, soul over body, male over female, adult over child, humanity over nature, civilized man over the primitive, conscious-ness over the unconscious, etc.) are all rejected. Apparent opposites are shown to interpenetrate, to complement one another, and to be necessary elements of a larger whole (which is, of course, also a nonwhole). The Daoist utopia, expressed as a mythical Golden Age to be reattained, is such a unity-in-diversity, in which self-realization is maximized for all beings.

The entire history of utopia that has unfolded over two and a half millennia is implicit in the opposition between these two primordial visions.

Utopia as Domination

Throughout history, there have been utopian expressions of the quest for domination. Such utopias project the existing system of domination into a perfected future order in which the contradictions that cannot be reconciled in the real world are resolved through an act of sovereign imagination. The resulting images of static perfection can then be used as weapons against the evil and the unenlightened, in short, against all the forces of resistance. Vaclav Havel, while writing as a dissident under actually existing dystopia, called such a utopia "a more or less rationalist attempt to think up an abstract better world, to conceive 'on paper' how it should be organized. It is an attempt to produce a blueprint of the best possible system and then to try to put it into practice." The Czechs, he says, have "lived through the failure of one great utopia, and this has given us a very skeptical and critical view of utopianism in general."[7]

The dystopia that they endured is only one specific form of the generic utopia of domination that lies at the imaginary core of civilization's project of universal conquest. It is closely allied to the conception of knowledge as power, a conception with roots at the beginnings of civilization, but which has only achieved fulfillment with the rise of the nation-state, transnational capital, and the global megamachine. Havel's critique touches on this relationship of utopia to the quest for unlimited domination, for a world of "total administration," in which all other realities, whether cultural, spiritual, psychological, or personal, are subordinated. Utopianism, he says, is "an arrogant attempt by human reason to plan life" that "inevitably ends up homogenizing, regimenting, standardizing and destroying life, as well as curtailing everything that projects beyond, overflows or falls outside the abstract project."[8] He concludes that there is "a direct and logical progression from beautiful utopias to concentration camps," which are "but an attempt by utopians to dispose of those elements which do not fit into their utopias."[9]

Havel is perceptive enough to have noted at times that the complementary utopianism of the corporate capitalist West leads in a direction similar to the one he detected in the state capitalist East. The utopia of consumption has not, of course, relied heavily on concentration camps (though it seems to be moving more in that direction lately) but its tactics are in many ways similar to those Havel points out. The elements that are most threatening to its utopian illusion are also concentrated—in ghettos, in reservations, in prisons, in human and ecological sacrifice zones—as the unthinkable horrors on the margins of utopia. However, such dystopian dimensions of the everyday can be ideologically banished in a world in which everyone who can shop at Walmart and dine at McDonald's can self-identify as middle class, and is convinced, in any case, that "There Is No Alternative." Thus, it becomes increasingly evident that totalitarianism reaches its greatest perfection in the utopia of consumption. Its only remaining rival of any consequence is the competing totalitarianism of religious fundamentalism. And though the battle between these totalizing systems continues to intensify, there is no doubt that the overwhelmingly more powerful one at this moment in history on a global scale remains the "empire of consumption."

Totalitarianism today is not on the deepest level a matter of sovereignty. Nor does it depend on the state's formal abolition of all competing forms of social organization (though the evils embodied in this political totalization process and its system of oppression and terror cannot be overemphasized). The ultimate totalitarian achievement is the capture of the imagination, and the reinforcement of that conquest, as the dominant order is legitimated through processes of sublimation and banalization. The consuming subject is overawed by the sublime consumptionist spectacle and automatized by the realities and rituals of everyday productionist and consumptionist life.

The economistic system's values are not yet universal, but are, however, hegemonic. This means that they are embedded in the reigning "common sense" and the dominant "reality principle." "Reality" is whatever is enshrined in the dominant ideology, imaginary, ethos, materiality, and institutional structure. Furthermore, these values are constantly extending their dominion, especially in their consumptionist dimension. The growing success of the totalitarian project depends heavily on the efficacy of the consumptionist utopia and its image of the good life. It is a life of happiness, health, love, sex, beauty, power, fun, and immortality. And it is available to all who buy the right commodities, and know how to perpetually *refashion* their very selves into the right kind of commodities. It is available, that is, in the form of the fundamental fantasy of the world of consumption. It is with good reason that a popular version of this fantasy is called "the American Dream."

Utopia as Elitism

The history of utopianism contains abundant evidence of its ideological use for purposes of power and manipulation. Plato, again, outlined the essentials of the program quite well. First, the utopian order is defined as a harmony in which all contradictions are resolved. Next, an ideology is devised in which the system of power is identified with an underlying order of natural and social domination and is redefined as universal self-realization. And, finally, the rule of the elite is mystified further as an expression of the divine will. This "noble lie" has been more than a mere philosophical fiction. Its basic structure has remained intact over history, requiring only an updating of the content, as when, for example, historical inevitability is substituted for divine will.

But utopian elitism has infected not only the more obviously authoritarian utopian ideals. It has been exemplified as well in seemingly libertarian tendencies, such as the Movement of the Free Spirit. In a sense, the Free Spirit was one of the most antiauthoritarian tendencies in European history. It followed Joachim of Fiore's teaching of the coming of the third stage of history, the Age of the Holy Spirit, which would see "the illumination of all, in mystical democracy, without masters and Church."[10] It proclaimed that the law of Church, state, and traditional morality were all abolished for those who enter into the Joachimite utopian realm. In its extreme antinomianism, the movement adhered in a sense to a most radically anarchistic position.

However, this anarchic rejection of law disguised certain profoundly authoritarian dimensions of the movement. In particular, there remained a hierarchy between its more advanced adepts and the masses drawn to it. According to Norman Cohn, "after 'becoming God,' a new adept began to seek contact with pious souls who wished to 'attain perfection.' From these he exacted an oath of blind obedience, which was made on bended knees . . . they gave a promise of absolute obedience to a human being and received in return an assurance that they could do no sin."[11] Moreover, there are serious problems even with the sexual iconoclasm and eroticism that have often been seen as evidence of the movement's libertarian rejection of traditional morality. One must judge as, to say the least, less than emancipatory the view that "just as cattle were created for the use of human beings, so women were created to be used by the Brethren of the Free Spirit."[12]

The tradition of utilizing utopian mythology to justify authoritarianism and domination has continued through the modern period. The vagaries of the Leninist manipulation of the vision of the utopia of communism are too familiar to repeat. A more instructive example is Bakunin, who, while launching an authentic and indeed powerful critique of various forms of domination, in turn used the myth of the anarchist utopia to justify elitism and personal power. He correctly described the goals of anarchism as the destruction of all the forces that restrain human freedom, and the achievement of a free, cooperative society of equals acting in solidarity. Yet in the name of this utopian ideal he was capable of advocating the control of the revolutionary movement by an enlightened elite of revolutionaries. He proposed for various secret societies an oath of "absolute obedience" to the group, fanatical and ascetic commitment from all members, and a hierarchical relationship between levels of organization. The justification for these authoritarian measures was their supposed temporary nature and their necessity as a means toward the imminent achievement of the utopian future.

Bakunin was finally capable of calling for an "invisible dictatorship" that is "all the stronger for having none of the paraphernalia of power."[13] It is true that he counterposes to his vanguardism a multitude of antiauthoritarian declarations. The danger, however, is that to the extent that the vanguardist project is realized, the antiauthoritarian utopia will remain in a state of complete invisibility, while the putatively invisible dictators will retain a certain degree of materiality.

Utopia as Escapism

It is clear that utopia may function to support an oppressive system of power, and it may also become a means to establish new forms of domination. But the dangers do not end there. For even when it is not used to dominate, it may still fail to liberate. Indeed, it may function merely as an inert and impotent illusion, a utopia of escape. The lure of escapist utopianism is great for those who profess a certain idealism, but who have been frustrated in their efforts to realize their dreams, and those whose situation in society renders the idea of praxis entirely unnatural.

The former situation is typical of various leftist sectarians, ranging from democratic centralists to libertarian municipalists, whose blueprint for the future demands only earnest and dedicated propagation of the correct set of ideas, which will certainly revolutionize the world if only the masses finally learn how to pay attention and fall in line with the intended course of history. According to such an abstract idealist worldview, the tenacity with which these masses continue to hold on to their unenlightened views only reinforces the need for more vigorous propagandizing and validates the virtuousness of those who fight the good fight.

The latter case pertains especially to many academic utopians. Such utopologists are the counterparts of the better-known Marxologists, who have found an even more firmly established intellectual niche. The logos of these "ologists" is not the "way of things" with which engaged dialectic concerns itself, but rather their own "words about things" that are always one step removed from the dynamism of the real. Utopologists are often the most well-intentioned and progressive of thinkers; however, they fail to bridge the gap between good intention and effective action or grasp the connection between the movement of ideas and the movement of reality.

Escapist utopianism of all varieties remains in the vacuous realm of what Hegel called the Beautiful Soul, the sphere of those dreamers of moral perfection who are unwilling or unable to cope with the ambiguities and uncertainties of the world and history, and therefore cling to a more manageable and immediately gratifying ideal world.

The utopia of escape has powerful attractions. So often we are inclined to believe because belief fulfills certain needs and satisfies, or even creates and then satisfies, certain desires. Accordingly, utopia can serve as a means of escape from the imperfections of the world and their inevitable reflection within our own being. It can be an escape from the exigencies of the real, from history and its unavoidable tragedies. It can be an escape from the minutiae of the everyday. It can offer an imaginary compensation for being denied real power or having real efficacy. In this sense, utopia is neurosis, a defense mechanism, a convulsive reaction against self and world. It offers an imaginary revenge against a recalcitrant reality.

Utopia as Critique

In opposition to the utopianism of domination and the utopianism of escape is a utopianism that is a critique of domination and a vision of a reality beyond it. Ricoeur contends that the "deinstitutionalization of the main human relationships" is "the kernel of all utopias," and that though it "may be an escape," it is also "the arm of critique."[14] Mannheim's classic definition of utopia also stresses its character as a challenge to the status quo. He contends that a utopian orientation is one that is, first, "incongruous with the state of reality within which it occurs," and that second, "transcends reality." When utopian perspectives "pass over into conduct," he says, they "tend to shatter, either partially or wholly, the order of things prevailing at the time."[15]

Ricoeur's analysis of the critical dimension of utopia is among the most profound, in that he situates it in relation to the social imagination. Utopia, in his view, is the corrective to that other powerful construct of the imagination, ideology. He refers to "the eccentric function of imagination as the possibility of the nowhere," and asks, "is not this eccentricity of the utopian imagination at the same time the cure of the pathology of ideological thinking, which has its blindness and narrowness precisely in its inability to conceive of a nowhere?"[16] Ideology is an expression of the conservative, systematizing processes of the social imagination. Utopianism, in contrast, expresses the creative, self-transcending, liberating tendencies.

In reality, no ideology is "pure" ideology, and elements of utopia are even embedded in ideology itself. It is for this reason that the process of "immanent critique" can move from ideological premises to utopian conclusions. Nevertheless, Ricoeur's point concerning the critical, oppositional nature of utopia is well taken. He notes that there are two distinct aims for the utopian imagination in its rejection of the established order: "to be ruled by good rulers—either ascetic or ethical—or to be ruled by no rulers. All utopias oscillate between these two poles."[17] The first utopian option has already been described. It is the dominant authoritarian and hierarchical utopian ideal from the *Republic* of Plato to the modern fantasyland of technological progress and endless consumption.

The second option is exemplified by what Marie Louise Berneri calls, in *Journey through Utopia*, "the libertarian utopia." Libertarian utopians "oppose to the conception of the centralized state that of a federation of free communities, where the individual can express his [or her] personality without being submitted to the censure of an artificial code, where freedom is not an abstract word, but manifests itself concretely in work."[18] Indeed, as illustrated in the utopias of Fourier and Morris (to be discussed shortly), one of the distinctive attributes of the most radically libertarian utopias is the emergence of a realm of freedom in which the very division between work and play dissolves, and does so not in some distant and endlessly mediated future, but here and now.

Utopia of Desire

The civilized order has always been faced with the problem of taming or repressing passion to serve the needs of exploitative and hierarchical institutions. A primary function of civilized morality has been to subordinate individual fulfillment to the requirements of domination, which is expressed in mystified form as the universal good or the moral law. Kant stated this first principle of civilization in section one of the *Foundations of the Metaphysics of Morals*, when he explained that if human happiness were the "real end of nature," then our destiny would most certainly be attained best through following our instincts (i.e., through the passions).

However, he continues, reason tells us that this is not our true end, which is to follow the moral law merely because we recognize it to be the law.[19]

Kant grudgingly admits that it would be possible for all the members of society to renounce repression and what he sees as their higher duties for the sake of "indulgence in pleasure." But he hastily adds that one "could not possibly will" that such a social order should exist, for it would mean that we would live a life "like the inhabitants of the South Sea Islands," that is, we would "allow our talents to rust" while we foolishly pursue a life of "idleness, indulgence, and propagation."[20] Significantly, Kant takes as his example of what a "rational" human being could never choose: an indigenous society, and specifically, Polynesian society, the society that perhaps more than any other inspired the imaginations of those (Diderot, Gauguin) who sought a world in which pleasure, beauty, freedom, and harmony could be reconciled. In rejecting in absolute horror the thought of any civilized person going Tahitian, Kant was exorcising the specter of an existing society that offered evidence that unrepressed passion and human self-realization could coexist, that utopia could have a material basis, that real world history could prefigure a new passionate order that would in turn inspire a new utopian social order.

In fact, such possibilities are precisely the premises on which Fourier bases his vision of a utopia of passionate attraction. He is the ultimate philosopher of "ne céder pas à son desire."[21] Much as Proudhon contends that "freedom is the mother, not the daughter of order," Fourier asserts that the passions, far from destroying social order, are the source of the most perfect harmony in society. The problem is not to bring the passions under rigid control, but rather to determine how their fullest expression can contribute to a sublime harmonization of the whole of society.

In Fourier's view, all the passions and inclinations of individuals can be directed freely toward activity that is beneficial for the community. He contends that under civilization, unbearably long hours of unfulfilling work activity have been imposed in the name of productivity and economic need, while, in reality, all the labor required to satisfy the needs of society, and, indeed, to produce abundance, can be furnished without the infliction of any such undeserved punishment. He notes that even highly pleasurable activities become boring after several hours, and asks quite sensibly how human beings can possibly be expected to engage even that long in labor that is only mildly agreeable, much less the kind that is truly unpleasant or even repugnant.

Such absurdities will end, he assures us, as humanity abandons obsolete Civilization and enters into Harmony. Through the creation of more fulfilling forms of labor, more voluntary choice of work activities, limitation of work periods, and rotation of tasks, work will become a form of expression of the passions, rather than a restraint on them. The same principle of maximal harmonization of passions that is applied to work will be applied to all areas of social life, and indeed will be even easier to realize in other realms of social interaction, such as personal relationships, recreation, and cultural activities.

William Morris is perhaps the one other figure who ranks with Fourier among nineteenth-century utopian imaginative geniuses. Morris's contribution to utopianism includes his political essays, his work in the creative arts, and his authorship of *News from Nowhere*, one of the most notable works of utopian fiction. He made an enduring contribution to the liberatory utopian tradition by emphasizing the crucial importance of art, aesthetic values, and the creative imagination to the achievement of the good society, and by illustrating their potentialities so capably in his own work. It is common for admirers of nineteenth- and early twentieth-century radical social theory to apologize for its economism and uncritical acceptance of high technology by noting that those who formulated the theories were a product of their time, in which astoundingly vast powers of production were unleashed, and seemingly miraculous material progress took place. Nevertheless, Morris was also a product of those times, and reacted to them not by internalizing the values embodied in the prevailing system, but rather by creating a vision of a qualitatively different society with radically different values.

He envisioned a social order in which the creative capacities of all would be allowed free expression. Human productive activity would be valued as a good in itself, rather than as a means toward accumulation of property and power. The goal of labor would be the collective creation of a community in which beauty, joy, and freedom would be realized. Morris's utopia is the quintessence of what Mumford described as "the community as a work of art." In imagining such ideals, utopian thinkers such as Morris and Fourier are important for creating a life-affirming, positive vision of the future as an alternative to the increasingly deadening, repressive, and mechanized society of their day.

These are notable achievements, in that they attest to the enduring capacity of human beings to see beyond the assumptions of their own age.

However, radical thought has become ineffectual in more recent times in part because it has often continued to conceive of the social dialectic in terms of this stark opposition between oppressive, restrictive forces and emancipatory, liberating ones. Many are still merely seeing beyond the limits of a previous age. Meanwhile, the dominant system has revolutionized itself as it has moved from the productionist to the consumptionist stage of capitalist society. Particularly in the most developed capitalist societies, it has passed beyond the highly repressive stage reflected in Kant's obsessive moralism into what Marcuse calls the stage of "repressive desublimation." In this stage, desire, instinct, and passion are "liberated," but only to the degree that they can serve the needs of an ideologically mystified system of domination.

Many anarchist and utopian thinkers have continued to depict the dominant order as if it were still the same repressive system that it was in the productionist age of capital accumulation. This approach fails miserably, since those who live within the late-capitalist consumptionist system find that the critique describes a world that simply does not correspond to their everyday life experience. An adequate critique must focus not only on the system's negative moment of domination but also on its positive utopian one that allows it to harness the social imagination. Thus, Bookchin's account of the system of domination, among others, suffers in large part from an inability to get beyond what Foucault called the "repressive hypothesis." Foucault contributes to a more subtle understanding of the mechanisms of domination by pointing out the ways in which various strategies and tactics made possible by the constraints of the system itself are sources of pleasure and gratification.[22] The Situationists and Castoriadis make further contributions in bringing "the spectacle" and the social imaginary, with their highly positive and constitutive dimensions, to the center of analysis. A consideration of the role of what Bourdieu calls "habitus," the repertoire of dispositions that internalize social structure, brings another essential dimension to light.

And finally, Žižek's Hegelian-Marxist-Lacanian theory goes perhaps furthest in uncovering the deepest mysteries of social subjectivity in his diagnosis of the role of the "fundamental fantasy" and of "enjoyment" within the social order. As Žižek has pointed out, the late-capitalist Superego abolishes all forms of "Thou shalt not," in favor of its ultimate categorical imperative, "Thou shalt enjoy!" Consequently, well-socialized "postmodern" subjects (alias "consumers") feel guilty not because of their fear of "transgression" against repressive law, but rather because their level of enjoyment is never quite up to par (and is usually miserably below). The most humiliating moral flaw in late capitalism is a failure to inhabit the imaginary consumptionist utopia.

If we take into consideration all these positive dimensions of the dominant utopian project, we can see how a utopianism of the passions and aesthetic sensibility in the tradition of Fourier and Morris, if decoupled from naïve antiauthoritarian ideology, offers certain elements that are needed for the development of an effective critical alternative. Such a utopianism, by confronting the dominant system on its own utopian ground, is capable of revealing the contradictions, limitations, and falsehoods of the utopia of consumption, and of then rechanneling in a liberatory direction the desires and passions that have been captured.

The Presence of Utopia

It would be a disastrous error to look to utopian thinking only, or even primarily, for visions of the *future*, no matter how libertarian, just, peaceful, ecological, or desirable in any other way that imagined future may be. For utopianism is above all about the *present*. The most utopian of utopianisms is also the most practical one. It demands Heaven on Earth and explores the extraordinary realities latent in the seemingly ordinary present.[23] Its ideal was expressed best by that most utopian of poets, Blake, when he asserted that when the doors of perception are opened, we perceive all things as infinite. The most utopian community would be one in which the members could find the kind of numinous reality that Blake was capable of discovering in a literally quotidian event, the rising of the sun: "What it will be Questiond When the Sun rises do you not see a round Disk of fire somewhat like a Guinea O no no I see an Innumerable company of the Heavenly host crying Holy Holy Holy is the Lord God Almighty I question not my corporeal or Vegetative Eye any more than I would Question a Window concerning a Sight I look thro it & not with it."[24] This does not mean that every single experience of each member of the community must be a Blakean mystical epiphany; however, it may very well mean that each would become the kind of "truly experienced person," who, according to Gary Snyder, "delights in the ordinary."[25]

The most liberatory utopianism affirms this existence of the eternal, the sublime, the marvelous, as a present reality and an object of present experience. It does not propose any "metaphysics of presence" that posits an unmediated essential reality that somehow reveals to us its full being. Rather it is a *radical empiricism of presence* that allows what is present to present itself, to give itself as a miraculous gift. What appears may be mediated, but the mediations, the layers of appearance, are also present, they are part of the gift. There is, however, no need for what is present to be mediated by various ideas of essence or ultimate reality, all of which take us one step away from what is presented.

Such a perspective breaks radically with the ideology of progress, which demands a continual alienation from *present* realities and repression of *present* experience for the sake of some future attainment of reality or value. This perspective negates the idea of the present as a realm of accumulation with a view to some ultimate cosmic payoff. It asserts the identity of means and ends. It thus uncovers the hoax of all utopias of power. It holds before us the lotus flower and invites us to look upon it, perhaps in serenity, perhaps in bliss, perhaps in laughter and amusement.[26]

This points to the profoundly surrealist dimension of utopia. Franklin Rosemont points out that in childhood we all dwell in a world of wonder, but the society of domination manages to reduce this world for most of us to certain rare moments in which we experience "fleeting eruptions of inspiration, sudden passions, dazzling encounters 'by chance.'"[27] However, he explains, "such moments, true glimpses of the Marvelous, secure themselves permanently in one's psychic life, in the depths of our inner mythology," and surrealism seeks "to extend these moments, to unite them, to hasten their proliferation, to arm them" so that "what had been only individual, sporadic, unconscious . . . becomes collective, systematic, conscious, invincible." The surrealist project is thus "to actualize the Marvelous in everyday life."[28]

Such a surrealist project is at the heart (and in both the conscious and unconscious mind) of the most radical forms of utopianism. It finds what is of infinite value, not in some higher realm or some indefinite future, but in the depths of our being and the heights of our experience. Indeed, it finds them even in the false, the evil, the ugly, and the profane. Utopia is present in all the creative play of energies, in spiritual and material voyages of discovery, and, of course, in everything touched by the transformative imagination.

Even if it can never be attained, utopia is already present or it is a fraud.

Hyper(topian) Text

If this is true, it might seem that literary utopias would not be of great significance, for they are about what is merely imagined, rather than what actually is. However, they cannot be dismissed in this way, for their value lies precisely in the fact that they bring us closer to what actually is. The greatest of the fictional utopias are as much about evoking the deepest of our past and present experiential realities as they are about envisioning future possibilities. Thus, the most powerful utopian works are also profoundly *topian*—they create a vivid sense of place, of topos, that is grounded in deeply experienced realities. Utopianism finds its fulfillment in topianism, indeed, we might even say in *hypertopianism*, the most intense sense of being somewhere, in a specific place at which reality shines forth.

One of the great achievements in this venture is Robert Nichols's anarchist-inspired series, *Daily Lives in Nghsi-Altai*.[29] In this remarkable tetralogy, Nichols envisions the nature of a communal yet highly individualized society in which decentralized democracy, ecological sensibility, bioregional principles, and liberatory technologies are integrated into a traditional culture. It is a vision of utopia emerging out of the rich particularity of history and lived experience. While *Daily Lives* has never gained the recognition it deserves, it is, in fact, an extraordinary contribution to both literary and theoretical utopianism.

Nichols creatively incorporates concepts of utopian anarchist and decentralist writers and imagines what they would mean in a rich cultural embodiment. In Nghsi-Altai they are realized not in a utopia of static perfection, but rather in a generally peaceful but still mildly chaotic world in which people live the good but still slightly messy life, and achieve an expansive yet communally bounded freedom. What is so compelling about this work is its extraordinary synthesis of utopianism with an acute sense of both the universals of the human condition and the specificity and particularity of culture. Nichols brilliantly creates a sense of the utopian *ethos*. It is not surprising that Ursula Le Guin has recognized the importance of Nichols's influence in her development of a utopian project that culminates in a social anthropology of utopia.

Le Guin has created a series of major landmarks in the history of utopianism. In *The Left Hand of Darkness* her protagonist confronts the challenge of relating personally and humanly to a literally androgynous species.[30] The work is of major significance for its confrontation of the question of otherness and difference with a subtlety rare not only in utopian writing but in literature in general. *The Dispossessed* quickly became a utopian classic for its exploration of the contrasts between the anarchist "ambiguous utopia," Annares, and the corrupt, earthlike planet, Urras.[31] Le Guin's grasp of anarchist social theory in the work, which is expressed as the teachings of Odo, the founding mother of Annares's political system, far surpasses that of most academic and partisan writers on the subject. But what is most notable about the work is the protagonist's ruthlessly anarchistic critique of Annares itself. It is, in effect, an anarchist critique of anarchism, and a utopian critique of the dangers of utopia.

But finally, in *Always Coming Home* Le Guin produced her masterpiece and, indeed, what is perhaps the masterpiece of utopian literature to date.[32] The work includes the familiar LeGuinian themes of the good society versus the corrupt society, and the departure from, and return to, one's spiritual center. It is also implicitly an anarchist utopia, though without the overt discussion of anarchist theory that is found in *The Dispossessed*. But the great achievement of the book is the richness of detail, the development of particularity and "suchness," at the level of the person, the group, and the culture. Le Guin's evocation of the good society is compelling because she has, more than any other utopian writer, succeeded in creating a topos and an ethos. Indeed, *Always Coming Home*, with its songs, stories, myths, legends, music, rituals, and accounts of lives, is less a utopian novel than an anthropological sourcebook of another world that tells us important things about the deepest truths of our own world.[33] Le Guin's great achievement is that she has given to utopia—nowhere—the strongest possible sense of place.[34] Utopian literature has finally become truly *topian*.

There is perhaps only one work of fiction that has made a comparable contribution to anarchistic utopianism since the appearance of Le Guin's classic work. This is Starhawk's *The Fifth Sacred Thing* in which she depicts a nonviolent, cooperative, communal anarchist society based on ecofeminist values.[35] Four of the "five things" alluded to in the title are the four elements that make up the natural world, and which must be treated with care and respect. A person or community that does so gains access to the "fifth sacred thing," which is spirit.

The book is remarkable in that it creates a powerful sense of a qualitatively different society through its convincing depiction of values, practices, and institutions in many spheres that reinforce one another. But though the society is in many ways quite distant dominant society of today, it does not seem as experientially distant from present reality as do most utopias. It is a world that is transformed through the amplification of certain elements that are very much present in our existing world. The characters and situations that express truths about cooperation, nonviolence, equality, freedom, love and care, creativity, sensuality, and joy do not seem so far from what many readers will have experienced if they have had some contact with the feminist, ecology, peace, and global justice movements, and particularly the more communitarian and anarchistic dimensions of these movements. *The Fifth Sacred Thing* suggests that a great many people and small groups are right now creating in their own lives the elements of a utopian world, and it offers a compelling vision of what that utopian world might be like if many such people were to join these elements together in a community that shaped them into an all-embracing way of life.

Utopia in History

Thus, the importance of literary utopias such as those just discussed should not be underestimated. However, it would be a mistake to focus (as the academic world usually does) on utopia primarily as a literary genre, as is often done today, and to neglect the ongoing history of real-world utopian communal experience. This immense legacy of utopian practice was first delineated in extensive detail by Elisée Reclus in his six-volume, 3,500 page magnum opus of social theory, *L'Homme et la Terre* (Man and the Earth).[36] Reclus showed that a fertile history of radical freedom has existed and developed alongside the long story of domination that has been so central to world history. This "other history" has included cooperative and egalitarian tribal traditions, anarchistic millenarian movements, dissident spiritualities, antiauthoritarian experiments in radical grassroots democracy and communalism, movements for the liberation of women, and the radically libertarian moments of many of the world's revolutions and revolutionary movements.

Millenarian movements, despite the elitist and authoritarian aspects that have been noted, illustrate the extent to which the utopian social imagination can inspire the absolute negation of apparently immovable social institutions, such as the state, the Church, patriarchy, and repressive morality. Ernst Bloch observes that in the Joachimite tradition, "the Kingdom" becomes radically immanentized. It is "more decidedly of this world than anything since the days of early Christianity. Jesus is once again the Messiah of a new Earth, and Christianity operates in reality, not just in ritual and empty promises; it operates without masters and property, in mystical democracy."[37] Such millenarian movements, for all their flaws, have shown the extent to which the utopian social imagination could radically subvert the dominant order, even during what have been thought of as the more conservative periods of history.

Particularly in their most radical early stages, many modern revolutions have contained a deeply utopian dimension. In these periods, a decisive break with existing systems of power has been undertaken, and hierarchy, domination, and authoritarianism have been vigorously combated. It is true that the system of domination, or some pseudo-revolutionary mutation of it, has always triumphed. This proves that the techniques of social domination are far more advanced than is the art of social liberation. But as a result of these "revolutions within the revolutions," we are left with a heritage of utopian practice that continues to inspire the radical imagination. The multitude of impressive historical examples in this tradition includes the direct democracy of the section assemblies of the French Revolution, the civic democracy and egalitarianism of the Paris Commune, the council democracy of the early Russian Revolution and the Hungarian Revolution, and the democratic self-management in the anarchist industrial and agricultural collectives of the Spanish Revolution.

What has been less evident but perhaps most important in these emancipatory moments has been the flowering of creativity on the microsocial level, which has been expressed in personal change and the transformation of intimate relationships, the proliferation of small action and affinity groups, and the emergence of liberatory social and cultural spaces at the grassroots level. Such phenomena have been accorded little attention by historians, whether of the mainstream or even radical varieties. For example, despite considerable historical work on Spanish anarcho-syndicalism and the role of anarchists in the Revolution, the multifaceted cultural movement that for well over half a century prepared the way for the Revolution has been relatively neglected. This anarchist cultural movement included diverse expressions, including circles or affinity groups, libertarian schools (*ateneos*), cooperatives, "free love" advocacy, feminism, vegetarianism, nudism, rationalism and "free thought," mysticism, and early ecological and pro-nature tendencies. In other words, many of most radically *utopian* dimensions of the movement have been overlooked.

A final important sphere of utopianism that has also been to a large degree neglected is the history of liberatory intentional communities. Ronald Creagh, in his definitive study *Utopies Américaines*, presents abundant evidence of the rich history of experiments in libertarian communalism carried out across the North American continent, from the Owenite and Fourierist colonies of the early nineteenth century to libertarian countercultural communes of the 1960s and beyond.[38] Many problems concerning the project of social emancipation can only be confronted through investigation and experimentation on the microsocial level. The social history of utopianism thus helps one to appreciate the centrality of personal life, in all its particularity, to the project of social emancipation.

Creagh shows that the North American intentional communities confronted in practice numerous issues related to interpersonal relations and everyday life that are often overlooked in theoretical analyses and sometimes only superficially touched upon in imaginative utopias. They posed questions concerning sexual and affectionate relationships, the nurturing of children, the balancing of solitude and community, the tensions between individuality and solidarity, the threats of charismatic authority, the complexity of achieving just and democratic decision-making in all spheres, and the problem of consciously confronting the heritage of domination carried in each psyche. The story of successes, and just as importantly, of failures, in the long tradition of liberatory striving is an invaluable legacy for inspiring the utopian imagination and guiding future utopian creation.

The End of Utopia

Utopia has had a long history, both as a form of visionary art and literature and as a political practice aiming at radical social transformation. However, for most of the past century, social commentators have been announcing the death of utopia, and the end of radically utopian thinking, at least in so far as it significantly affects history and social movements.

Mannheim argues that the modern period is an epoch of rationalization in which utopian thought must in the long run decline. He recognizes that this poses a threat to society, since "the complete elimination of reality-transcending elements from our world would lead us to a 'matter-of-factness' which would ultimately mean the decay of the human will."[39] Indeed, he goes so far as to judge that "with the relinquishment of utopias, man would lose his will to shape history and therewith his ability to understand it."[40] Yet he seems reconciled to the fact that utopia will play at most a minor role in the future of the modern world. In fact, he seems to think that in the European intellectual world the death of utopia was in his time already a fait accompli. He refers to "the complete disappearance of all reality-transcending doctrines—utopian as well as ideological,"[41] a situation that he believes to have resulted from the success that historicism, the critique of ideology, psychoanalysis, and other intellectual trends had in demonstrating the relativity of all values. He asks whether in an increasingly rationalized and disenchanted world such developments as "the gradual reduction of politics to economics," "the conscious rejection of the past and of the notion of historical time," and "the conscious brushing aside of every cultural ideal," will not result in "a disappearance of every form of utopianism from the political arena."[42]

However, the world has demonstrated a tendency to resist instrumental rationality and remain more "enchanted" than Mannheim imagined. He believes that "radical anarchism," which he calls the "relatively purest form of modern Chiliastic mentality" by his own time "disappears almost entirely from the political scene."[43] He concludes that the "disintegration of the anarchist ecstatic utopia was abrupt and brutal, but it was dictated with a fatal necessity by the historical process itself."[44] Ironically, Mannheim's obituary for anarchism was written in 1929, seven years before the Spanish Revolution, the period of the most extensive and socially creative experimentation in anarchist organization in the history of modern Europe. Despite the "fatal necessity" that dictated anarchism's demise, its supposed corpse not only quickly showed signs of life but also soon attained a condition of unprecedented vigor.

Utopia was to be reinterred several times in the half century after Mannheim, most notably by the "End of Ideology" theorists (Bell, Lipset, et al.) of the 1950s. According to this school, ideology in general and utopian ideology in particular had been superseded in the West, and was to be replaced elsewhere by a pragmatic, nonideological outlook typically embodied in the modern state and corporation. As Daniel Bell states in 1960, there had come "an end to chiliastic hopes, to millenarianism, to apocalyptic thinking—and to ideology."[45] So anarchism and utopianism were again buried by the theorists—only to reemerge shortly thereafter in the 1960s in a form that was even more challenging to conventional reality than the more traditionalist versions of the 1930s.

But the ferment of the 1960s did not put an end to grandiose speculation concerning the imminent end of both ideology and utopia. Not so long ago Francis Fukuyama, at the time the deputy director of the Policy Planning Department of the State Department, announced the latest end of ideology, and with it the end of any utopian aspirations. "What we may be witnessing is not just the end of the cold war, or the passing of a particular period of postwar history, but the end of history as such: that is, the end point of mankind's ideological evolution and the universalization of western liberal democracy as the final form of human government."[46]

As he says, *we may be witnessing* this. But as it turned out, we may not. For a brief triumphalist moment, history, viewed through the thick mist of neo-con ideology, could seem to Mr. Fukuyama and the Department of (Steady?) State to have reached its end. One could imagine a gathering of neoconservative intellectuals in 1992 to celebrate the end of history, perhaps under a huge banner declaring "Mission Accomplished!" But then history, with all its deep and complex contradictions, its dialectical reversals, its tragedies, and its absurdities, decided, as it always does, to move on.

The Return to Nowhere

So history goes on, as does the quest for utopia. If the history of utopianism shows anything, it is that the sources of inspiration for utopian visions are myriad. The idea that an end has already come to the quest for a reality that radically transcends the existing one was a naïve idea indeed. Not the least of its absurdities was that it ignored the dependence of the existing system upon its own vision of utopia, which drives it toward self-transcendence and self-destruction. But it is not only the utopia of domination that will live on. As long as the radical imagination exists, the anarchistic utopia, with its values of freedom, mutuality, joyfulness, and creativity, will continue to exist, and human beings will seek to realize it with diverse degrees of passion, imagination, and rationality. Whether it will in any given future epoch be successfully marginalized or instead realized to varying degrees through powerful upsurges of social creativity cannot be determined ahead of time.

What we do know from past history is that hunger, thirst, sexual desire, religious passion, the quest for truth, the desire for self-actualization, love, compassion, empathy, envy, resentment, maliciousness, hatred, will to power, neurosis, and psychosis of every variety can, by cultural alchemy, be transformed into, or expressed through, utopian striving. We do not know whether the future will be more a dream or more a nightmare, but we do know that it is quite likely that it will have a utopian dimension.

6

The Microecology of Community: Toward a Theory of Grassroots Organization

The Problem of Political Culture

In his fascinating work *Beer and Revolution*, Tom Goyens describes the place of the German beer parlor culture of New York in the immigrant revolutionary milieu, and in particular in the German anarchist community.[1] From today's perspective it might seem a bit bizarre to consider the revolutionary potential of saloons; however, they did indeed function during a certain epoch as important sites for working-class and revolutionary organizations, as centers of comradeship and community building among radicals, and as an important sphere for free expression and nonconformist discourse. The beer parlors were an integral part of a vibrant radical culture in which social activities, daily newspapers, political clubs and organizations, public meetings, popular music and arts, and many other factors worked together to create a richly textured fabric of relationships that nurtured both the personal lives and the revolutionary values of the community's members. This work adds another fascinating chapter to the story of radical and revolutionary culture that spans a considerable period of American history.

The immigrant revolutionary political culture largely declined with the increasing integration of the second and subsequent generations into the dominant social order. However, the quest to create a strong revolutionary working-class culture did not end, and once again achieved a certain degree of success in the late 1960s and early 1970s. Whatever the limitations of the radical movement of that period, it was possible at that time for a growing number of people to live much of their lives within a oppositional community with its own newspapers, magazines, radio stations, cooperatives, alternative schools, intentional communities, radical cafés and other "liberated" spaces, and distinctive music and art forms, to give just a few examples. The depth of the revolutionary dimension of the period has perhaps been exaggerated at times.[2] But the danger today comes not from the excesses of *soixante-huitard* romanticism but rather from the possibility that the lessons to be learned from the real social and political achievements of the period will be largely forgotten.

I once had a conversation with a political scientist and self-proclaimed leftist from a large university in New York City. I happened to mention the subject of the current expansion of corporate and state power as compared to the "retreat of the state in the 1960s." He reacted to this concept with complete incomprehension and utter disbelief that any such phenomenon could possibly have occurred. I suspect that what underlies such social amnesia is a kind of resigned, defensive, and at times cynical denial that an oppositional political culture can, in our historical epoch, in our sort of society, significantly challenge the dominant system of power. Yet not so long ago, Bolivian peasants successfully ousted a right-wing regime through massive protests and noncooperation. And more recently, mass movements in Arab countries have ousted dictators who had entrenched power for decades. Even deeper transformation has taken place in Chiapas and Rojava. Such examples may be dismissed by some in the "developed world" as coming from the global South, that other world that perhaps seems to many people too "other" and perhaps too peripheral to be relevant to a society such as their own.

But such a view is tragically mistaken. We have seen that even in the world that conceives of itself as the "first" among unequals, grassroots movements with effective social power can do more than merely exert a certain pressure on the dominant system through officially sanctioned means (elections, lobbying, letter-writing, etc.) that are rightly seen as "internal" to the system. They can also transform that system through an "external" influence, as the system recognizes and responds to various manifestations of their social power—including their implicit power of resistance and noncooperation, their power to shape wider public opinion, and their potential for direct political mobilization when antagonized adequately. The system acknowledges the significance of widespread resistance, of effective attacks on its legitimacy, and of significant costs that it incurs in attempts to impose policies on any large refractory segment of the population. It also responds by developing mechanisms to neutralize and co-opt centers of relatively autonomous power, since they are the most ultimately threatening and potentially delegitimating form of opposition.

In the 1960s, though there was certainly nothing like a revolutionary or even a pre-revolutionary situation in the United States, there was an assault on certain elements of the corporate-state system, an assault that caused a significant challenge to the power of that system. Examples of the resulting retreat of corporate-state power included a reduction in state control of reproduction, the elimination of direct state-enforced racial segregation, the relaxing of the direct control of the freedom of movement and behavior of minority-group members in many areas; the emergence of a strong antiauthoritarian education movement; reduced persecution of nonconforming sexual and gender expression in some areas; reduced enforcement of drug laws; relaxation of censorship and controls on personal behavior in general; greater restrictions on environmental destruction by corporations and the state; advances in citizens' rights to information concerning corporate and state activities; expansion of certain civil liberties and legal rights against the state; and stronger defense of the rights of so-called clients of state bureaucracies.

Over the past few decades there has been, on the other hand, a rather imperious reassertion and expansion of corporate and state power, expressed through both repressive apparatuses and ideological apparatuses, in direct proportion to the "withering away" of engaged opposition at the level of the social base. Despite the increasing proliferation of rhetoric concerning the significance of "civil society," most of what goes under this name poses no challenge to corporate-state hegemony, but constitutes, rather, an essential element of the steering mechanism of the corporate-state order. The American Left, beginning in the early 1970s, committed itself rather single-mindedly to a strategy of transformation of the state from within, and transformation of capitalism through the state. Though this slogan has little resonance today, the approach adopted was seen as a rather heroic, if also prosaic, "long march through the institutions." In effect, the development of a broad-based, potentially majoritarian participatory democratic social movement was abandoned for the sake of interest group politics. There is no doubt that there were enormous possibilities for democratizing the state and using the state to place limits on capital's exploitation and devastation of both human society and the natural world. However, it has become increasingly evident that those possibilities could not be realized through the means adopted: communication with the citizenry primarily through use of the dominant corporate media; acceptance of the monopolization of the political sphere by the two corporate political parties; and indirect political action, primarily through oppositional pressure groups seeking to influence state policy, and often focusing on a limited spectrum of single-issues campaigns.[3] In effect, the Left adopted a self-defeating strategy of becoming a coalition of interest groups within a putatively pluralistic and liberal democratic system that has in fact become increasingly oligarchic and corporate controlled. Any aspiration for the creation of a self-conscious, dissident political culture with its own ideals and its own growing, developing grassroots institutions was abandoned.

Some may dispute this interpretation. Left-liberal commentator Jim Hightower once made the claim (in an interview on Free Speech TV) that although the hard Right controls a certain segment of the big media, with Fox TV being the paradigm case, "progressive" forces are today more powerful than the Right at the grassroots level. He cited his own newsletter, which has one hundred thousand subscribers, alternative media such as FSTV, mushrooming progressive internet sites, and large, successful grassroots events as evidence of this grassroots power.

The examples he cites are indeed encouraging, but, nevertheless, the overall picture at the grassroots level is in reality quite the reverse of what he claims. However great the objective *potential* for the Left may be at the base, grassroots organization is overwhelmingly in the hands of reactionaries. As mentioned earlier, the fundamentalist churches, with their tens of millions of active members who can be found in significant numbers in almost every city, town, and rural area of the country, are the vanguard of grassroots right-wing organization. Each of these small communities embodies an *ideology*, an *imaginary*, and perhaps above all, an *ethos*—taken together, all this constitutes a highly articulated set of ideas, beliefs, images, symbols, rituals, practices, habits, and organizational forms. There is available to the members of these communities a complete social environment and ritualistic structure to organize their lives and their primary communal interactions. Not of least importance is the full spectrum of media that gives support to the values of these communities.

For masses of Americans, the most reactionary right-wing ideologies are the one "living option" in opposition to the dominant consumer society and the social disintegration it leaves in its wake. Once, I drove 350 miles across Louisiana, and I was able to tune in right-wing extremist talk-radio star Rush Limbaugh on a half dozen stations from one end of the state to the other. I would not have had to go much out of my way to find hundreds of fundamentalist churches that do their daily work of socialization and indoctrination at the microsocial level. But I certainly had little chance of hearing dissident voices from the Left. What was perhaps most discouraging was that much of my drive was through what was once populist central Louisiana—an area that in the early twentieth century saw radical, racially integrated timber workers' unions organized by the Industrial Workers of the World, whose largest city had a socialist mayor, and which was the site of the New Llano cooperative community, a thriving socialist experiment with six hundred members engaged in diverse agricultural and industrial endeavors over a period of several decades.[4] Severe social contradictions and the potential for radical social movements still exist across central Louisiana (as in so much of the country) but the organizational, ideological, and imaginary work needed to develop these contradictions creatively have not been realized.

By the late 1960s, the American Left was relatively large, affluent, well educated, and skilled. It was seemingly in an objective position to organize itself significantly both at the grassroots level (we might say, on the level of "the base" of concrete life-activity) and at the level of the means of communication (we might say on a certain "superstructural" or "ideological" level, in the nonpejorative sense of the latter term). At the same time, various groups on the religious Right were beginning to organize politically and to come under the influence of the society of consumption and mass media. A telling example is Pentecostalism, a religious movement that consisted of a marginalized, not very affluent, not very well-educated population. Members were held in contempt by much of mainstream culture, dismissed as backward, and derisively labeled "holy rollers." However, over a period of three decades they and other religious fundamentalists have created television and radio networks with daily audiences in the tens of millions, book publishing houses with extensive catalogues, magazines and publications with huge readerships, large systems of elementary, secondary, and higher education, and a base of local churches with a wide spectrum of activities and groups for people of all ages, with diverse needs and expectations.

After these three decades, the Left has no such media networks.[5] Neither has it created a thriving political culture at the grassroots level. The striking fact is that despite the American Left's professed concern for "the people" and "the grassroots," there is nothing presently at *the base* to compare with right-wing organization at that level. This is no way to deny that even across the most reactionary stretches of the American heartland there are many individuals who continue to read their Chomsky, tune in to *Democracy Now!*, and perhaps occasionally travel great distances to join antiwar and climate justice rallies. And I believe that many more will continue to do so. But for a long period of time there has been a disastrous lag in both base organization and organization of the means of communication. If the Left is to regain its radicality (in the sense of both transformative vision and rootedness in social reality) and its hope for long-term success in social and ecological regeneration, and, indeed, if it has a passionate concern that people have a chance to live good lives, its first priority must be the creation of strong, thriving *communities of solidarity and liberation.*

There is a need for an ethos that expresses hope and creativity in concrete form. There is great danger in the tendency of the Left to become a culture of opposition, of endless "struggle," and of reactivity. As Hegel points out, a consciousness that becomes consumed by its own ideals, cut off from concrete, creative historical self-expression,[6] is doomed to chronic unhappiness, or, as we might say, is headed for "burnout." In order to sustain hope, there is a need for the reality of a rich, vital, fulfilling, growing culture that embodies ideals of love, justice, and respect for the natural world. In searching for inspiration for such a culture, we can look not only to the political and labor movements of a century ago, but also to more recent movements that have a more integral and comprehensive approach to social transformation: the base communities of Latin American that have been inspired by liberation theology, the Sarvodaya movement of Sri Lanka, which embodies Gandhian and Buddhist ideals, and the struggles of tribal peoples who have synthesized deep communitarian and ecological values with the struggle for justice and liberation.[7]

Past history indicates that political radicalism is likely to intensify in times of traumatic social transition. We are in the midst of a period of rapid qualitative social change and recurrent crisis on a global scale. Today, we see an increasingly integrated world system, coordinated through the institutions of transnational capital and the global state system, revolutionizing societies everywhere at an increasingly rapid rate. It is no coincidence that one of the most noteworthy developments in the direction of a strong dissident political culture has arisen within the anticorporate globalization or "altermondialist" movement that has emerged precisely in opposition to this totalizing, homogenizing force. Pierre Clastres in *Society against the State* described the struggle of Amerindian peoples against the rise of a "One"—in the form of centralized, hierarchical political power—that threatened their traditional social and ecological relationships.[8] We might say that today "the One" is rising on an unprecedented global scale and that the key social and ecological question today is whether "the Many" will also rise to the occasion. Central to this issue is the crucial question of political culture. It may well be the case that "another world is possible" in the future only if a growing number of people begin living in another world at the present moment.

The contention here is that the matrix out of which that other world is most likely to emerge is a rich political culture rooted in transformative primary communities.

The Microecology of Community

Over the past generation of radical social theory, we have heard a great deal more about the "microphysics of power" than we have about the microecology of community. The dominance of the former approach is, I think, less a reflection of the inherent superiority of poststructuralist analysis than a symptom of the defensive nature of oppositional culture in our time. A heavy focus on the "physics" of the system of power, and the depiction of social action in terms of various "strategies" and "tactics" shaped largely in *reaction* to this system betrays a certain level of capitulation to a dominant mechanistic, objectifying order. There has been a widespread assumption—not only among postmodernist and poststructuralist theorists, but also among political activists—that the historical destiny of opposition is essentially a future of permanent struggle against the system of power. For many, the highest aspirations of oppositional culture seem to lie in small tactical gains within a fundamentally immovable system and in the forms of enjoyment and creativity possible through struggles within the vast labyrinth of power.

The ideology of permanent struggle embodies some important truths about our creative resources in the face of domination, but unless these truths are placed within a larger, more affirmative problematic, they easily become a recipe for disillusionment and nihilism. Such a larger problematic underlies the microecology of community. This approach undertakes a careful exploration of the nature and possibilities of community at the molecular level of society, and directs our hopes and efforts toward a project of regenerating human society and liberating human creative powers through engagement in that project. It sets out from the assumption that society, no matter how mechanized and objectified it might become, always remains an organic, dynamic, dialectically developing whole, the product of human creative activity in interaction with the natural world of which it is an inseparable part. Society is shaped by human thought, imagination, and transformative activity, and is not least of all, the result of the kind of primary relationships that human beings enter into with one another. Reflection on the processes (especially at the micro level) through which society and culture are generated can help change one's self-image from that of mere critical observer of the social system, the generalized social object, to that of active participant in shaping the world through the various contributions that one makes to social reproduction, social disintegration, social creation, and social regeneration.

It has been suggested that the most immediate concern in a renewed radical politics must be the creation of strong, thriving *communities of solidarity and liberation*. Such a form of community is one that is engaged deeply in the quest for communal freedom in the sense developed in a previous chapter. It is in the process of replacing a system of domination of the person and community through force, violence, and coercion with a system of voluntary, mutualistic cooperation. It is in the process of replacing the domination of the person and community through exploitation, manipulation, and instrumentalization for the sake of power with a system of personal and communal self-realization. And it is in the process of replacing the domination of the person and community through alienation and objectification with a system based on agency, self-determination, and free self-expression.

Such communities are described as communities of solidarity and *liberation*. It would be significant if the Western Left could once again speak the rather démodé language of "liberation." The respectable Left long ago decided that this discourse was too dangerous, and decided to label itself and its aims as "progressive." It is no secret that "progressive" was invented in part as a euphemism for "liberal," the political orientation that dares not speak its name. But the term has also become a generic label for virtually anything that is vaguely to the Left, or begins to look Left in a political culture increasingly dominated by the Right. Thus, the rise of "progressivism" has been an eminently regressive development.

The abandonment of terms such as "women's liberation," "black liberation," and "gay liberation," has coincided with the marginalization of the remnants of what were once called "freedom movements," and the co-optation of their issues by the dominant political interests. In the end, the discourse of "freedom" and "liberty" has largely been conceded to conservatives and right-wing "libertarians," with lamentable consequences. The dominance of the negative, individualist concept of freedom as "being left alone" goes almost unchallenged, while the positive, social concept of freedom as collective agency and participation in many-sided communal self-realization is seldom mentioned. It is in this context that the concept of the communities of solidarity and *liberation* takes on crucial importance.

It is essential that we look for inspiration for the emergence of such communities not only in certain neglected chapters in the long and diverse history of radical and revolutionary movements, but also in contemporary examples of grassroots, community-based social reorganization across the globe. It is also crucial that we understand how the successes of reactionary movements (and most notably those of the religious Right) have resulted in large part from their achievements in community building, in grassroots organization, and in the creation of organizational forms that fulfill primary social needs. We must understand the way in which both successful liberation movements and successful reactionary ones have created small communities that embody a highly articulated set of values, ideas, beliefs, images, symbols, rituals, and practices, and integrated these communities into a large social movement.

We might say that any microcommunity that possesses such qualities exemplifies a process of "social condensation." It makes manifest and available for practice aspects of social ideology and the social imaginary that usually remain largely unconscious, thereby intensifying the power and effectiveness of these important but usually inchoate and latent social forces. These forces are realized in a concrete organizational form and in a distinctive social imaginary object. In achieving a certain degree of social objectivity, the small community opens up new channels for social efficacy and new self-transformative possibilities for its members, though it always also runs the risk of rigidification and reification (the decline of group reciprocity into seriality, as Sartre called it). In view of the potential power of such communities and in the context of the increasingly apparent organizational impasse of the Left, there is an urgent need to investigate (not merely theoretically but through experimentation and experience) the possibilities for the creation of liberatory primary groups, the most basic communities of solidarity and liberation.

We will begin with a consideration of decentralist communitarian theory and two of the most extensive experiments in small-group organization—affinity groups and base communities. Later we will explore other dimensions of radical communitarianism, including the experience of indigenous communities, the communitarian potential of self-management projects, and various community-based movements for social transformation.

Toward a Community of Communities

The far-reaching contributions to Left communitarian politics made by Martin Buber have been noted, but might usefully be discussed in more detail. Buber's political philosophy is best known for his concept of the "full cooperative," which influenced the early kibbutzim.[9] When one hears the terms "cooperative" and "co-op" today, they most often refer to the consumer cooperative. Buber pointed out correctly that of the various forms, this kind of cooperative is the least transformative of the participants and of the larger society, but that nevertheless it can serve as a useful step in the direction of a larger system of social cooperation. Though the consumer cooperative creates certain social bonds and teaches lessons in common management, consumption is inherently a much less active form of cooperation than is production. Cooperative production employs a broad spectrum of human capacities on behalf of the community and gives concrete expression to collective creativity. The democratically organized producer cooperative is therefore a much more significant step toward a fully cooperative society. For Buber, however, the most important cooperative social form is the "full cooperative," which combines production, consumption, and living together communally. He believes, in the tradition of Landauer, that this would be ideally in the framework of an agricultural community with a close relationship to the land. Such a cooperative is less likely than others to adapt itself to the larger competitive, exploitative system, and is more capable of fundamentally reshaping the lives and values of the participants. In Buber's vision, the cooperative, communitarian movement would achieve its fulfillment through the establishment of a large number of diverse, fully cooperative communities that were rooted in the land, and which would federate with one another to create "a new organic whole."[10]

Buber sees such an organic society as the opposite of the dehumanized, mechanistic system that has increasingly come to dominate the world. He contends that society is "in the midst of crisis," indeed, a profound and unprecedented crisis of subjectivity, community, and the human spirit. Society, he says, has been mechanized as "the State with its police-system and its bureaucracy" has triumphed over "organic, functionally organized society."[11] People have increasingly given up their sense of personal responsibility, lost faith in their traditional communities, and abandoned their fate to a mechanized and automatized mass society. As a result of the ascendancy of a global system of concentrated economic power and hierarchical political power, humanity is faced with the greatest danger in history: "a gigantic centralization of power covering the whole planet and devouring all free community."[12]

For Buber, a regenerated free society can only be an "organic commonwealth" that constitutes "a community of communities."[13] Such a commonwealth would be regulated through "common management," that is, through a participatory, decentralized form of communitarian socialism. While Buber has not as far as I know been called an ecosocialist, it should be noted that he does state explicitly that the community must embrace both humanity and nature. He invokes on behalf of this idea the image of St. Francis, who "entered into alliance with all creatures."[14] Indeed, Buber's "organic commonwealth" is an ecological community in many ways, including its unity through diversity in its internal structure, and its intimate relation to the land. Furthermore, if the larger free society is conceived of as the "community of communities," it can only realize this goal as a human community within the larger community of nature.

Assuming that the transformation of a highly alienated and exploitative society into a "community of communities" might be a quite noble ideal, the question remains of where we might begin in pursuing such a goal. This is Marx's old question: "who will educate the educators?" to which we might add, "who will socialize the socialists," "who will communalize the communitarians," and even "who will utopianize the utopians." How can we break the dialectical cycle of domination, in which the dominant ideology, imaginary, ethos, institutional structure, and materiality all reinforce one another? Buber's social thought is based on the assumption that for any deeply transformative social change to take place there must be an immediate and radical break with the present social order on the level of the most concrete social practice. As long as one continues to live most of one's life within the institutional structures of an inhumane, objectifying system, it will be difficult to carry out or even conceive of carrying out any deep transformation of that system.

The self-proclaimed utopianism of Buber's approach may lead many to dismiss it as unrealistic, but it is in fact more realistic, that is, realizable, in the long term than are seemingly more pragmatic political positions. Buber contends that "common management"—whether it is called socialism, communism, anarchism, or cooperation—has no possibility of realization unless its roots are developed at the level of the social base. If it is imposed from above, through mere reform of existing social structures, through a seizure of centralized power, or even through mass organizations for social change, it will necessarily be subverted. What is variously seen as "revisionism," "betrayal," "deformation," et cetera is only the inevitable natural result of an attempt to create democratic, libertarian, communitarian, and organic transformation through hierarchical, authoritarian, technobureaucratic, and mechanistic means.

Buber is most famous philosophically for his distinction between the open, mutualistic "I-Thou" relationship, and the alienating, objectifying "I-It" relationship. This distinction has profound political implications. Long before the idea of the "personal as political" became a popular slogan, Buber placed the complex, living, developing person and the primary relationship between persons at the center of the "social question." He asks, in effect, how we can recreate ourselves as the kind of *persons* who can collectively constitute an authentic nondominating cooperative community and, ultimately, a global society consisting of such communities.

His answer is that if authentic community is to emerge on the level of the larger society, it must first emerge at a more primary level—in his terms, in the realm of the "Thou," the realm of the person, of the most concrete personal relationships, and of the most immediate experience of both human and natural realities. Such relationships and experience will be fostered by developments such as the cooperative intentional communities advocated by Buber and in democratically self-managed worker cooperatives, both of which consist of relatively small-scale primary organizational groups of perhaps several hundred members.[15] However, if Buber is right in his view that transformation must take place on the level of the most basic personal relationship and interactions, we might direct our attention first to the potentialities of even smaller primary groups on the most personal, molecular level of society.

The Resurgence of the Affinity Group

Recent history offers more evidence of the possible emergence of such transformative groups than many might suspect, considering the rather demoralized, less than visionary state of much of the contemporary Left. For example, we might look to one of the most significant and promising developments in oppositional politics, the often uncompromisingly radical global justice movement. The successes of the movement have resulted in large part from the fact that it created a strong oppositional culture, with its own powerful, if still embryonic, counterinstitutions, and from its reliance on small-group organization. In *We Are Everywhere: The Irresistible Rise of Global Anticapitalism*,[16] the work that perhaps best documents this movement, the editors cite many aspects of the movement's cultural milieu, which they call "wild autonomy." It includes a broad spectrum of education and health care projects, food and housing cooperatives, social centers, alternative media, transportation initiatives, independent media, art, and publishing projects. Together these activities "form a self-organized matrix dedicated to the construction of alternative social relationships."[17]

Central to the development of this matrix is even more basic self-organization on the molecular level, in the form of the affinity groups that have been perhaps the most distinctive aspect of the movement. The affinity group as a specific organizational form had its origin in the Spanish anarchist movement, though is part of a long tradition that includes various small religious communities (especially those of radical and dissident sects), numerous experiments in small intentional community, and the political "circles" of the nineteenth century. The affinity group structure was revived in the antinuclear movement of the 1960s and 1970s, and it has played a part in other recent social movements including feminism, gay liberation, the ecology movement, the Black Blocs, and the ZAD.

Francis Dupuis-Déri, a political scientist and participant-observer in the global justice movement, has done some of the most important empirically based research on affinity groups in the movement. He defines such a group as "an autonomous activist unit created by between five and twenty people on the basis of a common affinity with the goal of carrying out political actions together."[18] To say that the groups are based on affinity means that the members "decide among themselves the criteria for inclusion in or exclusion from their group" and that its "creation and functioning" is "to a large degree determined by ties of friendship."[19]

Dupuis-Déri coins the term "amilitant(e)s" to describe the members. This is a brilliantly dialectical concept, expressing in one term both negation and affirmation. On the one hand, it signifies that they are "militants," activists, who are "*a*-militants," that is, who are not militants in the traditional, rigid, hierarchical sense, while on the other hand, it indicates that they are "*ami*-litants," that is, that are friends (*amis*) and that their activism is based on friendship (*amitié*).

Such a group is "autonomous" in the sense that it is not under the direction of any larger organization, but is rather directed according to the interests and commitments of the members. It is basically a group of friends, but the members have much stronger common value commitments than do members of most other groups. In Dupuis-Déri's formulation, members of the group "share a similar sensibility regarding their choice of causes to defend and promote, targets to prioritize, type of actions to carry out and the manner of doing so, the degree of risk they are willing to take, etc."[20] All observers note that there is typically a pervasive ethos of egalitarianism, antihierarchy, participation, and commitment to the good of the group. Dupuis-Déri stresses the fact that the internally democratic nature of the affinity group makes possible a much higher level of political reflection and deliberation than is typical of the hierarchical and putatively representative institutions that most associate with democracy.

Dupuis-Déri recognizes that the majority of affinity groups in the global justice movement have not hitherto been based on "affinity" in its strong sense, since they are formed by participants who did not know one another before they came together for a particular protest or political action, and then found that they had common values and sensibilities. Some groups remain together only for the duration of a particular action or project, while others become permanent associations in which the members consciously plan their collective futures. Dupuis-Déri notes that the members accept the development of affinity as an ideal to pursue within the group and recognize that the group functions more effectively to the degree that this goal is attained.

One of the qualities that makes the affinity group an effective social agent is an internal division of labor in which members fulfill a broad range of functions that help strengthen the group and the larger movement in which it participates. Roles of the members typically include short-term group support (ranging from catering to "vibes-watching"), long-term group support (ranging from child care to fundraising), legal observation and arrestee support, police liaison activity and "cop-watching," communications and media relations, medical care, traffic control, entertainment, and direct participation in demonstrations and other political actions (as both "arrestable" and "non-arrestable" participants). In addition, entire groups may perform a variety of roles in the larger movement. For example, they may facilitate decision-making among networks of groups, function as study groups, or perform services for the movement or the larger community. Thus both internally and externally, the affinity groups seek to develop what Buber described as "organic" and "functional" organization related to the needs of the community at various levels.

Barbara Epstein notes the degree to which the most lively, vibrant, growing segment of the Left of today has been found precisely among the young radicals of the global justice movement who organize around values of decentralization, consensus decision-making, egalitarianism, antihierarchy, antiauthoritarianism, antistatism, and an emphasis on personal life and self-transformation.[21] Epstein observes that the movement has been far from doctrinaire ideologically and has often combined elements of Marxist economic analysis and anarchist politics with an immersion in popular movements and spontaneous struggles.[22] She cites possible weaknesses of the movement's approach, such as a dedication to principles that sometimes leads to a neglect for careful analysis of the practical consequences of actions, to difficulties in sustaining and developing organization based on radical egalitarianism, and to the danger that the movement's antileadership ideology will disguise hidden power-relations. Nevertheless, the movement has been the scene of the greatest growth and vitality on the Left in times that have been far from encouraging for its more traditional tendencies. This vitality comes in large part from the fact that the movement offers not only a political cause but a radically politicized and communalized culture and way of life. Authentic participation in the affinity group is an essential element of this synthesis of politics and everyday life.

The realization of the communitarian potential of the affinity group will depend on a deepening of the meaning of affinity and friendship. What does it mean to be what Dupuis-Déri calls an "amilitant," one who practices the radical politics of friendship? Agamben offers some beautiful and inspiring suggestions in his essay "The Friend,"[23] commenting on a well-known text of Aristotle, in which the philosopher says:

> For good people, "con-senting" [*synaisthanomenoi*, sensing together]
> feels sweet because they recognize the good itself, and what good
> people feel in respect to themselves, they also feel with respect to
> their friends: one's friend is, in fact, an other self [*heteros autos*].
> And as all people find the fact of their own existence [*to auton
> einai*] desirable, the existence of their friends is equally—or almost
> equally—desirable. Existence is desirable because one senses that it
> is a good thing, and this sensation [*aisthesis*] is in itself sweet. One
> must therefore also "consent" that his friend exists, and this happens
> by living together and by sharing acts and thoughts in common
> [*koinónein*]. In this sense, we say that humans live together [*syzén*],
> unlike cattle that share the pasture together.

Agamben points out certain presuppositions of such an analysis. One of
these is that the very experience of being and living can be something
excellent. We humans are fully capable of a good life in which the very
"sensation of existing is in itself sweet."[24] In addition to this sensation of
enjoyment of life, there is another "joint sensation, or a con-sent (*synaist-
hanesthai*) with the existence of a friend" and this gives friendship "an
ontological and political status."[25] Real friendship makes us fundamentally
a certain kind of being that we would not be in its absence, and being such
a being has larger political implications. "The friend is not an other I, but
an otherness immanent to selfness, a becoming other of the self," so that
"friendship is this desubjectification at the very heart of the most intimate
sensation of the self."[26] Friendship is thus a mutual sharing of the joy of
life in which one accedes to communal being. This may seem a bit abstract.
Much of this same idea was expressed perhaps more clearly by an old anarchist friend, longtime Bay Area activist and electrician David Koven, who
summarized his philosophy of life as "we deserve the best." His conviction
was that we (he and his friends, the community, people in general) are
capable of having very joyful, fulfilling lives and our project as anarchists
is to help one another realize this capacity. The affinity group (along with
the extended family, when it expresses similar values) is the most intimate
sphere in which we can practice such elemental mutual aid and solidarity.

Each affinity group can, then, constitute a small community of liberation, a sphere of freedom from the prison of the ego, and of freedom to
achieve communal self-realization. It is a primary expression of free life.
A crucial question is whether such small communities can develop more

generally throughout contemporary society, so that without losing their radicality, they will become less marginal. Can they expand their scope, so that they will become a generalized expression of the striving for a new just, ecological society, for a free life in common? Can they successfully incorporate a diversity of age groups, ethnicities, and class backgrounds? Fortunately, there is very good evidence that such primary communities have in fact had a more general appeal in some contemporary societies, and that they can have the potential to play a significant liberatory social role everywhere.

The Experience of Base Communities

The most familiar example of the socially transformative small group is offered by the base communities of Latin America that began to flourish in the 1960s and 1970s and ultimately grew into an international movement encompassing hundreds of thousands of small groups and many millions of participants. Influenced by liberation theology, they became central agents in a variety of social justice and revolutionary struggles in South and Central America. The project of these communities has been to achieve a synthesis of the Christian Gospel of love, the Hebrew prophets' message of social justice, and the class analysis of Marxism, within the fundamentally anarchistic context of a small, face-to-face community of solidarity and liberation.

Base communities are almost always identified with Latin America, and it has commonly been assumed that North American society has somehow been immune to such tendencies. It is indeed true that there has been no parallel in the United States with the massive participation of base communities in Left and revolutionary movements of Latin America. However, a significant number of base communities have in fact existed in North America. The crucial difference has been the absence of a large, coherently organized Left into which they might have been integrated, by which they might have been radicalized or revolutionized, and which they may in turn have even further radicalized or revolutionized. To the extent that a fragmental, dispersed American Left has expressed itself in interest-group politics focused on social justice issues (antiwar, prison reform, civil liberties, welfare rights, etc.), it is likely that the members of such communities have played a significant role in such activism.

Significant research has been carried out on an important segment of the communities, those associated with the Roman Catholic Church.

The results are surprising and instructive to anyone interested in social transformation. A study by Bernard Lee found that up to one million Catholics in the United States participated in more than thirty-seven thousand, and perhaps as many as fifty thousand, small base communities at the time of the study.[27] These communities typically consisted of thirteen to seventeen adults, and included over 60 percent women, in addition to children. The great majority met every week or two, usually in the homes of members. Lee found that the members of these groups were looking for a deeper level of community and spiritual experience than they found in more traditional religious institutions. The base communities offered them a more participatory mode of practice and a more personal and experiential expression of their religious faith. In comparison to Latin American base communities, North American communities had a more middle-class membership, though this was less true of Hispanic and other ethnic minority communities.

While these small communities have certainly not played as radical a political role as have their Latin American analogues, it is significant that one-fifth of them made an explicit commitment to social justice and social transformation. This means that at the time of the survey there were perhaps as many as ten thousand such politicized communities in the United States. These small communities experienced great vitality during a period in which American Catholicism in general was undergoing crisis and seeing a general decline in commitment and participation.

The recent history of radical political affinity groups and small religious communities shows that the social efficacy of the small community is not a mere hypothesis, but rather a demonstrated reality. The extent to which such communities can form the basis for far-reaching social transformation is unknown, yet it is clear that they can fulfill important needs in the lives of many millions of people (including millions in North America), and that they have played a significant role in recent social change movements in a number of countries.

Ecocommunity or Barbarism?

The creation of a new society consisting of a larger community based in such primary communities is perhaps, as Buber called it, and as some will label it dismissively, a "path in utopia." But it should be remembered that all the elements of such a society exist in some form in present-day groups and communities. The barriers in the way of that path are certainly not material, but are rather ideological, imaginary, cultural, and psychological. The dominant political ethos is reminiscent of the state of the stranded partygoers in Buñuel's film *The Exterminating Angel*. Though the crowd was ready to leave, it remained imprisoned by its own self-imposed immobility—a monumental though ultimately absurd failure of will.

One sometimes hears, especially from many ecological radicals, that the best hope for a wide-ranging transformation of society is a vast social and ecological catastrophe, one so great that even the well-indoctrinated and escapist segments of the public will have to conclude that something is fundamentally wrong with the dominant system. From this point of view we should perhaps be delighted by the current course of history, since we are headed for a level of global social and ecological disaster that will certainly make the need for drastic solutions glaringly obvious. However, the grim reality is that this kind of Messianic catastrophism is more likely a road toward fascism (especially eco-fascism) than toward a free society. Without the emergence of a strong and hopeful movement for the liberation of humanity and nature, severe crisis will only produce fear, reactivity, and a desperate cry for an authoritarian solution—though the tyranny may this time be dressed in some shade of green. The development of strong communities of liberation within a strong transfigurative culture dedicated to the liberation of humanity and nature is the only real barrier to continually intensifying social-ecological crisis and the authoritarianism it will necessarily breed.

We might still find a basis for optimism in the growing awareness of the contradictions of the existing order if we can begin immediately to channel this awareness into forms of organization that are truly both transformative and liberatory. Such consciousness (or at least the objective potential for its development) is destined to grow as the major contradictions within the system continue their development. If the dominant world system's drive toward ecological devastation reflects the second contradiction of capitalism, the drive toward a devastation of the human spirit and community reveal a third fundamental contradiction of capitalism that becomes ever more conspicuous.[28] As these contradictions play out in history, our increasingly repressed desires for both nature and community become increasingly revolutionary forces. Perhaps there is some truth in E.O. Wilson's thesis that because of our evolution in close relationship with the natural world we possess a deep "biophilia" that may be accessed in defense of nature. However, it seems even more likely that our many millennia of communal existence have produced in us a "sociophilia" or "communophilia," that is even more powerful and offers even more hope of being mobilized on behalf of the community.

The question of the degree to which the quest for community has revolutionary potential is an experimental one, and the experiment is one well worth undertaking. The long journey to the free ecological society requires a first step in the right direction. The most promising first step, the one that sustains most the possibility of further travel along the path, is the creation, through the efforts of each of us, here and now, of the small community of solidarity and liberation.

7

Bridging the Unbridgeable Chasm: Personal Transformation and Social Action in Anarchist Practice

One of the best-known polemics in the history of contemporary anarchism is Murray Bookchin's *Social Anarchism or Lifestyle Anarchism: An Unbridgeable Chasm.*[1] In this short work, Bookchin argues that two quite distinct and incompatible currents have traversed the entire history of anarchism. He labels these two divergent tendencies "social anarchism" and "lifestyle anarchism" and contends that between them "there exists a divide that cannot be bridged."

The idea that there is an "unbridgeable chasm" between two viewpoints that share certain common presuppositions and goals, and whose practices are in some ways interrelated, is a bit suspect from the outset. It is particularly problematic when proposed by a thinker such as Bookchin, who claims to hold a dialectical perspective. Whereas nondialectical thought merely opposes one reality to another in an abstract manner, or else places the two inertly beside one another, a dialectical analysis examines the ways in which various realities presuppose each other, constitute each another, challenge the identity of each other, and push each other to the limits of their development. Accordingly, one important quality of such a dialectical analysis is that it helps those with divergent viewpoints see the ways in which their positions are not mutually exclusive, but can instead be mutually realized in a further development of each.

Nevertheless, Bookchin contends that there is a bottomless abyss between these two tendencies within contemporary anarchism. On one side of the great gulf is an individualist and escapist current that he sees as increasingly dominating the movement, while on the other is a communally oriented and socially engaged standpoint, which he sees as in a process of continual retreat. Bookchin argues that this stark dichotomy typifies not only the present-day anarchist movement but also has deep roots in the history of anarchism, and that certain flaws that are inherent in anarchism itself have contributed to the ways in which the contemporary movement has gone astray. He presents his "unbridgeable chasm" thesis as follows. "Stated bluntly: Between the socialist pedigree of anarcho-syndicalism and anarcho-communism (which have never denied the importance of self-realization and the fulfillment of desire), and the basically liberal, individualistic pedigree of lifestyle anarchism (which fosters social ineffectuality, if not outright social negation), there exists a divide that cannot be bridged unless we completely disregard the profoundly different goals, methods, and underlying philosophy that distinguish them."

It will be argued here that this analysis is based on a fallacious reading of the history of both classical and contemporary anarchism. It will be shown that the anarchist tradition has been investigating the dialectic between the individual and social dimensions of freedom with considerable seriousness throughout its history. Alan Ritter's concept of "communal individuality" is an apt depiction of the traditional anarchist view of the relation between the personal and social dimensions. Ritter, a careful student of classical anarchist thought, explains that in espousing communal individuality, the anarchist tradition asserts that personal autonomy and social solidarity, rather than opposing one another, are inseparable and mutually reinforcing. He sees the theoretical defense of this synthesis to be "the strength of the anarchists' thought."[2] One might add that one of the great achievements of anarchist *practice* has been the actualization of this theoretical synthesis in various social forms, including personal relationships, affinity groups, intentional communities, cooperative projects, and movements for revolutionary social transformation. In the analysis that follows, Bookchin's critique of the record of anarchism in these areas is examined carefully and found to be wanting.[3]

One can find in Bookchin's text on lifestyle anarchism the seeds of his later break with anarchism itself. For in it he indicts not only the supposed "lifestyle" tendency, but also the anarchist tradition in general, for a failure to reconcile what he calls "autonomy" and "freedom." At the beginning of "Unbridgeable Chasm" he claims: "For some two centuries, anarchism—a very ecumenical body of antiauthoritarian ideas—developed in the tension between two basically contradictory tendencies: a personalistic commitment to individual autonomy and a collectivist commitment to social freedom."

Despite the centrality of this claim to his critique, Bookchin never produces significant evidence that what anarchists have historically and in recent times defended as "personal autonomy" and "social freedom" are "basically contradictory." To do so would have required him to take one of two approaches. First, he could have discussed the history of these two concepts as they are expressed by various thinkers and organizations in the tradition and shown that they are contradictory conceptually. He does not, however, do this. Second, he could have surveyed anarchist practice and demonstrated that the application of these two concepts in practice has led inevitably to contradictory results. He also fails to do this.

Conversely, the invalidity of Bookchin's claims could be demonstrated in two ways. First, one or more cases in which anarchists have developed concepts of individual autonomy and social freedom that are clearly noncontradictory could be presented. Second, one or more cases could be cited in which concepts of individual autonomy and social freedom have been applied in practice in complementary, noncontradictory ways. In the following discussion, Bookchin's contentions will be refuted in both of these ways. However, a mere refutation of Bookchin's claims would not do justice to the achievements of anarchism. I will therefore seek to show that not only can we find those "one or more cases" that minimally refute Bookchin, but also that there has been and still is today a rich and highly developed anarchist tradition that synthesizes the personal and social dimensions of freedom, rather than opposing them to one another.

Individual and Society in Anarchist Thought

According to Bookchin, "anarchism's failure to resolve [the] tension [between individual autonomy and social freedom], to articulate the relationship of the individual to the collective, and to enunciate the historical circumstances that would make possible a stateless anarchic society produced problems in anarchist thought that remain unresolved to this day." It would indeed be absurd to state that anarchist theory has entirely "resolved the tension" between the personal and social dimensions. In fact, only a nondialectical, abstractly idealist approach could imagine the dissolution of this tension in the real world or propose a theory that aims at "resolving" it.[4] However, anarchist thought and practice have certainly made significant contributions to "articulating the relationship between the individual and the collective." As mentioned, Ritter, in his study of classical anarchist theory, shows that a conception of "communal individuality" runs through the tradition. What is striking when one looks at this tradition is its consistency in upholding the importance of both poles of the individual-social polarity. Goldman is particularly notable for her incomparable manner of affirming of both social solidarity and personal individuality.[5] But many major anarchist thinkers, including those who are considered to be the most archetypal social anarchists, have maintained a very strong commitment to personal freedom and what Bookchin calls "autonomy."

William Godwin, who is often called "the father of philosophical anarchism," believed firmly that a free and just society must be based on the maximum liberty for each individual. Central to Godwin's entire political philosophy and ethics was what he called "the right of private judgment."[6] This right was based on the concept that each person's decisions on matters of crucial moral and practical importance should be guided to the greatest possible degree by his or her own reason and judgment, and that neither coercion nor social pressure should interfere with the exercise of this right. Godwin's carefully argued position constitutes one of the most extreme defenses of a kind of individual autonomy in the history of political theory. Nevertheless, he also held that the individual's judgment should in all cases be directed toward the greatest good for all of society. Indeed, he contended that one has no right to make personal use of *anything* that one happens to possess if it could create more good by being devoted to some larger social purpose. For Godwin, individual freedom and personal autonomy are intimately connected to social freedom and the common good. The affirmation of such an interrelationship pervades the mainstream of classical anarchist thought since Godwin and achieves a much higher level of development in the work of later thinkers.

Bakunin, perhaps the best-known anarchist theorist, is a paradigm case of a social anarchist who stresses both dimensions very strongly. While Bookchin claims that "Bakunin emphatically prioritized the social over the individual,"[7] in reality, one of Bakunin's central theses is that one does not ordinarily have to do such prioritizing, because the welfare of society and the self-realization of the individual person are complementary, rather than in conflict. In one of Bakunin's best-known passages, he addresses the compatibility between individual and social freedom. He says that the liberty that he defends is the only liberty worthy of the name, the liberty which implies the full development of all the material, intellectual, and moral capacities latent in every one of us; the liberty which knows no other restrictions but those set by the laws of our own nature. Consequently there are, properly speaking, no restrictions, since these laws are not imposed upon us by any legislator from outside, alongside, or above ourselves. These laws are subjective, inherent in ourselves; they constitute the very basis of our being. Instead of seeking to curtail them, we should see in them the real condition and the effective cause of our liberty—that liberty of each man which does not find another man's freedom a boundary but a confirmation and vast extension of his own; liberty through solidarity, in equality.[8]

Unfortunately, Bookchin completely ignores passages such as this one that conflict with the idea of "prioritizing." On the other hand, he cites the following statement by Bakunin on behalf of his position:

Society antedates and at the same time survives every human individual, being in this respect like Nature itself. It is eternal like Nature, or rather, having been born upon our earth, it will last as long as the earth. A radical revolt against society would therefore be just as impossible for man as a revolt against Nature, human society being nothing else but the last great manifestation or creation of Nature upon this earth. And an individual who would want to rebel against society . . . would place himself beyond the pale of real existence.[9]

One must wonder how carefully Bookchin read this passage before citing it, because it does not in fact support his view. Bakunin's point here is that any idea of revolting against society is an illusion. However, the concept that one cannot revolt against society does not imply the view that society should be "prioritized over the individual." Using Bookchin's fallacious method of reading this passage, one would be compelled to conclude that Bakunin also believed that *nature* should be "prioritized over the individual," since he says that we also cannot revolt against nature. But he did not hold such a position. The actual point of the passage is to lend support to Bakunin's general argument that the good of the individual and the social good, rather than conflicting, are compatible with one another. From such a perspective, the prioritization problematic adopted by both extreme individualists (who prioritize the individual) and authoritarians (who prioritize society) involves a false dilemma.

Elisée Reclus also affirmed the inseparable unity between personal and social freedom. He presents a very detailed defense of individual freedom regarding speech, conduct, association, and many other areas, but always in the context of growing communal ties based on mutual aid and social cooperation. In an early statement, he affirms that "for each individual man liberty is an end," but at the same time "it is only a means toward love and universal brotherhood."[10] Throughout his writings, he consistently stresses the theme that anarchism strives for a society based on both freedom and solidarity. Like Bakunin, Reclus rejects versions of socialism that "prioritize" the collective over the individual, rather than affirming both. He attacks "some communist varieties" that "in reaction against the present-day society, seem to believe that men ought to dissolve themselves into the mass and become nothing more than the innumerable arms of an octopus" or "drops of water lost in the sea."[11] He launches an extensive critique of authoritarian socialism based precisely on its failure to recognize the freedom and autonomy of each person. Reclus asserts that the anarchist ideal "entails for each man the complete and absolute liberty to express his thoughts in every area, including science, politics, and morals, without any condition other than his respect for others. It also entails the right of each to do as he pleases while naturally joining his will with those of others in all collective endeavors. His own freedom is in no way limited by this union, but rather expands, thanks to the strength of the common will."[12] Throughout his works, Reclus argues consistently that community and solidarity can never be separated from liberty and individuality.

Kropotkin had similar views. For example, he states quite specifically that communism is not only compatible with *individualism*, but is in fact the foundation for the only authentic form of individualism. "Communism," he says, "is the best basis for individual development and freedom; not that individualism which drives man to the war of each against all—this is the only one known up till now—but that which represents the full expansion of man's faculties, the superior development of what is original in him, the greatest fruitfulness of intelligence, feeling and will."[13] In another passage in which he expresses similar ideas, it is noteworthy that in doing so he invokes the value of individual *autonomy*. According to Kropotkin, "free workers would require a free organization, and this cannot have any other basis than free agreement and free cooperation, without sacrificing the autonomy of the individual to the all-pervading interference of the State."[14] Individual autonomy, in the context of free social cooperation is thus an essential value in the view of this great anarchist philosopher.

The Political Discourse of Freedom and Autonomy

Bookchin claims, however, that an *opposition* between personal autonomy and social freedom has plagued the entire anarchist tradition. He contends that individualists and lifestyle anarchists in particular "call for autonomy rather than freedom," and that as a result they "forfeit the rich social connotations of freedom." This is not, according to Bookchin, a marginal phenomenon limited to extreme individualists. Rather, he claims, there is a "steady anarchist drumbeat for autonomy rather than social freedom" and this "cannot be dismissed as accidental, particularly in Anglo-American varieties of libertarian thought, where the notion of autonomy more closely corresponds to personal liberty." He contends, moreover, that the "roots" of what he sees as the insidious concept of autonomy "lie in the Roman imperial tradition of *libertas*, wherein the untrammeled ego is 'free' to own his personal property—and to gratify his personal lusts. Today, the individual endowed with 'sovereign rights' is seen by many lifestyle anarchists as antithetical not only to the State but to society as such."[15]

Bookchin's discussion of autonomy and freedom is fundamentally flawed since he ignores the fact that actual usage simply does not correspond to his fanciful account. He holds that "while autonomy is associated with the presumably self-sovereign individual, freedom dialectically interweaves the individual with the collective." Neither claim is correct. The term "autonomy" does not denote a sovereign ego and is quite often used by its proponents in ways that explicitly reject an egoistic standpoint. Conversely, the term "freedom" is not necessarily related to any sort "dialectical interweaving" and is very often used in senses that contradict such a conception. The right wing, for example, incessantly stresses its commitment to a "freedom" that has no such connotations.

Though many anarchists throughout the history of the movement have used the term "autonomy," there has certainly been among them no "steady drumbeat" in which "social freedom" is rejected as contrary to "autonomy." Contemporary anarchists also do not often engage in this particular kind of tub-thumping. Rather, they usually consider the two concepts to be complementary, and indeed inseparable. A great many collectivist, syndicalist, and communist anarchists have used the term in a sense that is entirely compatible with their conception of social freedom. The Spanish sections of the First International in a statement in 1882 stated: "In our organization, we already practice the anarchist principle, the most graphic expression of Freedom and Autonomy."[16] Emma Goldman and Alexander Berkman were at one point members of a group called "Autonomy." A quotation that is found frequently on anarchist websites is communist anarchist Luigi Galleani's definition of anarchism: "The autonomy of the individual within the freedom of association."[17]

One of the most prominent usages of the term "autonomy" in the last few decades has been its reference to "autonomist Marxism," a direct actionist, decentralist tendency that emerged in Italy in the 1960s and has had a significant influence since then. It is also associated closely with the thought of Cornelius Castoriadis, who was one of the most important and sophisticated Left theorists of the last century, and was noted for his support for decentralism, self-management, and antistatism. It has also been used by the "Autonomes" in France, activists who were influenced by Socialism or Barbarism and other antiauthoritarian tendencies, and who have been important in grassroots struggles on behalf of the unemployed and immigrants, and in the global justice movement. Finally, it has been used by the German "Autonomen," who were strongly influenced by anarcho-communist ideas and have been known for militant direct actionist tactics. In all of these instances, the term has been associated with socially engaged, anticapitalist, antiauthoritarian movements that have rejected the strategy and practice of vanguard parties and left-wing unions and have advocated direct action, wildcat strikes, and other diverse forms of militant social struggle. Thus, the term has an extensive history in recent political movements on the Left, and its widespread usage in this connection has nothing to do with untrammeled egos, personal lusts, or the Roman Empire.

Bookchin's linguistic usage in this case is an unusually excellent example of what philosophers call "Humpty Dumpty Language." As that character says in *Alice in Wonderland*, "When *I* use a word . . . it means just what I choose it to mean—neither more nor less." While this strategy may have been appropriate in Wonderland, in rational discourse it is essential to consider what a word means for the language community in which it is used. And in cases in which a person's usage is to be used to determine what that person thinks, the crucial point to consider is obviously what that person intends by such usage.

A closely related element of Bookchin's critique of anarchist views of freedom is his contention that "essentially . . . anarchism as a whole advanced what Isaiah Berlin has called 'negative freedom,' that is to say, a formal 'freedom from,' rather than a substantive 'freedom to.'" This charge would be a quite significant charge against anarchism if Bookchin could substantiate it. However, anarchist theorists have argued correctly that one of the great strengths of the anarchist position is that it offers a more comprehensive and inclusive conception of freedom than the one-sidedly negative conception of freedom in classical liberalism, neoliberalism, and right-wing libertarianism, and the one-sidedly positive conception of freedom in welfare statism and various authoritarianisms of Right and Left. Anarchism can justly claim that it has to a greater degree than any other political theory strongly affirmed both the negative and positive aspects of freedom, and then gone beyond both.[18]

Anarchism's radical critique of force and coercion and its corresponding support for negative freedom are well known. Indeed, those who are unfamiliar with anarchist thought often identify anarchism with the mere belief in a voluntaristic society without coercive laws. However, one of the most striking aspects of anarchist thought throughout its history has been its very strong emphasis on the positive dimension of freedom. Bakunin is an excellent example. Though he emphasizes the threat to negative freedom posed by the coercive and repressive power of the state, his major focus is on the positive aspects. In a classic statement on this topic, he says that freedom is "something very positive, very complex, and above all eminently social, since it can only be realized by society and only through the strictest equality and solidarity of each with all."[19] He contends that the first "moment or element" of this freedom is also "eminently positive and social: it is the full development and the full enjoyment by each person of all human faculties and capacities, by means of education, scientific instruction, and material prosperity, all of which are things that can only be provided to each through collective labor . . . of the whole society."[20] He adds that there is also a "second element or moment of freedom" that is negative. It consists, he says, "of the *revolt* of the human individual against every authority, whether divine or human, collective or individual."[21] Interestingly, even Bakunin's "negative moment" of freedom does not correspond to what Berlin defined as "negative freedom," which, as important as it may be, nevertheless consists in itself of the basically empty and indeterminate condition of merely being uncoerced. Bakunin's "negative" moment of freedom is actually an expression of positive freedom, since it entails action and striving and has determinate content.

Bakunin is far from alone in the anarchist tradition in espousing such a positive conception of freedom. With the exception of some individualist anarchists and anarcho-capitalists, anarchist theorists consistently attribute a very strongly positive dimension to freedom. In his exhaustive (over 750 pages) survey of anarchist theory and practice, Peter Marshall concludes that while anarchists in general propose a considerable expansion of negative freedom, most also focus heavily on the positive conception, including, in particular, freedom as the ability "to realize one's full potential."[22] He explicitly points out that a hostile critic, Marxist Paul Thomas, "errs in thinking that anarchists are chiefly concerned with a negative view of liberty."[23] It is rather surprising that Bookchin, even when he still considered himself to be an anarchist, could so badly distort the historical anarchist position in a similar manner. On the other hand, the fact that he could imagine that he had invented a position (a strong libertarian concept of positive freedom) that was highly developed for over a century and a half suggests why he could finally reject anarchism rather contemptuously as being theoretically inadequate.

Bookchin on Classical Individualist Anarchism

In order to depict a supposed absolute dichotomy between his two forms of anarchism, Bookchin is compelled to present a highly distorted picture of individualist anarchism. According to his account, "as a credo, individualist anarchism remained largely a bohemian lifestyle, most conspicuous in its demands for sexual freedom ('free love') and enamored of innovations in art, behavior, and clothing," and "most often . . . expressed itself in culturally defiant behavior." In other words, it existed in a form that would have made it an ideal precursor to what Bookchin depicts as the "lifestyle anarchism" of more recent times.

But this one-sided individualist anarchism, convenient as it may be for Bookchin's argumentative strategy, exists much more in his imagination than in actual history. The classic American individualists—Josiah Warren, Lysander Spooner, Benjamin Tucker, and similar figures—simply do not fit into this mold.[24] One would never guess from his description that a figure like Tucker (the most important of the individualists) was concerned primarily with showing rent, profit, and interest to be forms of economic exploitation and with formulating proposals for a just economy. Neither would one imagine that the great American individualist "looked upon anarchism as a branch of the general socialist movement."[25] Ronald Creagh, author of the most comprehensive study of American anarchism, comments that "it is interesting to note that Josiah Warren and S.P. Andrews insisted on 'the sovereignty of the individual' but at the same time created the Modern Times community," and "perhaps under Warren's influence, one of the very first workers' associations called themselves 'sovereigns of industry.'"[26] Whether one agrees with their position, one must recognize that the individualist anarchists had highly developed ideas of social transformation and did not focus most of their energies on "Bohemianism." In the end, American individualist anarchism fits very poorly into Bookchin's model of "lifestyle anarchism" *avant la lettre*.

Moreover, much of the cultural radicalism that Bookchin depicts as typical only of individualist anarchism was in fact practiced widely by social anarchists also. Many communist and collectivist anarchists advocated "free love" and other forms of cultural nonconformity. For example, in the "Resolutions from the Zaragoza Congress of the CNT" (1936) one finds that "libertarian communism proclaims free love regulated only by the wishes of the man and the woman."[27] In addition, nudism, vegetarianism, and a kind of proto-ecologism spread within the Spanish anarchist movement, in part through the influence of communist anarchists such as Reclus, who harshly criticized authoritarian and bourgeois morality as repressive and hypocritical. Allan Antliff has done extensive and quite meticulous research that shows the ways in which anarchist avant-garde artists have long been engaged in the project of social liberation.[28] And one also finds in the American libertarian communalist movement the coexistence of anarcho-communist theory, support for revolutionary unionism, and cultural radicalism.[29]

Bookchin also tries to associate terrorism within the anarchist movement primarily with individualist currents. He claims that "it was in times of severe social repression and deadening social quiescence that individualist anarchists came to the foreground of libertarian activity—and then primarily as terrorists," and that "those who became terrorists were less often libertarian socialists or communists than desperate men and women who used weapons and explosives to protest the injustices and philistinism of their time, putatively in the name of 'propaganda of the deed.'"

Bookchin's understanding of the history of anarchist "terrorism" or propaganda of the deed, as exhibited in such statements, is highly defective.

Many of the most famous figures, such as Ravachol, Vaillant, and Émile Henry, were certainly "social anarchists" (generally anarcho-communists), and not individualists, as were well-known theorists such as Reclus, Kropotkin, Most, and Malatesta, who at times supported their acts or at least refused to condemn them.[30] Ravachol explained his actions as a result of both his "personal need" for vengeance against the bourgeoisie and his desire "to aid the anarchist cause" and "work for the happiness of all people."[31] Far from exemplifying Bookchin's self-indulgent "lifestyle anarchism," Ravachol offers a much better example of self-abnegating "revolutionary asceticism." Indeed, he proclaimed at his trial that he had "made a sacrifice of [his] person" for "the anarchist idea."[32] Vaillant, another well-known propagandist of the deed, described his bombing of the National Assembly in good class-struggle anarchist fashion as "the cry of a whole class which demands its rights and will soon add acts to words."[33] Émile Henry, an intellectually gifted young man, put aside his personal fortune to commit acts that would, he said, make the "golden calf" of the bourgeoisie "rock violently on its pedestal" until that class was finally overthrown. He proclaimed that his attentats were carried out in the name of "anarchy" with its "egalitarian and libertarian aspirations that strike out against authority."[34] Marshall, certainly one of the most painstaking chroniclers of anarchist history, concludes that "it is quite wrong and anachronistic to call the practitioners of 'propaganda by the deed' at the end of the 19th century 'life-style anarchists,'" since they were in actuality "part and product of a social movement which was consciously anarchist and socialist."[35]

A key claim in Bookchin's assessment of individualist anarchism is that it "came to prominence in anarchism precisely to the degree that anarchists lost their connection with a viable public sphere."[36] Bookchin's use of the word "precisely" implies that an examination of the historical evidence would clearly show a powerful, indeed a one-to-one correlation, between the decline of anarchist mass movements and the rise of individualist anarchism. In effect, he claims to have discovered a law-like regularity in the history of anarchism. It is noteworthy, however, that he makes not even the most cursory attempt to support his claim with historical evidence. His failure to do so is wise on his part, since the empirical evidence shows him to be quite precisely wrong.

American individualist anarchism, for example, clearly does not fit into his historical model. Perhaps the most important chapter in the entire history of individualist anarchism took place in the United States between the establishment of Josiah Warren's "Time Store" in the late 1820s and the suspension of publication of Benjamin Tucker's journal *Liberty* about eighty years later. Its emergence and flourishing did not in fact follow the decline of mass anarchist movements. Quite to the contrary, it was during the heyday of individualist anarchism that anarchism as a mass social movement in the United States also saw its most rapid development. The later decline in the fortunes of social anarchism had much to do with the assimilation of radical immigrant groups, and then with the growing ascendancy of communism on the Left after the Russian Revolution. It had nothing to do with its energy being sapped by rampant individualist Bohemianism.[37]

Neither does the history of European anarchism lend support to Bookchin's thesis. Individualist anarchism in Europe has roots in some aspects of thinkers such as La Boétie, Godwin, and Proudhon, but developed most under the influence of Stirner and Nietzsche in the latter half of the nineteenth century, and became a particularly prominent current around the turn of the century. Thus, its growth also did not follow any retreat of anarchists from the public sphere, but rather coincided with the spread of socially engaged anarcho-syndicalist and anarcho-communist movements. If Bookchin's thesis had any merit one would expect a significant development of European individualist anarchism to have taken place after the destruction of the Spanish anarchist movement in 1939 and the general decline and relative inactivity of anarchist social movements throughout the 1940s and 1950s. However, a flourishing of individualist anarchism did not take place in that period. Once again, Bookchin's thesis is clearly falsified.

Finally, we might consider the more recent revival of individualist anarchism in the United States. After a decline early in the twentieth century, it reemerged in the 1960s and early 1970s in the form of anarcho-capitalism. However, this growth of individualism was not followed by a decline of social anarchism. Rather, it occurred at the same time that social anarchism was having a revival in the United States and elsewhere. Individualist anarchist Murray Rothbard was developing a certain following at the same time that social anarchist Murray Bookchin was. Thus, in case after case, the kind of correlation that Bookchin's thesis would predict simply did not occur.

Lifestyle Anarchism as the New Individualism

We will now examine in more detail some significant aspects of Bookchin's attack on contemporary anarchism. He describes lifestyle anarchism and what he sees as its pernicious effects on contemporary anarchism as follows:

> Today's reactionary social context greatly explains the emergence of a phenomenon in Euro-American anarchism that cannot be ignored: the spread of individualist anarchism. In the tradition-ally individualist-liberal United States and Britain, the 1990s are awash in self-styled anarchists who—their flamboyant radical rhet-oric aside—are cultivating a latter-day anarcho-individualism that I will call lifestyle anarchism. Its preoccupations with the ego and its uniqueness and its polymorphous concepts of resistance are steadily eroding the socialistic character of the libertarian tradition.

Bookchin claims that not only is contemporary anarchism losing its tradi-tional leftist orientation, it is also in fact becoming "apolitical" under the influence of the egocentric, reactionary values of the dominant culture:

> Ad hoc adventurism, personal bravura, an aversion to theory oddly akin to the antirational biases of postmodernism,[38] celebrations of theoretical incoherence (pluralism), a basically apolitical and anti-organizational commitment to imagination, desire, and ecstasy, and an intensely self-oriented enchantment of everyday life, reflect the toll that social reaction has taken on Euro-American anarchism over the past two decades.

It was the supposed dominance of such individualist, apolitical, escapist, and self-indulgent qualities among today's anarchists that eventually led Bookchin to disassociate himself from anarchism and conclude that it is a failed project with no promise at this point in history. However, his depic-tion of contemporary anarchism is not accurate. Not only does he wildly exaggerate its weaknesses, he also overlooks the enormous strengths that have made it so important in the global justice movement and later in the Occupy movement.

According to Bookchin, "what passes for anarchism in America and increasingly in Europe is little more than an introspective personalism that denigrates responsible social commitment; an encounter group vari-ously renamed a 'collective' or an 'affinity group'; a state of mind that arrogantly derides structure, organization, and public involvement; and a playground for juvenile antics." He contends, moreover, that the political consequences of these alleged developments have been disastrous. He indicts "the insularity of lifestyle anarchism and its individualistic underpinnings" for "aborting the entry of a potential left-libertarian movement into an ever-contracting public sphere."

If Bookchin had been right in this diagnosis of anarchism in 1995, the past several decades would certainly have been a period of extreme quiescence for the movement. However, already by the late 1990s the kind of young anarchists whom he bitterly disparaged were at the forefront of the global justice movement, quite conspicuously taking a "left libertarian movement" into the center of an expanding global public sphere. History has passed judgment on his claims about contemporary anarchism's lack of potential for entry into the public sphere, and that we are in a period in which the public sphere continuously contracts. Recent movements across the globe to reclaim "public space" and radicalize it have made this judgment even more resounding.

But what of his most distinctive contentions concerning the attributes of this contemporary anarchism? Has the anarchist movement in general ("what passes for anarchism") in fact "denigrated" social commitment? Have anarchist collectives and affinity groups functioned primarily as "encounter groups"?[39] Have contemporary anarchists tended to reject structure, organization, and public engagement? It obviously cannot be denied that examples of the phenomena that Bookchin decries can be found within the anarchist movement today. Indeed, tendencies toward excessive individualism, adventurism, and detachment from social reality have always been present within anarchism and have always needed to be addressed by activists and groups within the movement. Well over a century ago, Reclus pointed out how some anarchists who initiate noble cooperative economic projects often become insulated in their small world: "One tells oneself that it is especially important to succeed in an undertaking that involves the collective honor of a great number of friends, and one gradually allows oneself to be drawn into the petty practices of conventional business. The person who had resolved to change the world has changed into nothing more than a simple grocer."[40] Yet it would have been absurd for anyone in Reclus's day to conclude that because of such tendencies the entire anarchist movement was turning into an association of simple grocers.

It is clear that the anarchist movement today also faces enormous challenges in its project of developing truly liberatory social forms, and many of those challenges are internal to the movement. Those who focus one-sidedly on the personal dimension or on their own small projects must be encouraged to think through the larger social and political dimensions and preconditions of what they value most in their own lives and endeavors. Correspondingly, those who overemphasize political programs and grand designs must be encouraged to understand the dialectical relationship between the transformation of subjectivity, the emergence of small primary groups and communities, and the possibilities for large-scale social transformation. Limited perspectives of both kinds certainly exist in anarchism today; but it must also be recognized that much is being achieved in the ongoing project of pursuing many-sided personal and social liberation that goes beyond such one-dimensionality.

When Bookchin observes the diverse efforts of primarily young anarchists to create liberatory social alternatives, he dismisses their endeavors as entirely worthless: "all claims to autonomy notwithstanding, this middle-class 'rebel,' with or without a brick in hand, is entirely captive to the subterranean market forces that occupy all the allegedly 'free' terrains of modern social life, from food cooperatives to rural communes." In Bookchin's dogmatic assessment, such activists are not merely *influenced* by the dominant system but are *entirely captive* to it. Projects such as cooperatives and intentional communities do not merely sometimes go wrong, but "all" such projects are "occupied" by capitalist forces. Any freedom supposedly attained there is not real but merely "alleged." This is Bookchin's version of Margaret Thatcher's "There Is No Alternative." For anarchists and Left libertarians there is simply no alternative to his strategy of libertarian municipalism. We are to believe that this is so obvious that no real analysis of the empirical evidence of experiences in cooperatives, intentional communities, collectives, or affinity groups is necessary.

On Consensus as Disguised Egoism

An area in which Bookchin attacks the contemporary anarchist movement particularly harshly is its commitment to consensus decision-making. He has long been very hostile to this procedure, which he has criticized as a form of minority tyranny that is a barrier to creating a viable movement for social change. In his view, consensus exaggerates the importance of personal self-actualization and group transformation at the expense of political effectiveness, and is a misguided assault on democracy itself.

In his arguments against consensus, Bookchin often assumes invalidly that it is incompatible with democratic decision-making. He also concludes falsely that its advocates are extreme individualists and elitists. This is true of his attack on Susan Brown for her arguments for consensus and against the inherent right of the majority to make decisions, and more specifically for her agreement with Peter Marshall that according to anarchist principles "the majority has no more right to dictate to the minority, even a minority of one, than the minority to the majority."[41] Most anarchists who affirm this principle and advocate consensus as the ideal also recognize the need to use decentralized direct democracy to make decisions on some levels of organization, about certain matters, and in certain situations. What they reject is any absolute, inherent, or unconditional right of the majority to make decisions for the group. This position is based on recognition of the fallibility of majorities and of the dangers of social pressure and conformist impulses. It is also an acknowledgment that majority rule is at best a necessary evil, and that even if it is accepted in some cases, it is always better to find more libertarian, voluntaristic means before resorting to less libertarian, more coercive ones.

Whether they have labeled any enforcement of the will of the majority a form of "dictating," anarchists have always been concerned about the inevitable possibility that majority decisions might conflict with deeply held values of some group members. Most have stressed the importance of recognizing, and indeed nurturing, what Godwin called "the right of private judgment." This is why the anarchist tradition (contra Bookchin) has placed so much emphasis on the right of secession. For most anarchists, this is also not an absolute, inherent, or unconditional right. Nevertheless, anarchist groups and communities often try to build into their structures provisions for dissenting members to opt out of particular policies and activities to which they have strong principled objections. As voluntary associations, and unlike states, they accord members who wish to end their association the greatest practically possible opportunity to disassociate without penalty. For similar reasons, anarchist groups and communities seek the greatest possible consensus decision-making (or when possible, consensual cooperation without formal decision-making) before resorting to majoritarian democracy. Such procedures have become increasingly familiar to the general public in many countries because of their widespread adoption (under anarchist influence) in the global justice and Occupy movements.

In Bookchin's view, the advocate of consensus, by "denigrating rational, discursive, and direct-democratic procedures for collective decision-making as 'dictating' and 'ruling' awards a minority of one sovereign ego the right to abort the decision of a majority." There are a series of false assumptions in this short statement. It is simply not true that support for consensus implies that one opts for irrationality. Both consensus and majority rule are rational decision-making processes that can be debated coherently. On the other hand, the failure to recognize that the imposition of the will of a majority on a minority (whether justified or not) is a form of "ruling" indicates either confusion or bad faith. Furthermore, Bookchin fails to grasp the fact that even if one supports the institution of democratic decision-making, one can still uphold the principle that one must ultimately follow one's own conscience and in some cases disobey the majority. Such recognition of the need to follow one's conscience does not imply an appeal to some "sovereign ego." Far from appealing to egoism, advocates of consensus usually base it on respect for persons, and the belief that consensus leads to more cooperative relationships and a more authentic and developed expression of the group's judgment and values. In the real world, an anarchist who finds it necessary to reject the will of the majority is much more likely to base that rejection on the *good of the community* than on the *sovereignty of the ego*.

Bookchin also argues that consensus decision-making "precludes ongoing dissensus—the all-important process of continual dialogue, disagreement, challenge, and counterchallenge, without which social as well as individual creativity would be impossible." However, in reality there is nothing inherent in consensus that must preclude these things, and there *is* something inherent in it that encourages them. If consensus is to be reached by finding an alternative that is acceptable to all, it will sometimes be necessary to continue dialogue when it might have been cut off by majority vote. Furthermore, the fact that a consensus decision is reached in no way implies that differences in outlook will completely disappear from that point on, or that differences of opinion will be less likely to occur. Indeed, there is some reason to think that the respect for diversity inherent in consensus processes will in fact encourage and reinforce such multiplicity.

Bookchin's strong defense of majority rule as the privileged mode of decision-making and his dismissal of other possible processes reflect the fact that he is much less concerned than many anarchist theorists about the dangers of social pressure and conformist mechanisms within groups. His fear that people might decline into a "herd," a peril that he incongruously associates with individualism, seems to dissolve when he turns his attention to an institution like the municipal assembly.[42] The anarchist commitment to seeking consensus is on the other hand based on a realistic recognition that conformism, instrumentalist thinking, and power-seeking behavior are ever-present dangers in all decision-making bodies.

Finally, Bookchin claims that consensus decision-making inevitably fails. "If anything," he remarks, "functioning on the basis of consensus assures that important decision-making will be either manipulated by a minority or collapse completely." This conclusion amounts to no more than a hasty generalization based on very little evidence concerning groups actually using it (e.g., Bookchin's personal recollections of the Clamshell Alliance almost twenty years earlier). If one wishes to assess accurately the practice of the contemporary anarchist movement it is necessary to look at empirical studies and careful documentation of this practice.

The Role of Affinity Groups and Primary Communities

Bookchin's attack on contemporary anarchist practice is based in large part on a basic assumption about the nature of society. He contends that it is the municipality that is "the living cell which forms the basic unit of political life . . . from which everything else must emerge: confederation, interdependence, citizenship, and freedom."[43] He also claims that "like it or not" the city is "the most immediate environment which we encounter and with which we are obliged to deal, beyond the sphere of family and friends, in order to satisfy our needs as social beings."[44] However, there is in reality no one privileged "basic unit of political life" and to seek one results in a very nondialectical reduction of the political problematic. Furthermore, there are in fact many overlapping natural and social and environments "with which we are obliged to deal," all of which are mediated in many ways. The city or municipality is neither the "most immediate" social environment nor "the living cell" on which all else depends.[45]

A dialectical approach recognizes that deeply transformative social change must take place at many levels of society simultaneously. This implies the flourishing of local economic alternatives such as worker cooperatives, consumer cooperatives, labor-exchange systems, land trusts, cooperative housing, and other noncapitalist initiatives—in short, of an emerging solidarity economy. It implies neighborhood and local radical, direct actionist political organization (including a movement for strong town and neighborhood assemblies) that helps generate a radically democratic grassroots politics. It implies the existence of cooperative, democratic media, including strong dissident and community-based radio, television, and print media. It implies the creation of local institutions such as bookstores, cafes, theaters, art galleries, music venues, and community centers for the nurturing of liberatory arts and forms of cultural expression. It implies the establishment of local alternative schools, educational centers, skills and knowledge exchanges, colleges, and universities. It implies the flourishing of cooperative households, small intentional communities, and affinity groups. None of these activities should be dismissed a priori as forms of self-indulgence or as tangential or contradictory to some single privileged political strategy.

It is in fact in many of these areas that a large part of grassroots anarchist activism is taking place today. While Bookchin bases his stereotypes of contemporary anarchism at best on impressionistic observations, others have engaged in careful research on the movement and its practice. One should note the careful observations of Québécois political scientist Francis Dupuis-Déri, who has studied affinity groups and other forms of anarchist organization during many years of experience as a participant-observer in the global justice movement.[46] Dupuis-Déri shows that one reason why that movement has grown rapidly is that it has created "in the shadow of the black flag" (as he phrases it) a strong radical political culture, a growing system of counterinstitutions in which this culture is expressed, and small group structures in which members can begin to transform their own relationships in accord with the ideals of the movement. Members have initiated a spectrum of projects fitting into many of the forms of liberatory social expression just mentioned. In the words of the News from Nowhere group, these diverse activities "form a self-organized matrix dedicated to the construction of alternative social relationships."[47] Central to the development of this "matrix" is the most basic self-organization on the molecular level, in the form of the affinity groups that are perhaps the most distinctive aspect of the movement.

As discussed in Chapter 6, affinity groups have a long history within the anarchist movement and have become even more significant in recent years. Dupuis-Déri cites anarchist writer and pedagogue Sébastien Faure's statement that affinity is "the only principle that is in keeping with the spirit of anarchism, since it threatens neither the aspirations, the character, nor the freedom of anyone."[48] Dupuis-Déri explains that the basis of these groups in affinity implies "reciprocity and common interests, indeed common activities that friends engage in and which maintain and reinforce the bond of friendship."[49] It is ideas such as these that have led many anarchists to consider the possibility that such groups could be the most crucial elements of an anarchist organization or society. The affinity group structure offers the possibility of a sphere in which the members can practice in their most personal interactions their values of egalitarianism, antihierarchy, mutual aid, love, and generosity. It is a basic community of solidarity and liberation out of which the larger communities might emerge.

Whereas Bookchin has attacked consensus as hyper-individualist and ineffectual, anarchist affinity groups have tended to make consensus decision-making central to their ethos. Dupuis-Déri shows that real-world affinity groups have explored consensus as a means of achieving both group solidarity and practical efficacy. According to his interviews, group members "feel that the primary affinitive or amical bond at the heart of their group more or less naturally implies a desire and will to seek consensus."[50] In his view, consensus is a purely anarchist form of decision-making, while majority-rule compromises anarchist principles. "Anarchy is distinct from (direct) democracy in that decisions are made collectively by *consensus* in anarchy and by *majority vote* in democracy."[51] The widespread anarchist option for consensus is based on both principle and practicality. "Stories and personal accounts concerning affinity groups show that the participants generally prefer anarchy to direct democracy, both for moral reasons (democracy is perceived as synonymous with majority tyranny) and political ones (consensus promotes greater group cohesiveness, a spontaneous division of labor, and a feeling of security)."[52]

While Bookchin charges that current affinity group practice and consensus processes encourage self-absorption and quietism, Dupuis-Déri's research shows that affinity groups and other forms of microsocial organization have served to expand the public (or rather, communal) sphere and create a forum for participatory deliberation. He observes that "small-scale political communities—a squat, an activist group, a crowd of demonstrators, and an affinity group—provide political spaces where decision-making processes can be egalitarian and can function by means of deliberative assemblies, in which a meeting room, an auditorium, or even a street occupied by demonstrators may serve as the agora."[53] The import of Dupuis-Déri's findings is that the contemporary anarchist movement has been engaged in an important experiment in the libertarian tradition of communal individuality. It is an endeavor to unite a politics of direct action, inspired by a sense of social justice and solidarity, with a practice of participatory, egalitarian community based on love and respect for each person. Far from fostering irresponsible individualism, they constitute a project for making shared responsibility a reality in the everyday lives of the group members.

A crucial issue is whether affinity groups and other small communities of liberation can spread throughout all levels of society, moving beyond their present marginality without losing their radicality. Can they expand their scope, so that while they may remain in part a manifestation of oppositional youth culture they will also become a more generalized expression of the striving for a new just, ecological society? Can they successfully incorporate a diversity of age groups, ethnicities, and class backgrounds? Can they become more enduring, long-term nuclei of communal life for a growing number of people? It is not possible to investigate these issues in detail here, but experience in and research on small primary communities (including affinity groups, base communities, small intentional communities, and cooperatives) provides evidence of their ability to play a significant liberatory role in the future.

The extent to which this potential will be realized remains to be seen; however, it is clear that the contemporary anarchist movement has already made important contributions to this developing experiment in communal individuality. I have focused here on anarchist participation in the global justice movement; however, my close observation of the anarchist-influenced recovery effort in the first few years since Hurricane Katrina has led me to conclusions similar to those of Dupuis-Déri. Among the volunteers there were perhaps many thousands who were committed to or at least significantly influenced by anarchism. I met many of them and worked closely with some. Though most have qualities that Bookchin associates with the lifestyle anarchism that he vilifies, what has struck me most about them and moved me deeply is their commitment to solidarity and mutual aid and their love and respect for the people and communities they serve.[54] A detailed analysis of this post-Katrina experience of "Disaster Anarchism" is the topic of Chapter 8.

It must be concluded that Bookchin's thesis that there is an "unbridge-able chasm" between forms of anarchism that stress individuality and those that stress social solidarity is refuted by the history of both anarchist theory and anarchist practice. The bridge is crossed many times each day by those who practice the anarchist ideal of communal individuality in their everyday lives.

Disaster Anarchism: Hurricane Katrina and the Shock of Recognition

The following reflections on the Hurricane Katrina disaster and its after-math consider the contradictory, radically divergent dimensions of crisis and traumatic experience. The first section is based (with only minor changes) on a text written for an international conference in Milan on Elisée Reclus, the foremost geographer of his time and a major commu-nitarian anarchist political theorist. I was scheduled do a presentation at the conference, but six weeks before it took place, the Hurricane Katrina disaster hit. I was still too heavily involved in the recovery to attend the conference, so I quickly composed this text and sent it as my contribu-tion. It was written very much in the midst of crisis, as was the second section, a postscript written nine months later, on the first day of the next hurricane season. The central theme of these reflections is that although the Katrina disaster offers abundant evidence of how crisis creates ideal opportunities for intensified economic exploitation, what has since then come to be called "disaster capitalism,"[1] and also for increased repression, brutality, and ethnic cleansing, which might be called "disaster fascism," it also creates the conditions for an extraordinary flourishing of mutual aid, solidarity, and communal cooperation, something we might call "disaster anarchism."

Reclusian Reflections on an Unnatural Disaster (October 2005)

I was in Dharamsala, India, in late August when I heard that a major hurricane was approaching New Orleans. I was there with the Louisiana Himalaya Association, a local group that works with Tibetan refugees. I soon discovered that I was to leave the Tibetan refugee community to return to what had itself become a city of refugees. When I arrived home, I found a city of empty streets, fallen trees, debris scattered everywhere, abandoned cars, flood-ravaged houses, and eerie silence. Since then I've been working with the recovery effort in my neighborhood and with several grassroots organizations around the city. Over the past month the city has slowly begun to come back, as symbolized by the "second line" jazz funeral parade that marched through the city Sunday—the first time this has happened since the hurricane.

These reflections are a bit in the spirit of a jazz funeral. They mourn our collective tragedy but speak out also for our collective hope. I believe that they are also very much in the spirit of Reclus, who will frequently be quoted in what follows. If Reclus, despite all his social and ecological prescience, didn't actually predict the Hurricane Katrina disaster a century in advance. Much of what he said is rather prophetic in relation both to this particular event and to the state of the world in which we live today.

Writing in the mid-nineteenth century, during his two-year stay in Louisiana, Reclus commented on the ecologically precarious condition of the city of New Orleans. "One has only to dig a few centimeters, or during dry spells, one or two meters, to reach muddy water. Also, the slightest rain is enough to flood the streets, and when a heavy rain beats down over the city, all of the avenues and plazas become rivers and lagoons. The steam engines work almost constantly to rid New Orleans of its stagnant waters and to discharge them through a canal into Lake Pontchartrain, four miles north of the river."[2] He noted further that "the districts far from the Mississippi are only a few centimeters above sea level, and people's homes are separated from the alligator nests only by drainage pools of stagnant and always iridescent water."[3]

Since the time of Reclus, the city has spread far beyond the natural levees of the Mississippi and the few so-called ridges or higher ground on which it was first constructed. Much of it now lies well below sea level, at times as much as three meters or more. As the city has grown, it has expanded to areas more and more susceptible to flooding. The job of pumping out water has become increasingly difficult, and, as we now know, sometimes impossible. Furthermore, the destruction of Louisiana's coastal cypress forests and the massive erosion of coastline (ultimately reaching the level of forty to fifty square miles, or about 100 to 130 square kilometers, per year) have resulted not only in the loss of great natural beauty, but also in the elimination of the city's natural protective barrier against the destructive force of hurricanes.[4]

The Social Ecology of Disaster

Reclus notes that throughout history despots have "placed cities in areas in which they would never have grown up spontaneously," so that "once established in such unnatural environments, they have only been able to develop at the cost of an enormous loss of vital energy." Today, he says, such "unnatural" urbanization is caused not by mad tyrants but rather by the despotism of the market: by "powerful capitalists, speculators, and presidents of financial syndicates."[5] The site of our "unnatural metropolis" (as it has been aptly labeled in one geographical work[6]) was chosen in accord with the needs of Empire and colonial conquest. Since the colonial period it has grown irrationally and antiecologically as a result of the tyranny of capital, with its imperious dictates of profit, growth, development, and blind, opportunistic exploitation.

The local media have repeated the refrain that the true destructive potential of a major hurricane was ignored not only by the politicians and other major decisions-makers but also by the population at large. In short, nobody really caught on and nobody really warned us. Nobody is really guilty because everybody is equally guilty. This is, however, far from the truth, and implicitly a recognition of the depth of fetishistic disavowal. Environmental writers such as John McPhee and Christopher Hallowell[7] have written eloquently of the coming disaster, official hearings have been held in which its details have been discussed, and eventually even the popular media have occasionally chimed in. Moreover, ecological activists, and especially the most radical and political ones, have continually stressed the dangers of ecologically irrational urban sprawl, deforestation and coastal erosion, pointed out the aggravating effects of global climate change, with the consequent likelihood of increased storm activity and intensity and rising sea levels, and called for an immediate change of direction. These supposed prophets of doom have now been proven to be the true realists, for this year has already seen the second-highest number of tropical storms in history, and the season is not yet over.[8]

A century and a half ago Reclus saw these destructive social forces at work and suggested what their consequences might be. He observed that "foremost among the causes that have vanquished so many successive civilizations" has been "the brutal violence with which most nations have treated the nourishing earth." He specifies among the evils that have led to this result that they have "cut down forests" and "caused rivers to overflow."[9] In another telling passage from the same early work (1866) he writes of a "secret harmony" that exists between humanity and the natural world and warns that "when reckless societies allow themselves to meddle with that which creates the beauty of their domain, they always end up regretting it."[10]

What they come to regret is called disaster. As in the case of Thanatos in general, disaster is the Thing that *haunts* everyone: the Thing that they spend their lives thinking about by not thinking about it. Reclus was struck by the fact that New Orleans was a city plagued by disaster. And he was perplexed by the seeming complacency of its inhabitants in the face of its ongoing disasters and occasional catastrophes. Soon after his arrival, he was to be stricken in one of the epidemics of yellow fever that periodically killed a large percentage of the city's population. But what made a greater impression on him at the time of his arrival were the spectacular fires that constantly plagued the city and ultimately destroyed almost all the structures dating back to the eighteenth century. "In New Orleans . . . the total destruction caused by fires is equivalent to half of the loss due to similar catastrophes throughout France."[11] He was understandably astounded that New Orleans, a city of two hundred thousand at that time, could have half as much destruction by fire as his own country, with its many millions of inhabitants.

Reclus was also shocked by the terrible ongoing loss of life that took place on the river. He observes that "from the construction of the first steamboat up to the present time, more than forty thousand persons have been burned or drowned in the Mississippi because of accidents of all sorts, including explosions, collisions, or fires—an average of one thousand victims per year."[12] One of the most striking passages in his "Voyage to New Orleans" is his description of a fire on the river in which seven large steamships in a row were consumed in flames and destroyed.

New Orleans has continued to live with disaster and the threat of catastrophe, along with its continued propensity to think about the unthinkable by resolutely refusing to think about it. It has long been known on some level that a powerful hurricane directly hitting the city or coming close to it would produce a major disaster and possibly even destroy the city. In 1965, the relatively large Hurricane Betsy caused massive destruction and flooding and a number of deaths in and around the city and became part of local legend. Over the next forty years the conditions for catastrophe intensified. All along there were a few voices crying out in the wilderness (and sometimes on behalf of the wilderness), but their sound was so faint that few noticed their existence. Local officials and media discussed the coming cataclysm only occasionally and exerted little pressure on behalf of adequate preventive measures. Requests for increased funding for hurricane protection were made, but both Congress and a "fiscally conservative" administration could safely ignore the problem and fund imperialist adventures instead, given the lack of outcry for a solution on the part of the seemingly willing victims of imminent catastrophe.

A Heritage of Violence

Another phenomenon that astounded Reclus was the level of crime and violence in antebellum New Orleans. He said that apart from one town in the Wild West, the violence of New Orleans was unsurpassed globally. "The night watchmen are far too few in numbers to be very effective in preventing disasters. . . . The most notorious criminals are hardly ever arrested, except when, emboldened by long success, they have the audacity to kill in broad daylight. Each year, several hundred murders are committed and duly reported by the press, but they are rarely pursued by the judges. However, criminal activity is so excessive that, in spite of the casual nature of justice, twenty-five to thirty thousand arrests are made each year."[13] Nostalgic southerners, as they wave their little confederate flags, still fantasize about an Old South that was all magnolias and mint juleps, rather than murder and mayhem. Fortunately, we have Reclus to remind us of the deep roots of our heritage of violence, which was itself rooted in long traditions of racism, complacent conservatism and entrenched social injustice.

The local traditions that shocked Reclus a century and a half ago continue today. There are still several hundred murders per year in New Orleans (in the worst year there were four hundred), in addition to similarly astronomical rates for many other crimes. So it was not entirely surprising that in the chaos of the aftermath of Katrina there should be an outbreak of crime and violence. Many were shocked by scenes of widespread violence and looting in the city after the storm and by later stories of massive desertions by the police and police participation in looting and theft.

New Orleanians were appalled to see scenes of crowds carting off entire shelves of merchandise from stores as the police looked on (or joined in), and to hear reports that a military helicopter had been fired on, and that one of the major shopping malls been emptied and then set on fire. Some stories were the result of paranoid delusions, as the claim that hundreds of bodies of shooting victims piled up in the Superdome, though the coroner's office later reported that not a single body was actually found there. Yet all the horror was not the product of fantasy. Reports of rapes and other acts of violence, in addition to the tragedy of large numbers of the elderly being abandoned to drown helplessly or die in attics of heat exhaustion proved accurate.

The issue of looting ultimately proved to be more complex than the media images implies. The great majority of the public recognized the simple justice of foraging for necessities in the wake of disaster, despite the media's often racist images depicting it as looting. However, the ugly side of the free enterprise system was seen in frantic plunder of consumer goods for later resale, followed by legalized plunder as price-gouging took effect for essentials such as emergency repairs on roofs. Large corporations and other businesses raked in windfall profits from juicy contracts as they subcontracted the actual work to hardworking but underpaid laborers. As always, the most insidious violence is the systemic violence. The worst looting is the looting that is quite legal.

Games of Chance

The mayor of New Orleans stated several days ago that it will be necessary for decision-makers to "think outside the box" if the city is to recover successfully. He then proposed that the key to recovery would be reliance on tourism and shipping, the precise industries that the city has depended upon most heavily for most of the past century. His one slightly innovative idea was to build more gambling casinos for the tourists, since hitherto there were only two within the city limits, plus a few more in the suburbs. So much for the boxed-in mind of his honor the mayor.

The mayor's desperate hope that the city's fortunes could be improved by putting the money on games of chance recalls Reclus's comment on a certain economic delusion that he saw spreading in mid-nineteenth-century America. "The American," he noted "is constantly on the lookout for opportunities, waiting for fortune to pass by so he can hop on and be carried away toward the land of El Dorado."[14] There is a sort of pathologically perverse logic to the mayor's gamble. Year after year we bet against the inevitable disaster—and lost. Maybe if we keep betting on (and in) the casinos, we'll finally win.

To many, indeed to the masses of the populace, the world usually seems like a game of chance. Accordingly, catastrophe always appears like something out of the blue. It seems like something rather catastrophic! The reason for this is that the rules of the game remain carefully hidden. They are hidden by design, a design we call social ideology, and by a deeper design we call the social imaginary. However, if we make the effort we can gain insight into the nature of these designs, and into the character of the rules of the game. Catastrophe will then appear a bit less catastrophic in one sense, that of an overwhelming disaster that seemingly comes from nowhere. But it will appear more catastrophic in the root sense of the term. "Catastrophe" comes from the Greek for "overturning." A catastrophe thus overturns what has been built up, and it is more or less "catastrophic" according to the nature of the structures that have been built up. So in order to understand the context of catastrophe we need to understand the structures of domination that have created the conditions of catastrophe.

Reclus made an important contribution to just this kind of understanding. In reflecting on the problems of the city he concluded that what he called the "urban question" is inseparable from the more fundamental "social question." This question, as posed by classical anarchist theory, concerns the nature of the existing system of social domination and the possibilities for the creation of a free, just, ecological society to replace it. If we apply such an analysis to the present question, we will see that the true nature of the Hurricane Katrina disaster in New Orleans can only be understood in relation to the development of underlying, long-term social conditions. We will find that the disaster reflects in very specific ways the interaction of major forms of domination that were analyzed in great detail by Reclus, especially in his magnum opus of social geography *L'Homme et la Terre*,[15] but also throughout his works.[16]

It relates especially to three of these forms of domination. The first of these forms is the state. Reclus attacked the state apparatus and its bureaucracy for being hopelessly inefficient, for aggravating the problems it claimed to solve, for oppressing people through arbitrary and abusive actions, and for concentrating power in the hands of irresponsible and often arrogant officials. The second relevant form is racism. Reclus was unusual among classical radical theorists in grasping racism as a major form of domination, an understanding that resulted in large part from his experiences in Louisiana. And the third form is capitalism. Though Reclus was scathing in his critique of the state, racism, patriarchy, and other forms of domination, he was careful to identify capital as the overriding form in the modern period.

The Hurricane Katrina disaster reflects very clearly the dialectic between these forms of domination. The most obvious aspect has been the blatant bureaucratic inefficiency of the various levels of government and of traditional aid agencies such as the Red Cross, in addition to the oppressiveness of the police. Only slightly less obvious has been the systemic racism that is reflected in the greater impact of the disaster on the black community: the scandalously slow rate at which essential aid reached it; the comparatively low level of aid that was given; the long delays in restoring basic services; and the prevention of community members from returning to their neighborhoods.

Further below the surface, but even more deeply determining, are the effects of the priorities of capital. In New Orleans we see a failure to invest in the social (and social ecological) infrastructure (the social ecological base) as is quite appropriate from a capitalist standpoint for a community that works primarily in unskilled, labor-intensive, "service" industries such as tourism, food and beverage, entertainment, and gambling. The larger southeast Louisiana region, with its reliance not only on tourism, but also on highly polluting, socially undesirable petrochemical and extractive industries, must be seen as a semi-peripheral sector, a sphere of greater exploitation relative to investment, within a core economy. Furthermore, racist patterns of urban development have resulted in an extreme concentration of personal wealth outside the city limits, and reinforced segregation within it, so that the city and the poorer areas within it become increasingly less significant from the standpoint of economic and political power—and thus more dispensable socially. At least this is how things must necessarily appear from the systematically distorted perspective of the dominant system of power. Of course, that system does not grasp the organic connection between social and ecological phenomena. Occasionally, however, an event such as a major disaster offers some renewed hints that things are indeed interconnected.

A State of Disaster

Thus, the Katrina disaster revealed strikingly the connection between social and ecological crisis and the disastrous mode of functioning of the modern nation-state. It offered abundant evidence on behalf of Reclus's contention that bureaucracy "impedes individual initiative in every way, and even prevents its emergence" and "delays, halts, and immobilizes the works that are entrusted to it."[17] Media around the world commented with amazement on the shocking ineptitude of the US government in helping victims of the disaster. The huge gap between the imperial state's ability to destroy life and its ability to save it became painfully evident. For those caught in the midst of the disaster, it was galling to realize that the state can in a matter of minutes call in precision (or, tragically, not so precision) bombers to destroy a building on the other side of the planet suspected of containing enemy combatants, while for days on end it proved unable or unwilling to rescue storm survivors seen everywhere on global news media begging for help.[18]

For a long time, there was very little aid of any kind to some of the most devastated areas, which were most often in poor and black communities. The city administration gave no official recognition or assistance to citizens' efforts at mutual aid and grassroots cooperation but instead actively created obstacles to such cooperation. Citizens attempting to enter the city were turned away at the city limits. At one point I was taking an injured volunteer to a hospital outside the city limits (since none were open inside the city) and was told that if we left we couldn't return. The same problem arose when leaving the city to seek supplies. For weeks on end it was often necessary to try several routes back into the city before finding police or National Guard members who were flexible enough to allow volunteers through roadblocks.

Barring citizens from their homes and neighborhoods for over a month added to the initial devastation of the hurricane. Further needless destruction of homes and possessions took place during Hurricane Rita, which hit the city only a month after Katrina, as rainwater poured through damaged roofs, wind caused additional damage, mold continued to grow in water-damaged houses, and further looting took place in some areas. If there had not been a drought for the six weeks after Hurricane Katrina (with the exception of one day of heavy rain from Rita) destruction would certainly have been enormously greater.

During the crisis, the state wreaked havoc not only by its exclusion of citizens from the city and its failure to deliver aid to storm victims, but also through its active persecution of those citizens who sought to save and rebuild their communities. Reclus in his chapter of *L'Homme et la Terre* on "The Modern State," notes that "minor officials exercise their power more absolutely than persons of high rank, who are by their very importance constrained by a certain propriety." Consequently, he says, "the uncouth can give free rein to crass behavior, the violent can lash out as they please, and the cruel can enjoy torturing at their leisure."[19] Such behavior, which is so common on the part of those who govern us, was given free rein during the Katrina disaster.

For example, both local and out-of-state police harassed Seventh Ward community leader Mama D for remaining in her neighborhood, which was under an evacuation order, and operating an autonomous community self-help project. The police cursed at her, called her a prostitute, and threatened her with arrest. Community activists Jeffrey Holmes and Andrea Garland created in their Upper Ninth Ward neighborhood a "Toxic Art Exhibit," consisting of damaged art works and political slogans, on the neutral ground (the New Orleans expression for "median") in front of their home and art gallery. The exhibit was vandalized by the military that was patrolling the area, and later removed by the authorities. The police later raided the house and arrested Jeffrey on the ludicrous charge of "disturbing the peace." Three young volunteers in the Seventh Ward, who were taking photos of the effects of looting and vandalism, were confronted by police, the police forced them to the ground, kicked one of them (the only African American in the group) and accused him of looting, held guns to their heads, subjected them to verbal abuse, and then falsely arrested them all for trespassing. They spent the rest of the day and night on the concrete floor of the makeshift Greyhound station prison and were told they had to plead guilty and do forced labor or be taken immediately to a state prison a hundred miles away. Similar stories of abusive behavior by police and arrests without cause are common in post-Katrina New Orleans.

On a Street Named Desire

So far I have dwelled primarily on the negative—what we might call the disastrous side of the disaster. However, I would like to turn to the positive and hopeful side of this experience: the extraordinary and inspiring efforts of local and outside volunteers; the reemergence and flourishing of grassroots community; and the creation of hope for a qualitatively better future. Despite the suffering and tragedy around us, the time that I've spent in New Orleans since the hurricane has undoubtedly been one of the most gratifying periods in my life. Seldom have I felt such a sense of the goodness of people, of their ability to show love and compassion for one another, and of their capacity to create spontaneous community.

Out of this disaster has come extensive evidence of the power of voluntary cooperation and mutual aid based on love and solidarity that Reclus described so eloquently. Mutual aid, he said, is "the principle agent of human progress."[20] In his view, the practice of mutual aid would begin with small groups of friends (affinity groups, in effect), and extend out to larger and larger communities, ultimately transforming society as a whole. "Let us found little republics within ourselves and around ourselves. Gradually these isolated groups will come together like scattered crystals and form the great Republic."[21] Elsewhere, he says that the anarchist must "work to free himself personally from all preconceived or imposed ideas, and gradually gather around himself friends who live and act in the same way. It is step by step, through small, loving, and intelligent associations, that the great fraternal society will be formed."[22] Reclus believes, based on his study of the vast sweep of the human story since its beginning, that such free association fulfills a deep longing that is deeply rooted in our nature and history.

"Anarchy," for Reclus means much more than such negative dimensions as antistatism, anticapitalism, and rebellion against arbitrary authority. It is, above all, a positive practice of social transformation and social regeneration based on nondominating mutual aid and cooperation. Furthermore, it refers not only to the free, cooperative society of the future, but also to every aspect of that society that can be realized in the present, "here and now." Reclus explains that "anarchistic society has long been in a process of rapid development," and can be found "wherever free thought breaks loose from the chains of dogma; wherever the spirit of inquiry rejects the old formulas; wherever the human will asserts itself through independent actions; wherever honest people, rebelling against all enforced discipline, join freely together in order to educate themselves, and to reclaim, without any master, their share of life, and the complete satisfaction of their needs."[23] The free community has enormous potential for "rapid development" precisely because it satisfies fundamental human needs—and above all, the long-suppressed need for that community itself.

I have found a great deal of this spirit of voluntary cooperation and concern for people's real needs (in short, the spirit of the gift) in New Orleans over the past month. The most inspiring aspect of the recovery has been this grassroots, cooperative effort to practice mutual aid and community self-help. A vast spectrum of local and outside grassroots organizations have been at work in the recovery effort. These include the Rainbow Family, Food Not Bombs volunteers from several states, the Common Ground Collective in Algiers, the Bywater neighborhood collective, the Soul Patrol in the Seventh Ward neighborhood, the Family Farm Defenders from Wisconsin, the Pagan Cluster, and groups from Prescott College in Arizona, Appalachian State in North Carolina, and other colleges and universities. Individual volunteers have come from throughout the United States, from Canada, and from other countries, often linking up with local community groups or groups of volunteers from outside the state who are working with local groups. I felt great satisfaction when one young volunteer from a distant state said to me explicitly: "We came here to practice mutual aid." The idea is still very much alive!

For the first week after my return I worked primarily with the collective in the Bywater neighborhood of the city, which was inspired by the Common Ground project across the river in the Algiers neighborhood. My friend Leenie Halbert volunteered her house on Desire Street as the center for the group, which focused on preparing and distributing food to residents who remained in the city. A dozen or so volunteers stayed there or camped nearby and many more came by to help. A Food Not Bombs group from New Haven joined the project, along with many other local and outside volunteers, including many anarchists. Leenie's house became a focus of social activity and hope in a largely deserted neighborhood and city. The food deliveries lifted the spirits of many and were essential to others who were isolated, such as the elderly man who had not heard about the hurricane and flood several weeks after the events.

A reporter from the New York daily newspaper *Newsday* did an article on the group, describing his first encounter with "communitarian anarchists." The reporter explained that Leenie "had come back into town with some of the aforementioned communitarian anarchists—people who believe in do-it-yourself action within small groups.... Her aim was to feed the hungry and bring water to the thirsty, to fix the broken homes of her neighbors and to offer a sense of community in their deserted streets."[24] He conceded that "whatever Leenie and her friends called themselves and whatever they believed, though, they were doing a good thing," and quoted Leenie's own explanation of what our group was doing: "I just wanted to bring love back to my neighborhood."[25] This may be an offense to the militants and foolishness to the postmodernists, but it's as good a description of communitarian anarchism as I have heard.

What might we conclude from these reflections? Reclus's philosophy of life was based on a deep love of humanity and nature, and on a profound faith that the community of humanity and nature can be regenerated and liberated through personal and small-group transformation based on the practice of mutual aid and social cooperation. Though the Hurricane Katrina disaster has demonstrated the irrationality of the system of domination that Reclus analyzed so perceptively, it has also, in the forms of mutual aid and grassroots community that have emerged in the midst of crisis, offered powerful evidence of the viability of his vision of a future society based on love, justice, and freedom.

Facing the Future (May 2006)

It is now exactly nine months since Hurricane Katrina. The past months have only reinforced the lessons that were learned in the first weeks after the storm. The abject failure and utter irrationality of the dominant system of state and corporate power have only become more obvious with the passage of time. On the other hand, we have seen growing evidence of the extraordinary and inspiring achievements possible through mutual aid and solidarity.

As we enter the new hurricane season, the situation in New Orleans remains very dismal. The social crisis continues. Most of the members of our community remain scattered around the country in exile, dreaming of return while their homes and neighborhoods lie abandoned and rotting. As we watch the spectacle of hundreds of billions of dollars being squandered on wars of aggression, it is quite clear that the means to assure our exiled citizens the ability to return are abundantly available. Yet there has been no large-scale, official effort to enable them to come home. Instead, we find a policy of de facto ethnic cleansing in which the generally poor and black majority of New Orleanians remain stranded in distant cities with few resources at their disposal. At the same time, vast areas of our city remain ruined, depopulated, and deteriorating. The means have also been available for a major rebuilding program to save these neighborhoods, but no such program has been undertaken. Even the piecemeal approach that would help a certain segment of needy homeowners has been plagued by delay and under-funding.

What is even more troubling from a long-term perspective is that the city remains vulnerable to further massive devastation by the hurricanes and tropical storms that are expected to increase in frequency and intensity because of global climate change. Even if the repairs and reinforcement of the levees that are underway are completed, they are unlikely to prevent flooding, should another storm at the level of Katrina hit us in the coming months. Most disquieting of all (to those few who are capable of thinking about it) is the real possibility that the long-predicted "Big One" might finally hit the city before a comprehensive protection plan is completed. In the worst-case scenario, twenty feet of water might cover even the higher ground and the city could remain underwater for months. No effective plan to protect us from such a killer storm has been adopted, much less put into effect. Neither has any plan been undertaken for comprehensive restoration of wetlands, which are our first line of defense against the kind of storm surge that was so devastating during Katrina. The games of chance continue.

We have just seen a farcical political campaign for mayor and city council in which the enormity of the tragedy and the dangers of imminent catastrophe were not faced. The major candidates were all representatives of business interests and had no intention of raising any difficult questions about social injustice, racism, exclusion of the citizens from decision-making concerning their own communities, and, needless to say, the bankruptcy of the political and economic systems that caused the Katrina disaster. None really confronted the issue of the criminal negligence of the Corps of Engineers, the criminal ecovandalism of coastal wetlands by the oil industry, or the disgrace of condemning a large segment of our citizenry to indefinite exile. Instead, they engaged in mindless and trivial quibbling over which of them has superior "leadership ability." Each covets the distinction of leading this great and historic city, though the direction in which they plan to lead us only takes us further into the abyss of social and ecological disaster.

The Social Crisis in New Orleans

It is difficult even to begin to summarize the diverse forms of injustice that we have seen over the months since Katrina. They have included de facto ethnic cleansing, mistreatment and exploitation of migrant workers, widespread police brutality, denial of prisoners' rights, collapse of the courts and legal system, unfair evictions, price gouging on rent, discriminatory housing policies, discriminatory reorganization of the school system, and gutting of the health care system, to mention some of the more important problems.

Perhaps none of these problems illustrates the depth of the crisis more than does the issue of housing. Lack of available and affordable housing has been one of the major obstacles to the return of evacuees. While thousands of units of public housing suffered little damage, officials exaggerated that damage and have kept the vast majority of public housing residents (who have no other immediate options) from returning. In addition, landlords have often forced residents out of scarce rental units, at times through fraud and subterfuge, to enable them to raise rents drastically. This has effectively driven some residents out of their neighborhoods and prevented others from returning to the community.

Some neighborhoods have even been threatened with complete destruction. HUD secretary Alphonse Jackson notoriously questioned whether the entire Lower Ninth Ward neighborhood should even be rebuilt, though he later backtracked on this position. For the time being, residents who are homeowners are free to begin repair and rebuilding with the hope that sufficient density will be achieved to make their immediate neighborhoods viable. However, the difficulties that residents have experienced in moving back into many areas (lack of jobs, schools, and health care; inadequate funds for rebuilding, repairs, or rent; etc.) makes the future of these neighborhoods questionable.

In addition, we have seen the promotion of a "New Urbanist" agenda for rebuilding that puts priority on creating "diverse," mixed-income neighborhoods in place of predominantly poor, African American ones. The New Urbanism was already applied before Katrina in the demolition of the St. Thomas Housing Project, which was replaced by an ersatz "urban village" development called "River Garden." While St. Thomas residents were promised a large share of the new housing, in the end they received only 20 percent or less of the new units and the vast majority of the community was displaced.

In a city with a 70 percent African American, and heavily poor, population, the redevelopment of neighborhoods into overwhelmingly affluent white enclaves has obvious implications. It is a strategy for re-appropriating desirable real estate that the white elite foolishly abandoned during the white flight hysteria, by displacing a large segment of the poor African American population that now occupies much of these areas. As whites began to move out of deteriorated, obsolete older suburbs, room was created for a segment of the displaced black population to be relocated from historic and architecturally valuable areas ripe for redevelopment.

However, the convenient post-Katrina exile of most of the black popu-lation to distant cities has been an even more effective solution to any displacement problem that might stand in the way of the New Urbanist ethnically cleansed utopia.

Post-Katrina housing problems have offered vast opportunities for profiteering. One of the most pressing needs in the effort to preserve our housing stock after Katrina was adequate tarping of roofs to prevent further water damage. Official policy has consistently subordinated community needs to exploitative programs that favor large corporations. In this particular case, large companies were paid $150 to $175 per one hundred square feet to install temporary tarps for roofs. After several layers of subcontracting and skimming of profits, the workers who finally installed the tarps were sometimes paid as little as $10 per hundred square feet for doing the actual physical work. Thus, there has been up to a 1,750-percent markup on actual productive labor, an absurd increase that even defies credibility. The companies at the top of the pyramid justified their plunder in the name of overhead, but it is in fact a clear case of opportunistic exploitation of disaster. Furthermore, considerable funding that could have subsidized permanent roofing for residents who are in need, and who deserve restorative justice, was squandered on what is essentially corporate welfare.

It is tragic that an image that sticks in the minds of many TV viewers is the "looter" walking out of a store with a case of beer or a boom box in the few days after Katrina. These viewers miss the more complex issues that remain invisible in the mainstream media. This is the tragic story of the ongoing plunder of billions of dollars by rapacious capitalists, while real grassroots recovery receives sadly inadequate funding.

The Environmental Crisis in New Orleans

The criminal negligence of the federal government in its levee design policies has become blatantly evident, as careful analysis of the disaster has progressed over the past months. Corps of Engineers commander Lieutenant General Strock told Congress that that the levees were designed to protect the city from a category 3 storm but not a category 4 storm such as Katrina.[26] In fact, Katrina turned out to be a strong category 3 storm, and the Corp did not protect it from a storm at that level either. However, whatever the intensity of Katrina the general's statement is in itself damning, since the charge of the Corps has been to protect the city from catastrophic flooding, yet it indicates that the Corps had no plans to protect the city from inevitable category four or five hurricanes, which are becoming increasingly more likely in view of global warming and generally increased storm activity. In fact, the Corps's "Standard Project Hurricane," which is defined as "the most severe storm that is considered reasonably characteristic of a region" was based on ridiculously obsolete data and assumed a level of storm activity that had already been exceeded several times in very recent Gulf Coast climatic history. However, the effects of Hurricane Katrina itself we now know were only those of a low category three hurricane. So the Corps not only failed to prepare for the climatic realities of the region, but also failed to achieve even the inadequate protection that it claimed to have as its goal.

On April 5, General Strock told the United States Senate Subcommittee on Energy and Water: "We have now concluded we had problems with the design of the structure."[27] This ludicrously ironic understatement is not much of a concession, given the level of negligence and malfeasance by the Corps and the enormity of the resulting disaster. Studies based on information that has long been available now show numerous design flaws in many levees. To mention only the most outrageous one, the Corps designed levees in which sheet metal extended only a short distance down into layers of sand that were susceptible to seepage and undermining by canal water, rather than using longer sheets that would have reached a layer of impervious clay.

While Strock and the Corps continue to claim that such problems didn't come to light prior to Katrina, in reality, studies by the Corps as early as 1986 suggested the possibility of failure based on inadequate wall design. Anyone interested in the details of the greatest engineering disaster in US history should read Ivor van Heerden's excellent analysis *The Storm*, which presents all the shocking details.[28] It is clear that the Corps of Engineers, in alliance with its corporate contractors, caused the Katrina disaster through its malfeasance, and thus the federal government should be fully liable for damages to the lives and property of the victims.

Evidence of the role of wetland loss in the disaster is also now quite clear. If we still had the wetlands that existed fifty years ago and that have been destroyed in the pursuit of maximizing economic exploitation, flooding from Hurricane Katrina resulting from the storm surge from the south and east would have been, at worst, moderate rather than catastrophic. It is now known that the Mississippi River Gulf Outlet (MRGO), which was constructed at a huge cost to benefit a few corporations, has eaten up an enormous expanse of wetlands and during Katrina acted as a funnel for storm surge, and vastly increased devastation and deaths. However, the greatest single factor in overall wetlands loss has been the canalization of coastal areas by the oil industry to support drilling and movement of equipment.

Over two thousand square miles of wetlands, an area the size of the state of Delaware, have been lost in the last half century as the result of this activity. On the other hand, in the same period the oil industry has produced tens of billions of barrels of oil on Louisiana's coastline and in its offshore waters. Enormous wealth has been generated for the national and global economies; however, Louisiana has on balance reaped few economic benefits, while suffering the consequences of massive pollution, destruction of the natural beauty of coastal areas, and the loss of its natural protection from hurricane disasters. There is an enormous issue of restorative justice here. Justice requires minimally that the oil industry be required to undo the harm that it has inflicted on Louisiana in the course of its reckless pursuit of profit by underwriting a significant portion of the cost of restoration programs.

A viable plan to restore Louisiana's coastline has long existed, and its price tag has been estimated at $14 billion, a small fraction of the $200 to $300 billion estimated cost of Hurricane Katrina's damage. Van Heerden estimates that a comprehensive program to build effective levees and flood gates and also to restore wetlands would cost a total of $30 billion. In September 2005, newspapers featured a headline announcing the Bush administration's proposal for $250 million for wetlands restoration. Perhaps many readers thought that this was a generous step in the right direction, but what most of them did not grasp was that this allocation was less than 1 percent of the total funds needed to restore our wetlands and complete the public works projects necessary to protect the region. In view of the responsibility of the federal government for creating the disaster, such a level of response is grotesque.

Mike Tidwell, author of *Bayou Farewell*,[29] has been one of the few commentators to describe our current dilemma with stark clarity: "To encourage people to return to New Orleans, as Bush is doing, without funding the only plan that can save the city from the next Big One is to commit an act of mass homicide."[30]

Mutual Aid and Solidarity in New Orleans

At the same time that the state and corporate capitalism have shown their ineptitude in confronting our fundamental social and ecological problems, the grassroots recovery movement has continued to show its strength, its effectiveness, and its positive vision for the future. Most importantly, within this large and diverse movement, some have begun to lay the foundation for a participatory, democratically self-managed community based on mutual aid and solidarity.

The Common Ground Collective has been at the heart of this recovery movement from the beginning, and has been the major force within it that has focused on putting a transformative vision into practice. Common Ground was founded in the Algiers neighborhood of New Orleans only one week after Hurricane Katrina, when, according to a now legendary account, three friends sitting around a kitchen table, with only a cell phone, $50, and their own energy, imagination, and compassion to work with, decided to take direct action to save the community.[31] The former Black Panther leader and longtime Green activist Malik Rahim is one of Common Ground's strongest guiding spirits and its main visionary. Malik's vision includes not only the immediate disaster relief and first response for which Common Ground initially became well known, but also more far-reaching programs such as sustainable and environmentally sound rebuilding and a solidarity economy based on workers' cooperatives and other forms of mutual aid.

Over eight thousand volunteers have participated in Common Ground's projects over the nine months since Katrina, and its aid programs have helped eighty thousand people.[32] Common Ground volunteers range from students who have come for a week at Thanksgiving or spring break to long-term relief workers who have stayed for months or even moved to New Orleans for long periods to work as permanent staff members. In March alone, 2,600 volunteers from 220 colleges, fifty states, and at least eight countries came to work with Common Ground. During that single month volunteers gutted 232 houses, four schools and one church. This work alone saved the community and residents the equivalent of $1.5 million in paid labor.

Common Ground is now an important presence in a number of neighborhoods and has instituted a wide spectrum of programs to serve diverse needs of the community. Its main center has moved three times to accommodate its rapidly expanding activities and is now located at St. Mary of the Angels School in the city's ravaged Ninth Ward. Every classroom in the school building is filled with cots and the center can now house up to five hundred volunteers at one time. Common Ground operates several distribution centers, two media centers, a women's center, a community kitchen, several clinics, and various sites for housing volunteers. Its current projects include house gutting, mold abatement, roof tarping, tree removal, temporary housing, safety and health training, a community newspaper, community radio, bioremediation, a biodiesel program, computer classes, childcare co-ops, worker co-ops, legal assistance, eviction defense, prisoner support, after-school and summer programs, antiracism training, and wetlands restoration work.

Portraits of Tragedy and Hope

Francesco di Santis is an "embedded artist," "visual folklorist," and longtime Common Ground volunteer. He arrived in New Orleans on September 11, 2005, less than two weeks after Hurricane Katrina, and I met him a week later on Desire Street. He had already begun talking to survivors, evacuees, and volunteers and sketching their portraits. He went on to create the "Post-Katrina Portrait Story Project," a collection of over a thousand powerful and expressive portraits, on each of which the survivor or volunteer has written his or her story. The project became one of the official projects of the Common Ground Collective, and collections of portraits could be found on the walls of various Common Ground sites. Francesco also put hundreds of pages of these images and texts online.[33]

Francesco's work is a beautiful and eloquent expression of communitarian anarchist values of communal solidarity and voluntary cooperation based on mutual aid. In the foreword to the collection, he describes the outlook that guided his project:

> Respecting the heritage of those displaced or dispossessed by disaster is mandatory for disaster relief work. Awareness of regionality is a crucial dimension of politics. . . . New Orleanians in particular tend to have a very strong sense of neighborhood and local culture sadly lacking in lands overtaken by suburban and ex-urban sprawl, car culture, corporate monoculture and mass media consolidation. And recognizing this upon arrival won my heart over.[34]

Even a few brief excerpts from the Portrait Story Project say more than many pages of analysis possibly could about tragedy and hope, trauma and transcendence, and the practical meaning of "disaster anarchism."

Many passages in the Portraits evoke the experience called "the Dark Night of the Soul," the descent into the depths of one's being that for ages has been seen as the harbinger of spiritual rebirth and awakening. A volunteer relates such an experience powerfully, strikingly juxtaposing images of darkness and light, waking and reawakening. "At night, it gets dark. Darker than I ever knew a city could become. Now the stars can finally be seen. Last night, I woke to the shaking of my room. The walls were rattling and the whole house moved. I clung to my bed. The earth was quaking and I thought, 'this is it.' Pieces of the world were coming apart and I tried to grasp onto the remaining fragments of reality—before it was all gone. I woke again." It is an experience of the world coming apart.

A survivor tells of the trauma of her waking nightmare:

> You are looking at the face of a traumatized Katrina survivor! Katrina came and uprooted my family and community like a thief in the night. Been to so many places. You can never know what it was like for me and my child to see everything disappear right in front of our faces. The media lies! So did the people that told me they were taking me somewhere safe, but instead tossed us under a bridge, held at gunpoint without food or water for days on end. I WAS LIED TO when they told me my child and I would be transported to the same place—they lied and separated us.

It is an experience of the seeming disappearance of everything.

Other passages recount the traumatic confrontation with death or the threat of death, along with the disintegration of everyday normality. A volunteer at Charity Hospital describes his horror at finding a Katrina diary written on a marker board in the flooded hospital during the first days after the flood. The tone of the entries by the trapped survivors changes from hopeful expectation the first day to panic and despair by the sixth. "Day 1: We are all ok. . . . Day 2: We are all ok. . . . Day 3: Help is on the way. . . . Day 4: Where is the help? . . . Day 5: Bodies *floating in the water!* WHERE IS THE HELP? . . . Day 6: WE ARE ALL GOING TO DIE!!" It is the experience of the reality of mortality and abandonment.

The Portraits are the story of this trauma. But their deepest and most pervasive message concerns what emerged from this devastating, disorientating experience. As Hegel teaches, the confrontation with contingency and death can free one from the empire of the everyday. It can allow a distracted and superficial everyday self to recognize, to respond to, and to give way to a larger reality.

The woman who was mistreated and separated from her child moved beyond the trauma to activism. She says in the end: "this is my home. I want to return to and give back to and help rebuild my community. My name is Miss Donna and I am a survivor of Katrina, the U.S. gov't, FEMA & media." Miss Donna went on to become a key figure in Common Ground and to coordinate its Women's Center. Similarly, the Charity Hospital volunteer responded to his encounter with human tragedy with resolution to help. He says that the thought of the desperation experienced by the flood victims still moves him to tears, but "this is why I'm still here!"

Repeatedly, one finds images of awakening, and references to a new awareness. A survivor says: "My eyes have been opened wide to those of you who have come from afar to help us. I see your eyes open to us and our lives. I see the hope and promise of a new day." A volunteer says: "There is something special about living in a disaster zone. I would explain it as a change in the perception of reality. Mundane events become far more meaningful." The extraordinary, the marvelous, and even the miraculous are found at the heart of the ordinary.

A photographer from the mainstream media writes of "working in a devastated area in the Ninth Ward," and of finding realities beyond the reach of that mainstream. "I realized that I was in a place that had been invisible to me, the rest of white America, and to the world before Katrina tore the lid off it." He was one of many volunteers who was haunted by his experience, and irresistibly drawn back to New Orleans. "I came back in December because I did not want the darkness and neglect, my own and everyone else's, to descend on this place again."

A volunteer who had previously worked with the Red Cross writes of her experience of personal and political change. She says that in working with Common Ground she found "authenticity" and "a model of people being the power instead of the bureaucracy." She says: "This one week experience struck me so much that for three months at home I just wanted to come back." She returned, and is moved by "seeing flowers and birds coming back literally and figuratively." She concludes that "out of deep hurt can come beautiful transformation personally and collectively." Many volunteers expressed such a feeling of engagement with people and communities, and with their needs, their problems, and their possibilities. They began to realize that such active involvement was something that they had consciously or unconsciously longed for. I spoke to a nurse with Common Ground Health Clinic who said that she had been waiting all of her professional life for this experience.

Volunteers and survivors often described the experience of a break with conventional reality, and the emergence of a new time and space of possibility. A volunteer who rushed from the Aegean coast immediately after Katrina, says that he learned that "what matters most" in the wake of Katrina is that there was a "system crack" in which new realities had become possible. As a result of this "crack" or break, "we now have the chance to help enact a transformation." He, like many, found that in the midst of disaster there is a reappearance of the outside, that powerful otherness that challenges the official reality and creates previously unimaginable possibilities. He found renewed faith in the possibility of widespread social change, as he imagined the effects of "all points radiating out from this our swampy heaven."

One survivor, in the midst of suffering and disaster, was able to say: "I have had and am having one of the greatest experiences ever," and, of her still largely destroyed city: "I love this place!" Similar sentiments were expressed by many. What such often-expressed sentiments signify is, in part, that out of disaster has come an ability to experience the beauty, the wonder, and the sacredness of the place, and of the people of the place. Once again, perhaps for the first time since the enchanted world of childhood, one achieves the capacity to perceive the extraordinary within the ordinary. The trivial aspects of life are pushed to the side and one appreciates the intrinsic value of persons and things. Such sentiments are also a response to qualitatively different forms of activity that had begun to take place in that place. One could become deeply immersed in action that expresses values such as mutual aid, solidarity, love of the community, compassion, sharing, the spirit of the gift, equality, antihierarchy, the quest for justice, and outrage against the manifold abuses of racism, capitalism, sexism, authoritarianism, bureaucratism, and all forms of oppression, exploitation, and domination. One could experience one's own activity as intrinsically valuable.

After an account of desperate and often frustrating struggles against overwhelming challenges, one volunteer concluded that "a revolution is being born." This is easy to dismiss as hyperbole, the naïve enthusiasm of someone caught up in the moment. But that's precisely the point. There is a transformative moment that can become a powerful reality, if one has the negative capability to be caught up in it. It becomes the decisive moment, the moment of insight. It becomes the revolutionary moment, the moment in which things begin to turn around. The crucial question is whether this moment will lead to many other such moments. The answer is in the lives of the thousands who were caught up in those moments. Who knows where they will lead? How caught up are they?

There are hints about the extent of such possibilities. Sometime after Katrina, a young woman from Romania contacted me, saying mysteriously that she was on her way to New Orleans from England, that she needed to talk to me, and that she would tell me why when she got here. When we met, she told me that she had been a student in Oxford, and her room-mate there had been a volunteer in New Orleans after Katrina, and had spoken very movingly to her of that experience. She said that she did not want to return to Romania, and that she felt that England was spiritually dead. She had crossed the ocean looking for spiritual life, for meaning-ful engagement in the world. What she had heard about post-Katrina New Orleans had inspired her. She decided that she had a vocation here, perhaps to study philosophy, but above all to become immersed in the life of the community and to serve it.

I don't know what she is doing now, but her story is only one of many like it. The best are full of passionate intensity! There is a convergence of such stories, in which a personal quest becomes more and more a collective reality. There develops (in Proudhon's words) a *force collective*, which is also a *force imaginaire*. It draws together many in whom dwells (to use Landauer's words) the same spirit. It makes possible the impossible community.

The few excerpts from the Portraits quoted here only begin to convey the depth, the beauty, the humanity, and the spirit of hope expressed in these works. What they and many similar experiences show is that the trauma of disaster can lead in very divergent directions. One direction is the "disaster capitalism" that is exhibited in rampant profiteering, exploita-tion of migrants and other workers, and predatory development projects. Another is the "disaster fascism" that is manifested in police brutality, racist stereotyping of survivors, and ethnic cleansing of neighborhoods and communities. In a certain sense, both of these developments are merely an extrapolation and intensification of business as usual.

But finally, there is a "disaster anarchism" that breaks radically with this ordinary course of things. It consists of an extraordinary flourishing of love, compassion, solidarity, mutual aid, and voluntary cooperation. Within it there emerges a strong sense of the possibility of a qualitatively different way of life, through the actual experience of that other way of living. Through crisis, people are shocked into a renewed awareness of their shared humanity, of what is, on the deepest existential level, of most value to them as human beings. They grasp the simple truth that the young Marx expressed so well when he said that the "greatest wealth" for the human being is "the other human being."

As a well-worn cliché tells us, crisis is a time of both danger and opportunity. The danger lies in the familiar depredations of disaster capitalism and disaster fascism. The opportunity lies in the often neglected possibilities of transformative disaster anarchism.

9

The Common Good: Sarvodaya and the Gandhian Legacy

The Sarvodaya Movement in India

One of the most brilliant and powerful diagnoses of the tragedies and contradictions of what is called "development" is Arundhati Roy's article "The Greater Common Good."[1] In it, she delineates the catastrophic effects of the dam-building program in India that has constructed four thousand dams while displacing perhaps forty million people. This vast undertaking has benefitted some, most particularly the more powerful and the more affluent. But their gain has been at the expense of the poorest and the most oppressed, and above all, the *adivasi*, or tribal people of India. These victims of maldevelopment have seen only growing immiseration and deracination, as their traditional communities and forms of livelihood have been destroyed. All this devastation has been carried out, Roy observes sardonically, in the name of "the greater common good." Her account of this tragedy impels us to think about the meaning of concepts such as "common" and "good," and the ways that they are at the center of global struggles everywhere today.

Looming in the background of the struggle in India over dams and displacement are the towering figures of Mohandas Gandhi, the "Father of the Indian Nation," and Jawaharlal Nehru, the first prime minister of India and the founder of a powerful political dynasty. Roy cites the famous dictum of Nehru that "Dams Are the Temples of Modern India." This is a telling pronouncement, one of those rare occasions when power speaks truth to everyone else, revealing much more than it intended. What it betrays in this particular case is that the global struggles over "the common" and "the good" are struggles over what we hold to be most sacred. To use Kantian terminology, they are struggles over what we see as being beyond mere price and as having a higher dignity. For Nehru, the sacred was embodied above all in the massive infrastructure of the industrializing economy. For Gandhi, it dwelled in the life activity of the seven hundred thousand villages of India that for him constituted the true "India," the Indian nation as a community of communities.

However, this traditional world of the village was destined to become marginalized, to become "the part of no part," the constitutive exception to Nehru's triumphant "Modern India." It is a hardly trivial exception, since it still makes up nearly two-thirds of India. And it has reproduced its exceptionality on a massive scale in the urban "villages that are no villages" of today into which so many displaced rural people have crowded. These are the sprawling, densely packed slum villages of the megalopolises, the villages of shacks and makeshift huts, the roadside villages of tarp dwellings, the open-air villages of sidewalk-dwellers and roof-dwellers. These urban villages, like their neglected counterparts across the Indian countryside, have never gotten the message that "the world is flat" and that the bounty of equal opportunity capitalism is now trickling down upon them.[2]

Today, there is no official debate about which temples are appropriate for globalized humanity. According to the dominant consensus, it is assumed that all must worship at the altar of Superpower, and that its temples are not only its megadams, but also its skyscrapers, its nuclear reactors, its industrial "parks," its hypermalls, its military installations, and its supertankers. The only remaining question, at least for the officials and the opinion-makers, is the degree to which these temples should be administered by the state, by the corporations, or by an alliance between the two. However, "on the ground," where people actually live, the debate is not over. *Arche*, the realm of domination, is certainly dominant, but the Gandhian legacy lives on in community-based movements for radical decentralization, grassroots participatory democracy, the solidarity economy, and the defense of land and place. It is time to reexamine the roots of this tradition.

The Gandhian movement is called *Sarvodaya*. Literally, this means "the welfare of all." However, it would not be incorrect to say that its deepest meaning is the "common good," in the ethical sense of that term. The Gandhian tradition opposes a radically libertarian and communitarian conception of this common good to the dominant one that identifies it with the demands of economic and political power, and with the logic of instrumental rationality. In some ways, the entire global struggle today between local communities and hierarchical systems of power reflects this opposition, and might still be symbolized by these emblematic figures of Gandhi and Nehru.

The Roots of Revolution

One of the cardinal principles of Sarvodaya is *swadeshi*, or devotion to one's land. Swadeshi is usually identified with the idea of economic self-sufficiency, as exemplified by Gandhi's anticolonial campaign against imports from England, and by his movement for village economic self-reliance. However, as historically significant as these applications have been, the concept has much wider implications. As Gandhi stated it, swadeshi implies that "I should make use of the indigenous institutions and serve them by curing them of their proved defects."[3] Gandhi taught, in accord with this principle, that one should work with, develop, and improve indigenous cultural and spiritual traditions, traditional participatory political practices, and deeply rooted, local forms of production. In Hegelian terms, Gandhianism presupposes that there is an invaluable reservoir of ethical substantiality upon which the movement for liberation can draw. Social transformation today thus has a material and historical basis in existing values, ideals, practices, and institutions. Such transformation is at once a form of radical social revolution and a form of organic social evolution, synthesizing a radical break with the system of domination in the major spheres of institutions, ideology, imaginary, ethos, and materiality, with a radical continuity in all these spheres, stemming from the community's deep roots in the Earth, the land, and in its own history. *Sarvodaya* is therefore a libertarian, communitarian vision of the quest for Another World (*altermondialisme* in the strongest sense of the term), a seemingly impossible world, which, like the Impossible Community, is in fact *possible*, because it is and has been in so many ways *actual*.

An example of Gandhian radicalism as rootedness is offered by its relation to the ancient institution of the *chaupal*. The chaupal is a traditional space in the Indian village that is sacred, common, and open to all. Pranaw Jha summarizes its basic characteristics as follows:

> [The *chaupal* is] a common place . . . owned by the all villagers . . .
> No individual or family can claim to have the individual ownership
> of the place identified as *chaupal*. It is a place where villagers of
> all rank, age, castes, and faith sit together and discuss serious and
> non-serious issues. It is a place where usually the village elders

and traditional panches[4] sit to solve the individual or communal disputes. Sometimes the *chaupal* has no fixed venue. The place where the village elders and panches sit to sort out some disputes or to take some collective decisions for the welfare of the villagers is called the *chaupal*.[5]

Jha notes that the chaupal has had many uses, including educational activities, religious rituals, shamanic rites, and healing processes. However, there is one quality shared by all forms: "It is open for everybody."[6]

Jha claims that Gandhi's whole program of *swaraj* or local autonomy is rooted in the tradition of chaupal, in that it is based on the active, direct participation of all in the life of the village community. Moreover, many other aspects of Sarvodaya, the "*ashrams* and camps," the "*khadi* spinning and weaving centers," and the "prayers and meetings and dining" were all to take place "in a *chaupal* like atmosphere."[7] This exemplifies the fact that the Gandhian movement has been much more than a break with or reactive response to the dominant imperial system. Rather, it has been a positive development of underlying indigenous traditions and practices upon which the imperial system was superimposed. It has also not been a mere return to and reaffirmation of what had been suppressed by empire. Rather, it has been a radicalization of traditional institutions so that they could take on liberatory forms that had never before been achieved.

Gandhian Anarchism

The fact that Sarvodaya is firmly rooted in Indian traditions is perhaps less surprising than the degree to which it is rooted quite specifically in the anarchist tradition. It will therefore be useful to focus in some detail on its explicitly anarchistic dimensions. The depth of the anarchist roots of Sarvodaya are seldom appreciated even by its many anarchist admirers. Yet it would not be an exaggeration to describe it as the largest movement of anarchist inspiration since the destruction of the Spanish anarchist organizations at the end of the Spanish Civil War. Thomas Vettickal, in one of the most comprehensive studies of the movement, summarizes Gandhi's ultimate goal for India as an anarchist society "in which there would be no state, no private property, no police, no military, no law courts and no organized religion." He concludes that "the pure ideal of Gandhi is an ideal of philosophical anarchism, a stateless, classless society marked by voluntary cooperation."[8] There is abundant evidence for this conclusion, in the ideas of Gandhi himself, in those of his foremost successor, Vinoba Bhave, and in many aspects of the Sarvodaya movement's organizational structure and practice.

Ostergaard and Currell, in one of the most comprehensive studies of Sarvodaya, state that though they conceptualize the movement as "an Indian version of anarchism," it might also be thought of as "an Indian expression of 'communitarian socialism.'"[9] It follows that one might also describe it as "communitarian anarchism." They point out many areas of convergence and a few points of divergence between Sarvodaya and traditional Western anarchism. Common points include a rejection of private property, the ideal of synthesizing freedom and equality, an affirmation of the dignity and value of all forms of work, a belief in political and economic decentralization, stress on the centrality of the local community and assembly, the rejection of parliamentary politics and representative government, and support for direct action by the people. They also mention some ways in which Sarvodaya diverges from many forms of Western anarchism, including the central place that the former accords to religion and spirituality, its often extreme asceticism, the place of nonviolence in its worldview, its focus on the immediate realization of a radically transformed way of life, and its willingness to tolerate existing institutions as the new society progressively grows and replaces them.[10]

Most of these points of difference do not make Sarvodaya any less anarchistic. They do, however, show that it is closer in many ways to the communitarian anarchism of Landauer and the position of many so-called utopian socialists than it is to the better-known forms of Western anarchism (e.g., Proudhon's mutualism, Bakunin's collectivism, and anarcho-syndicalism). One can see a striking similarity to many of Landauer's ideas, such as his emphasis on the centrality of spirit in social transformation, his belief in social change through cooperative experiments, and his focus on the immediate creation of a sphere of nondominating, nonexploitative, nonstatist relationships. Landauer's conception of revolutionary practice has much in common with Gandhi's program of direct action through assertive satyagraha and the creation of positive cooperative alternatives. Landauer's best-known idea, that of displacing the state progressively through the creation of nonstatist relationships, parallels Gandhi's idea of replacing the state with a growing sphere of Sarvodaya organizations and villages. A significant point of divergence is Gandhi's promotion of extreme asceticism (which, it should be noted, came in for considerable criticism within the Gandhian movement itself at an early date). Landauer's communitarianism, like Sarvodaya, emphasizes the importance of dedicated work and constructive activity, but it also places much more emphasis on the need for an affirmative ethos of joy and personal fulfillment.

Gandhian Antistatism

The popular image of the Gandhian movement as being primarily a form of struggle for national liberation and independence is a serious misconception. It is, of course, true that one of the movement's central goals was the deliverance of India from British imperial domination. However, its ultimate purpose was far from the creation and perpetuation of an Indian nation-state, much less the nationalistic glorification of such a state. In reality, the central focus of Gandhianism is on replacing the centralized nation-state with a decentralized society consisting of free, self-managed communities working together through voluntary cooperation. As Vinoba states, "where the power is centralized, democracy in the true sense cannot function properly."[11] According to Gandhi, *swaraj*, or self-rule, "means continuous effort to be independent of government control, whether it is foreign government or whether it is national."[12] Thus, the questioning of the very form of the centralized nation-state is intrinsic to the Gandhian political outlook.

Gandhian antistatism, though not widely understood, follows directly from what is perhaps the best-known tenet of the Gandhian philosophy, the principle of ahimsa, or nonviolence. As Ostergaard and Currell point out, "the anarchism of Sarvodaya is, in fact, arrived at largely, if not wholly, by spelling out the social and political implications of Gandhi's re-interpretation of the principle of Non-violence."[13] Gandhi emphasized the obvious (but commonly repressed) truth that if violence is a great evil, then there is no greater social evil than the centralized state, the systematic organization of massive force and violence. In Gandhi's words, "the State represents violence in an organized and concentrated form. The individual has a soul, but as the State is a soulless machine, it can never be weaned from violence to which it owes its very existence."[14] For Gandhi, the alternative to such concentrated violence and coercion is a system of noncoercive, voluntary cooperation, that is, "anarchy." Accordingly, he states, echoing Thoreau, "that State will be the best governed which is governed the least," and defines "the ideally non-violent State" as "an ordered anarchy."[15]

Gandhi also shares the anarchist tradition's deep skepticism concerning political parties and party politics. His "Last Will and Testament," written just the day before he was assassinated, is an astounding document in which he advocates a radical change of direction for the Congress Party, the dominant political force in newly independent India. He proposed to "disband the existing Congress organization" so that it would "flower into a *Lok Sevak Sangh.*" This means that it would transform itself into an association for the service of the people that would promote the far-reaching Sarvodaya program in each village, rather than focusing on electoral politics. He sees this service as including such endeavors as the promotion of racial, religious, and sexual equality, local self-reliance, and universal education, and that this would be the primary work of the movement.[16]

Gandhi's successor, Vinoba Bhave, held such antistatist convictions at least as vehemently as did Gandhi himself. Vinoba judges that "if the world is afflicted with any malady, it is that of government."[17] Sarvodaya envisions, he says, "a social order which will be free not only from every form of exploitation but also from every form of governmental authority."[18] He qualifies this by explaining that for the foreseeable future this will mean primarily the abolition of centralized government. "The powers of the Government," he says, "will be decentralized and distributed among the villages. Every village will be a state in itself; the center will have only nominal authority over them."[19] However, for Vinoba also, the long-range goal is a radically anarchistic one—not only the withering away of the centralized state, but an end to all governmental authority, at every level. He foresees that "gradually, we shall reach a stage when authority in every form will have become unnecessary and will therefore fade away, giving rise to a perfectly free society."[20]

Vinoba seeks to rehabilitate the concept of "anarchy" as the alternative to statism, and to combat the negative use of that term. He notes that "administrators have spread fear of anarchy everywhere in order to make people submit meekly to their rule, however bad it may be," and remarks that if the state "produces economic inequality, it will be right to destroy it and to establish anarchy."[21] He is particularly critical of the evils of government bureaucracy, no doubt partly in reaction to the strongly statist direction the Indian regime took after independence. He judges that "the chief cause of all the turmoil and unrest found in the world is the managerial class,"[22] and that "the present democracy is a slave of bureaucracy."[23] Vinoba, like Gandhi, is thus very clear about the meaning of Sarvodaya's anarchism: it is a movement for power at the base, in the local communities and workplaces of India, and a movement against domination, in the form of concentrated economic power, and the power of the violent, centralized bureaucratic state.

Satyagraha as Revolutionary Direct Action

The famous guiding principle of Gandhian social struggle is satyagraha. The term comes from the roots *satya*, which means "truth," and *agraha*, which means "firmness," "insistence," or "holding to." Gandhi also described it as "love force" or "soul force." He stresses that it is the opposite of "passive resistance," in that it is an active and affirmative force for truth and justice. He recognizes its connection with Thoreau's concept of "civil disobedience," which strongly influenced him, though he says that he began to develop his concept before he discovered Thoreau's ideas. He observes that it might also be called "civil resistance." Satyagraha has many links with the anarchist tradition of direct action, and makes a major contribution to that tradition. Some forms of anarchist direct action have been criticized for exhibiting tendencies toward individualism, adventurism, and machismo. Satyagraha shows that uncompromising direct action does not have to fall into any of these traps, and offers a powerful historical example of direct action that is community-based and grounded in careful reflection on the common good.

Gandhi holds that satyagraha is effective because it awakens the community to the enormous reserve of power that it possesses but ordinarily fails to recognize. He echoes the great libertarian thinker Étienne de la Boétie, who in his *Discourse on Voluntary Servitude* explained that the few who monopolize concentrated power can only do so with the tacit acceptance, and, indeed, active cooperation of the vast majority who unwittingly alienate that power to them.[24] According to Gandhi, "The rich cannot accumulate wealth without the co-operation of the poor in society. If this knowledge were to penetrate to and spread amongst the poor, they would become strong and would learn how to free themselves by means of non-violence from the crushing inequalities which have brought them to the verge of starvation."[25] It is this belief in the vast power of an activated, solidaristic community that is the basis for the Gandhian commitment to revolutionary direct action.

Satygraha is often defined as "nonviolent action," and this certainly describes much of what it means in practice. However, it is not *identical* with nonviolence, and it would be a mistake to identify it with dogmatic, absolutist pacifism. Gandhi certainly taught that the most diligent pursuit of peace, nonviolence, and a noncoercive society was central to the idea of *sarvodaya*. However, he realized there are cases in which violence is the only means of minimizing coercion and harm. For example, he concedes that in the short term a village might have to accept paying taxes to a coercive centralized state, even while working to create a nonviolent, nonstatist world. This is, in effect, a compromise with massive organized violence (a fact that is seldom recognized by most nonviolence advocates who habitually fund large-scale violence). In the following passage, Gandhi also concedes that there are cases in which individual acts of violence are justified. He states, for example, that:

> I do believe that where there is only a choice between cowardice and violence I would advise violence. Thus when my eldest son asked me what he should have done, had he been present when I was almost fatally assaulted in 1908, whether he should have run away and seen me killed or whether he should have used his physical force which he could and wanted to use, and defended me, I told him that it was his duty to defend me even by using violence. . . . I would rather have India resort to arms in order to defend her honor than that she should in a cowardly manner become or remain a helpless witness to her own dishonor.[26]

Arundhati Roy has commented aptly on the inapplicability of "Gandhian nonviolence" in the case of tribal people of the forests who have recently been attacked by tens of thousands of paramilitary troops. They have been subjected to mass slaughter, rapes, and the burning of their villages. Roy asks rhetorically whether these impoverished, oppressed, malnourished people should perhaps stage a hunger strike. She adds that if they did undertake such a futile strategy, there would be no mass media lurking around in the forest to report it to the public. Roy's point is, of course, well taken. Nonviolence is a powerful strategy (and, indeed, much more than a strategy), but there are times when it will result in more violence taking place than if violence is used to prevent that greater violence. A strong case can be made that Gandhi's own principles can be used to reject a rigid adherence to "Gandhian nonviolence" in many such situations.

Swaraj and the Structure of Communal Autonomy

The pivotal Gandhian concept of swaraj means self-rule or self-management. In the context of Sarvodaya it means direct action embodied in
communal practices and institutions. In his most detailed concise expression of the meaning of swaraj, Gandhi outlines a vision of a relatively
autonomous village republic. It is only "relatively autonomous" primarily
because of the extent to which it must, for the near future, operate within
the confines of the existing nation-state. However, Gandhi observes, "any
village can become such a republic today without much interference even
from the present Government, whose sole effective connection with the
villages is the exaction of the village revenue."[27] Beyond paying this tribute
to whatever remains of the system of domination, the village can make
far-reaching advances toward becoming a free, self-governing, relatively
self-sufficient, cooperative community. As Gandhi describes it:

> My idea of Village Swaraj is that it is a complete republic, independ-
> ent of its neighbors for its own vital wants, and yet interdependent
> for many others in which dependence is a necessity. Thus every
> village's first concern will be to grow its own food crops and cotton
> for its cloth. It should have a reserve for its cattle, recreation and
> playgrounds for adults and children. Then if there is more land avail-
> able, it will grow *useful* money crops, thus excluding *ganja*, tobacco,
> opium and the like. The village will maintain a village theater, school
> and public hall. It will have its own waterworks, ensuring clean
> water supply. This can be done through controlled wells or tanks.
> Education will be compulsory up to the final basic course. As far as
> possible every activity will be conducted on the co-operative basis.[28]

In his description of this village republic, Gandhi focuses on the central
importance of the *panchayat*, or democratic village committee, as an organ
of swaraj. The panchayat consists of a council of five persons responsible for making ongoing decisions about the functioning of the village.
In Gandhi's version, this council, which would be elected annually by
all adults in the village, both male and female, would be the major body
exercising ongoing oversight of the affairs of the community. It will have
"all the authority and jurisdiction" necessary to carry out "the government
of the village" and will in effect be "the legislature, judiciary and executive combined to operate for its year of office."[29] Gandhi believes that
a democratically based, communally responsive panchayat could be a

major step toward a nonviolent cooperative community. He says that "if panchayats could help people avoid disputes and settle them fairly," then villagers "would need neither the police nor the military."[30] His analysis is very much in accord with Landauer's idea that to the extent that we successfully institute cooperative, nonstatist relationships and practices within our communities, the statist relationships of violence and domination can be eliminated.

The panchayat was far from being an invention of the Gandhian movement. Rather, it is a deeply rooted traditional institution with a long history in South Asia. Classically, it was a village council consisting of five elders who mediated disputes between individuals, families, and villages. Today, the panchayat (which often consists of a committee of five within a larger council) is an official part of the Indian political system. There are hundreds of thousands of panchayats operating today in India. However, the Gandhian concept is distinctive, in that quite unlike the situation of today, it would operate within a system in which most political and economic power would have devolved to the level of the local community. The panchayat would thus become a crucial organism in carrying out the will of the community as expressed democratically. For projects at higher levels, there would be second- and third-order panchayats made up of representatives elected by the lower level panchayats.

As important as the panchayat is in Gandhi's vision of swaraj, there is another institution that expresses Sarvodaya's commitment to direct democracy in an even more radical form. Gandhianism proposes that the most important organ of self-rule, the ultimate political authority, should be the *gram sabha* or village assembly. It is the gram sabha that elects the panchayat each year to oversee the ongoing administration of the decisions of the assembly, which are the most direct expression of the power of the community. Vettickal states: "The gram sabha is the basic unit of the edifice of decentralized democracy, not gram panchayat. This gram sabha would be completely autonomous, self-regulating and self-determining in its internal matters and self-sufficient in respect to its essential requirements. The panchayat will be completely subservient to it."[31] Thus, despite the key role of the village council for Sarvodaya, the movement is not in the end an Indian version of "councilism," but rather a more radical vision of participatory direct democracy.

The radically democratic vision of Sarvodaya is able at times to move even beyond the limits of majoritarian democracy. Direct democracy at the level of base organizations is the most fully realized form of democratic decision-making; however, it still entails the evil of the subordination of the minority to the majority. Vinoba, recognizing this problem, argues not only for the most participatory forms of direct democracy, but also for choosing consensus over majority rule whenever possible. He says that majority rule is an idea that has been imported from the West, where it is still considered "progressive." He judges that in reality this form of decision-making is "totally crude," and that "things will go rightly only when we accept the idea of unanimity."[32] He thus remains true to the anarchist ideal of fully voluntary agreement as the ultimate goal, and the standard by which to judge existing institutions.

The Problem of the Transition

One of the most challenging problems for any radically transformative social movement is the creation of intermediary practices and institutions that are capable of successfully taking the steps from what exists to what is hoped for. There must be a plan for effective transitional institutions that are adequate to create the new social order, or the movement's program will collapse into abstract idealism.[33] For the Sarvodaya movement, the panchayat and gram sabha are the primary political organs of the village republic or autonomous grassroots community to come. To a certain degree, the transition can progress as these institutions are established in existing villages and neighborhoods and as they begin to take on increasing power as the movement spreads through the society. However, there has been awareness in the Sarvodaya movement that other additional means toward social transformation will be needed. For Gandhi, the most powerful catalyst for such transformation is the *ashram*. According to Vettickal, "Gandhi's 'experiments with truth' start in the ashrams. Ashrams become the laboratories of experiments: truth, nonviolence, satyagraha, self-reliance, *brahmacharya*."[34]

The goal of the ashram is to initiate and put into practice many of the activities that would be at the heart of the future transformed village community. Thus, it would engage in cooperative production, develop forms of self-sufficiency, utilize humane, participatory forms of technology, such as the *charkha* or spinning wheel, promote the equality of women, reject all remnants of caste distinction, pursue spiritual realization, and, in general, exhibit solidarity and mutual aid in all endeavors. To take one example, the principles of the Satyagraha Ashram, founded May 25,

1915, in Ahmedabad, included vows of truthfulness, nonviolence, celibacy, vegetarianism, nontheft, nonpossession, the wearing of *khadi*, fearlessness, and the rejection of untouchability.[35] Not surprisingly, the requirement of celibacy is disconcerting for most observers today; however, as Vettickal notes, even in Gandhi's day this "created confusion and conflict among his co-workers" and "diverted attention unnecessarily from the main question of village uplift."[36] However, the precise details of the Gandhian version of the transformative base community are not what is most important. The primary lesson to be learned from the ashram is the need to establish small exemplary communities that practice diligently the (probably apocryphal) Gandhian injunction to "be the change you want to see" as a step toward the full realization of the autonomous local community or "Village Republic."

Another important element of the Gandhian strategy for change is the formation of a body of dedicated, trained Sarvodaya workers. The goal was that these workers, called *gram sevaks*, would become numerous enough so that every village could have at least one such full-time activist. Ostergaard and Currell estimate that in the 1960s there were perhaps five thousand permanent, full-time Sarvodaya workers and twenty thousand more who worked for the movement regularly part-time, or full-time for short periods of time.[37] One of the basic problems of an oppositional movement is educating the community and propagating transformative values in a context in which the dominant system has a relative monopoly on education and socialization. It is highly unlikely that purely informal and spontaneous efforts at education will allow a movement to proliferate to the point at which it could challenge the dominant system. The training of such a corps of Sarvodaya workers was a significant step in the direction of the creation of an effective agency of social transformation, and was in part responsible for the movement's success in spreading from village to village. The more general lesson that can be learned from this experience is that the quest for the free community will require many dedicated activists who will make it their vocation, their life's work, to develop skills that will help them facilitate the organization of the affinity groups, base communities, and transformed town and neighborhood communities that will form the fabric of the new society.

A final important Gandhian organizational idea that addresses the question of the transition is the *Shanti Sena*, or Peace Army. This organization consists of a body of volunteers who work for peace and apply nonviolent methods to conflict resolution. By 1969 this organization had twelve thousand members.[38] The Shanti Sena is an attempt to change the nature of everyday practice, to begin at once applying the values of the new society, and to demonstrate that these values are applicable and beneficial even within the existing one. This idea can also act as inspiration for a new libertarian communitarianism. As the free community develops, it will require a large number of community-based activists trained in mediation, conflict resolution, and cooperative decision-making. If we are to follow Landauer's communitarian anarchist vision of replacing all statist, coercive, and authoritarian relationships with cooperative, caring, and loving ones, we will need to put concerted effort into the daunting project of confronting a pervasively violent system of domination, and the effects of violence within our own character-structures. The Gandhian idea that some should engage in special training and devote a significant amount of their time to helping in this process is eminently realistic.

The institution of such roles and institutions as the gram sevak and the Shanti Sena exhibit the Sarvodaya movement's deep understanding of many of the prerequisites for social transformation. There is often in contemporary anarchist movements a neglect of the hard work of forma-tion of activists and movement workers. Such formation might even be questioned, based on a fundamentally valid interest in combating exces-sive division of labor, on a wise concern that essential skills should be dispersed widely throughout the community, and on a healthy fear of the emergence of vanguardism, militantism, and elitism. However, such opposition can also reveal excessive faith in pure spontaneity and an exaggerated individualism, and can itself become a new form of rigid-ity and dogmatism. Marx's nagging question of "who will educate the educators" must be taken very seriously. As Gandhians have recognized, even revolutionaries are, like everyone else, the product of the system of domination that they abhor, and its traces are deeply embedded within their own being. A successful break with that system can only be achieved through diligent collective work of self-transformation and, at times, the development among some of special skills that can contribute to that communal transformation.

Sarvodayan Technology

For Gandhi and Sarvodaya, the question of economy is inseparable from that of technology. Gandhi rightly rejects the ideological conception of a neutral technology that can be a mere means toward any possible social goal. He realizes that some technologies have been developed specifically because they have served the ends of domination and exploitation, and it is far from self-evident that these same technologies would by some miracle be ideally suited for communal autonomy and liberation. Gandhi was not afraid to state his perhaps shocking conclusion that the dominant system of industrial technology had to be abolished. Technology must be returned to the position of being a means, rather than an end in itself. That is, it must become an instrument for nurturing the life and facilitating the self-realization of the person, the family, and the larger community.

The symbol of Gandhi's critique of industrial technology and his vision of a humane, cooperative economy was the *charkha* or spinning wheel. It would be easy to dismiss this concept as a naïve idealization of the past, if one interprets it simplistically as "back to the spinning wheel." However, what is important about this image is not this technological object, narrowly conceived, but the entire system of values that it symbolizes. First, the charkha represented a form of production that was free from the control of empire. British imperial policy demanded that India grow cotton, export it to England, and buy back expensive manufactured fabric. The use of the charka to produce homespun fabric defied this system of colonial exploitation. Second, the charkha represented a form of production that is community-controlled. Production could take place in the village and even in the household, at the sacred hearth that is the antithesis of the accursed empire. Third, spinning can be an intimate communal activity and even a meditative one. Thus, it expresses the need for forms of production that are inherently good for the person and the community, rather than instrumentally valuable for certain powers and authorities. Finally (and this list should not be considered exhaustive), the product of the charkha, *khadi*, or homespun fabric, is good for the community. It is beautiful in its simplicity, it is useful and durable, and it is a powerful expression of the communal imaginary. To wear khadi became a symbol of communal solidarity and participation in the struggle for justice and liberation.

Today, the spinning wheel could not possibly have the imaginary force, even in India, that it did in Gandhi's time. We might say that there is an empty imaginary space that the spinning wheel and khadi once occupied. Vandana Shiva makes a powerful case that today, in the world of TNCs and GMOs, in India, and perhaps in many other places, the seed can now occupy the imaginary space and exercise the imaginary power once possessed by Gandhi's charkha and by the momentous pinch of salt that he collected on his Salt March. In her book *Earth Democracy*, which contains many quotes from Gandhi and ideas of Gandhian inspiration, she says:

> The seed is starting to take shape as the site and symbol of free-dom in the age of manipulation and monopoly of life. The seed is not big and powerful, but can become alive as a sign of resistance and creativity in the smallest of huts or gardens and the poorest of families. In smallness lies power. The seed also embodies diversity. It embodies the freedom to stay alive. Seed freedom goes far beyond the farmer's freedom from corporations. It represents the freedom of diverse cultures from centralized control. In the seed, ecological issues combine with social justice. The seed could play the role of Gandhi's spinning wheel—a symbol of freedom during India's independence movement—in this period of recolonization through free trade.[39]

During the more than seventy years since Gandhi, the possibilities for ecologically sound and socially liberatory technology have expanded greatly. There is no need to adhere dogmatically to his specific proposals (though some still have great value). What is important is the spirit of his ideas, and their underlying rationale, as in the four points just mentioned. This was, in fact, his own advice. He sometimes sounds as doctrinaire a critic of dominant technologies as are the most extreme neo-primitivists. He says that "this industrial civilization is a disease" and that "it is all evil."[40] However, he does not, in fact, hold that each element of the industrial system must necessarily be destroyed. While the assumption of technological neutrality must be thrown out, individual technologies, for example, "steamships and telegraphs" must be considered individually. While "they are in no way indispensable for the permanent welfare of the human race," nevertheless "we should be able to use them on due occasion," provided "we have learnt to avoid industrialism."[41] What is necessary is "to destroy industrialism at any cost."[42] We can translate "industrialism" as "domination by the technological system." In Gandhi's view, many technologies may have to be eliminated, but when power is made democratic and decentralized to the local level, some technologies that have previously been used to dominate and exploit might then be used in some form to serve the common good.

The Sarvodaya Solidarity Economy

The work of the Sarvodaya movement should be recognized as one of the most important chapters in the struggle for economic democracy and the self-managed economy. Its ideal is an economic system in which land is held communally at the local level and in which production is organized through direct democratic decision-making by all the members of the local community and administered by their elected delegates. The limited degree to which that ideal has been realized must be admitted. However, the fact that such ideas were spread widely across a nation of hundreds of millions of people, and that they have been put into practice by many thousands of people on millions of acres of land is an achievement that deserves greater recognition in the history of the cooperative movement and the movement for economic self-management.

Sarvodaya's vision of economic transformation focuses on two key concepts, *bhoodan* and *gramdan*, which developed into guiding ideas of the movement under the influence of Gandhi's successor Vinoba. Bhoodan means "the gift of land." In carrying out the bhoodan program, Sarvodaya workers across India solicited donations of land from those who possess it, for use by the landless and for cooperative cultivation by the village. Bhoodan was to lead ultimately to gramdan, which means "the gift of the village." According to this concept, bhoodan would progress to the point at which at least 70 percent of the people in a village had pooled their land. The common land would then be looked upon as a gift of the community members to the entire village, which would manage it cooperatively under conditions of equality for all.

The achievements of such programs were impressive, and they should be looked upon as a great inspiration for all who believe in cooperative production and the restoration of the commons. By 1970, over half a million donors had given 4.2 million acres for bhoodan, and somewhat over a million acres had been effectively transferred to nearly a half million landless workers. In addition, by about the same time, 140,000 villages, one-fourth of all those in India, had officially declared support for gramdan.[43] But declaring support is not the same as taking serious steps in the direction of achieving it. Ostergaard and Currell report that by 1965 only about five hundred villages had shown significant signs of social transformation, and that by 1970 the situation was much the same.[44] Moreover, while possibly several million acres of redistributed land is an encouraging achievement, it does not add up to a fundamental transformation in a country in which hundreds of millions of people live in poverty, and a large segment of these remain in absolute poverty.

The Sarvodaya strategy for land redistribution became focused almost entirely on a policy called "trusteeship." Gandhi contends that ultimately the wealthy property-owners will have to "make a choice between class war and voluntarily converting themselves into trustees of their wealth."[45] He speculates that they will opt for rationality and fairness and choose trusteeship, a system in which they "would be allowed to retain the stewardship of their possessions and use their talent to increase the wealth, not for their own sakes, but for the sake of the nation and therefore without exploitation."[46] In return for their contribution, "the state would regulate the rate of commission which they would get commensurate with the service rendered and its value to society."[47]

It is largely out of his extreme fear of state power that Gandhi advocated this policy of trusteeship. In his view, "the violence of private ownership" is less dangerous than "the violence of state ownership," though he admitted that if necessary he would "support a minimum of state ownership."[48] There are a number of problems with this strategy. First, relatively few of the wealthy would ever agree to such a voluntary end to exploitation. Second, in an increasingly complex corporate economy, decisions are not in any case made by old-fashioned individual proprietors, but rather by an upper management that has strictly defined "fiduciary" responsibilities that do not include the possibility of giving away the company. Finally, a consistent antistate position would resort to state action at most to facilitate the transfer of control to democratic self-management, rather than proposing an ongoing policy of state micromanagement of economic distribution.

Ostergaard and Currell note that in some ways, as Vinoba made gramdan and bhoodan central to Sarvodaya, he moved it in a more "revolutionary" and "utopian" direction. By proclaiming the ideals of direct democratic decision-making, and the communalization of property "the doctrine has now become an explicit and avowed gospel of revolution, a call for the total reconstruction not only of Indian but of all human society."[49] However, they also note that Vinoba did not "sanction attempts to achieve the movement's objectives by the use of nonviolent resistance on the lines made familiar in Gandhi's Satyagraha campaigns," and that "this eschewal of 'negative' satyagraha (except in limited situations) has enabled the movement to avoid a direct struggle with the existing power-holders."[50]

The result has been a Gandhianism that is perhaps more revolutionary in theory, but decidedly less revolutionary in practice.

The difficulty is that Vinoba "eschewed" precisely the strategies that were so successful in overthrowing the power of the British Empire and achieving independence for India. Abandoning more militant and assertive forms of satyagraha, the movement adopted an ineffective, idealist strategy of appealing moralistically to the new ruling class to voluntarily turn over its wealth and power to the oppressed. In his statements on trusteeship, Gandhi speculated that the rich might be convinced to give up much of their wealth in large part out of self-interest and desire to be part of a better society. However, it is clear that the conditions of trusteeship hardly seem to be enough of an incentive to convince them on grounds of maximizing their own good. After all, the elites were not part of the Gandhian movement, and their lives and values continued to be shaped primarily by the old world of which they remained a part.

Gandhi was moving in a much more realistic direction when he observed, a decade before his statements on trusteeship, that if in militant strikes owners "have to face the destruction wrought by strikers" these owners might be convinced "that they should at once offer the strikers full control of the concern which is as much the strikers as theirs."[51] His point is that the threat of severe losses, or even a pyrrhic victory that would mean economic disaster, might convince the owners to give up control. This is similar to the rationale behind Gandhian campaigns of resistance, noncooperation, boycotts, and blockades under colonialism. In reality, Gandhian tactics that have used such "negative contingencies" have been much more effective than those that have pinned their hopes solely on "positive reinforcement." The two contrasting experiments in Gandhian revolutionary strategy have contributed useful evidence to the inquiry into the relative utility of various practices as means of social transformation. The results of these experiments offer hope that active satyagraha might be effective not only for achieving national liberation and the overthrow of dictatorship, but also for winning the struggle for economic democracy and the self-management of production that is so central to Sarvodaya.

The Gandhian Legacy

Sarvodaya has made an enormous contribution to communitarian anarchism through its notable achievements in creating a sphere of ethical substantiality, by generating liberatory institutional forms and practices that have to a certain degree taken the form of material, historical realities. It also presents a vision of a free, communal society that might fulfill the promise inherent in its inspiring but incomplete experiments. Thus, it has made great advances in the areas of social institutions, the social ethos, and social ideology. In view of its strong traditionalist dimensions, one might question whether it has gone equally far in expressing the radical social imagination. However, in reality, its breakthroughs in the sphere of the social imaginary are quite astounding, if placed in historical context.

Sarvodaya emerged in a society that had been subject to imperial rule by foreign conquerors for centuries, and which was suffering under the weight of both traditional and externally imposed hierarchical institutions. Yet, amazingly early in the twentieth century, Gandhi and the Sarvodaya movement could begin to imagine, and then to begin pursuing as real-world goals, a free India, the abolition of the caste system, active participation of women in decision-making processes, a system of humane and ecologically sound technology, a politics of direct participatory democracy, democratic self-management of production, and a radically decentralized system of power. The inspiring history of Sarvodaya challenges us to carry on its legacy, and by learning from both its achievements and its shortcomings, to discover what the liberation of the radical imagination and the creation of a transformative ethos could mean today. Fortunately, there are those who have taken up this challenge, and carried on the good work of Sarvodaya with very impressive results.

The Sarvodaya Shramadana Movement in Sri Lanka

There is a growing awareness of the failures of the dominant model of development that has been imposed on the global South and a growing movement of opposition to its consequences, which have aptly been labeled "maldevelopment" (though perhaps "malignant growth" would be even more appropriate). We often hear of popular resistance movements, for example, the antidam movement in India or antisweatshop campaigns around the world. Yet with a few notable exceptions, such as the Zapatistas' liberated municipalities, we hear far less about the extensive positive achievements of communities around the world that have found alternatives to the neocolonial, neoliberal development programs of global capital.

If one were to mention that there is a community-based, participatory, ecologically conscious development movement that has involved millions of people in its programs, has engaged participants in close to half of its country's villages, has created more than five thousand preschools, and has established several thousand community banks and savings societies, many, even among those with an interest in global justice, might have some difficulty identifying either this movement or its country in which such things have been achieved. Nevertheless, all this has in fact occurred. The movement is called Sarvodaya Shramadana and the country is Sri Lanka.[52]

Sarvodaya Shramadana is a grassroots development movement founded in 1958 by a high school teacher, Dr. A.T. Ariyaratne. It began when Dr. Ariyaratne recruited a few of his students to organize work camps with the goal of helping people in impoverished villages help themselves provide for their own needs. The movement teaches an impressive lesson concerning the enormous power of a few dedicated people with an extraordinarily good idea. When reading of its history, one is reminded of the project began by Fr. José Maria Arrizmendiarrieta in Mondragon, Spain, in the late 1940s. That project grew from an idea of one visionary person and a few idealistic young people into the world's largest experiment in worker self-management, and the seventh-largest enterprise in Spain.[53] Sarvodaya has grown from similar modest beginnings into a major social force in its country and a powerful example for the rest of the world.

What is distinctive about this most successful of grassroots social movements is that it is at once a politics of material transformation, a politics of community, and a politics of spirituality. The classic work on the relationship between politics and spirituality is Joel Kovel's *History and Spirit*.[54] In that profound work, Kovel explains that spirit concerns "what happens to us when the boundaries of the self give way."[55] It relates to the transformation that occurs when egoic consciousness is overcome through the power of love for the other: for other human beings and for the larger communities of humanity and nature. Such love the power to restore the primordial but broken connection between an abstracted, narrowed self and its larger context in society, nature, and the matrix of being. Such an impulse toward the restoration of wholeness involves the entire person and is necessarily expressed not only in thought and feelings, but also in transformative action. Spirit is thus a revolutionary force. As Kovel states it, "the force of love has a material reality."[56] To the extent that Sarvodaya bases social action on a critique of the egoic self and a practice of engaged compassion and loving kindness, it is to a large degree a case study in the practical application of such profound truths.

Dr. Ariyaratne redefined the Gandhian concept of sarvodaya as "unity of welfare" to stress its character as "the unity of awakening," or "the awakening of all." This redefinition, though entirely consistent with the spirit of the Gandhian conception, reflects more specifically the Buddhist doctrine that the awakening of the person to the reality of the world and the practice of love and compassion that follows from such an awakening is the central challenge for every human being and every human community.

To this extended concept of sarvodaya was added the term *shramadana*. *Shrama* means energy or labor and *dana* means giving or sharing. Shramadana thus means shared labor or collective energy. This concept is also an expression of the core of Buddhist values, since "right livelihood" or good work is one of the points in the Noble Eightfold Path (the core of all Buddhist practice), and the perfection of giving is one of the six *paramitas* (the Buddhist perfections or virtues). The concepts of sarvodaya and shramadana taken together express the aspiration that the awakening of all might be carried out through shared, cooperative labor for the common good.

Awakening: The Theoretical, Ethical, and Spiritual Basis

Although Sarvodaya is inspired by Buddhism, there is active participation in its programs by the Hindu, Muslim, and Christian minorities that together make up almost a third of Sri Lanka's population. This is made possible in large part by the fact that what Sarvodaya takes from Buddhism has nothing to do with sectarian religious dogma or unverifiable beliefs about supernatural realities. Rather it looks to "Buddhism" in the root sense of awakening, a practice that now constitutes a 2,500-year tradition of experience of and experimentation with meditation, non-egocentric thinking, and compassionate action. In accord with this tradition, the movement assumes that success in social transformation depends on success in the practice of personal self-transformation. It applies this practice to contemporary realities such as the pursuit of peace in a society torn by ethnic conflict, and the quest for communal self-determination in a society beset by the neocolonial global economy.

Awakening involves a broad spectrum of values and practices. Dr. Ariyaratne identifies as central values of the movement *dana* (giving or generosity), *sila* (basic morality, which traditionally includes prohibitions against injuring, stealing, lying, exploiting sexually, and dulling one's consciousness), and *samadhi* (concentration or meditation).[57] According to Joanna Macy, one finds "on the lips of every village organizer and painted on the walls of village centers" the Buddhist virtues called the four "Buddha Abodes." These consist of *metta*, or loving kindness and goodwill toward all beings; *karuna*, or compassion for the suffering of all beings; *mudita*, or sympathetic joy for those who are benefited and freed from suffering; and *upekkha*, equanimity or mental balance, which is often thought of as the prerequisite for the others. Macy notes that "every meeting, whether it is a village gathering or a committee on latrines, begins with two minutes of silence for *metta* meditation, extending loving thoughts to all beings."[58]

Some might be tempted to dismiss what Macy describes as a form of naïve idealism in which "sending out good vibes" becomes a substitute for engagement in real social transformation. However, awakening is never seen by Sarvodaya as a mere process of subjective personal change, cut off from material and social reality. It is an *awakening to* the most basic realities that we often ignore in everyday (egocentric, instrumentalizing, objectifying) consciousness. Thus, it implies an acute awareness of basic human needs and the suffering that exists all around us as the result of the neglect of those needs. Sarvodaya recognizes ten such primary needs, which it calls "prerequisites for awakening," and uses them as a point of reference when formulating collective work projects. These needs include material ones for water, clothing, food, health care, housing, and energy; social ones for communication, education, spiritual life, and shared cultural values; and ecological ones for a healthy and beautiful natural environment.

Sarvodaya teaches that the process of awakening and the generous and compassionate action that flows from it begin at the most basic levels of the person and small group and move upward and outward through the various levels of society. According to Dr. Ariyaratne, "personal awakening is seen as being interdependent with the awakening of one's local community, and both play a part in the awakening of one's nation and of the whole world."[59] This approach is in accord with the communitarian principle taught by Landauer and Buber that the only way that a truly cooperative human community can ever exist is as an integral part of a larger cooperative community consisting of many smaller cooperative communities. We might add that it also shows awareness of the need for these smaller communities to be made up of cooperative primary groups and cooperative people, ideas already developed considerably within the Gandhian Sarvodaya movement.

One might in this view find echoes of the simplistic cliché that exhorts us to "think globally, act locally" but for Sarvodaya Shramadana there is a very complex relationship between the local and the global, and there are many significant levels of social reality between the local and the global. The possibility of *vishvodaya* (global awakening) depends on processes of *deshodaya* (national awakening), which depends on *gramodaya* (village awakening) and *nagarodaya* (city awakening), which in turn depend on *kutumbodaya* (family awakening), and ultimately *paurushodaya* (personal awakening). Though Sarvodaya Shramadana may hold that in the last instance the most basic levels of the person and the local community are the most powerful determinants of successful social transformation, there is nevertheless a reciprocal relationship between the levels: no personal awakening can take place without expressing itself in the concerns of the community, no village can achieve awakening without addressing the needs of other villages and confronting national and international issues. Though developing its organization "from the bottom up," Sarvodaya shramadana is a practice of thinking and acting at all levels from the personal and local to the global, from the singular and particular to the universal. What appears at the level of universality cannot be separated from what appears at the levels of singularity and particularity; all is dialectically identical.

Nevertheless, giving and care flowing from basic social and communal ties, compassionate practice rooted in place, lies at the core of Sarvodaya Shramadana. In this, it carries on the values of original Buddhism as part of what both Lewis Mumford and Karl Jaspers called the "Axial Revolt" against the society of the megamachine and the culture of domination.[60] This revolt was a reaction to the exploitation, hierarchy, inequality, and obsession with material accumulation that were expanding rapidly at this stage in human history and undermining earlier communal, egalitarian traditions. The Axial sages looked back not only with a certain nostalgia but also with an awareness of the radically critical import of the values of the tribe and the autonomous Neolithic village, values such as the gift and noncalculating, spontaneous care for the needs of each member of the community. Sarvodaya Shramadana carries on these ancient traditions and demonstrates their relevance today.

The Commonwealth of Villages

Sarvodaya Shramadana explicitly rejects virtually every aspect of the dominant models of development. It expresses an "uncompromising insistence on a form of development which is wholly indigenous" and "comes entirely out of the perceptions of the village community."[61] Lest this be seen as a form of naïve spontaneism, it should be remembered that the institutions and practices of a Sri Lankan village reflect several millennia of highly developed spiritual and ethical practice, and an even longer history of communal self-organization.

Dr. Ariyaratne says that the dominant economic systems today are founded on fallacious, destructive principles concerning land, labor, and capital. He criticizes a commodified view of land that separates it from nature; the reduction of labor to a means of acquiring money; and the dominance of financial capital to the detriment of the social capital (or anticapital) consisting of a wealth of knowledge, skills, and abilities that has in large part been passed on as a gift from prior generations. He notes that in the course of his own political evolution he first adopted ideas of political transformation taken from Western revolutionary theory and Third World movements influenced by the West. After seeing the failures of centralized, state-oriented, technocratic, economistic approaches, he turned to the spiritual and ethical traditions of Sri Lankan culture and to the practical traditions of cooperation and self-help in its villages and communities.

In this same spirit, Sadeeva Ariyaratne identifies the conventional top-down hierarchical system of decision-making as the basis for what she calls "the post-colonial crisis of democracy" and argues that it is "the core reason for many ills in the contemporary Sri Lankan society, including the ethnic conflict."[62] It is ironic that the neocolonial powers still talk of their responsibility to "bring democracy" to the "less developed" world when many in that world are well aware of the fact that it was colonialism and neocolonialism that undermined the most popular, democratic and participatory aspects of their traditional communities and replaced them with oppressive and manipulative power structures. Dr. Ariyaratne states that Sarvodaya Shramadana has "the political objective of converting Sri Lankan polity into a commonwealth of villages or community republics" in which "every village should enjoy maximum self-government."[63] Sarvodaya Shramadana is based on respect for the value and uniqueness of each community and the principle of achieving unity through diversity.

Its conception of unity-in-diversity is both social and ecological, stressing the importance of preserving and fostering social diversity while at the same time protecting biodiversity and ecological integrity. Because of this ecological concern, Sarvodaya Shramadana has made use of the "Effective Micro-organism (EM) Method," a form of agriculture that is ecologically sound, increases crop yields significantly, and is particularly well suited for communities with limited economic resources.[64]

Sarvodaya Shramadana rejects the idea that it can communicate effectively through use of the dominant media, which have goals contrary to its own aspirations. Sadeeva Ariyaratne contends that the mainstream media in Sri Lanka as elsewhere "serve as an outlet for the expressions of dominant ideologies" and create a "public opinion" that is "a construct of dominant groups."[65] It is unlikely that the public will be motivated to become active participants in the community through the passive consumption of information distorted by such systems of power. Sarvodaya Shramadana therefore seeks to reach out to people primarily through its own activities. It looks to the power of learning through doing, that is, to education and communication through the practical example of collective work, democratic decision-making, and self-transformative activities in the communities in which people live their everyday lives.

Based on these participatory, decentralist ideas and its long experience in grassroots organization, Sarvodaya Shramadana has developed a "Five Stage Development Process." In the first stage, members of a village community perceive a problem and ask for help. Sarvodaya Shramadana field workers go to the village and discuss the problem with villagers and community leaders in order to determine what is to be undertaken. A shramadana camp is then organized to plan the project and begin the village "awakening" process. Hundreds of volunteers join together, including local community members, people from other Sarvodaya villages and from various levels of the organization, young people, including school groups, Buddhist monks, and sometimes volunteers from international programs and support groups.

The second stage includes the formation of local groups and training programs to support the work to be undertaken. This process elicits the efforts of a diverse spectrum of participants that might include, for example "a children's group, a youth group, mother's group, elders, farmers," in addition to creating such projects as "a child development center, community kitchen, community center, a village library, or a plant and tool bank."[66]

In the third stage, the participants carry forward the planning and initiation of the grassroots development projects that are the core of the work. The programs are guided by an analysis of how the "Ten Basic Human Needs" are reflected in local conditions. An official Sarvodaya Shramadana Society is formed, enabling the community to secure loans from banks and programs within the movement to help finance the projects. In addition, microcredit programs are established within the communities. As mentioned, Sarvodaya Shramadana has already created thousands of village community banks and savings societies, and plans are underway for many more, with an ultimate goal of fifteen thousand.

In the fourth stage, the various projects are brought to fruition. They are supported through training programs and appropriate technologies (e.g., "hand pumps for wells, solar energy, or high efficiency ceramic cooking stoves and better building methods"[67]) to create a thriving, self-reliant local economy.

Finally, in the fifth stage, the community begins to reach out to other communities with similar needs and offers them its labor, skills, experience, technical abilities, and material aid. The "unity of awakening" arising from their participation in the process leads them to offer a compassionate "gift of labor" to others.

Creating Peace amid Strife

One of the most central concerns of Sarvodaya Shramadana has been the attainment of peace in a war-torn society, for Sri Lanka is a classic case of a society deeply divided by violent ethnic conflict. Sarvodaya Shramadana was founded well before civil war broke out in 1983 between the Buddhist Sinhala majority and the Hindu Tamil minority, but through most of its history it has had to face the challenge of civil strife. At the end of the war in 2009, it was estimated that between eighty and one hundred thousand people had been killed over the decades of brutal conflict.

Sarvodaya Shramadana holds that lasting peace, whether within the family, the village, or the larger society, can only be attained if each person works diligently to achieve peace within him or herself, while at the same time working together with others for the good of these larger communities. It is noteworthy that Dr. Ariyaratne does not distinguish between "legal violence" and "illegal violence." He notes quite astutely that a truly *nonviolent* society has neither.[68] This means that the solution to violence, including even civil war or terrorism, cannot be to resort to massively coercive repression (the violence of the state, which is the dominant mode of violence globally). It is necessary instead to confront the roots of violence in the personality and in social conditions, and to create real alternatives to it on every level.

The most striking of Sarvodaya Shramadana's peace activities has been its huge peace meditations. The first such meditation was held in 1999 at Vihara Maha Devi Park in Colombo, with 200,000 participants. An even more impressive 650,000 participated in a meditation in Anuradhapura in 2002. Many other smaller meditations have been held across the island, often with thousands or tens of thousands of participants. These events are designed to bring together the members of the various ethnic groups in order to heal the divisions that lie at the root of civil war. Representatives of various religious communities are given a place at the front of these assemblies. The participants, whatever their backgrounds may be, see Buddhist monks, Muslim imams, Christian priests, and Hindu leaders joining together to show their solidarity in support of peace.

As described in A.T. Ariyaratne's "Peace Meditation Program Introduction and Guide to Participants," peace meditations are aimed at creating a spirit of forgiveness and acceptance of others and a desire to overcome one's own shortcomings. A typical mass peace meditation lasts for three hours and includes walking and sitting meditation. The meditation is carried out in complete silence. The idea of hundreds of thousands of people coming together to walk and sit in peaceful silence is rather remarkable. There are few signs, banners, chanting of slogans, speeches, or cheering. The only exceptions are that each participating organization may carry a sign identifying itself and a few concluding words are said during the last ten minutes. Preparation for the meditation often includes special efforts in the practice of *sila* (basic Buddhist moral principles such as kindness, truthfulness, etc.), following a vegetarian diet, eating in moderation, and dressing in simple white clothing. In addition, participants are instructed in Buddhist meditation practices such as concentration on the breath and loving kindness meditation.

Another area of Sarvodaya Shramadana peace activity has been a wide range of grassroots organizations to improve understanding and cooperation between villages. One of the primary organizational strategies is to involve groups of people from differing ethnic and religious backgrounds in face-to-face discussions concerning peace and conflict resolution. This approach is applied through "People's Peace Dialogues" and "Youth Peace Camps" in which thousands of young people participate each year. It also inspires a "People-to-People Exchange Program" involving young people from communities in different areas of the country. A program called "Village to Village—Heart to Heart" goes one step further and partners villages from different regions, so that a thousand villages in the north are paired with a thousand in the south. In addition to exchanges of visits there are also exchanges of voluntary labor for grassroots development projects. Rapid Language Learning Programs are used to improve communication between communities.

Finally, the movement has established "People's Peace Tables," which are workshops in which representatives of local communities come together to discuss basic problems and look to their collective futures. The consensus of these workshops has been that the dominant political system is incapable of solving major problems and engaging local communities actively in the process of creating a better society, and that these communities have been excluded from any real decision-making. It has been found that people of all communities want peace, but they do not think that the centralized state can achieve it. There has emerged from the workshops an awareness "that there is a need for a deep process of political, social and ethical renewal through which people transform themselves from passive subjects to active citizenry."[69] This is, of course, precisely the kind of need that Sarvodaya Shramadana's programs seek to fulfill.

As one looks at the accomplishments of Sarvodaya Shramadana, one must include that in some ways, especially as a grassroots development movement, it has gone beyond the achievements of the Gandhian Sarvodaya movement. It has certainly made progress in showing how to sustain the momentum and widen the scope of diverse village-based projects. On the other hand, it has not so far developed the far-ranging program of social transformation envisioned by Gandhi. But the most useful approach is not to waste much time comparing the two movements or rating them against one another. Rather, it is to see what lessons each has to teach, and to discover how the Sarvodaya legacy can be carried forward in struggles for freedom and justice today.

Foreign Aid

I once attended a meeting of "progressive" organizations, held in the wake of a presidential election, at which a speaker suggested that if the United States were to undertake certain procedural reforms in its electoral system, it might become an "example" for the rest of the world politically. One must certainly agree that the US should clean up its electoral act as quickly as possible. But after doing so it would still be far from a good example for the world. For the act would still remain what it essentially is: an act, a spectacle that is very remote from the needs of people and the aspirations of communities. Mere reform of voting procedures would succeed in bolstering the aura of legitimacy of a fundamentally unresponsive and depoliticized decision-making process, but the system would nevertheless remain a corporate-dominated, oligarchical, highly centralized, and undemocratic one.

If one reflects on the achievements of a broad-based, participatory social movement like Sarvodaya and Sarvodaya Shramadana, it becomes apparent that it is countries like the United States that constitute in many ways the "underdeveloped world" of politics. For all their material wealth they are poor in authentic communal life and poor in techniques by which people can shape the destinies of their own communities. One must look to places such as the villages of Sri Lanka that are engaged in Sarvodaya Shramadana projects to discover the "developed world" of contemporary politics. Perhaps someday such villages will send teams of advisors to the West to help it come to terms with its communitarian underdevelopment, and begin to discover a way out of its political poverty.

Meanwhile, we in the overdeveloped world can begin to make more serious attempts to learn from societies in which a long history of communal practice and a deeply rooted sense of social solidarity make possible exemplary experiments in social cooperation.

10

Beyond the Limits of the City:
A Communitarian Anarchist Critique
of Libertarian Municipalism

Social ecologist Murray Bookchin's theory of libertarian municipalism was one of the most theoretically developed anarchist political programs in the twentieth century. Though Bookchin in his final years renounced the term "anarchism" in favor of what he called "communalism," he was still working within the broad framework of anarchist thought, and he continued to be recognized by many as the foremost anarchist theorist of his generation in the English-speaking world.[1] His politics of libertarian municipalism is the most notable example of what might be called the programmatic tendency in recent anarchist political thought.

In the following discussion, a detailed critical analysis of libertarian municipalist politics will be presented from the perspective of communitarian anarchism and dialectical social ecology. This analysis is an implicit defense of social ecology, which still has much to offer to anarchism and to political thought and practice in general. Indeed, the contention here is that a dialectical social ecology, combined with a radical communitarian anarchist politics, is the strongest position in contemporary anarchist thought.[2]

The ecocommunitarian anarchist perspective presented here is inspired by a vision of human communities achieving their fulfillment as an integral part of the larger, self-realizing Earth community. If social ecology is an attempt to understand the dialectical movement of society within the context of the larger dialectic of society and nature, ecocommunitarian anarchism is the project of creating a way of life consonant with that understanding, that is, a world of free, just, ecologically responsible communities. Setting out from this philosophical and practical perspective, it will be argued that although Bookchin's politics possesses an important core of truth embodied in its vision of grassroots direct democracy, it also contains certain theoretical inconsistencies, and also lacks the historical grounding necessary for it to be a reliable guide for an ecological communitarian practice.

One of the main claims that will be defended here is that because of certain ideological and dogmatic aspects, this politics remains in some ways on the level of abstract moralism, rather than reaching that of the ethical. The latter requires a serious engagement with the historical and material conditions that form a basis for ethical substantiality, the embodiment of ethical ideals in institutions, practices, and forms of life. In terms of the conceptual framework developed here, his politics has focused too narrowly on the generation of alternative ideology and certain specific institutional forms, but has, like many other programmatic tendencies, neglected crucial questions concerning the social ethos, the social imaginary, and larger social institutional structures. As a result of its moment of abstract idealism, it has in practice tended to divert the energies of its adherents into an ideological sectarianism, and away from an effective confrontation with crucial dimensions of history, culture, and the psyche. Bookchin's politics ultimately takes a strongly voluntarist turn, in which the projects of propagation of ideology and of sectarian organization, which quickly reveal their limits, are supplemented by an appeal to the power of the will.

In this respect, Bookchin's politics carries on certain dimensions of the Bakuninist tradition in anarchism. It is in many ways an expression of the masculinist moment of anarchism. It focuses on the importance of establishing the correct set of ideas and principles (the program) and then organizing institutions (the movement) through which these ideas can be willed into reality through the decisive act. There is a feminist moment of anarchism, on the other hand, that is associated with the patient, diligent work of nurturing libertarian and communitarian sensibilities and relationships, and fostering communities of solidarity that care for the needs of the members and help them realize their human capacities. Neither moment should be emphasized to the exclusion of the other. However, an underlying theme of the present analysis is that the latter moment must be central to ecocommunitarian anarchism, and that the neglect of this moment has had lamentable consequences for anarchist political thought.

Democracy, Ecology, and Community

The idea of replacing the state with a system of localized, participatory, community-based political institutions has a long and very rich history in anarchist thought. As early as the 1790s, William Godwin proposed that government should be reduced essentially to a system of local juries and assemblies that would perform all the functions that could not be carried out voluntarily or enforced informally through public opinion and social pressure.[3] A century later, Elisée Reclus presented an extensive history of the forms of popular direct democracy, from the era of the Athenian polis to modern times, and proposed that these principles be embodied in a revolutionary system of communal self-rule.[4] Bookchin has been one of the most uncompromising advocates of this tradition of radical democracy in recent times, presenting an often inspiring defense of local direct democracy through his theory of libertarian municipalism.[5] For many years, he was, along with a few other thinkers such as Benjamin Barber, among the few Anglo-American theorists to carry on the tradition of serious theoretical exploration of the possibilities for decentralized, participatory democracy.[6] This critique recognizes the importance of Bookchin's contribution to ecological, communitarian, democratic theory and investigates the issues that must be resolved if the liberatory potential of certain aspects of his thought is to be freed from the constraints of sectarian dogma.

A strong point in Bookchin's politics is his attempt to ground it in ethics and the philosophy of nature. In viewing politics fundamentally as a sphere of ethics, Bookchin carries on certain aspects of the Aristotelian-Hegelian tradition of politics as collective or communal self-realization. Aristotle saw politics, the pursuit of the good of the polis, the political community, as a branch of ethics, the pursuit of the human good in general.[7] He called the ultimate goal for human beings *eudaimonia*, which, though often translated as "happiness," has a broader connotation of "the good life" or "self-realization." Bookchin expands this concept of the larger good even further to encompass the natural world. Beginning with his early work, he argues that the development of a political ethics requires both "a moral community" and "an ecological community," and implies "a political culture that invites the widest possible participation."[8]

For Bookchin, politics is an integral part of the process of evolutionary unfolding and self-realization spanning the natural and social history of the planet. Social ecology looks at this history as a developmental process that has continually produced greater richness, diversity, complexity, and rationality. The political, Bookchin says, must be understood in the context of humanity's quality of being "nature rendered self-conscious."[9] From this perspective, the goal of politics is the creation of a free, ecological society in which human beings pursue self-realization through participation in a nondominating human community, and further planetary self-realization by playing a cooperative, nondominating role within the larger ecological community. A fundamental political task is thus the elimination of those forms of domination that hinder the attainment of greater freedom and self-realization for humanity and nature, and the creation of new social forms that are most conducive to these ends.

This describes "politics" in the larger, classical sense of a political ethics, but leaves open the question of which "politics," in the narrower sense of determinate social practice, best serves such a political vision. Bookchin has expressed considerable enthusiasm at different times for a variety of approaches to political, economic, and cultural change. In the early essay "The Forms of Freedom," he envisions a radically transformative communalism rapidly creating an alternative to centralized, hierarchical, urbanized industrial society. Employing terms reminiscent of the great communitarian anarchist Gustav Landauer, he suggests: "we can envision young people renewing social life just as they renew the human species. Leaving the city, they begin to found the nuclear ecological communities to which older people repair in increasing numbers," as "the modern city begins to shrivel, to contract and to disappear."[10] The almost apocalyptic and millenarian aspects of Bookchin's views in this period reflect both the spirit of the American counterculture at that time, and his strong identification with the utopian tradition.

During this early period, Bookchin inspired many with his depiction of the possibilities for radically democratic ecocommunities in which a deeply libertarian, ecological, and communitarian culture would emerge. In "Toward a Vision of the Urban Future," for example, he looks hopefully to a variety of popular initiatives in contemporary urban society. He mentions block committees, tenants associations, "ad hoc committees," neighborhood councils, housing cooperatives, "sweat equity" programs, cooperative day care, educational projects, food co-ops, squatting and building occupations, and alternative technology experiments as making contributions of varying importance to the achievement of "municipal liberty."[11]

In the whole of his earlier work, Bookchin situates participatory democracy, and municipal democracy in particular, within the context of a larger, profoundly revolutionary cultural movement aimed at transforming the whole of the political culture. A compelling quality of such a movement is its promise of realizing immediately many diverse aspects of the free, cooperative world of the future. To use more recent terminology, it was the vision of a deeply prefigurative movement. It was on the basis of this ecocommunitarian vision that Bookchin gained a considerable degree of influence within the radical ecology and cooperative movements, beginning in the late 1960s and continuing through the 1980s.

However, by the late 1980s, Bookchin's thought takes a strongly programmatic turn. While he had always stressed the great importance of the municipality, he now gives much stronger priority to municipal politics, he prescribes political strategies much more rigidly, and he deem-phasizes or in some cases even rejects other approaches to change that he previously advocated. For example, he dismisses ecofeminism as irra-tionalist and essentialist (unless it is the "social ecofeminist" dimension of social ecology), and he rejects bioregionalism as politically regressive. He proclaims the municipality the central political reality, and municipal assembly government the preeminent expression of democratic politics. The result is libertarian municipalism, a political ideology that Bookchin continued to develop and promote tirelessly over the last twenty years of his life. It is this ideology that is the subject of this critique.

Citizenship and Self-Identity

Bookchin contends that the "nuclear unit" of a new politics must be the "citizen," which is, as he says, "a term that embodies the classical ideals of *philia*, autonomy, rationality, and above all, civic commitment."[12] He rightly argues that the revival of such an ideal would be politically a signif-icant advance in a society dominated by values and self-images based on consumption and passive participation in mass society. To think of oneself as a citizen contradicts the dominant representations of the self as egoistic calculator, as profit maximizer, as competitor for scarce resources, or as narcissistic consumer of products, images, experiences, and even other persons. It replaces narrow self-interest and egoism with a sense of ethical responsibility toward one's neighbors, and identification with a larger whole: the political community. Furthermore, it reintroduces the idea of moral agency on the political level, through the concept that one can in cooperation with others create social embodiments of the good. In short, Bookchin's concept challenges the ethics and moral psychology of economistic, capitalist society and presents an edifying image of a higher ideal of selfhood and community.

Yet this image has serious limitations. To begin with, it seems unwise, particularly if one adopts a dialectical perspective, to make any single role into such a "nuclear unit of society," or to see any as the privileged form of self-identity, for there are many important self-images with profound political implications. A notable example is that of personhood. While civic virtue requires diverse obligations to one's fellow citizens, respect, love, and compassion are feelings appropriately directed at all persons. If (as Bookchin has himself at times agreed) we should accept the principle that "the personal is political," we must explore the political dimension of personhood and the process of recognition of the personhood of others. In addition, the political significance of our roles as members of the Earth community and of our particular ecological and bioregional communities can hardly be overemphasized. We conceive of these roles as expressing a kind of citizenship, in the quite reasonable sense of the practice of responsible membership in a community with which we can meaningfully act in solidarity. Such an outlook is similar to the ecofeminist view expressed by Ariel Salleh, when she argues that ecofeminism "reaches for an earth democracy, across cultures and species."[13] A fully developed social ecology similarly sees our political ties and responsibilities as extending to all our human and biotic communities and ultimately to the entire Earth community.

However, Bookchin shows little patience with any investigation into the boundaries of citizenship. He contends that the concept of citizen "becomes vacuous" and is "stripped of its rich historical content"[14] when the limits of the concept's privileged usage are transgressed. In addition, he argues, somewhat contradictorily, that, rather than being *vacuous*, such more expansive concepts as bioregional citizenship and Earth citizenship have an *absurd excess of content*, and imply that various animals, including insects, and even inanimate objects, including rocks, must be recognized as citizens. But such contentions are clearly invalid. Just as we can act as moral agents in relation to other beings that are not agents (in ethics, they are called "moral patients"), we can exercise duties of citizenship in relation to other beings who are not citizens.

The term "citizen" simply does not have the limited connotations that Bookchin absolutizes. In ordinary usage, it connotes membership in a nation-state and subdivisions of nation-states, including states that are in no way authentically democratic or participatory. The privileged locus of citizenship in the present-day world is the state, and not the municipality. When someone is asked "What is your citizenship?" it is highly unlikely that they would reply something like "Burlington" or "the Bronx." The creation of a shared conception of citizenship in Bookchin's sense is a *project* that must be judged in relation to the actually existing fund of meanings and the possibilities for social creation in a given culture. The creation of a conception of citizenship based on participation in the Earth community or in a bioregional community is no less a project, and one that has a liberatory potential that can only be assessed through processes of cultural creativity, and historical practice, and by critical reflection on the results of these processes.

Although Bookchin often invokes Hegel, he neglects that philosopher's distinction between an abstract and a concrete universal and its application to political ideas. Any political concept that is not both articulated theoretically and also developed historically and practically remains a mere abstract universal. In themselves, concepts such as "citizen of a municipality," "citizen of a state," and "citizen of the Earth" are inevitably "vacuous"—that is, they remain on the level of abstraction. Their abstractness cannot be negated merely by appealing to past historical usage or to one's hopes for an improved usage in the future. They can be given richer *theoretical content* by exploring their place in the history of ideas and in social history, by engaging in a conceptual analysis, and by reflecting on their possible relationship to other emerging theoretical and social possibilities. Yet they will still remain abstractions, albeit now more fully articulated ones. They gain *concrete universality*, on the other hand, through their embodiment in the history of society, or, more precisely in the practice of a community—in its *institutions*, its prevailing *ethos*, its ruling *ideas*, and its dominant *images*.

Bookchin often confuses such historical concreteness with relatedness to concrete historical phenomena. In this he is typical of many radical and utopian political thinkers. Badiou's theory of "fidelity to the event" is one of the most extreme examples, but at least that thinker does not entirely hide his implicit Platonic idealism.[15] When Bookchin finds certain political forms of the past to be inspiring, they take on a certain numinous quality for him. Various models of citizenship become relevant today not because of their relation to real historical possibilities (including real possibilities existing in the social imaginary realm), but because they present an image of what our epoch assuredly *ought* to be. Their numinous presence shines out across history and transforms present reality. It is for this reason that he strangely thinks that certain historical usages of the term "citizen" can dictate proper usage of the term today.

Of course, Bookchin is aware on a certain level that the citizenship that he advocates is not a widespread living reality, but rather a proposed ideal. Thus, he notes that "today, the concept of citizenship has already undergone serious erosion through the reduction of citizens to 'constituents' of statist jurisdictions or to 'taxpayers' who sustain statist institutions."[16] Since he clearly has American society in mind when he makes this historical observation, one might ask when there was a Golden Age in American history when the people actually constituted a body of "citizens" in Bookchin's strong sense of "a self-managing and competent agent in democratically shaping a polity."[17] The closest approximations of such citizenship in American history is found in certain aspects of Democratic-Republican Societies of the 1790s, the most radical elements of the populism of the late nineteenth and early twentieth centuries, and other similar phenomena that remained outside the mainstream of American political history.[18] Thus, we find a remarkable form of "erosion," a phenomenon possible only in the realm of ideological geology, in which an ideal type based on discontinuous historical phenomena erodes into the actually existing institutions of contemporary society.

As symptomatic as such analysis may be, a more substantive problem for Bookchin's politics concerns his claim that the adoption of the municipalist concept of citizenship will result in an end to conflicts between particularistic interests. He argues that "we would expect that the special interests that divide people today into workers, professionals, managers, and the like would be melded into a general interest in which people see themselves as *citizens* guided strictly by the needs of their community and region rather than by personal proclivities and vocational concerns."[19] Yet his very formulation preserves the idea of particularistic interest, since it focuses on the needs of one's own particular "community and region," needs that could (and, in the real world, certainly would) conflict in some ways with the needs of other communities and regions. There will always be communities that possess in relative abundance certain natural goods that fulfill real needs of the community but that would fulfill even greater needs of other communities lacking these goods or having special conditions that render their needs more pressing. Of course, one might hold that in the best of all possible libertarian municipalisms, the citizens' highest and deepest need would be to contribute to the greatest good of humanity and the Earth. But such an achievement is at best a long-term goal, dependent on an enormous evolution of communitarian values. It can certainly not be seen as a reality that will emerge quickly once decision-making is placed in hands of municipal or neighborhood assemblies.

Bookchin has not thought through the strong tension in his thought between universality and particularity. Such a tension is inherent in any ecological politics that is committed to unity-in-diversity and which seeks to theorize the complex dialectic between whole and part. For Bookchin, this creative tension rigidifies into contradiction, as a result of his territorializing of the political realm at the level of the particular municipal community. The contradiction between particular and particular is resolved by the mere invocation of universality, not by the working out of the contradiction in a manner by which universality can emerge organically. In some ways, his version of "citizenship" is, on the practico-theoretical level, a regression from the universality of membership in the working class, whatever limitations that concept may have had. The classical anarchist and Marxist conceptions of being a worker involved a certain degree of concrete universality. On the one hand, one's privileged being *qua* worker consisted of membership in a *universal* class, but on the other it required a very concrete translation of that universality into particularity through local struggles and acts of solidarity. It became clear that mere abstract membership in the working class could not produce practical solidarity, and that contradictions based on trade, ethnicity, sex, and other factors needed to be worked out in practice (industrial unionism, the general strike, working-class cultural organizations, rituals and celebrations, working-class art and music, and daily papers and other publications, not to mention working-class parties).

Bookchin never devoted adequate attention to the ways in which such contradictions can be worked out and the larger communal dimensions can be expressed concretely. Libertarian municipalism faces the fundamental problem that it defines one's being *qua* citizen above all as being a member of a *particular* group: the class of citizens of a given municipality. And this generates inevitable contradictions between the interests of citizens of different municipalities. Of course, this does not exclude the achievement of universality through such particularity. In this connection, Bookchin's concept of confederalism begins to point in the right direction, but even after years of discussion the content of confederalism remained very vague and sketchy. In the end, many of the dimensions of citizenship that are essential for effective social transformation are absent from his practical politics, being largely displaced into a distant utopian future, as part the theory of the imagined confederalist system.

The "Agent of History "

Bookchin asks at one point the identity of the "historical 'agent' for sweeping social change."[20] In a sense, he has already answered this question in his discussion of citizenship. However, his specific response focuses on the nature of the social whole constituted by the entire body of citizens. It is "the People." He describes this emerging "People" as a "'counterculture' in the broadest sense," and suggests that it might include "alternative organizations, technologies, periodicals, food cooperatives, health and women's centers, schools, even barter-markets, not to speak of local and regional coalitions."[21] While this concept is obviously shaped and in some ways limited by the image of the US counterculture of the 1960s, it reflects a broad conception of cultural creativity as the precondition for liberatory social change. This is its great strength. It points to a variety of community-oriented initiatives that develop the potential for social cooperation and grassroots organization, and thus for a many-sided transformative movement in which there is a mutually reinforcing dialectical development of major social determinants.

The idea of "the People" as the preeminent historical agent is central to Bookchin's critique of the traditional leftist choice of the working class or proletariat for that role. He, along with other anarchists, was far ahead of most Marxists and other socialists in breaking with a one-sidedly economistic conception of social transformation. Indeed, some postmodernist Marxists and other au courant leftists now sound much like Bookchin of thirty years ago, when they run through the litany of oppressed groups and victims of domination who are now looked upon as hoped-for agents of social transformation, or as it is more likely to be expressed in the culture of resignation, agents of "resistance" and "struggle." Bookchin can justly claim that his concept is superior to many of these current theories, in that his idea of "the People" maintains a degree of unity within the diversity, while leftist victimology has often degenerated into incoherent, divisive forms of identity politics.

However, in the end, Bookchin (like various postmodernists, post-structuralists, post-Marxists, and post-anarchists with whom he would have little else in common) goes too far in dismissing the role of economic class analysis. He claims that while "the People" was "an illusory concept" in the eighteenth century, it is now a reality in view of the contemporary importance of various "transclass issues like ecology, feminism, and a sense of civic responsibility to neighborhoods and communities."[22] He is, of course, right in stressing the general, transclass nature of such issues and movements. But as a proponent of dialectical thinking, Bookchin should have recognized that they have *both* a class and a transclass nature, in the strong sense of each term, since they all have a quite specific meaning, not only in relation to gender, ethnicity, community, and nature, but also in relation to economic class. The growing concern for environmental justice and the critique of environmental racism have made this reality increasingly apparent in relation to the "transclass" issue of ecology. Without addressing the particular class dimensions of an issue (along with its ethnic, gender, and cultural dimensions), a movement for radical social transformation will fail to understand it both in concrete detail and also within its larger context. It will therefore lose its ability to communicate effectively with those intimately involved in the issue, and more importantly, it will lose its capacity to learn from them. The fact is that Bookchin's social analysis has had almost nothing to say about the evolution of class in either American or global society. Indeed, he seems in his own theory and practice to have equated the obsolescence of the classical concept of the working class with the obsolescence of any detailed class analysis.

While Bookchin identifies "the People" as the emerging subject of history and the agent of social transformation, he also identifies a specific group within this large social category as essential to its successful formation. The "agent of revolutionary change," in the strongest sense of the term "agency," will be the "radical intelligentsia," a social stratum which in his view has always been necessary "to catalyze" such change.[23] He does not discuss the nature of this intelligentsia in great detail. What is clear is that it would include theoretically sophisticated activists who would lead a libertarian municipalist movement. Presumably, it would also include activists in a variety of cultural and intellectual fields who would help spread revolutionary ideas, as has historically been the case in radical movements.

Bookchin is certainly right in emphasizing the need within a movement for social transformation for a sizable segment of people with developed political commitments and theoretical grounding. However, it

is essential that a movement's forms of expression and modes of communication not be directed exclusively at recruiting such a group. Libertarian
municipalist politics has been based on the valid assumption that a
precondition for effective social action is widely dispersed theoretical
grounding. But it has overlooked the fact that theory can be embodied
in many forms of expression that go far beyond the bounds of narrow
theoretical discourse. In addition, it has increasingly focused on Bookchin's
own theoretical position as the definitive new synthesis of revolutionary
thought. Thus, there has been too narrow a conception of theory, and too
narrow a spectrum of theory, even within the confines of that conception.

A heavy emphasis on the role of a narrowly defined radical intelligentsia threatens to overshadow the crucial importance of cultural
creativity by those who would not identify themselves as intellectuals.
This includes those who create grassroots cultural institutions, cooperative social practices, and transformed relationships in personal and
family life. The nonhierarchical, cooperative principles of social ecology
should lead one to pay careful attention to the subtle ways in which large
numbers of people contribute to the shaping of all social institutions,
whether traditional or transformative ones. Bookchin himself recognized
the importance of such activity when he describes the "reemergence of
'the People'" through the development of a "counterculture" consisting of
a variety of cooperative and communitarian groups and institutions.[24] He
does not explain why this entire developing culture is not equally entitled
to be called the "historical agent." One must suspect that the answer lies in
the fact that he realistically sees that the majority of participants in such
a culture would be highly unlikely to have a firm grounding in a highly
ideological and programmatic outlook such as libertarian municipalism.

The Municipality as Ground of Social Being

The institutional goal of the process of historical transformation is, for
Bookchin, the libertarian municipality. He often describes the municipality
as the fundamental political reality, and indeed, the fundamental social
one. He states that "conceived in more institutional terms, the municipality
is the basis for a free society, the irreducible ground for individuality as
well as society."[25] Even more strikingly, he says that the municipality is
"the living cell which forms the basic unit of political life . . . from which
everything else must emerge: confederation, interdependence, citizenship,
and freedom."[26] This assertion is a response to the need for a liberatory

political identity that can successfully replace the passive, disempowering identity of membership in the nation-state, and a moral identity that can successful replace the amoral identity of consumer. For Bookchin, the municipality is the arena in which political ethics and the civic virtues that it requires can begin to germinate and ultimately achieve an abundant flowering in a rich municipal political culture. This vision of free community is in many ways a very inspiring one, and contains a powerful kernel of truth.

It is far from clear, however, why the municipality should be considered such a privileged social reality. Bookchin attributes to it alone a role in social life that is in fact shared by a variety of institutions and spheres of existence. Communitarian anarchists have stressed the fundamental nature of the most intimate personal sphere, whether identified with the affinity group, the familial group, the base community, or the small intentional community. Many critical social analyses show the importance of the dialectic between this personal dimension and a variety of institutional spheres in the shaping of the self and values, including political values.[27]

Significantly, in Bookchin's own argument for the priority of the municipality he claims that it is "the one domain *outside of personal life* that the individual must deal with on a very direct basis" and that the city is "the most immediate environment which we encounter and with which we are obliged to deal, *beyond the sphere of family and friends*, in order to satisfy our needs as social beings."[28] It should be noted that these statements actually recognize the priority of the family and, perhaps, the affinity group in social life, for the city is identified as the *next most important* sphere of life. But beyond this rather large problem, Bookchin's case for the greater "immediacy" of the city does not stand up to a careful analysis of the actual experience of contemporary city-dwellers.

Even if we bracket the immediacy of the family and the circle of personal friends, it is not true that the individual deals in a somehow more "direct" way with the municipality than with other social spheres. Many millions in modern society deal at least as directly with the mass media, by way of their television sets, computers, radios, newspapers, and magazines, until they go to work and deal with bosses, coworkers, and various technologies, after which they return to the domestic hearth and further bombardment by the mass media. The municipality remains a generalized background to this more direct experience. This becomes increasingly the case, as a growing number wander through the urban landscape absorbed in their iPods, doing their texting, or talking on their cell phones. Of course, the municipality is one social and spatial *context* in which all the other more direct experience takes place. But this is also the case for a series of larger contexts: various political subdivisions such as states and provinces, the nation-state, the whole of society, the planet. In the case of each, everything that goes on within its limits can be said to be "part" of it, thereby attesting to its great importance. But this is mere formalistic, nondialectical argumentation. The fact is that there are few "needs as social beings" that are satisfied uniquely by "the municipality" in strong contradistinction to any other source of satisfaction, and those that are (and which are enormously important, as in the case of those related to the urban imaginary) are not a significant concern for libertarian municipalism.

In fact, Bookchin has at times recognized the need for this more dialectical and contextual view of the city that is defended here. In arguing against the kind of reification of the "bourgeois city" that takes place in traditional city planning, he states that "to treat the city as an autonomous entity, apart from the social conditions that produce it [is] to isolate and objectify a habitat that is itself contingent and formed by other factors. Behind the physical structure of the city lies the social community—its workaday life, values, culture, familial ties, class relations, and personal bonds."[29] It is important to apply this same kind of dialectical analysis to the conceptualization of the city in libertarian municipalism. The city must be seen as a relative social whole consisting of constituent relative social wholes, interrelated with other such relative wholes, and also as forming a part of even larger ones.[30] Add to this the natural relative wholes that are inseparable from the social ones, and then consider all the mutual determinations between all of these relative wholes and all of their various parts, and we begin to see the complexity of a dialectical social ecological analysis.

The Social and the Political

Bookchin is unfortunately at his weakest in one of his most fundamental theoretical undertakings, the articulation of the concept of "the political." He contends that he makes "careful but crucial distinctions between the three societal realms: the social, the political, and the state,"[31] and claims that his idea "that there could be a political arena independent of the state and the social . . . was to elude most radical thinkers."[32] His social and statist realms cover almost everything that exists in present-day society. The *statist sphere* subsumes all the institutions and activities through which the state operates. The *social sphere* includes everything else in society, with the exception of "the political." This final category encompasses activity in the *public sphere*, a realm that he identifies "with politics in the Hellenic sense of the term."[33] By this, he means the kind of participatory democratic institutions that are proposed by libertarian municipalism, and which have emerged at various points in history. Libertarian municipalists, he says, "are concerned with what people do in this *public or political sphere*, not with what people do in their bedrooms, living rooms, or basements."[34]

There is, however, a degree of unintentional irony in this statement. For it implies that whatever they may hope for in the future, for the present they should not be concerned with what people do *anywhere*, since the political realm does not yet exist to any significant degree. Bookchin's "political" resides at most within the tiny libertarian municipalist movement, though strictly speaking, it cannot *now* constitute even a "public sphere" considering how distant it is from any actual exercise of public power. Thus, Bookchin's *defense* of the political against those who would "denature" and "dissolve it" culminates in the effective *abolition* of the political as a meaningful description of anything of significance in existing society.

This definition has problematical implications for practice. Bookchin argues that "it is precisely the *municipality* that most individuals must deal with directly, once they leave the social realm and enter the public sphere."[35] But since what he calls "the public sphere" consists of his idealized "Hellenic politics," it will be impossible for "most individuals" to locate it anywhere in the real world. Instead, they find only the "social" and "statist" realms, into which almost all aspects of the actually existing municipality have already been dissolved, not by any theorist, but by the course of history itself. Thus, unless Bookchin is willing to find a public sphere in the existing statist institutions that dominate municipal politics, or somewhere in that vast realm of "the social," there is simply no public sphere, for the vast majority of people to "enter."

Embarrassing as these implications may be for Bookchin's position, his predicament is in fact much worse than this. For in claiming that the municipality is what most people "deal with directly," he is condemned to defining the actually existing municipality in terms of the social, a conclusion that he wishes to avoid. Moreover, the more he forsakes abstract theory for description of actual social reality, the more he undermines his own position. He concedes that "doubtless the municipality is usually the place where even a great deal of *social* life is existentially lived—school, work, entertainment, and simple pleasures like walking, bicycling, and disporting themselves."[36] He might have expanded this list considerably, for almost *anything* that he could possibly invoke on behalf of the centrality of "the municipality" will fall in his sphere of the "social." The actually existing municipality will thus be shown to lie overwhelmingly in his "social" sphere, and his argument thus becomes a demonstration of the centrality not of the political, but of the social realm. And obviously, what doesn't fall into the "social" sphere must lie in the actually existing "statist" sphere, rather than in the virtually nonexistent "political" one.

A problem for Bookchin is that his argument for municipalism works even more effectively as a defense of statism. For when one walks, bicycles, or "disports oneself," either *within* or *outside* a municipality, one almost inevitably finds oneself within a nation-state.[37] After he lists the various *social* dimensions of the municipality, and as the implications of his argument perhaps begin to dawn on him, he protests rather feebly that all this "does not efface its distinctiveness as a unique sphere of life."[38] Quite true, but that was not, of course, the point in dispute. It is perfectly consistent to accept the innocuous propositions that the municipality is "distinctive" and that it is "a unique sphere of life" while rejecting every one of Bookchin's substantive claims about its relationship to human experience, the public sphere, and the "political."

A more dialectical view of the political would see it not as simply located in certain narrowly defined political institutions, but as dispersed through much of what Bookchin calls the social, and even as lying within certain dimensions of the complex and self-contradictory sphere that he dismisses as the "statist." Gundersen suggests certain ways in which such a more dialectical approach might be taken to various questions posed by Bookchin. Gundersen discusses the significance of deliberation in Athenian democracy, one of the most important historical paradigms for Bookchin's libertarian municipalism. He notes that while the official institutions of democracy consisted of such explicitly "political" forms as the assembly, the courts, and the council, the "political" must also be seen to have existed *outside* these institutions, if the role of deliberation is properly understood. "Much of the deliberation that fueled their highly participatory democracy," he says, "took place not in the Assembly, Council, or law courts, but in the agora, the public square adjacent to those places."[39] He might also have mentioned the ways in which social institutions like patriarchy and slavery were not external to the political, but rather conditioned the nature of the political even in the narrower formal institutional sense (reinforcing oligarchical and agonistic tendencies, and impeding the functioning of the democratic institutions).

Bookchin's inadequately dialectical approach to the social and the political is also exemplified by his discussion of Aristotle's politics and Greek history. He notes that "the two worlds of the social and political emerge, the latter from the former. Aristotle's approach to the rise of the polis is emphatically developmental. The polis is the culmination of a political whole from the growth of a social and biological part, a realm of the latent and the possible. Family and village do not disappear in Aristotle's treatment of the subject, but *they are encompassed* by the fuller and more complete domain of the polis."[40] But this exemplifies one of the weakest aspects of Bookchin's thought, his espousal of a very simplistic, "developmental" view of dialectic, in which the mere "unfolding of the potentiality within a being" is described as the core of dialectical movement.[41] The result is a destruction of the radical nature of dialectic. Radical negativity is reduced to an innocuous process of self-realization. The idea that dialectical movement always produces a subversive remainder disappears completely in Bookchin's account.

To the extent that Aristotle (much like Bookchin) maintains a sharp division between the social and the political, his thought reflects a hierarchical dualism rooted in the institutional structure of Athenian society. This is expressed in the concept of a "ruling part" that is found within the self, the family, the village, and the state, and also in his idea that some peoples are born to be free and others to be slaves. Since the household is founded on patriarchal authority and a slave economy, it cannot constitute a political realm, a sphere of free interaction between equals. But somehow a realm of freedom can emerge at the political level, without transforming the social realm out of which it emerges. This is, of course, a self-contradictory project, and a dialectical account must theorize and not merely ignore all of the contradictory elements.

A truly dialectical approach sees change not as mere unfolding of potentiality, but as transformative movement driven by the contradictions inherent in phenomena and existing between phenomena, and by the continuous production not of reconciliation and synthesis, but of a surplus, an excess, an irreconcilable remainder. An authentically dialectical analysis recognizes that as the political dimension emerges within society, it does not separate itself off from the rest of the social world to embed itself in an exclusive sphere. Rather, as the social whole develops, there is a transformation and politicization of many aspects of what Bookchin calls "the social" (a process that may take a liberatory, an authoritarian, or even a totalitarian direction). Our goal must be a conception of the political that is less ideological than Hegel's, but equally dialectical. If we, in such a Left Hegelian spirit, take an essential moment of the political to be the self-conscious self-determination of the community with its own good as the end ("strong agency"), the emergence of the political in any sphere will be seen both to presuppose and also to imply its emergence in other spheres. In short, the social will be the political.[42]

Paideia and Civic Virtue

One of the most appealing aspects of Bookchin's politics is his emphasis on the possibilities for self-realization through active participation in the political sphere. His image of engaged citizenship is inspired perhaps above all by the classical Athenian polis, which "rested on the premise that its citizens could be entrusted with 'power' because they possessed the personal capacity to use power in a trustworthy fashion. The education of citizens into rule was therefore an education into personal competence, intelligence, moral probity, and social commitment."[43] These are the kind of qualities, he believes, that must be created today in order for municipalism to operate successfully. The process of *paideia* or political formation must instill such civic virtues in each citizen, so that the process of individual self-realization can be reconciled with the pursuit of the collective good of the community.

As valuable as these qualities may be, it is important to note the one-sidedness of the list of virtues that Bookchin attributes to his citizens. The unfortunate fact is that highly competent, very intelligent, morally scrupulous, and socially committed people are sometimes not the best community members. On the other hand, qualities such as care, compassion, sensitivity, patience, generosity, and humility that ecofeminists and other care ethicists have emphasized heavily are often typical of those who contribute most to the community. Bookchin occasionally mentions some of these virtues, but they remain in the background, much as they have generally in traditional masculinist ethics. This is not to say that the civic virtues that he lists are not essential ones. Indeed, one could hardly imagine participatory assemblies functioning effectively without them, and one often sees them succumb to weaknesses and failures precisely because of the lack of formation in such areas.

But even if Bookchin's conception of civic virtue is revised into a more balanced one, his conception of paideia still poses major problems. Paideia, though often translated as education, is fundamentally a question of social formation. A theory of radical social transformation must start with a clear recognition that the processes of socialization are not now in the hands of those who would promote such transformation, including the programs of libertarian municipalism or anything vaguely related to it. Rather, they are dominated above all by economic power and the economistic culture, which, in alliance with the state, aim to train workers, employees, and managers to serve the existing system of production, and to produce a mass of consumers for the dominant system of consumption. Municipalism proposes that a populace that has been profoundly conditioned by these processes should become a "citizenry," both committed to the process of self-rule and also fully competent to carry it out.

This is certainly a very admirable goal. However, Bookchin's programmatic formulations sometimes seem to presuppose that such a citizenry has already been formed and merely awaits the opportunity to take power. He states, for example, that "the municipalist conception of citizenship assumes" that "every citizen is regarded as competent to participate directly in the 'affairs of state,' indeed what is more important, encouraged to do so."[44] But the success of participatory institutions would seem to require much more than either an assumption of competence or the mere encouragement of participation in civic affairs. What is necessary is that an increasing segment of the existing populace that has great potential for competence should be transformed into a body of effective and responsible members of a self-determining community. This would require the mobilization of transformative forces that pervasively shape all aspects of their lives, including, as has been argued here, the most fundamental institutional, imaginary, theoretical, and ethotic ones.

To equate such socialization or paideia primarily with the institution of certain elements of libertarian municipalist politics hardly seems to be an adequate approach. Indeed, to implement aspects of its program before the cultural and psychological preconditions have been developed may very well lead to failure and disillusionment. A program of libertarian municipalism that focuses primarily on the decentralization of power to the local level might have extremely reactionary consequences within the context of the existing political culture of the United States and some other countries. One might imagine a "power to the people's assemblies" that would result in harsh anti-immigrant laws, extension of capital punishment, intensified repression and police brutality, expanded restrictions on freedom of speech, imposition of regressive religious practices, repressive enforcement of morality, and punitive measures against the poor, to cite some proposals that have widespread public support in perhaps a considerable majority of municipalities in the United States (not to mention the numerous parts of the world where religious fundamentalism, neofascism, other forms of right-wing extremism prevail). It is no accident that localism has appealed much more to the right wing in the United States, than to the dominant Left or to the general population, and that reactionary localism has become both more extremist and more popular. As discussions in previous chapters have shown, the Far Right has worked diligently for decades at the grassroots level in many areas to create the cultural preconditions for reactionary grassroots democracy.

Bookchin has stated, in response to naïve ideas of localism and decentralization, that "small is not necessarily beautiful."[45] It is equally true that in the real world of social domination, "municipalism is not necessarily beautiful." It may indeed be quite ugly, if the preconditions for beauty do not exist. Of course, Bookchin would quite reasonably prefer to see his popular assemblies established in more "progressive" locales, so that they could become a model for a new democratic, and, indeed, a libertarian and populist, politics. But the possibility of far-reaching proliferation of such developments depends on a significant evolution of the larger political culture at the level of the base. To the extent that activists accept Bookchin's standpoint of hostility toward, or at best, unenthusiastic acceptance of diverse approaches to social change, this will restrict the scope of the necessary paideia, impede the pervasive transformation of society, and undercut the possibilities for effective local democracy.

The fatal flaw in Bookchin's politics is expressed very clearly by Bookchin himself. He states that according to the libertarian municipalist analysis, "be they large or small, the initial assemblies and the movement that seeks to foster them in civic elections remain the only real school for citizenship we have."[46] His politics reaches an ultimate impasse in the absence of any account of how participation in assemblies could possibly effect the far-reaching changes in the character of human beings that are necessary for the free community to emerge. Instead, we find generalizations such as that the assembly is the "social gymnasium" in which his masculinist citizens "forge" their selfhood and achieve "muscularity of thought." One finds little deep philosophical psychology or cultural critique anywhere in Bookchin's works. Such areas of inquiry must necessarily be repressed, for they are a threat to his municipalism. The very discussion of the issues they pose leads to a consideration of the larger context of social questions that he seeks to answer within the confines of a narrow and artificially bracketed "political" sphere.

The Municipalist Program

Libertarian municipalism has always claimed to be not only a theoretical analysis of the nature of radical democracy, but a workable, practical program for change. At one point, Bookchin proposed the program of libertarian municipalism as the basis for potential organization of the green movement in North America. The municipalist program is presented as a viable strategy for creating and mobilizing activist movements in present-day towns and cities in the United States. Yet one must ask what the real possibilities for organizing groups and movements under that banner might be, given the present state of political culture, given the existing public to which appeals must be addressed, and, not least of all, given the system of communication and information that must be confronted in any attempt to persuade the public.

Bookchin recognizes as significant political advances structural changes (such as neighborhood assemblies or municipally run services) that move in the direction of municipal democracy or economic municipalization, electoral strategies for gaining political influence or control on behalf of the municipalist agenda, and, to some degree, alternative projects that are independent of the state. On the other hand, he rejects, either as irrelevant or as a dangerous form of co-optation, any political proposal for reform of the nation-state, beyond the local (or sometimes, the state) level. Thus, he has judged the neighborhood planning assemblies in Burlington, Vermont, as an important advance, even though these assemblies do not have policy-making or law-making authority. On the other hand, he has rejected the legitimacy of certain rather far-reaching demands by the green movement because they propose action at the national level.

Bookchin criticizes very severely all strategies that do not lead toward municipal direct democracy and municipal self-management, since he sees these approaches as forms of capitulation to the dominant system. He rejects the active participation by municipalists, social ecologists, Left Greens, and anarchists in movements for social justice, peace, and other "progressive" causes when the specific goals of these movements are not clearly linked to a comprehensive liberatory vision of social, economic, and political transformation, which he essentially limits, at this point in history, to the libertarian municipalist program. It is doubtful whether, if Bookchin had been on the scene at the time, he would have encouraged libertarian municipalists to become active in as broad and nonprogrammatic a movement as Occupy Wall Street, despite its anarchist and "horizontalist" dimensions.

Bookchin and Biehl's critique of the Left Greens shows the implications of this antireformist position. They attack this tendency for its demand to "cut the Pentagon budget by 95 percent," and its proposals for "a $10 per hour minimum wage [in 1991 dollars]," "a thirty-hour work week with no loss of income," and a "workers' superfund."[47] They hold that the failing in these proposals is that they do not eliminate the last 5 percent of the military budget, thus supporting the nation-state, and that they perpetuate economic control at the national level. Bookchin dismisses the Left Greens' proposals as "commonplace economic demands."[48] He distinguishes between his own efforts "to enlarge the *directly democratic* possibilities that exist within the republican system" and the Left Greens' "typical trade unionist and social democratic demands that are designed to render capitalism and the state more palatable."[49]

It is true that the Left Greens' proposals are reformist, rather than revolutionary (though they might fairly be described as radically reformist). It is impossible, however, to deduce a priori the conclusion that all efforts to make national economic policy more just and to demilitarize the nation-state are inherently regressive or cooptative. The empirical evidence on such matters is far from conclusive. For example, reforms producing improvement in conditions for the less privileged segments of society may lead them to become more politically engaged and facilitate their radicalization. Successful fights for decent primary, secondary, and higher education have sometimes intensified social contradictions by producing a well-educated populace that rebels against institutions that deny them the better life for which their education has prepared them.

There is, in fact, an inspiring history of struggles for limited goals that did not betray the more far-reaching visions, and indeed revolutionary impulses, of the participants. Success in these limited struggles sometimes contributes to the development of the communities of solidarity and liberation on which the emergence of the free communitarian society will depend.

For example, the anarchists who fought for the reformist goal of the eight-hour workday did not give up their revolutionary goal of the abolition of capitalism. Bookchin holds that the eight-hour demand was made *only* because it was part of the pursuit of "the goal of insurrection" and "was designed to reinforce what was virtually an armed conflict"[50] However, this is an inaccurate reading of history. The goals of the anarchists in the eight-hour-day movement were complex. One was, indeed, the radicalization of the working class. A second was the eight-hour day itself, which was considered by many to be a real gain for the workers. A third was the achievement of a growing solidarity with the workers and their struggles, which was considered a good, apart from any immediate pragmatic gains. This identification transcended the kind of strategic thinking that Bookchin emphasizes. A notable exponent of the latter two justifications was Emma Goldman, who originally followed Johann Most in rejecting the significance of such limited demands. She attributes her change in outlook to the moving words of an elderly worker in the audience at one of her lectures.[51]

There is no reason why Left Greens today cannot similarly fight for a thirty-hour work week without giving up their vision of economic democracy. Indeed, it seems important that those who have utopian visions should also *stand with ordinary people* in their fights for justice and democracy—even though many of these people may not have yet developed such visions, and may not have learned yet how to articulate their hopes in theoretical terms. Unless this occurs, the prevailing dualistic split between reflection and action will continue to be reproduced in movements for social transformation, and the kind of "People" that libertarian municipalism presupposes will never become a reality. To reject all reform proposals at the level of the nation-state a priori reflects a lack of sensitivity to the issues that are meaningful in relation to the lives and aspirations of actual people now.

Bookchin is correct in his view that groups like the Left Greens easily lose the utopian and transformative dimension of their outlook as they become focused on reform proposals that might immediately appeal to a wide public. It is true that the Left Green proposal to "democratize the United Nations" seems rather outlandish from the radically decentralist perspective of the Left Green movement itself. Yet it is inconsistent for Bookchin to dismiss *all* proposals for reform, merely because they "propose" something less than the immediate abolition of the nation-state. Libertarian municipalism itself advocates, *for the immediate present*, working for change within subdivisions of the nation-state, as municipalities (and states, including small ones like Vermont) most certainly are at present.

Social ecological politics requires a dialectical approach to social phenomena, and this implies a careful analysis of the political culture, situated in relation to its larger natural and social context, and an understanding of the possibilities inherent in it. The danger of programmatic tendencies, which are endemic to the traditional Left and to all the sectarianisms it has spawned, is that they rigidify one's view of society, reinforce dogmatism, inflexibility, and attachment to one's ideas, limit one's social imagination, and discourage the open, experimental spirit that is necessary for creative social change.

While libertarian municipalism has taken a narrow, sectarian form, it can also be understood as a more general orientation toward radical grassroots democracy in towns and neighborhoods. Looked at in this broader sense, the concept can make a significant contribution to the development of a vision of a free, cooperative community. Bookchin sometimes presented a far-reaching list of proposals for developing more ecologically responsible and democratic communities. These include the establishment of community credit unions, community-supported agriculture, associations for local self-reliance, and community gardens.[52] Elsewhere, he includes in the "minimal steps" for creating "Left Green municipalist movements" such activities as electing council members who support "assemblies and other popular institutions"; establishing "civic banks to fund municipal enterprises and land purchases"; creating community-owned enterprises; and forming "grassroots networks" for various purposes.[53]

In a discussion of how a municipalist movement might be initiated in the state of Vermont, he presents proposals that emphasize cooperatives and even small, individually owned businesses.[54] He suggests that the process could begin with the purchase of unprofitable enterprises to create worker self-managed cooperatives, the establishment of land trusts, and support for small-scale enterprises. This could be done, he notes, without infringing "on the proprietary rights of small retail outlets, service establishments, artisan shops, small farms, local manufacturing enterprises, and the like."[55] He concludes that in such a system, "cooperatives, farms, and small retail outlets would be fostered with municipal funds and placed under growing public control."[56] He adds that a "People's Bank" to finance the economic projects could be established, buying groups to support local farming could be established, and public land could be used for "domestic gardening."[57]

These proposals present the outline of an admirable program for promoting a vibrant local economy based on cooperatives and small businesses. Yet it is precisely the "municipalist" element of such a program that might be least practical for quite some time, given the political culture of the United States. It seems likely that for the present the members of cooperatives and the owners of small enterprises would have little enthusiasm for coming under "increasing public control," if this means that the municipality (either through an assembly or local officials) would increasingly take over management decisions. Whatever might evolve eventually as a cooperative economy develops, a program for change in the real world must either have an appeal to an existing public, or must have a workable strategy for creating such a public. There is certainly considerable potential for broad support for "public control" in areas like environmental protection, health and safety measures, and greater economic justice for workers. However, the concept of "public control" of economic enterprises through management by neighborhood or municipal assemblies is, to use Bookchin's terminology, a "nonsense demand" at present, since the preconditions for making it meaningful do not exist. The demand certainly *should* be meaningful, but only *will* be to the degree that growing communities of solidarity and liberation create those preconditions.

Beyond the Fetishism of Assemblies

While Bookchin sees the municipality as a whole as the most important political realm, he identifies the municipal assembly as the privileged organ of democratic politics, and puts enormous emphasis on its place in both the creation and functioning of free municipalities. "Popular assemblies," he says, "are the minds of a free society; the administrators of their policies are the hands."[58] However, as central as assemblies may be to the realization of participatory democracy, this metaphor distorts and exaggerates their possible significance. One hears echoes of the dualistic and hierarchical Aristotelian idea of the "rational element" as "the ruling part" of the person—in this case the social organism. In reality, the "mind" of a society will always be widely dispersed throughout all social realms. Not only is it not *necessary* that a society's most significant thought and reflection should take place in popular assemblies, it is *inconceivable* that most of it should occur there. Particularly in a community that encourages creative thought and imagination, social intelligence will operate through the ongoing reflection of individuals in their everyday lives, through diverse, thriving networks of small groups and grassroots institutions in which these individuals formulate their ideas and aspirations, and through vibrant democratic media of communication in which citizens exchange ideas and shape the values of the community.[59]

Bookchin fails to confront adequately certain important issues concerning the scope of decision-making by assemblies. He clearly believes that *all* important policy decisions can and should be made in the assembly, even in the case of emergencies. He confidently assures us that, "given modern logistical conditions, there can be no emergency so great that assemblies cannot be rapidly convened to make important policy decisions by a majority vote and the appropriate boards convened to execute these decisions—irrespective of a community's size or the complexity of its problems. Experts will always be available to offer their solutions, hopefully competing ones that will foster discussion, to the more specialized problems a community may face."[60] But this is hardly convincing. Are we to believe that all issues concerning education, social aid, health, (neighborhood, town, and regional) community planning, energy, sanitation, conflict resolution, self-defense, agreements with other communities or bodies, and a multitude of other major concerns can be resolved and largely administered by an assembly consisting of the whole body of the citizens? In a densely populated, technologically complex, intricately interrelated world, every community will need to make difficult, complex decisions concerning this entire spectrum of issues that can hardly be dealt with on an ad hoc basis by large assemblies. It is impossible to imagine assemblies formulating directives on such matters that are so specific that administrators would have no significant role in shaping policy, or that they could carry out policies without reflection and deliberation.

All complex systems of social organization require developed forms of administration of rules and policies. A just, democratic system will devote much attention to shaping administration in accord with its basic values and structuring it to minimize typical dangers. It seems rather remarkable that Bookchin never explores the basic question of whether any formal, codified system of local law should exist to give direction to the administration of policy.[61] If such laws, or, indeed, any general rules and policy decisions are adopted by an assembly, they must then be applied to particular cases and articulated by judicial and administrative agencies. It is inevitable that these agencies will have some share in political power. But this alternative is inconsistent with his many affirmations of the supremacy of the assembly. On the other hand, if no explicit general rules are adopted by the assembly, then it will have the impossibly complex task of applying its implicit rules to all disputed cases and formulating all important details of programs. We are left with a purgatorial vision of hapless citizens condemned to listening endlessly to "hopefully competing" experts on every imaginable area of municipal administration and then desperately struggling to micromanage all the affairs of the community.

It is possible that if Bookchin's proposals were instituted, the policy-making power of administrators might even be greater than in other systems, in view of the fact that he does not propose any significant sphere for judicial or legal institutions that might check administrative power. Unless we assume that libertarian municipalist communities will become and remain quite simplified (an assumption that is inconsistent with Bookchin's ideas concerning technology, cities, etc.), then it would in reality be impossible for all decisions concerning the application of policy decisions to specific cases to be made in the assembly, or to be supervised directly by the assembly. A popular judiciary and administration might be one way of solving such problems.[62] However, the judicial and administrative realms remain almost a complete void in Bookchin's political theory, despite his fleeting references to popular courts in classical Athens and other historical cases. Among the possible libertarian and democratic procedures to perform judicial and administrative functions are popular juries, as proposed by Godwin two centuries ago, and citizens' committees, as suggested by Burnheim.[63]

Bookchin dismisses proposals for popular juries and citizens' committees as unacceptable *"systems of representation."*[64] However, this assessment does not reflect the true nature of proposals such as those of

Godwin and Burnheim. In fact, neither system includes "representation" in the sense of the creation of a specific group of elected officials separate from the body of citizens. One of the appealing aspects of such juries and committees is that since membership is determined through random selection, all citizens have an equal opportunity to exercise decision-making power. It is an exemplary case of keeping "the empty place of power" as empty as possible. Some of the possible corrupting influences of large assemblies (encouragement of egoistic competition, undue influence by power-seeking personalities, etc.) are much less likely to emerge in such a context. Both the application of general decisions to specific cases at the local level and collective decision-making beyond the local level pose difficult challenges to direct democracy.

Popular committees and juries offer participatory democratic means of performing functions that cannot possibly be carried out effectively by assemblies. Moreover, there is a sense in which democratic bodies consisting of randomly selected citizens are the most radically democratic and most radically anarchistic form of communal self-determination and self-administration. Rancière has presented a powerful case to this effect. He contends that democracy "first of all means this: anarchic 'government,' one based on nothing other than the absence of every title to govern."[65] It is anarchistic in two senses, in that it is most inimical to any form of domination, and in that all, no matter what real or pretended advantages they may have over others (including personal charisma or rhetorical ability), must "bow before the law of chance."[66] The drawing of lots is the most radical "power of the people," because it does not mean rule by the majority, or by any group or segment of society, but rather "the power of anyone at all, the equality of capabilities to occupy the positions of governors and the governed."[67] Rancière argues that the reason the drawing of lots now seems "contrary to every serious principle for selecting governors" is "because we have at once forgotten what democracy meant and what type of 'nature' it aimed at countering."[68] What democracy meant was what classical political theory attacked it for, in the name of social order and reason, and what modern political theory attacks it for, usually in the name of "democracy": that it was a process leading to the overthrow of all forms of *arche*. And the "nature" that it sought to counter was the ideological conception of nature, in which hierarchy and domination were inscribed into the nature of things. In short, the Great Book of Nature was (re-)written in language of *arche*.

So there is challenging work of remembering at hand, work that will only succeed to the degree that it is transformed into active experimentation with the neglected participatory forms of association; experimentation that fortunately is beginning to occur on a much wider scale. Some empirical support for the promise of popular committees and administrative groups emerged in the Occupy movement, in which the most important work was often done not in general assemblies, but rather in diverse committees that were sometimes called working groups or workshops.[69] For example, participants in Occupy Slovenia reported that committees or "workshops" became more basic expressions of direct action and of the diversity of the movement than were the assemblies. "Of particular importance is the way that the democracy of direct action, with its empowerment of decentralized workshops rather than the central assembly, encourages new initiatives, even initiatives that the majority of those at the assembly might not actively support."[70] Most of my own work in Occupy New Orleans focused on helping coordinate a working group, the Solidarity Economy Group, which acted independently of the general assembly, though in accord with the movement's common values, and was able to do outreach and focused grassroots organizing that was beyond the scope of the assembly. It is clear that the future success of grassroots democracy will depend on experimentation with various participatory forms and our ability to learn from the sharing of, and reflection on, our engaged experience.

We must pay careful attention to the many places in the world where such experimentation is taking place. For example, very significant evidence concerning the balance between assemblies and other democratic organs is offered by the experience of the Bolivian indigenous social movements. Zibechi reports that during the insurgency of 2003 in El Alto, neighborhood governments "supplanted the delegitimized and absent state," and "actions were carried out directly by the residents of the neighborhoods, overriding all other institutions and organizations, even the ones created by them beforehand."[71] The grassroots participatory assemblies were extremely important, but were not the privileged locus of popular power. They "acted as structures of territorial identity within which other kinds of loyalties, organizational networks, solidarities, and initiatives are deployed in an autonomous manner."[72] Significantly, within the "neighborhood microgovernments" that were organized, "all social leadership was revolved."[73] Also, in the Indian Army, assignment of positions was "rotating, cyclical, using the same system of rotation as the *ayllu* [rural community]. Everyone has an equal chance to be a commander."[74] In both the "civil" and "military" spheres, decision-making and administration of communal affairs were divided between the community assembly and other bodies that were based on rotation of membership. This experience offers important lessons on how a community can act democratically and effectively in areas that necessarily go beyond the scope and capacities of assemblies.

Another issue that must be faced by advocates of popular assemblies is that even within the formally democratic assembly itself, true participatory democracy is not necessarily realized. It is important that disguised power-relations should not achieve legitimacy through the ideology of an egalitarian, democratic body in which "the People" supposedly act in an "unmediated" fashion, and in which their will is considered "transparent." In fact, in assemblies with hundreds or thousands of members, or even with tens of thousands of potential members (as proposed by libertarian municipalism), there is an enormous potential for manipulation and power-seeking behavior. If it is true that power corrupts, as anarchists more than anyone else have stressed, then one cannot look with complacency on the power that comes from being the center of attention of a large assembly, from success in debate before such an assembly, and from the quest for victory for one's cause. Rousseau's classic critique of the dire effect on democratic assemblies of factions and parties was well-founded. To minimize these dangers, it is necessary to avoid idealizing assemblies, to analyze carefully their strengths and weaknesses, and to experiment with processes that can bring them closer to the highest ideals that inspire them.

The scale of the assembly is one of the key questions that participatory democrats must confront. Bookchin recognizes that given the size of existing municipalities, there will be a need for even more decentralized decision-making bodies. He suggests that "whether a municipality can be administered by all its citizens in a single assembly or has to be subdivided into several confederally related assemblies depends much on its size," and he proposes that the assembly might be constituted on block, neighborhood, or town level.[75] The majority of the world now lives in urbanized areas, over 20 percent in urban agglomerations of over one million, and over 5 percent in megacities of over ten million that are growing rapidly. In such a global context, the idea of "municipal assemblies" becomes increasingly less viable.[76] In highly urbanized sectors of global society, the creation of democratic assemblies at the level of the neighborhood (or even smaller units) seems to be a more promising approach. Zibechi notes that between 1988 and 2005 the number of neighborhood assemblies in El Alto tripled but the size of the neighborhoods decreased from 2,000 to between 1,300 and 1,400 people. He observes that as the assemblies got smaller they became stronger and less subject to co-optation.[77]

It must be recognized that the concept of the neighborhood is itself a problematical one. The term "neighborhood" can refer to anything ranging from an arbitrary administrative unit to a rather clearly defined, historically and culturally determined community. Bookchin claims that New York City, for example, still consists of neighborhoods that are "organic communities."[78] It is true that in many contemporary American cities with long histories there remains a significant degree of identification with neighborhoods that can contribute to the creation of neighborhood democracy. Yet to describe the neighborhoods of New York or other present-day cities as "organic communities" is not realistic. These cities have been thoroughly transformed according to the exigencies of the state, bureaucratic administration, surveillance and control, capitalist production, marketing, and real estate speculation, with all the atomization, fragmentation, and privatization that this implies. Natives of many great historic cities with strong neighborhood traditions (e.g., Paris) complain that traditional neighborhoods have been almost completely destroyed by commercialization, land speculation, and displacement of the less affluent to the suburbs. Furthermore, neighborhood tradition itself is at once "organic" and "inorganic," containing both the history of commonalities and the history of social contradiction. The political significance of urban tradition does not imply a mere defense of that which is simply "there," but a process of contestation and social creativity based on that which both is and is not there. It is not that when we go there, there's no there there. There is something there, and there are ghosts of what has been there. There are radical fragments, and perhaps revolutionary absences.

In the United States, much of traditional urban neighborhood life has been undermined by social atomization, institutionalized racism, and the migration of capital and economic support away from the center. Bookchin correctly cites my own city of New Orleans as an example of a city that has a strong tradition of culturally distinct neighborhoods that have endured with clear identities until recent times.[79] But it is also a good example of the culturally corrosive effects of contemporary economistic society, which progressively transforms local culture into a commodity for advertising, real estate speculation, and tourism, while it destroys it as a lived reality. Thus, the neighborhood "organic community" is much more an imaginary construct that is entangled with nostalgic feelings and idealistic aspirations than it is an objective social reality. Rather than seeing the neighborhood as an idealized "organic community," we should instead see it as "a dialectical community." This means that it is a *social project* in which citizens create and recreate the neighborhood community, by grounding it in and reaffirming certain actually existing "organic" elements, igniting communal indignation through a shared realization of loss, generating new elements founded on the creative interpretation of needs and aspirations, and, finally, transforming all these elements through their mutual interaction as this developing project gains coherence.

We live in a world that is experiencing the rapid growth of cities, and especially megalopolises, which have now reached populations of up to forty million. Radical changes are taking place in global urban society and these pose crucial questions for the libertarian municipalist model. What would a local assembly look like in the Third World megalopolises that are the fastest-growing segment of global society? Could delegates from hundreds or thousands of block or neighborhood assemblies come to an agreement with "rigorous instructions" from their assemblies, as Bookchin's municipalist program suggests? He is certainly right when he states that "one of our chief goals must be to radically decentralize our industrialized urban areas into humanly-scaled cities and towns" that are "ecologically sound."[80] But a social ecological politics must not only aim at such far-reaching, visionary goals but also offer effective political options for the increasing proportion of humanity that lives in highly populated urban areas, and, above all, the inhabitants of the rapidly growing slums and shanty towns of the global South, who face catastrophic crises requiring practical responses as soon as possible.[81] It seems difficult to avoid the conclusion that such cities will require a combination of democratic assemblies and forms of committee, jury, and council decision-making that must be made as democratic and as responsible to the whole community as is possible. If social ecological politics and communitarian anarchism are to be meaningful today, they must confront this real urban world and offer hope for effective liberatory action.

It is clear that in this real world direct participatory democracy will imply local assemblies of considerable size. Consequently certain well-known dangers of large deliberative bodies must be taken seriously. Among the problems that often emerge in such bodies are competitiveness, egotism, theatrics, demagogy, charismatic leadership, factionalism, aggressiveness, obsession with procedural details, domination of discussion by manipulative minorities, and passivity of the majority. These are ever-present dangers, but they are likely to be aggravated by the size of the local assembly, which will be many times larger than most traditional legislative bodies. Moreover, the gap in political sophistication between individuals in local assemblies will no doubt be much greater than in traditional bodies composed of members of the political class, who must develop a certain degree of political expertise to succeed politically. Finally, the local assembly would lose one important advantage possessed by systems of representation, for all their other drawbacks. Elected representatives can be chastised for betraying the people when they seem to act contrary to the will or interest of the community. On the other hand, those who emerge as leaders of a democratic assembly, including those who take power by default if most do not participate actively in managing the affairs of the community, might be able to disguise undemocratic behavior more effectually, since they can claim to be acting as equal members of a popular democratic body.

It will be instructive to listen again to Zibechi on the lessons about power to be learned from indigenous experience. He quotes Clastres on the implicit forces of hierarchy and domination within any culture or social structure that have always threatened to give rise to the state if not combated:

> Yes, the state exists in primitive societies, even in the tiniest band of nomad-hunters. It exists, but it is constantly being warded off, it is constantly being prevented. It is ceaselessly prevented from becoming a reality. A primitive society directs all its efforts toward preventing its chief from becoming a chief (and that can go as far as murder) . . . the history of societies without classes is that history of their struggle against the latent State; it is the history of their effort to code the flux of power.[82]

Zibechi concludes that "the state exists, effectively, in every neighborhood council, in every practice organized in a structured way," but notes further that "the residents have also developed mechanisms to address this," ranging from noncooperation to overt insurrection, and including tactics they have been using for five hundred years.[83]

An authentically democratic movement will honestly and openly recognize the considerable potential for the emergence of disguised and mystified elitism and power-seeking within assemblies. It will deal with this threat not only through formal procedures within assemblies, but above all by creating a communitarian, democratic culture that will express itself in decision-making bodies and in all other institutions. For the assembly and other organs of direct democracy to contribute effectively to a free, cooperative community, they must be purged of the competitive, agonistic, masculinist aspects that have often corrupted them. They can only fulfill their democratic promise if they are an integral expression of the cooperative community that embodies in its institutions a spirit of solidarity with that community itself, and with the larger communities of humanity and nature. Such a community will only be realized if the movement to create it is itself a transformative community that reshapes, through its own self-consciously liberatory and solidaristic processes and institutions, the values, feelings, sensibilities, and relationships of its members.

The meaning of such personal transformation has been elaborated perhaps most explicitly in feminist, and especially ecofeminist, ethics, which has pointed out that the dominant moral and political discourses have exhibited a one-sided emphasis on ideas and principles, and neglected the realm of feeling and sensibility. The feminist call for an expansion of the borders of the moral through an *ethics of care* has been developed further into the ecofeminist *politics of care* for humanity and nature. In its most radical version, materialist ecofeminism as a political vision is rooted historically and experientially (given *ethical substance*) through an analysis of the subsistence labor and care-giving activities of women and indigenous peoples around the world. Ariel Salleh points out, in a passage specifically aimed at Biehl's implicitly masculinist position, that for ecofeminism "politics is no longer focused exclusively on the mechanics of public order and justice, but seen to penetrate the recesses of daily life and the very fabric of the discursive medium itself."[84] In this spirit, we must explore the ways in which the transition from formal to substantive democracy depends not only on the establishment of more radically democratic *forms*, but also on the establishment of cultural *practices* that foster a radically democratic, egalitarian, mutualistic, and communitarian ethos.

Municipal Economics

One of the most compelling aspects of Bookchin's political thought is the central role of an ethical critique of the dominant economistic society, and the call for the creation of a "moral economy" as a precondition for a just ecological society. He asserts that such a moral economy implies the emergence of "a productive community" to replace the amoral "mere marketplace," that currently prevails. Further, it requires that producers "explicitly agree to exchange their products and services on terms that are not merely 'equitable' or 'fair' but supportive of each other."[85] He believes that if the prevailing system of economic exploitation and the dominant economistic culture based on it are to be eliminated, a sphere must be created in which people find new forms of exchange to begin successfully replacing capitalist relations, and this sphere must be capable of ultimately displacing the capitalism system entirely. He sees this sphere as above all that of the municipalized economy. He states that "under libertarian municipalism," property becomes "part of a larger whole that is controlled by the citizen body in assembly as citizens."[86] Elsewhere, he explains that "land, factories, and workshops would be controlled by popular assemblies of free communities, not by a nation-state or by worker-producers who might very well develop a proprietary interest in them."[87]

Communitarian anarchists must agree with Bookchin that democratic community control of production is an essential element of the ultimate social ideal. The free community will be a realization of what Buber called "the full cooperative," that is the synthesis of cooperative production, cooperative consumption, and cooperative living. For the immediate future, at least, it is not at all clear that a municipalized economic sector should be looked upon as the *primary* focus of economic transformation, rather than as *one area* among many in which significant economic change should take place. It is possible to imagine a broad spectrum of self-managed enterprises, individual producers, and small partnerships that would enter into a growing cooperative economic sector that would incorporate social ecological values. The extent to which the communitarian principle of distribution according to need can be achieved will be proportional to the degree to which cooperative and communitarian values have evolved, and to which the institutional structures within which they exist will have emerged.

Bookchin is certainly right in his view that participation in a moral economy will be "an ongoing education in forms of association, virtue, and decency" through which citizens develop cooperative, communitarian qualities and relationships.[88] And it is true that ideally "price, resources, personal interests, and costs" will "play no role in a moral economy" and that there will be "no 'accounting' of what is given and taken."[89] However, social transformation always begins with historically determined persons in a historically determined cultural context. Though an anarcho-communist system of distribution is the most ethically justifiable one as a long-term goal, the attempt to put such a system into practice in the short run, without developing the psychological and institutional preconditions for its successful functioning, would be a certain recipe for disillusionment and economic failure. Moreover, while the free community will certainly reject "accounting" in the individualist, propertarian sense of reducing every exchange to a quantifiable monetary transaction, nevertheless, the community may very well find it desirable to take account of exchanges in relation to both social and ecological needs and to available means, even with a degree of specificity that is unimaginable under capitalism.

Bookchin and Biehl sometimes attribute to the process of municipalization an almost miraculous power to abolish or render innocuous with great rapidity all egoistic and particularistic interests that have been deeply inculcated by the culture of late capitalism. They attack proposals for worker self-management on the grounds that such a system does not, as in the case of municipalization, "eliminate the possibility that *particularistic* interests of *any* kind will develop in economic life,"[90] and contend that in "a democratized polity" workers would develop "a general public interest,"[91] rather than a particularistic one of any sort. But it is also quite possible for the citizens of a municipality (or neighborhood) to put their own interest above that of the members of other communities, or that of the larger community of nature. The mere fact of being a "citizen of a municipality" does not in itself assure identification with "a general public interest." On the other hand, the condition of being such a citizen poses the problem of reconciling *particular* (local, neighborhood, municipal) interest with *general* (federative, regional, bioregional, global) interests.

Furthermore, libertarian municipalism has not confronted adequately the problem of possible conflict between the *particularistic* perspective of the worker in a productive enterprise and the *particularistic* perspective of the citizen of the municipality. Bookchin and Biehl have proposed that "workers in their area of the economy" be placed on advisory boards that are "merely technical agencies, with no power to make policy decisions."[92] But this would do little if anything to solve the problem of conflict of interest. Bookchin calls the "municipally managed enterprise" at one point "a worker-citizen controlled enterprise,"[93] but the actual control is effectively limited to members of the community acting as citizens, not as workers. Shared policy-making between the community-members qua community-members and the workers qua workers, despite its complexities, would seem to be a much more promising short- to medium-term option. In either case (pure community democracy or a mixed system of community and workplace democracy), it seems obvious that there would be a continual potential for conflict between workers who are focused on their needs and responsibilities as producers and assembly members who are focused on the needs and responsibilities of the local community as a whole, and this problem cannot be solved through a merely theoretical affirmation of the priority of the community.

Another area of possible conflict between the community and the workplace concerns small, nonexploitative enterprises. Bookchin suggests that for a certain period of time, municipalist policies would "not infringe on the proprietary rights of small retail outlets, service establishments, artisan shops, small farms, local manufacturing enterprises, and the like."[94] The question arises, though, of why this sector should not continue to exist in the long term, alongside more cooperative forms of production, if some citizens voluntarily choose this alternative. Would the assembly at a certain point abolish such enterprises by fiat, even if they had not evolved in an exploitative direction? A precedent for their continuation as an "individualist sector" within a larger communal economy is the experience of the collectives in the Spanish Revolution. Collectives that often included the majority of people in a village existed alongside small farms and enterprises of "individualists" who did not join.[95] There is no conclusive evidence that such small enterprises are necessarily exploitative or that they cannot be operated in a socially and ecologically sound manner within a larger solidarity economy. This would be the case to the degree that the community democratically establishes just and effective parameters of social and ecological responsibility.[96]

However, Bookchin vehemently rejects this possibility. He claims that if any sort of market and any individual enterprises continue to exist, then "competition will force even the smallest enterprise eventually either to grow or to die, to accumulate capital or to disappear, to devour rival enter-prises or to be devoured."[97] Yet he has noted that historically the existence of a *market* has not been equivalent to the existence of a *market-dominated society*. He has not explained why such a distinction cannot hold in the future. He has himself been criticized by "purist" anarchists who attack his acceptance of municipal government as a capitulation to "archism." Yet he rightly distinguishes between the mere existence of governmental institutions and *statism*, the system of political domination that results from the centralization of political power in the nation-state. Similarly, one may distinguish between the mere existence of market exchanges and *capitalism*—the system of economic domination that tends toward the concentration of economic power in large corporate enterprises, based on the structural possibility of capital endlessly reproducing and expanding itself through exchange.

But whatever the long-term future of the market may be, it is in fact the economic context in which present-day experiments take place. If municipally owned enterprises are established, they will at present neces-sarily operate within a market, if only because many of the resources they need for production will be produced within the market economy. It is also likely that they would choose to sell some or most of their prod-ucts within the market, since the vast majority of potential consumers, including those most sympathetic to cooperative experiments, would still be operating within the market economy. Indeed, it is not certain that even if a great many such municipal enterprises were created that they would choose to limit their exchanges entirely to the network of similar enterprises, rather than continuing to participate in the larger market.[98] Whatever may be the case in the future, to the extent that municipalized enterprises are proposed as a real-world practical strategy, they will necessarily constitute (by Bookchin's own criteria) a "reform" within the existing economy. Thus, it is inconsistent for advocates of libertarian municipalism to attack proposals for self-management as mere reformism. These proposals, like Bookchin's, are incapable of abolishing the state and capitalism by fiat or by some automatic process of gradual growth and absorption. But were they adopted, they would represent a real advance in expanding the cooperative and democratic aspects of production, while at the same time improving the economic position and effective freedom of the exploited and disenfranchised. Moreover, they can be part of the larger process of developing growing communities of liberation and solidarity that can ultimately act collectively for fundamental social transformation.

The Confederative Principle

Anarchist political thought has usually proposed that social cooperation beyond the local level should take place through voluntary federations of relatively autonomous individuals, workplaces, or communities. While classical anarchist theorists such as Proudhon and Bakunin called such a system "federalism," Bookchin calls his variation on this theme "confederalism." He describes its structure as consisting of "above all a network of administrative councils whose members or delegates are elected from popular face-to-face democratic assemblies, in the various villages, towns, and even neighborhoods of large cities."[99] Under such a system, power will remain entirely in the hands of the assemblies. "Policymaking is exclusively the right of popular community assemblies," while "administration and coordination are the responsibility of confederal councils."[100] Councils therefore exist only to carry out the will of the assemblies. Toward this end, "the members of these confederal councils are strictly mandated, recallable, and responsible to the assemblies that chose them for the purpose of coordinating and administering the policies formulated by the assemblies themselves."[101] The administrative councils are thus not democratic decision-making bodies in any sense; they are strictly limited to carrying out the directives of such democratic bodies.

It is not clear how this absolute division between policy-making and administration could work in practice. How, for example, is administration to occur when there are disagreements between assemblies on policies or the means of administering policies? Since there can be no delegation of policy-making authority, effective collective activity would seemingly depend in many cases on a *consensus* of assemblies that is expressed in the administrative councils. The only other solution would be for only those communities that are in agreement to administer policies collectively. However, this option would work only for those policies that could succeed even with the noncooperation of a segment of the confederated communities. Many endeavors, such as road-building projects, flood protection programs, and conservation plans, would require cooperation of contiguous communities in order to succeed. Thus, much would depend on the achievement of consensus. It should be noted that Bookchin is quick to attack "the tyranny of consensus" as a decision-making procedure within assemblies, in which small numbers of dissenters can delay or defeat collective action. Yet, ironically, he seems obliged to depend on consensus (and, in fact, depend on absolute consensus rather than the modified consensus often adopted by assemblies) for decision-making in bodies whose members are rigidly mandated to vote according to previous directions from their assemblies.

He seems, at least, to be committed to such a position until he comes to the question of what should occur when some communities do not abide by certain fundamental principles. He states that "if particular communities or neighborhoods—or a minority grouping of them—choose to go their own way to a point where human rights are violated or where ecological mayhem is permitted, *the majority* in a local or regional confederation has every right to prevent such malfeasance through its confederal council."[102] However, this proposal blatantly contradicts his requirement that policy be made only at the assembly level. If sanctions are imposed by a majority vote of the council, this would be an obvious case of a quite important policy being adopted above the assembly level (no single assembly could adopt collective action by many communities).

A very crucial, unanswered question is by what means the confederal council would exercise such a "preventive" authority. Presumably Bookchin has in mind various forms of coercion. But whatever his answer might be, such action would constitute policy-making above the assembly level in important areas. There is clearly a broad scope for interpretation of what does or does not infringe on human rights, or what does or does not constitute an unjustifiable ecological danger. If the majority of communities, acting confederally through a council, uses coercion to deal with such basic issues, then certain *statelike functions* would clearly emerge at the confederal level. Whether they should is an issue that must be considered by anarchists. However, what is clear is that is the possible emergence of such functions should be recognized and judged without illusions.

It would seem that the only way to avoid this result is to take a purist anarchist approach, in which collective action could only be taken above the assembly level through fully voluntary agreements of the communities, and that communities would have full rights of noncooperation or secession on any issue. According to such an approach, a community would have the right to refuse to cooperate, even in order to pursue goals that other communities think unjust or ecologically destructive. Under this form of confederal organization, everything would be decided by consensus, and the majority of confederating communities would have no power of enforcement in any area. This option would be consistent with Bookchin's initial claim that no decision-making should be made at the confederal level, though very few would consider it a viable way of solving problems in a complex world.

There are other aspects of Bookchin's confederalism that raise questions about the practicality or even the possibility of such a system. He proposes that activities of the assemblies be coordinated through the confederal councils, and that members of these councils must be "rotatable, recallable, and, above all, rigorously instructed in written form to support or oppose any issue that appears on the agenda."[103] But could such instruction be a practical possibility in highly populated, complex, technologically sophisticated societies? Could this system function at the equivalent of the national level, at the regional level, or even at the municipal level?

Paris, the city that produced the revolutionary "sections" that are one of the great inspirations for municipalism, might be taken as an example. Metropolitan Paris has today roughly twelve million people. If government were devolved into assemblies for each sizable neighborhood of twenty-five thousand people, there would be nearly five hundred assemblies in the metropolitan area. If it were decentralized into much more democratic assemblies for areas of a few blocks, with about one thousand citizens each, there would then be twelve thousand assemblies. If the city thus had hundreds or even thousands of neighborhood assemblies, and each "several" assemblies (as Bookchin suggests) would send delegates to councils, which presumably would have to form even larger confederations for truly municipal issues, could the chain of responsibility hold up? If so, how? And if not? If municipalism is not practicable in the kind of society in which real human beings happen to find themselves, then the question arises of what other political arrangements might be practicable and which also move in the direction of the admirable goals that Bookchin seeks to realize through municipalism.

Municipalizing Nature?

As Bookchin increasingly focused on the idea of *municipalist* politics, the theme of *ecological* politics faded increasingly further into the background of his thought. In fact, the idea of a *bioregional* politics was never incorporated into his version of social ecology. Yet there are two fundamental social ecological concepts that essentially define a bioregional perspective. One is the recognition of the dialectic of nature and culture, in which the larger natural world is seen as an active coparticipant in the creative activities of human beings. The other is the recognition of unity-in-diversity, in which the unique, determinate particularity of each part is seen as making an essential contribution to the unfolding of the developing whole. While Bookchin has done much to stress the importance of such general conceptions, what has been missing in his municipalist politics is sensitivity to the details of the natural world and the quite particular ways in which it can and does shape human cultural endeavors, and a sense of inhabiting various natural wholes, whether ecosystems, bioregions, or the entire biosphere. This is exactly what bioregionalism contributes to ecological politics.

One finds in Bookchin's writings little detailed discussion of ecological situatedness and bioregional particularity. Typically, he limits himself to statements such as that there should be a "sensitive balance between town and country"[104] and that a municipality should be "delicately attuned to the natural ecosystem in which it is located."[105] Elsewhere, he says that ecological communities should be "networked confederally through ecosystems, bioregions, and biomes," that they "must be artistically tailored to their natural surroundings," and that they "would aspire to live with, nourish, and feed upon the life-forms that indigenously belong to the ecosystems in which they are integrated."[106] These statements show concern for the relationship of a community to its ecological context, but the terms chosen to describe this relationship do not make bioregional realities central to the culture. Furthermore, Bookchin's discussions of confederalism invariably base organization on political principles and spatial proximity. He does not devote serious attention to the importance of bioregional realities to processes of imagining and shaping our communities and associations of communities. On the other hand, the bioregional imagination and the politics of place are central to ecocommunitarian anarchism.

It is likely that an underlying reason why Bookchin's does not focus on bioregional realities, or, indeed, on communal traditions in the strong, historically grounded sense is his fear that such natural and communal connections threaten the freedom of the individual. Such bonds are in conflict with Bookchin's Promethean, masculinist conception of heroic citizens shaping their own destiny. On the other hand, an ecocommunitarian approach values natural and social situatedness. Rather than threatening our freedom, such situatedness helps give it concrete substantiality. The free creative activity of a community gains richer and more determinate content within the context of a strong sense of place, in the midst of a continuity of natural and cultural history. The bioregional sensibility is based on a kind of commitment that Bookchin steadfastly rejects; that is, a giving oneself over to the other, a recognition of the claim of the other on the deepest levels of one's being. Bookchin describes his ideal community as "the commune that unites individuals by what they choose to like in each other rather than what they are obliged by blood ties to like."[107] However, when one develops and affirms one's membership in a human or natural community, one is hardly concerned with "choosing what to like and not to like" in the community (though one may certainly judge one's own human community quite harshly out of love and compassion for it).[108] The community helps constitute and is also an expression of one's very form of life and mode of being. Individualist concepts of choice, rights, justice, and interest lose their validity in this context.

There are times when Bookchin seems to come a bit closer to a bioregional and ecocommunitarian perspective. For example, he says that in an ecological society, "land would be used ecologically such that forests would grow in areas that are most suitable for arboreal flora and widely mixed food plants in areas that are most suitable for crops."[109] Culture and nature would seemingly both get their due through this simple division. But even here there are difficulties. A major ecological problem results from the fact that, except in the case of tropical rain forests, most areas that are quite well suited for forests (or prairies, or even wetlands) can also be used in a highly productive manner for crop production. A bioregional approach would stress heavily the importance of biological diversity and ecological integrity, and have much less enthusiasm for the further development of certain areas on grounds that they are "suitable for crops," in cases in which such development is not strictly necessary to provide adequately for human needs.

Bookchin comes closest to an authentically bioregional approach when he explains that "localism, taken seriously, implies a sensitivity to specialty, particularity, and the uniqueness of place, indeed a sense of place or *topos* that involves deep respect . . . to the areas in which we live and that are given to us in great part by the natural world itself."[110] Such admirable general principles need, however, to be developed into a comprehensive bioregional perspective that would give them a more concrete meaning. This perspective would address such issues as the ways in which bioregional particularity can be brought back into the town or city, how it can be discovered beneath the transformed surface, and how it can be expressed in the symbols, images, art, rituals, and other cultural expressions of the community. Bioregionalism gives content to the abstract concept that the creation of the ecological community is a dialectical, cooperative endeavor between human beings and the natural world. A bioregional politics expands our view of the political, by associating it more with the processes of ecologically grounded cultural creativity and with a mutualistic, cooperative process of self-expression on the part of the human community within the larger community of nature. It is a fundamental dimension of the project of realizing universal particularity.

Conclusion: A Politics of Liberty, Ecology, And Solidarity

The many questions raised here about libertarian municipalism do not in the slightest way cast doubt on the crucial importance of participatory, grassroots communal democracy to the realization of the free community of solidarity. Rather, they imply that if we value such democracy we will recognize the need for diverse, multidimensional experiments in democratic processes, and acknowledge the fact that many of the preconditions for a free and democratic culture lie in areas beyond the scope of what is usually called "democracy." Communes, cooperatives, collectives, and various other forms of organization are sometimes dismissed by Bookchin as "marginal projects" that cannot challenge the dominant system.[111] It is true that they have not successfully challenged that system thus far. However, there is no evidence that such diverse undertakings have any less potential for liberatory transformation than do local assemblies, nor is there evidence that a multidimensional politics that includes both assemblies and these other forms of organization will not have much greater potential than a politics that focuses almost exclusively on assemblies. An ecocommunitarianism that claims the legacy of anarchism will eschew any narrowly defined programs that would make municipalism, self-management, cooperatives, communalism, or any other approach the *royal road* to social transformation. On the other hand, it will see experiments in all of these areas—experiments that push each of those forms to their liberatory limits—as valuable steps toward discovering the way to a free, ecological society.

Proposals to create town and neighborhood assemblies have great merit, and should be a central element of an ecocommunitarian anarchist politics. But we must take into account the fact that they, and other counterinstitutions, are unlikely to become the dominant political processes in the near future. Unfortunately, we find that at times their partial adoption (in the form of virtually powerless "neighborhood planning assemblies" and "town meetings," or citizens' committees with little authority, or participatory budgeting that remains marginal) may even serve to deflect energy or diffuse demands for more basic cultural and personal changes. On the other hand, major advances in libertarian communitarianism can be made immediately through the establishment of affinity groups, base communities, internally democratic movements for change, and cooperative endeavors of many kinds. Advocates of radical democracy can do no greater service to this cause than to demonstrate the value of democratic processes by embodying them in their own forms of self-organization. Without imaginative and inspiring experiments in the practice of ecological, communitarian democracy by the radical democrats themselves, calls for "municipalism," "demarchy," or any other form of participatory democracy will have a hollow ring.

Bookchin made an important contribution to such efforts insofar as his work helped inspire many participants in ecological, communitarian, and participatory democratic projects. To the degree that he reduced ecological politics to a narrow, sectarian program of libertarian municipalism, he also created obstacles to the attainment of many of the very ideals he proclaimed. These ideals of liberty, ecology, and solidarity, remain, however, the guiding inspiration for theory and practice. They are indispensable for the development of a fully critical and dialectical social ecology, and for a renewed and reinvigorated practice of ecocommunitarian anarchist politics.

On Grassroots Revolution

In the following interview, intermedia conceptual/sound artist and scientist Alyce Santoro poses crucial questions about the most fundamental issues raised in the original edition of this book.

Alyce Santoro: Are you suggesting that social transformation can happen now, without waiting for radical change in the dominant political structure? Do you see "the impossible community" as a viable next phase in the evolution of the Occupy movement?

John P. Clark: Change can only happen now. That's when we do all our living, thinking and acting. So, we need to focus on how we can be most effective in creating forms of social transformation now. We need to rethink the temporality of change and also the spatiality of change. This means rethinking the old cliché "think globally, act locally." The challenge is to think and act locally and globally at the same time. In fact, we can't avoid acting locally and globally simultaneously, since global phenomena are largely made up of local ones and the magnitude of the global impacts of local action are constantly increasing. But there's another crucial dimension to this issue.

We need to continue to occupy, in the sense of truly liberating putatively public spaces, but we also have to consider carefully the ways in which we are occupied, in the sense of being dominated. To change the dominant structures, we need to find a way to break free from their dominance, which is not only institutional, but also ideological, imaginary, and practical. Our lives are determined powerfully by our shared systems of ideas, our collective fantasies, and our common forms of social practice, or ethos. The only effective way to short circuit this order of determination is to create, and then live, moment-to-moment, other institutional, ideological, imaginary, and practical realities—realities that embody freedom, justice and solidarity. To be effective, this must take place above all on the level of our most basic, primary communities.

The idea of "the impossible community" is that the community of solidarity and liberation appears as an impossibility within the confines of these structures of domination. So, the only viable alternative is to create—here and now—those very impossible communities. We need to stop demanding the impossible and simply do what is impossible. The strongest evidence for the possibility of something, including the impossible, is its actual existence. So, we have to do some serious anarchaeology, uncovering the rich history of free community that lies under layers of domination and the ideology of domination. But, above all, we have to get in touch with the practice of free community that is very much alive today, so that these living traditions can be nurtured and realized further.

I have in mind, historically, the enormous legacy of cooperative community, including many tribal traditions, the caring labor of women and traditional peoples, historical practices of local direct democracy, movements for workers' self-management, the vast history of intentional community, and the multitude of experiments in cooperative production, distribution, consumption, and living. This history continues today, especially on the margins of and in the gaps within the system of domination, and thus provides the "ethical substantiality," the realized and embodied social good, that is our best source of hope, guidance, and inspiration.

Occupy has been part of the process that I am describing. I devoted a lot of time to Occupy, and believe that, whatever its limitations, it has been enormously significant in engaging large numbers of people at the grassroots level, and giving them experience in participatory, directly democratic and consensual forms of decision-making. This kind of experience is invaluable to the kind of libertarian communitarian project described in the book. In such a project, the primary focus is on the regeneration of communities of solidarity and liberation through such specific forms as affinity groups, base communities, and intentional communities. At the same time, it requires expanding our efforts horizontally, through complementary cooperative projects in spheres such as the workplace, education, media and cultural creation, and vertically, through federative efforts at successive levels from the local, through the regional, to the global. Protest, occupation, and various forms of direct action must of course continue. But the creative, regenerative dimension must become our primary focus. Bakunin said, famously, that "the urge to destroy is a creative urge also." There is truth in this; however, we need to avoid lapsing into the leftist pitfalls of reactivity and the culture of permanent protest. Above all, we must not forget that that "the urge to create is a creative urge also."

AS: It seems the words "libertarian" and "anarchy" can be broadly interpreted; "communitarian," on the other hand, seems somewhat less ambiguous. Can you provide some basic definitions/current context for these constantly morphing terms?
JPC: Libertarians are people who are dedicated to defending and expanding freedom. However, "freedom" is a floating signifier, a flexible concept that can be appropriated for diverse and often conflicting purposes. It's also a master signifier, in that it has a kind of ineffable charismatic power that everyone wants to latch on to. So, the big question is what we mean by freedom.

The "Third Concept of Liberty" that I discuss in the book proposes that freedom has several crucial dimensions. One of these, the one that seems almost intuitive for Americans, is "negative freedom," or freedom from coercion, often epitomized as "not being told what to do." This idea must be developed into a larger conception of freedom from all forms of domination. While domination functions through overt force and the threat of force, it also (and more usually) operates through other diverse strategies and tactics of control. The second dimension of freedom is personal and communal self-determination. This means, above all, that we are able to live in a community that is a collective expression of our social being and our social ideals, rather than being an obstacle to them. Finally, and most significantly, freedom means personal and communal realization or flourishing, the achievement of the good in our personal and communal lives.

The term "libertarian" was invented in New Orleans in the 1850s by the French anarchist philosopher Joseph Déjacque. While he was here, Déjacque wrote his most important work, *L'Humanisphère*, and an important letter to Proudhon, the most famous anarchist thinker of the time. Despite their agreement in opposing the centralized state, Déjacque harshly criticized Proudhon on two grounds, first, for his sexism and support for patriarchy, and secondly, for his belief that the contribution of each individual to the value of a product could be determined. For

Déjacque, true freedom requires the abolition of all historic forms of domination, including, obviously, the age-old system of domination of women by men. It also requires that production and distribution be designed to fulfill the needs of all, rather than being based on a spurious individualist theory of value and entitlement. Déjacque concluded in his letter that because of Proudhon's acceptance of patriarchy and economic injustice, he was not a true *libertaire* or libertarian.

Déjacque's analysis also explains the meaning of anarchism in its deepest sense. This is discussed in the chapter of *The Impossible Community* entitled "Against Principalities and Powers." Anarchism is not merely an opposition to coercion or to any particular form of domination, such as the centralized state. Rather, it is the quest for freedom from all forms of domination—capitalism, the state, patriarchy, racial and ethnic oppression, bureaucratic and technological domination, gender and sex role oppression, and the domination of other species and of nature.

Which brings us to "communitarianism." In the United States, this term usually has a relatively conservative connotation, and is juxtaposed to liberalism in mainstream political thought. In South Asia and Britain, it's a more popularized term, often with pejorative undertones, and is linked to strong ethnic and religious identification and group conflicts. As I, and many others, use it, it is an affirmation of the age-old tradition of free, self-determining community. This might also be termed "communism," and often has been, though unfortunately this term has been co-opted by the forces of domination, just as the word "libertarian" has.

Nevertheless, I like to pose the seemingly paradoxical question: "Why is communism so good in practice, but it never seems to work in theory?" What most people think of as "communism" has not been communism at all, but rather a form of oppressive state capitalism or techno-bureaucratic despotism, justified through an ideology (a theory that doesn't work) that disguises it as "communism." Such a system has often been very effective as a form of domination, but not as a free, just or humane form of social organization. We might call it "authoritarian communism," but in reality, not only is it not really communism, it is in a very precise sense a form of anticommunism, the negation of communal autonomy. Historically, it has always feared real communities, taken power away from them, and done its best to crush or dissolve them.

There is, on the other hand, a long tradition of libertarian communism, which is the form of organization taken by communities of solidarity and liberation. It has been practiced in indigenous societies, in intentional communities (such as the most radical early kibbutzim in Israel and the Gandhian ashrams or cooperative ecocommunities in India), in the self-managed collectives during the Spanish Revolution, in affinity groups, in base communities, and in many families. It has constituted communism, in the sense of the autonomous self-determination of the community. It has often worked quite well.

We can also call this form of social organization "communitarianism." I find this term to be politically crucial today, above all, because I see the key step in personal and social transformation to be at the level of the person-in-community and each person's moment-to-moment practice within that community. We show that another world is possible by making another world actual. We need to rethink politics as world creation, though it is equally a process of world preservation. I think this is why much of the most effective communitarian anarchist practice has come from groups with a strong spiritual basis that generates an all-encompassing ethos. This is true of groups that come out of long traditions, like the Catholic Worker movement, the Gandhian Sarvodaya movement, engaged Buddhism and Daoism, and indigenous people's movements. But it is also true of small groups that draw on many communal and spiritual traditions and the great libertarian communitarian heritage, while finding their own way.

The emphasis on the primary community in no way excludes the need for simultaneous action at every other level. The quest for direct participatory democracy, for worker self-management, and for liberation from imperialist occupation, for example, cannot wait. However, the only way that these struggles can avoid co-optation is if they are rooted in liberatory transformation at the personal and communal level.

AS: On page 7 of your book you say, "What emerges out of traumatic marginalization and exclusion is liberatory communitarian potentiality, not any historical necessity." Could you talk about disaster-as-catalyst and about New Orleans as a particularly striking model of the inherent interconnectedness of the social and the ecological?
JPC: We can be in the midst of crisis without noticing it. Disaster came to New Orleans long before Hurricane Katrina, but its true severity wasn't noticed. Before Katrina New Orleans was already the incarceration capital of the world, it had one of the highest murder rates in the country, the education system was devastated, medical care was a disgrace for a large

segment of the community, and there were growing ecological threats such as massive coastal erosion—we had already lost an area of wetlands the size of the state of Delaware. Before Katrina, one saw bumper stickers that said, "New Orleans: Third World and Proud of it." After Katrina, we understood better what it means to be "Third World," or more accurately, to be on the Periphery, on the margins of Empire. The awareness is more akin to horror than to pride.

In New Orleans, as in the world in general, we have been faced with the tragic problems of denial and disavowal. Denial is the inability to allow an idea to enter consciousness, though it always enters in strange, distorted forms. Disavowal is the inability to keep in one's mind what one knows. It's the problem of the elusive obvious. People often can manage to remember everything except the most important thing. This mechanism often operates in families that have major problems such as violence, sexual abuse, betrayal, victimization. Sometimes the problem cannot even be recognized. Sometimes everyone knows but learns how to forget that they know. The same mechanism works on the global level. In fact, the single most important development taking place on our planet is met with denial and disavowal.

At the beginning of each semester I tell every one of my classes, no matter what the topic of the course may be, that I want to mention one thing: We are living in the sixth great mass extinction of life on Earth. If an extraterrestrial came to visit the earth and went back to report on what was happening here, this would certainly be the number one item. News from Earth: "They're going through a kind of planetary disaster that has only happened six times in several billion years!" Yet when I go through this routine, I find that most of my students have never been told this news in their twelve-plus years of formal education. Denial and disavowal reign supreme.

One thing that I learned from the Katrina experience is that the traumatic event can sometimes undo processes of denial and disavowal and awaken us to the gravity of our predicament. Such trauma can result in regression, which can be expressed in fundamentalism, reactionary movements, racism, nationalism, fascism, and the clamor for an authoritarian leader. We saw this in post-Katrina New Orleans, in the form of racist vigilantes, police repression, and prison atrocities. Or, it can result a new breakthrough, a new awakening, a new inspiration to act creatively and communally.

The Katrina disaster was the most devastating experience I have lived through, but also the most uplifting and inspiring one. Post-Katrina New Orleans was a horrifying, heartbreaking and post-apocalyptic world in many ways. But the communities of compassion and solidarity that developed in the wake of the disaster were the closest thing to my social ideal that I have ever experienced. I feel fortunate to have spent a significant period of time living and working with groups of people devoting themselves fully to serving the real needs of people and communities. In such times of communal solidarity, we can see the emergence of that "Beloved Community" that Martin Luther King spoke about. This experience was a major inspiration for what I described in the book as "The Impossible Community."

Many traditions have recognized the importance of the traumatic breakthrough. In the Buddhist tradition, the primary teaching is that one must be shaken out of complacency and come to the shocking realization of the universality of sickness, aging, and death, if one is ever to attain wisdom and compassion. In the Jewish tradition, a break with everyday reality and the traumatic experience of the sacred is described the beginning of wisdom. In the vision quest of indigenous traditions, extreme stresses are part of the path to a spiritual breakthrough. Both European and Asian mysticism describe a traumatic "Dark Night of the Soul" that is part of the path to spiritual awakening. Finally, dialectic is a kind of philosophical vision quest that works through traumatic challenges to all stereotyped thinking. In each case, trauma releases the ability to look at the gaps in our supposed reality and the incoherence in our conventional accounts of the world. Trauma is an encounter with death, but it is also an opportunity for rebirth. It helps us to see the possibility of the impossible and to think the unthinkable.

Notes

1   Introduction: In Search of the Impossible Community

1   See chap. 3 in this book for extensive discussion on this topic.

2   Slavoj Žižek, *The Ticklish Subject* (London: Verso, 1999), 113.

3   Žižek, *The Ticklish Subject*, 113. Libertarian communitarian ethical substantiality always is what it is not and *includes* the excess.

4   Slavoj Žižek, *Less Than Nothing: Hegel and the Shadow of Dialectical Materialism* (London: Verso, 2012), 442.

5   Žižek, *Less Than Nothing*, 205–6. This also repeats a certain moment of Marx's account of "man's" historical *Bildung*.

6   Žižek, *The Ticklish Subject*, 101.

7   As the discussion of agency below will show, it is also a deeply Hegelian moment. On Cornelius Castoriadis, see especially his magnum opus, *The Imaginary Institution of Society* (Cambridge, MA: MIT Press, 1987). For a brief analysis of Castoriadis's importance for many of the themes discussed here, see John P. Clark, "Cornelius Castoriadis: Thinking about Political Theory" in *Capitalism Nature Socialism* 49 (2002): 67–74.

8   It is in this regard that certain questions arise concerning Žižek's formulation of the Hegelian "ultimate goal" of the break with "substantial ethical unity." First, the unity is never a mere unity, and to represent it as such usually reflects either its idealized affirmation or its idealized negation. Second, this (non-)unity is never merely "dissolved" when it is sublated, but rather also preserved as a moment of dialectical development. Third, the idea of "full autonomy" is questionable to the degree that it might be read as implying a total transcendence of determining conditions. Finally, the "assertion" of this full autonomy against the supposed unity might imply a one-sidedly reactive stance. The communitarian anarchist conception of free community attempts to avoid all these (Oedipal, Promethean, Marxian, Bakuninist, etc.) pitfalls.

9   Colectivo Situaciones, "Epilogue: Notes about the Notion of 'Community,'" in Raúl Zibechi, *Dispersing Power: Social Movements as Anti-state Forces* (Oakland: AK Press, 2010), 137.

10   Zibechi, *Dispersing Power*, 138.

11   Mike Davis, *Planet of Slums* (London: Verso, 2006).

12   Andrei Codrescu has brilliantly explored certain dimensions of being the part of no part through his analysis of the importance of "the outside" within a given society. See *The Disappearance of the Outside: A Manifesto of Escape* (Reading, MA: Addison-Wesley, 1990).

13   Zibechi, *Dispersing Power*, 12.

14   Antonin Artaud, *The Theater and Its Double* (New York: Grove Press, 1958), 123.

15 Rebecca Solnit, *A Paradise Built in Hell: The Extraordinary Communities That Arise in Disaster* (New York: Viking, 2009), 18.

16 These areas, and especially the ecological, will be addressed in a forthcoming work on dialectical social ecology that will discuss the social ecological dimensions and implications of the present theoretical project in much greater detail.

17 On Reclus's enormous contribution in this area, see "The Dialectic of Nature and Culture," in John Clark and Camille Martin, eds., *Anarchy: Geography, Modernity: Selected Writings of Elisée Reclus* (Oakland: PM Press, 2013), 16–34. Another version of this analysis, "The Dialectical Social Geography of Elisée Reclus," can be found at https://theanarchistlibrary. org/library/john-clark-the-dialectical-social-geography-of-elisee-reclus.

18 David Graeber, *Fragments of an Anarchist Anthropology* (Chicago: Prickly Paradigm Press, 2004), 17. See also Lewis Hyde's *The Gift: Imagination and the Erotic Life of Property* (New York: Vintage Books, 1983) for a further development of the anarchistic implications of the gift economy, including the idea of the gift as "anarchist money."

19 Michael Tomasello, *Why We Cooperate* (Cambridge, MA: MIT Press, 2009), 6.

20 Ibid., 9.

21 Ibid., 52.

22 Ibid., 53.

23 Elinor Ostrom and Harini Nagendra, "Insights on Linking Forests, Trees, and People from the Air, on the Ground, and in the Laboratory," *Proceedings of the National Academy of Sciences* 103 no. 51 (December 19, 2006): 19224–31.

24 Mark J. Plotkin, *Tales of a Shaman's Apprentice: An Ethnobotanist Searches for New Medicines in the Amazon Rainforest* (New York: Viking Press, 1993), 273. He adds that "the beauty of ethnobotany is that it brings people into the forest picture, showing that tribal peoples can help provide us with answers on the best ways to use and protect the forests."

25 Emile Durkheim, *Selected Writings*, ed. Anthony Giddens (Cambridge, MA: Cambridge University Press, 1972), 138–39.

26 Ibid., 138–39.

27 Ibid., 140.

28 Sherwin B. Nuland, *The Wisdom of the Body* (New York: Alfred A. Knopf, 1997), xviii.

29 Max Weber, *The Theory of Social and Economic Organization*, ed. Talcott Parsons (New York: Free Press, 1964), 328.

30 Georg Simmel, "Group Expansion and the Development of Individuality," in Donald N. Levine, ed., *Georg Simmel on Individuality and Social Form* (Chicago: University of Chicago Press, 1971), 283.

31 Ibid., 280.

32 Ibid., 279.

33 Ibid., 280.

34 Ibid., 286.

35 Ibid., 289.

36 Ibid., 280.

37 This restriction of freedom is systematically overlooked in liberal conceptions, especially the "negative concept of liberty," as will be discussed at length in chap. 3.

38 Ibid., 284–85.

39 Jacques Rancière, *Hatred of Democracy* (London: Verso, 2006), 62.

40 See chap. 10 in this book. For a detailed critique of Bookchin's conception of dialectic, see John Clark, "Domesticating the Dialectic: A Critique of Bookchin's Neo-Aristotelianism," *Capitalism Nature Socialism* 19, no. 1 (March 2008): 51–68.

41 For a discussion of Papuan issues, see John Clark, "The Indigenous Struggle against Violence and Oppression: Resistance to State and Corporate Domination, Colonialism and Neo-Colonialism in West Papua," in Santi Nath Chattopadhyay, ed., *World Peace:*

Problems of Global Understanding and Prospect of Harmony (Kolkata, India: Punthi Pustak, 2005).

42   See Murray Bookchin, *Urbanization without Cities: The Rise and Decline of Citizenship* (Montreal: Black Rose Books, 1996). This is also true of his other main work on cities, *The Limits of the City* (New York: Harper Colophon Books, 1974) in which non-Western cities are barely mentioned, and even then primarily in the context of Western theories concerning the premodern and precapitalist world.

43   Nathan Jun, *Anarchism and Political Modernity* (New York: Continuum Books, forthcoming), chap. 6. See also his very perceptive article "Deleuze, Derrida, and Anarchism," *Anarchist Studies* 15, no. 2 (Fall 2007): 132–56.

44   Jun, "Deleuze, Derrida, and Anarchism," 143.

45   Ibid., 144.

46   Todd May, *The Political Philosophy of Poststructuralist Anarchism* (University Park: Pennsylvania State University Press), 13.

47   Ibid., 61.

48   The seemingly paradoxical determinism of some forms of anarchism is a major theme in Daniel Colson's *A Little Philosophical Lexicon of Anarchism from Proudhon to Deleuze* (Colchester: Minor Compositions, 2019).

49   William Godwin, *Enquiry Concerning Political Justice* (Philadelphia: Bioren and Madan, 1796), 1:457; http://etext.virginia.edu/toc/modeng/public/GodJust.html.

50   G.P. Maximov, *The Political Philosophy of Bakunin* (New York: Free Press, 1964), 153.

51   Ibid., 260.

52   Mikhail Bakunin, *God and the State*; https://theanarchistlibrary.org/library/michail-bakunin-god-and-the-state.pdf.

53   Lewis Call, "Postmodern Anarchism in the Novels of Ursula K. Le Guin," *SubStance* 36, no. 2 (2007): 87–105.

54   However, we might equally use a less violent depiction such as "nurture their own self-transformation."

55   In a forthcoming work presenting and defending a dialectical social ecology, the nature of dialectical social theory will be discussed in greater detail. Some of the important aspects are analyzed further in the discussion of Hegel, Marx, and the Frankfurt School in chap. 4 in this book.

56   Theodor W. Adorno, *Negative Dialectics* (New York: Seabury Press, 1973), 5.

57   Roland Dalbiez, *Psychoanalytic Theory and the Doctrine of Freud* (London: Longmans Green & Co., 1941, vol. 1; 1948, vol. 2).

58   Slavoj Žižek, "Hegel and Shitting: The Idea's Constipation," in Slavoj Žižek, Clayton Crockett, and Creston Davis, eds, *Hegel and the Infinite: Religion, Politics, and Dialectic* (New York: Columbia University Press, 2011), 230.

59   Ibid.

60   Murray Bookchin, *Social Anarchism or Lifestyle Anarchism: An Unbridgeable Chasm* (San Francisco: AK Press, 1995).

61   See John P. Clark, "Domesticating the Dialectic: A Critique of Bookchin's Neo-Aristotelianism" in *Capitalism Nature Socialism* 19, no. 1 (March 2008): 51–68.

62   See John P. Clark, "Lessons of the Rojavan Revolution," in *Between Earth and Empire: From the Necrocene to the Beloved Community* (Oakland: PM Press, 2019), 126–39.

2   Critique of the Gotham Program: From Libertarian Socialism to Communitarian Anarchism

1   Gustav Landauer, *Revolution and Other Writings: A Political Reader*, ed. and trans. Gabriel Kuhn (Oakland: PM Press, 2010), 170. This is from his book *Revolution* (1908).

2   The Fifteenth Street Manifesto Group, *Manifesto for a Left Turn: An Open Letter to U.S. Radicals* (New York: Fifteenth Street Manifesto Group, 2008); https://www.asanet.org/

sites/default/files/savvy/sectionmarxist/assets/pdf/ManifestoforaLeftTurn-oct.'08.pdf. See this online text for all quotes from the document.

3   From Brecht's *Threepenny Opera*. "We would be good [green, red] and not so low/ But the conditions don't make it so." See Bertolt Brecht, "Erstes Dreigroschenfinale (Über die Unsicherheit menschlicher Verhältnisse)"; https://lyricstranslate.com/en/bertolt-brecht-erstes-dreigroschenfinale-lyrics.html.

4   G.W.F. Hegel, *The Philosophy of History* (Kitchener, Canada: Batoche Books, 1900), http://www.marxists.org/reference/archive/hegel/works/hi/history3.htm.

5   More precisely, he says that "it is the bad side that produces the movement which makes history, by providing a struggle." Karl Marx, *The Poverty of Philosophy* (Moscow: Progress Publishers, 1955), http://www.marxists.org/archive/marx/works/1847/poverty-philosophy/ch02.htm.

6   Karl Marx and Friedrich Engels, *Die deutsche Ideologie* (Moscow: Marx-Engels-Lenin Institute, 1932), http://mlwerke.de/me/me03/me03_017.htm.

7   Louis Althusser, "Contradiction and Overdetermination," in *For Marx* (London: Penguin, 1969), http://www.marxists.org/reference/archive/althusser/1962/overdetermination.htm.

8   All quotations are from René Pascal, *Pensées* (New York: Dutton, 1958); http://www.gutenberg.org/files/18269/18269-h/18269-h.htm.

9   This is why Laurie Anderson's "O Superman" is the ideal postnational anthem for the state-capitalist system. It expresses the demonically androgynous nature of the system so perfectly. It concludes: "So hold me, Mom, in your long arms. Your petrochemical arms. Your military arms. In your electronic arms."

10 It is abstracted for analytical purposes from its expression in the other spheres, though they are not, of course, ultimately or in any substantive way separate, but rather are dialectically identical. This should be kept in mind in regard to each instance of analysis of only provisionally separate spheres or institutions. Thus, it will not seem so paradoxical that the project of "the abolition of the state" is inseparable from the project of ruthless critique of the ideology of "civil society," and of various "anti-state" ideologies.

11 Martin Buber, *Paths in Utopia* (Boston: Beacon Press, 1958).

12 Since then, the Occupy movement has often focused precisely on confronting problems such as foreclosures, evictions, and repossession (e.g., through disrupting auctions), and consciously strove to develop a language that ties systemic problems together. Such developments have been related to practices of horizontalism and direct action, and resulted in large part from anarchist influence in the movement. Obviously, this tendency has much in common with the participatory, solidaristic communitarian anarchist position that is being developed here.

13 See chap. 9, first section.

14 See chap. 9, second section.

15 Henry David Thoreau, "Walking," http://thoreau.eserver.org/walking2.html.

16 Kojin Karatani, *Transcritique: On Kant and Marx* (Cambridge, MA: MIT Press, 2005).

17 The Invisible Committee, *The Coming Insurrection* (Los Angeles: Semiotext(e), 2009).

18 Julien Coupat, "Interview with Julien Coupat" from *Le Monde* (May 5, 2009); translation at http://tarnac9.wordpress.com/2009/05/28/interview-with-julien-coupat/.

19 Peter Linebaugh, *The Magna Carta Manifesto* (Berkeley: University of California Press, 2008).

3   The Third Concept of Liberty: Theorizing the Free Community

1   G.W.F. Hegel, "The Earliest System-Programme of German Idealism," trans. H.S. Harris in Stephen Houlgate, ed., *The Hegel Reader* (Malden, MD: Blackwell Publishing, 1998), 28. The early Hegel sees the state as on the side of mechanism and domination, while the true community is on the side of spirit and freedom.

2   Isaiah Berlin, "Two Concepts of Liberty" in *Four Essays on Liberty* (London: Oxford University Press, 1969).

3   Ibid., 121–22.

4   Ibid., 122.

5   Ibid., 121–22.

6   Ibid., 131.

7   Ibid., 144. Berlin's polemical goals, which strongly conditioned the direction of his analysis, are not a central concern here.

8   T.H. Green, *Works of Thomas Hill Green* (London: Longmans, Green, 1889), 3:371.

9   T.H. Green, *Lectures on the Principles of Political Obligation* (Ann Arbor: University of Michigan Press, 1967), 210.

10   Ibid., 4–5.

11   Ibid., 2–3.

12   Green, *Works*, 3:371.

13   L.T. Hobhouse, *Liberalism* (New York: Oxford University Press, 1911), 21–49.

14   John Dewey, *Liberalism and Social Action* (New York: G.P. Putnam's Sons, 1963), 48.

15   Ibid., 56.

16   Ibid., 92.

17   Amartya Sen, *Development as Freedom* (New York: Knopf, 1999). See especially chap. 1: "The Perspective of Freedom." Nussbaum accepts Sen's view of freedom, but objects that the content of such freedom must be specified more clearly through a detailed discussion of the capabilities involved, something that she has, in fact, herself undertaken. See her article "Capabilities as Fundamental Entitlements: Sen and Social Justice" in *Feminist Economics* 9 (July 2003): 33–59.

18   The "central human functional capabilities" are listed and discussed many times in Nussbaum's recent works. See, for example, *Women and Human Development: The Capabilities Approach* (Cambridge: Cambridge University Press, 2000), 70–86. The list of capabilities with an explanation of each point is widely available. See, for example, http://www.iep.utm.edu/ge-capab/.

19   The merits and demerits of human capabilities theory cannot be investigated in great detail here. For a more extensive discussion of some of its strengths and weaknesses, including its lack of a critical dimension with regard to many crucial issues, see John P. Clark, "Capabilities Theory and the Limits of Liberal Justice: On Nussbaum's *Frontiers of Justice*" in *Human Rights Review* 10, no .4 (2009): 583–604.

20   Berlin, *Four Essays on Liberty*, lvi.

21   I am grateful to Prof. Jonathan Peterson of Loyola University for pointing out the importance of this objection.

22   In his *New Yorker* column, "The Wayward Press" (May 14, 1960).

23   Quentin Skinner, "A Third Concept of Liberty," in *Proceedings of the British Academy* 117 (2002): 261.

24   Ibid., 262.

25   Ibid., 262–63.

26   Ibid., 248.

27   In effect, Skinner concedes this point when he states that "if we are to speak of dependence as a source or form of constraint, it cannot be the case that we *know* that our absolute ruler will never in fact interfere. For in that case we are not under any constraint" (257).

28   Hegel, *Philosophy of Right*, trans. T.M. Knox (London: Clarendon Press, 1952), §123, 83.

29   *Enzyclopädie der philosophischen Wissenschaften im Grundrisse* I.24, Z.2, quoted in M.J. Inwood, *Hegel* (London: Routledge and Kegan Paul, 1983), 478.

30   This point is repeatedly made by Žižek in *Less than Nothing: Hegel and the Shadow of Dialectical Materialism* (London: Verso, 2012), which is a sustained critique of an interpretation of Hegel that reduces his dialectic to mere teleological unfolding or

development within a closed or reductively deterministic system, overlooking novelty and emergence. He stresses the important but seldom observed connection between dialectical movement and autopoesis (157–58).

31   Hegel, *Philosophy of Right*, 30–31.
32   *Enz.* III.424 Z, quoted in Inwood, *Hegel*, 480.
33   Robert Pippin, *Hegel's Practical Philosophy* (Cambridge, MA: Cambridge University Press, 2008).
34   Ibid., 4.
35   Ibid.
36   Ibid., 5.
37   Ibid., 36–37.
38   Ibid., 43.
39   Ibid., 113.
40   Ibid., 265.
41   Ibid.
42   Ibid., 270.
43   Ibid.
44   Ibid.
45   Ibid.
46   Ibid., 270–71.
47   *Encyclopedia*, §431, Zusatz, quoted in Robert R. Williams, *Hegel's Ethics of Recognition* (Berkeley: University of California Press, 1997), 76.
48   *Encyclopedia*, §436, quoted in ibid., 80.
49   *Encyclopedia*, §436, quoted in ibid.
50   *Encyclopedia*, §436, quoted in ibid.
51   *Encyclopedia*, §436, Zusatz, quoted in ibid, 79.
52   Hegel mentions three other elements: autonomy, union, and self-overcoming.
53   Williams, *Hegel's Ethics of Recognition*, 84.
54   Ibid., 76.
55   Hegel, *Philosophy of Right*, §260, 160–61.
56   Ibid., §260, 161.
57   Ibid., §156, Addition, 261.
58   Ibid., §132, 87.
59   Paul Redding, *Hegel's Hermeneutics* (Ithaca, NY: Cornell University Press, 1996), 241.
60   Z.A. Pelczynski, "Political Community and Individual Freedom in Hegel's Philosophy of State"; http://www.marxists.org/reference/subject/philosophy/works/ot/pelczyns.htm.
61   David Kolb, *The Critique of Pure Modernity: Hegel, Heidegger, and After* (Chicago: University of Chicago Press, 1986), 266–67.
62   *Encyclopedia*, §433, quoted in Williams, *Hegel's Ethics of Recognition*, 77.
63   Ibid.
64   Williams, *Hegel's Ethics of Recognition*, 76.
65   Kolb, *Critique of Pure Modernity*, 114.
66   *Encyclopedia*, §540, quoted in Kolb, *Critique of Pure Modernity*, 114.
67   Hegel, *Philosophy of Right*, §268, 164.
68   Kolb, *Critique of Pure Modernity*, 115.
69   Hegel, *Early Theological Writings*, trans. T.M. Knox (Chicago: University of Chicago Press, 1948), 277.
70   Ibid., 277–78.
71   Ibid., 305.
72   Ibid., 304.
73   Hegel, *Science of Logic*, trans. A.V. Miller (New York: Prometheus Books, 1969), 603.
74   Hegel, *Philosophy of Right*, §7. Addition, 228.

75 Gustav Landauer, *For Socialism* (St. Louis: Telos Press, 1978), 4–5, 34. In quotes from Landauer, I have used the lower case for the word "spirit," contrary to the translation cited. Nouns are not ordinarily capitalized in English, unlike German, so the use of the upper case might be taken to imply more metaphysical baggage than Landauer intended. However, there are plausible arguments for either choice.

76 Ibid., 55.

77 Ibid., 45.

78 Ibid., 34. Note, in his juxtaposition of "despair and courage, psychic distress and joy," Landauer's implicit recognition of the relation between crisis, trauma and liberatory breakthrough, a topic that will be discussed in some detail in chap. 8 of this book.

79 Gustav Landauer, *Revolution and Other Writings: A Political Reader*, ed. and trans. Gabriel Kuhn (Oakland: PM Press, 2010), 123. Landauer wrote this in 1908, near the end of the period of almost unquestioned Eurocentric progressivist optimism that has been called the "long nineteenth century."

80 Landauer, *For Socialism*, 33. One should always be suspicious of "immediacy," but Landauer's view can be salvaged if one interprets it as a call for social relations that are *less mediated* by mechanistic, manipulative, objectifying institutional structures.

81 Ibid., 42.

82 Ibid., 33.

83 Ibid., 61.

84 Ibid., 63.

85 Ibid., 64.

86 Buber developed ideas similar to Landauer's, in a libertarian socialist though not specifically anarchist direction, especially in his classic work *Paths in Utopia* (Boston: Beacon Press, 1958).

87 Landauer, *For Socialism*, 125. In the original, Landauer says: "Gesellschaft ist eine Gesellschaft von Gesellschaften von Gesellschaften; ein Bund von Bünden von Bünden; ein Gemeinwesen von Gemeinschaften von Gemeinden; eine Republik von Republiken von Republiken." The original German text of *Aufruf zum Sozialismus* can be found http://www.anarchismus.at/txt2/landauer3.htm.

88 Ibid., 126. The deep insights of Gandhianism and the Sarvodaya movement in these areas is discussed in chap. 9 in this book.

89 Landauer, *Revolution*, 168.

90 Landauer, *For Socialism*, 141.

91 Ibid., 141. Interestingly, Žižek notes: "Lacan shares with Nietzsche and Freud the idea that justice as equality is founded on envy: the envy of the other who has what we do not have, and who enjoys it. The demand for justice is ultimately the demand that the excessive enjoyment of the other should be curtailed, so that everyone's access to enjoyment will be equal." Slavoj Žižek, *How to Read Lacan* (New York: Norton, 2006), 37. Landauer recognizes the power of envy, but for him the goal of free community (what "should be") implies a break with such ideas of justice and equality, and with envy itself. Much of Landauer's analysis is aimed at overcoming the reactivity of the Left, and the politics of *ressentiment*.

92 In fact, this "envy for the community" could be translated into "inspiration by the community," but something would be lost in the translation. People seem to be inspired by all sorts of things today without being very deeply moved or transformed by the inspiration. Even greeting cards are "inspirational." "Envy," on the other hand, retains the connotation of the exertion of traumatic force, and of the arousal of intense desire.

93 Landauer, *Revolution*, 214.

94 Ibid.

95 Ibid., 166.

96 Slavoj Žižek, *In Defense of Lost Causes* (London: Verso, 2008), 337.

97 Ibid., 482 (in the afterword to the 2009 edition).

98 As Hegel says in *The Science of Logic*, "There is nothing, nothing in heaven, or in nature or in mind or anywhere else which does not equally contain both immediacy and mediation, so that these two determinations reveal themselves to be *unseparated* and inseparable and the opposition between them to be a nullity." *Hegel's Science of Logic*, trans. A.V. Miller (New York: Humanity Books, 2004), 68.

99 Landauer, *Revolution*, 169. It is not clear that Landauer foresaw the implications of his statement, which points to the need for an anarchist politics of the transitional state, the very thought of which constitutes a heresy for many purist anarchists, but which demands theoretical investigation. The possibility of such a transitional state would depend on socially transformative activity making the state in practice what it has been only in theory, as depicted in some forms of historical materialism: a purely superstructural phenomenon. It would, incidentally, realize precisely what Marx proposed in the "Critique of the Gotha Program," that is, "converting the state from an organ superimposed upon society into one completely subordinate to it." See Karl Marx, "Critique of the Gotha Program," at http://www.marxists.org/ archive/marx/works/1875/gotha/ch04.htm.

100 One could imagine various possible means of attaining this goal, depending on the diverse social, political, economic, and cultural contingencies that constitute the realities of historical struggle. There is no one privileged strategy for revolutionary struggle, for evolutionary struggle, or for the attainment of a condition of "dual power." See chap. 10 in this book for a critique of the most notable recent example of such ahistorical privileging of strategy within anarchist and libertarian social theory, Bookchin's "libertarian municipalism."

101 Ibid., 160.

102 This is reminiscent of the theme of the dialectic of evolution and revolution that runs through the work of Reclus. See Elisée Reclus, "Evolution, Revolution, and the Anarchist Ideal" in John P. Clark and Camille Martin, eds., *Anarchy, Geography, Modernity: Selected Writings of Elisée Reclus* (Oakland: PM Press, 2013), 138–55.

103 It is at this point, in its connection to the ethics and politics of care, that the necessarily ecofeminist nature of communitarian anarchism can be seen most clearly.

104 Landauer, *For Socialism*, 133.

105 I would like to thank Prof. Jonathan Peterson of Loyola University for noting the relevance of this aspect of Berlin's argument.

106 Berlin, *Four Essays on Liberty*, 169.

107 Ibid., 171.

108 Personal correspondence.

109 Consumer society's version of this spiritual nightmare would be something like "the Dark Night of the Soul in which all cows are Big Macs."

110 The global justice movement, the Occupy movement, and mass anti-austerity movements are signs of the possible emergence of a serious legitimation crisis.

111 Joel Kovel, *History and Spirit: An Inquiry into the Philosophy of Liberation* (Boston: Beacon Press, 1991), 1.

112 Ibid., 192.

113 For the "Manifesto" and the "Belem Ecosocialist Declaration" that developed out of it, see http://green.left.sweb.cz/frame/Manifesto.html and https://climateandcapitalism.com/2008/12/16/belem-ecosocialist-declaration-a-call-for-signatures. Unlike the "Declaration," I formulate one alternative of the dilemma as "ecobarbarism," rather than merely "barbarism," for a specific reason. I agree that if the ecosocialist alternative of a society of shared abundance and reconciliation with nature is not chosen, humanity will enter an era of intensifying crisis, and ultimately social and ecological collapse, the result of which can only be described as a new barbarism. However, the more immediate dilemma is between such an ecosocialism and emerging forms of instrumentally rational ecofascism that will attempt to resolve the social and ecological crises through

authoritarian and repressive means combined with strategies of manipulation through the consumptionist imaginary. Ecofascism in this sense is the trajectory of state capitalism, and should be conceived of as an institutional form. In a cyber-consumptionist era it can take the form of a relatively rational barbarism with a relatively human face. It is the most likely future for humanity, in the absence of a historic reversal in the direction of ecosocialism.

4 Against Principalities and Powers: Critique of Domination Versus Liberalization of Domination

1 The particular theory to be discussed is labeled "republican" in supposed contradistinction to liberalism. However, it remains in every significant tenet well within the traditional bounds of the Western liberal tradition.

2 Reclus developed his social geography and communitarian anarchism in a series of major works beginning in the 1860s and culminating in his magnum opus *L'Homme et la Terre* (Man and the Earth), published at the time of his death in 1905. For a survey of Reclus's extensive analysis of forms of domination, see "The Critique of Domination" in John Clark and Camille Martin, eds., *Anarchy, Geography, Modernity: Selected Writings of Elisée Reclus* (Oakland: PM Press, 2013), 74–98.

3 Elisée Reclus, "Anarchy" (1894), in Clark and Martin, *Anarchy*, 138.

4 Elisée Reclus, "The History of Cities" (1905), in Clark and Martin, *Anarchy*, 188.

5 Elisée Reclus, "To My Brother the Peasant" (1893), in Clark and Martin, *Anarchy*, 133.

6 Ibid.

7 Dialectical thought challenges, as pernicious ideology, the ubiquitous contemporary cliché: "It is what it is." From a dialectical perspective: "It is what it isn't," and "It isn't what it is."

8 Theodor W. Adorno, *Negative Dialectics* (New York: Seabury Press, 1973), 5.

9 Money is used to produce a commodity, which is used to produce money. The driving force in production becomes the expansion of value through this process, rather than the satisfaction of needs, as in subsistence production.

10 Karl Marx, "The General Formula for Capital," chap. 4 in *Capital: A Critique of Political Economy*, vol. 1, http://www.marxists.org/archive/marx/works/1867-c1/ch04.htm.

11 Karl Marx, "The Fetishism of Commodities and the Secret Thereof," chap.1, sec. 4, in *Capital*, vol. 1; http://www.marxists.org/archive/marx/works/1867-c1/ch01.htm#S4.

12 Ibid.

13 Ibid.

14 In the end, the latter may unconsciously and nonproductively produce not only the unintentional but the unthinkable, for example, universal barbarism, their own gravediggers, or even everyone's gravediggers.

15 Henri Lefebvre, *The Production of Space* (Oxford: Blackwell Publishers, 1991), 26.

16 Ibid.

17 Jacques Ellul, *The Technological Society* (New York: Vintage Books, 1964); Lewis Mumford, *Technics and Human Development* (San Diego: Harcourt Brace Jovanovich, 1967) and *The Pentagon of Power* (San Diego: Harcourt Brace Jovanovich, 1970); Langdon Winner, *Autonomous Technology* (Cambridge, MA: MIT Press, 1977); David Watson, *Against the Megamachine: Essays on Empire and Its Enemies* (Brooklyn: Autonomedia, 1998).

18 Lewis Mumford, "Authoritarian and Democratic Technics," in *Technology and Culture* 5, no.1 (Winter 1964): 1–8.

19 The familiar phrases from the "Movement" of the late 1960s, "That's what *They* want you to do," and "That's what *They* want you to think," captured the complexity of the system of domination better than much of contemporary political theory does. Of course, there were specific powerful people and political enemies who "wanted" these things, but the impersonal *They* reflected the systemic quality of the forces of

domination. *They* could no more be reduced to a class of specific individuals than "The Man" (like *das Man*) could be identified by a social security number.

20   Herbert Marcuse, *Eros and Civilization: A Philosophical Inquiry into Freud* (Boston: Beacon Press, 1966), 98.

21   Herbert Marcuse, *One-Dimensional Man: Studies in the Ideology of Advanced Industrial Society* (Boston: Beacon Press, 1964), 144.

22   Ibid.

23   Theodor Adorno, "Fragmente über Wagner," in *Zeitschrift für Sozialforschung*, 8, no. 1–2 (1939): 17; quoted in Walter Benjamin, *The Arcades Project* (Cambridge, MA: Harvard University Press), 699.

24   Guy Debord, *The Society of the Spectacle* (Detroit: Black and Red, 1970), sec. 36.

25   Guy Debord, *Comments on the Society of the Spectacle* (London: Verso Books, 1990); http://www.notbored.org/commentaires.html.

26   The enormous imaginary force of the film *The Matrix* derived in large part from the widespread recognition, at various levels of consciousness, of the spectacle as the truth of late capitalist society.

27   As mentioned above, recent efforts to revive the republican tradition are included within the liberal tradition, despite certain differences with the more dominant tendencies in liberal theory. Contemporary republican theorists are liberals to the degree that they defend versions of the liberal democratic nation-state and the liberal capitalist market economy, and work within a general conceptual framework, and utilize concepts of individual rights, individual freedom, rule of law, sovereignty, etc., that are quite similar to that of other liberals. Obviously, should any of these republican theorists break decisively with the major tenets of the liberal tradition they should not be classified this way. Philip Pettit, the republican theorist who will be discussed in detail here, certainly makes no such break.

28   Bruce Ackerman, *Social Justice in the Liberal State* (New Haven, CT: Yale University Press 1980), chap. 4.

29   Michael Walzer, *Spheres of Justice: A Defense of Pluralism and Equality* (New York: Basic Books, 1983). Among the many shortcomings of his position is his short-circuiting of deep systemic analysis through his typical liberal assumption that "distribution is what social conflict is all about" (11); his abstract, ahistorical conception of how systems of power develop; his assumption of the necessity of actual structures of domination; and his consequent reduction of the problem of domination to a problematic of "reduction of dominance" (17). In one of his few uses of the term, he labels the result "rule without domination."

30   Philip Pettit, *Republicanism: A Theory of Freedom and Government* (Oxford: Oxford University Press, 1997).

31   Richard Dagger, "Autonomy, Domination, and the Republican Challenge to Liberalism," in John Christman and Joel Anderson, *Autonomy and the Challenges to Liberalism: New Essays* (Cambridge: Cambridge University Press, 2005), 177–203.

32   Dagger defends a form of "republican liberalism," explicitly situating republicanism within the tradition of liberal political thought. This position is developed in Dagger's *Civic Virtues: Rights, Citizenship, and Republican Liberalism* (New York: Oxford University Press, 1997).

33   Paul Gowder, "The Liberal Critique of Domination," presented at 2012 Western Political Science Association conference, http://wpsa.research.pdx.edu/meet/2012/gowder.pdf.

34   Frank Lovett, *A General Theory of Domination and Justice* (Oxford: Oxford University Press, 2010). The publisher describes the book as the "first ever systematic and structural account of this much discussed topic in political theory." Though it certainly goes much further than Pettit in addressing systemic and structural issues, it typically, and symptomatically, misconceives the issue of impersonal systemic domination as the

issue of whether there can be domination without the existence of persons who are in a dominant or privileged position.

35 Michael J. Thompson, "Reconstructing Republican Freedom: A Critique of the Neo-Republican Concept of Freedom as Non-Domination," *Philosophy and Social Criticism* 39, no. 3 (2013): 277–98.

36 Pettit, *Republicanism*, 11. This claim is not accurate. Dialectical thought rejects such an approach as precritical and naïvely ideological. Of course, one might reply that this is merely evidence of its lack of grandeur.

37 Ibid.

38 Ibid.

39 From *idios*, meaning "private." We are idiots when we impose the private on what is inherently common. This problem was identified by the great dialectician Heraclitus at an early date in Western philosophy.

40 Ibid., vii–viii.

41 Ibid., 53.

42 Ibid. Pettit thinks that this is "a category that was not salient in earlier centuries." However, there is certainly evidence from previous centuries of both manipulation and the awareness of its significance. Etienne de La Boétie's *Discourse on Voluntary Servitude* (ca. 1552) is the classic work defending the view that most submission is the result of "manipulation," rather than overt coercion or the threat of coercion. See *The Politics of Obedience: The Discourse on Voluntary Servitude* (New York: Free Life Editions, 1975); http://mises.org/rothbard/boetie.pdf.

43 Pettit, *Republicanism*, 53.

44 Thus, theoretical invisibility will mirror social invisibility.

45 Philip Pettit, "Keeping Republican Freedom Simple: On a Difference with Quentin Skinner," in *Political Theory* 30, no. 3 (June, 2002): 340.

46 He would be particularly averse to Lacan's revelation that ultimately the "Discourse of the University" is only the most advanced form of the "Discourse of the Master," and plays a key (covert) role in social domination. In fact, liberal theory pays little attention to the ways in which domination is embodied in language itself. It is incapable of considering the possibility that under a system of domination we find the roots of that domination in the accession to the order of language itself, a process that Lacan calls "symbolic castration."

47 Ibid., 341.

48 Pettit, *Republicanism*, 53.

49 This is a direction of analysis taken up in detail by Lovett in *A General Theory of Domination and Justice*.

50 Pettit, "Keeping Republican Freedom Simple," 341–42.

51 Pettit, *Republicanism*, 78.

52 According to Anti-Slavery International, over forty million people are enslaved today, including twenty-five million who are forced workers or debt slaves. See https://www.antislavery.org. Pettit might reply that he only had "advanced" Western countries in mind when he referred to "traditional" relationships. However, in that case (putting aside the issue of the Eurocentricity of his thinking), his insensitivity to the degree to which overt interference exists under Western patriarchy and capitalism would be no less disturbing.

53 Ibid., 144.

54 Ibid.

55 Ibid.

56 Irving Thalberg, "Visceral Racism," *The Monist* 56 (1972): 43–63.

57 Joel Kovel, *White Racism: A Psychohistory* (New York: Columbia University Press, 1984).

58 Ibid., xi.

59 Pettit, *Republicanism*, 54.

60 Ibid., 205.

61 Ibid.

62 Ibid.

63 Ibid., 35.

64 Raúl Zibechi, *Dispersing Power: Social Movements as Anti-state Forces* (Oakland: AK Press, 2010), 36.

65 There has been extensive discussion of this issue in the literature on Mondragon and worker self-management in general. See, for example, George Benello, "The Challenge of Mondragon" in Howard J. Ehrlich, *Reinventing Anarchy, Again* (San Francisco: AK Press, 1996), 211–20.

66 Robert Michels, *Political Parties: A Sociological Study of the Oligarchical Tendencies of Modern Democracy* (New York: Hearst's International Library, 1915). The original German edition was published in 1911.

67 Pettit, "Keeping Republican Freedom Simple," 339.

68 Ibid., 345.

69 One could imagine a future republican tract, *The Not-So-Wretched of the Earth*.

70 It would be far less puzzling if Pettit were perhaps thinking of "benign colonialism" as a description of the relatively noninterfering relationship between the "mother country" and the white settlers in certain colonies. However, in this case, the terms "benign" and "noninterference" would become ideological euphemisms for "conquest," "genocide," and "slavery."

71 Pettit, *Republicanism*, ix.

72 Ibid., 63.

73 Pettit's presumption that the likely victims of domination are primarily members of marginalized groups is further evidence of the extent to which he ignores the pervasive, systemic nature of political, economic, and technological domination. He states that "unless such contestability is assured, the state may easily represent a dominating presence for those of a certain marginalized ethnicity or culture or gender" (ibid.). The implication is that in Pettit's idealized republican polity, not only is actual consent not necessary, but even contestability is not ordinarily necessary to protect the society at large from domination.

74 Ibid.

75 Ibid.

76 Jean-Jacques Rousseau, *The Social Contract*, book 3, chap. 15; http://www.marxists. org/reference/subject/economics/rousseau/social-contract/ch03.htm#015.

77 Pettit, *Republicanism*, 188.

78 Ibid.

79 Ibid.

80 This is not to say that in such systems actual contestation is necessarily dead. When large masses of people abandon their workplaces, shopping centers, schools, and homes and flood the streets, disabling the system, one can then see what "contestation" in a strong sense still means in a mass society. Such contestation is actual, not merely ideologically hypothetical, but is still no substitute for a many-sided movement of social transformation that is rooted in primary communities and confronts the major spheres of social determination.

81 Ibid., 199.

82 Ibid.

83 Ibid.

84 Ibid., 200.

85 Rancière, *Hatred of Democracy* (London: Verso, 2006), 92.

86 Frank Lovett, "Republicanism," in *Stanford Encyclopedia of Philosophy* (article revised May 18, 2010) at http://plato.stanford.edu/entries/republicanism/.

87 Ibid.

88   Iseult Honohan, *Civic Republicanism* (Abingdon, UK: Routledge, 2002), 184–85.
89   In fact, elsewhere, Honohan recognizes the importance of "John Rawls's magisterial interpretation of liberalism" (9) within the liberal tradition, which contradicts her generalization concerning its view of freedom and state action.
90   Quentin Skinner, *Liberty before Liberalism* (Cambridge, MA: Cambridge University Press, 1998), ix.
91   Ibid., 18, 26–30, 66, 74.
92   Quoted in Peter Marshall, *William Godwin* (New Haven, CT: Yale University Press, 1984), 77. Shortly thereafter, he would incorporate his "republican" sentiments into his *Enquiry Concerning Political Justice*, in Britain, the most notoriously radical political work of its time.
93   Ibid., 84.
94   G.W.F. Hegel, *The Phenomenology of Spirit* (Oxford: Oxford University Press, 1977), 118.

5   Anarchy and the Dialectic of Utopia: The Place of No Place

1   This concept of splace should not be confused in any way with Badiou's idea of "l'es-place." In fact, it should be seen as the precise opposite of his conception, which should perhaps be written "l'esp(~l)ace" or "sp(~l)ace." According to Badiou's strange neo-Pythagorean post-Maoism, all realities of place are dissolved in an abstract mathematical reductionism and a romantic fetishism of the heroic event. The "(~l)" in "l'esp(~l)ace" should be read as "non-lieu," or "no-place," which designates, in this case, Badiouian utopian nowhereism, but is also the French term for "case dismissed."
2   For a more extensive discussion of the *Daodejing* as an anarchist and utopian classic, see my "Master Lao and the Anarchist Prince" in John Clark, *The Anarchist Moment: Reflections on Culture, Nature and Power* (Montreal: Black Rose Books, 1984), 165–90.
3   It represents all this except to the degree that the project, because of its internal contradictions and self-transcending moments, also subverts itself.
4   Allan Bloom, ed. and trans., *The Republic of Plato* (New York: Basic Books, 1968), 439–40.
5   Of course, the work is also about justice, but in the end the two values are identified, for Plato adopts the maxim "justice is the interest of the stronger." Of course, along the way he rejects this principle in its vulgar Sophistic form, only to embrace it in its sublated, perfected form. One of the most exquisite expressions of Socratic irony is Socrates' brutal demolition of Thrasymachus's flimsy parody of this principle in order to throw the naive reader off the track and disguise Plato's own argument for this principle of power in its most sublime form.
6   In recent anarchist history, the best example was Murray Bookchin, who (before he himself renounced anarchism) reiterated repeatedly the theory that Laozi was not only not an anarchist, but, indeed, an authoritarian manipulator of peasants who sought to instill in them a quietistic, "passive-receptive" outlook to the benefit of their feudal overlords. Bookchin failed to offer much evidence of Laozi's fronting for feudalism.
7   Vaclav Havel, "Conversation with Vaclav Havel," *East European Reporter* 2, no. 3 (1986): 15.
8   Ibid., 17.
9   Ibid. It should be noted that despite this scathing attack on "utopia," Havel praised the early green movement (which had at the time a distinctively utopian dimension that has largely been lost since) for raising issues that "concern the meaning of life, such as whether there is any reason in the constant drive for increased production when it is to the detriment of future generations."
10   Ernst Bloch, *The Principle of Hope*, vol. 2 (Cambridge, MA: MIT Press, 1986), 509.
11   Norman Cohn, *The Pursuit of the Millennium* (New York: Oxford, 1970), 181.
12   Ibid., 179.
13   Michael Bakunin, *Selected Writings*, ed. Arthur Lehning (New York: Grove Press, 1973), 180.

14   Paul Ricoeur, *Lectures on Ideology and Utopia* (New York: Columbia University Press, 1986), 300.

15   Karl Mannheim, *Ideology and Utopia* (New York: Harcourt, Brace and World, 1936), 192.

16   Ricoeur, *Lectures on Ideology and Utopia*, 17.

17   Ibid., 299.

18   Marie Louise Berneri, *Journey through Utopia: A Critical Examination of Imagined Worlds in Western Literature* (Oakland: PM Press, 2019), 8.

19   Immanuel Kant, *Foundations of the Metaphysics of Morals* (Indianapolis: Library of Liberal Arts, 1959), 11.

20   Ibid., 41.

21   Referring to Lacan's dictum of not "ceding" one's desire.

22   This is not to say that Foucault's insights are in any way a complete break with the anarchist and utopian tradition. Fourier stated that "the passions cannot be repressed," that "passion stifled at one point reappears at another," and that "every passion that is suffocated produces a counterpassion." Jonathan Beecher and Richard Bienvenu, *The Utopian Vision of Charles Fourier: Selected Texts on Work, Love and Passionate Attraction* (Columbia: University of Missouri Press, 1983), 98, 40, 41. Thus, passion or desire is not simply lying latent, waiting to be liberated, but rather continues with its full power, though invested in different objects, under the system of domination.

23   We might still say that the present will always be in some ways haunted by the absence of the fully realized ideal that we imagine, yet the greatest reality of that absent ideal is that aspect of it that is already present here and now.

24   William Blake, notes to "A Vision of the Last Judgment," in David Erdman, ed., *The Complete Poetry and Prose of William Blake* (Garden City, NY: Doubleday, 1982), 565–66.

25   Gary Snyder, *Practice of the Wild* (San Francisco: North Point Press, 1990), 153.

26   This moment of immediacy is not only mediated but is also a mediation. The next day we may find ourselves standing in the way of those who trample on lotus flowers.

27   Franklin Rosemont, *Revolution in the Service of the Marvelous* (Chicago: Charles H. Kerr, 2004), 14.

28   Ibid.

29   Robert Nichols, *Daily Lives in Nghsi-Altai* (New York: New Directions, 1977–79). The series consists of *Arrival*, *Garh City*, *The Harditts in Sawna*, and *Exile*. It was preceded by an introductory work, *Red Shift* (Thetford, VT: Penny Each Press, 1977). A new (unfortunately abridged) edition appeared as *Travels in Altai* (Enfield, NH: Glad Day Books, 1999).

30   Le Guin, *The Left Hand of Darkness* (New York: Berkeley Publishing Group, 1969). Le Guin is profoundly influenced by Daoism, as she recognizes in various essays and in her own version of the *Daodejing*. Her work is perhaps the most notable contemporary expression of the anarchistic utopian tradition founded (and not founded) by the great (and possibly nonexistent) sage Laozi.

31   Ursula Le Guin, *The Dispossessed* (New York: Harper and Row, 1974).

32   Ursula K. Le Guin, *Always Coming Home* (New York: Harper and Row, 1985).

33   The book is consciously influenced by Nichols's work, which more explicitly draws on anarchist and decentralist ideas. In *Always Coming Home*, when "The Five People" ask where they came from, and "The Wise Old Man" and "The Talking Woman" give rather unsatisfying metaphysical replies, Coyote finally answers, "From the west you came, from the west, from Ingasi Altai, over the ocean, dancing you came, walking you came," 170. So when the Five People migrated across the ocean long ago they brought along many of the libertarian and decentralist values Nichols describes in *Nghsi-Altai*.

34   It is for this reason that the novel, with its emphasis on person, community, culture, nature, and place, has been an inspiration to those interested in bioregionalism, the project of reinhabiting the land, and the reestablishment of the connections between self, culture, and nature.

35   Starhawk, *The Fifth Sacred Thing* (New York: Bantam Books, 1993).

36   Elisée Reclus, *L'Homme et la Terre* (Paris: Librairie Universelle, 1905–8). This monumental work was the culmination of half a century of research in radical social geography. Discussion of this history and extensive translation from this work can be found in John Clark and Camille Martin, eds., *Anarchy, Geography, Modernity: Selected Writings of Elisée Reclus* (Oakland: PM Press, 2013).

37   Bloch, *The Principle of Hope*, 511.

38   Ronald Creagh, *Utopies Américaines* (Marseille: Agone, 2009). Sadly, this essential work is still unavailable in English, more than thirty-five years after the original edition, titled *Laboratoires de l'Utopie*, was published.

39   Mannheim, *Ideology and Utopia*, 262.

40   Ibid., 263.

41   Ibid., 255.

42   Ibid., 256.

43   Ibid., 248.

44   Ibid., 244.

45   Daniel Bell, *The End of Ideology* (Glencoe, IL: Free Press, 1960), 370.

46   Francis Fukuyama, "The End of History," *The National Interest* 16 (1989): 3.

6   The Microecology of Community: Toward a Theory of Grassroots Organization

1   Tom Goyens, *Beer and Revolution: The German Anarchist Movement in New York City, 1880-1914* (Urbana and Chicago: University of Illinois Press, 2007).

2   I remember being asked sometime after that era, "What were you doing during the Revolution?"

3   Ironically, one finds "progressive" forces lamenting the rather unsurprising fact that corporate-owned media represent the corporate interest rather than that of the public. Neither should it be surprising that when war is declared, a safely domesticated and anemic alternative such as NPR can so easily mutate into what has only half-humorously been labeled "Nationalistic Puppet Radio."

4   See the fascinating and inspiring documentary film *American Utopia* for the story of this community and the lessons that can be learned from its achievement and its weaknesses. Beverly Lewis, *American Utopia* (Baton Rouge, LA: Firefly Productions and Louisiana Public Broadcasting, 1994).

5   With some notable exceptions such as Free Speech TV, which is available to more than forty million homes through satellite and cable providers and other sources. Air America, the liberal radio network, went bankrupt after less than six years of operation, though moderately liberal talk has remained alive over the past few years on MSNBC, with some success.

6   That is, one that remains, in Hegel's terminology, on the level of abstract morality (*moralität*), as opposed to that of the concrete ethical (*sittlichkeit*).

7   See John P. Clark, "Papua Merdeka: The Indigenous Struggle Against State and Corporate Domination" in *Between Earth and Empire: From the Necrocene to the Beloved Community* (Oakland: PM Press, 2019), 140–53.

8   Pierre Clastres, *Society against the State* (New York: Zone Books, 1987).

9   Taking inspiration from Buber's utopian socialism does not mean ignoring the extent to which he compromised his position on behalf of the system of social oppression in Israel. See, for example, Uri Davis's "Martin Buber's Paths in Utopia: The Kibbutz: An Experiment that Didn't Fail?" *Peace News* no. 2446 (March–June 2002). Davis, who describes himself as a "critical Buber disciple," discusses Buber's theoretical and practical shortcomings in accepting and indeed participating in a process of ethnic cleansing after 1948. He also analyses the use of the kibbutz (described by Buber as "the experiment that did not fail") as a tool of colonialism and oppression.

10   Martin Buber, *Paths in Utopia* (Boston: Beacon Press, 1958), 79.

11   Ibid., 131.

12   Ibid., 132.

13   Ibid., 136.

14   Ibid., 135.

15   The Mondragon federation of worker cooperatives has attempted to limit the size of each to five hundred members to assure democratic decision-making processes. The average size of a kibbutz has been slightly under five hundred members and few have had over one thousand.

16   Notes from Nowhere, ed., *We Are Everywhere: The Irresistible Rise of Global Anticapitalism* (London: Verso, 2003).

17   Ibid., 113.

18   Francis Dupuis-Déri, "Manifestations, altermondialisation et 'groupes d'affinité'. Anarchisme et psychologie des foules rationnelles," presented at the international conference on "Les mobilisations altermondialistes," December 3–5, 2003; *Proceedings* (Paris: Fondation Nationale des Sciences Politiques), 3; http://www.afsp.msh-paris.fr/activite/groupe/germm/collgermm03txt/germm03dupuis.pdf. The translations from Dupuis-Déri are mine. For other descriptions of affinity groups from within the global justice or altermondialiste movement, see Starhawk, "Affinity Groups" at https://www.nonviolence.wri-irg.org/en/node/5164; Rise Up/ Direct Action Network Los Angeles, "Affinity Group Information and Resources" at http://www.d2kla.org/dan_affinty.html; Freedom Rising Affinity Group, "What is an Affinity Group?" at http://www.freedomrising.org/article.php?id=14 and *We Are Everywhere*, 88.

19   Dupuis-Déri, "Manifestations," 3.

20   Ibid.

21   Barbara Epstein, "Anarchism and the Anti-Globalization Movement," *Monthly Review* 53, no. 4 (September 2001): 1–14. A future discussion will explore the topic of the convergence of important elements of the Marxist and anarchist traditions subsequent to the decline of the most doctrinaire and sectarian tendencies within these traditions.

22   This eclecticism and the heavy emphasis on practice may produce a certain degree of theoretical incoherence, but it has also no doubt helped the movement escape the self-destructive sectarian strife that has plagued almost every Left tendency from the First International to the present-day green movement.

23   Giorgio Agamben, "The Friend" in *What Is an Apparatus? And Other Essays* (Stanford, CA: Stanford University Press, 2009), 25–37.

24   Ibid., 33.

25   Ibid., 34.

26   Ibid., 34–35.

27   Bernard J. Lee et al., *The Catholic Experience of Small Christian Communities* (New York: Paulist Press, 2000). See also Arthur Jones, "Small Communities Bear Big Gifts, Study Shows," *National Catholic Reporter* (May 28, 1999); http://annhernandez.com/?page_id=907. Gary MacEoin, "Communities Offer Hope for Church, Society," *National Catholic Reporter* (September 20, 2002); http://natcath. org/NCR_Online/archives2/2002c/092002/092002z.htm.

28   The first contradiction is between the forces and relations of production while the second is between the forces and relations of production and the (ecological) conditions of production. This third contradiction should be seen as that between the forces and relations of production and realities that are not merely superstructural "forms of consciousness" but forms of life that are basic to the constitution of human society.

7 Bridging the Unbridgeable Chasm: Personal Transformation and Social Action in Anarchist Practice

1 Murray Bookchin, *Social Anarchism or Lifestyle Anarchism: An Unbridgeable Chasm* (San Francisco: AK Press, 1995). I would like to express my appreciation to David Watson, Ronald Creagh, Spencer Sunshine, Peter Marshall, and Mark Lance for their very helpful suggestions, which improved this chapter considerably.

2 Alan Ritter, *Anarchism: A Theoretical Analysis* (Cambridge: Cambridge University Press, 1980), 3.

3 This discussion will not cover Bookchin's extensive claims in *Social Anarchism or Lifestyle Anarchism* concerning neoprimitivist and antitechnological tendencies in contemporary anarchism. These claims have been analyzed very carefully and refuted quite effectively in David Watson's chapters "Dreams of Reason and Unbridgeable Chasms" and "Social Ecology and Its Discontents" in *Beyond Bookchin: Preface to a Future Social Ecology* (Brooklyn: Autonomedia: 1996), 189–248.

4 In fact, one weakness of some anarchist theories, and certainly of Bookchin's own thought, is the tendency to exaggerate the degree to which this tension can be largely dissolved if certain institutional changes were introduced.

5 An excellent statement of Goldman's position is found in her essay "The Individual, Society and the State," in *Red Emma Speaks: Selected Writings & Speeches by Emma Goldman*, ed. Alix Kates Shulman (New York: Vintage Books, 1972), 86–106.

6 See John P. Clark, *The Philosophical Anarchism of William Godwin* (Princeton, NJ: Princeton University Press, 1977), 134–47.

7 Murray Bookchin, *Social Anarchism or Lifestyle Anarchism: An Unbridgeable Chasm* (San Francisco: AK Press, 1995), 5.

8 Michael Bakunin, "The Paris Commune and the Idea of the State" at https://www.marxists.org/reference/archive/bakunin/works/1871/paris-commune.htm.

9 Bookchin, *Social Anarchism or Lifestyle Anarchism*, 5.

10 John Clark and Camille Martin, eds., *Anarchy, Geography, Modernity: Selected Writings of Elisée Reclus* (Oakland: PM Press, 2013), 10.

11 Ibid., 53–54.

12 Ibid., 158–59.

13 Peter Kropotkin, "Anarchism: Its Philosophy and Ideal" at https://theanarchistlibrary.org/library/petr-kropotkin-anarchism-its-philosophy-and-ideal.

14 Peter Kropotkin, "Anarchist Communism: Its Basis and Principles" at https://theanarchistlibrary.org/library/petr-kropotkin-anarchist-communism-its-basis-and-principles.

15 Bookchin, *Social Anarchism or Lifestyle Anarchism*, 12.

16 Quoted in Robert Graham, ed., *Anarchism: A Documentary History of Libertarian Ideas, Volume 1: From Anarchy to Anarchism (300 CE–1939)* (Montreal: Black Rose Books, 2005), 125.

17 For example, "The End of Anarchism?" The Anarchist Library, https://theanarchistlibrary.org/library/luigi-galleani-the-end-of-anarchism.

18 Chapter 2 of the present work is an extended defense of the resulting "third concept of liberty."

19 Bakunin, *Oeuvres*, vol. 1 (Paris: Stock, 1895), 313. My translation. This is from his vast, mostly unpublished text, *The Knouto-Germanic Empire and the Social Revolution*, in the section called "God and the State." This text should not be confused with another one that was published as a book under the same title.

20 Ibid., 313–14.

21 Ibid., 314.

22 Peter Marshall, *Demanding the Impossible* (London: HarperCollins, 1992), 36.

23 Ibid., 670.

24 The standard history of American individualist anarchism is James J. Martin's *Men against the State* (DeKalb, IL: Adrian Allen Associates, 1953; Colorado Springs, CO: Ralph Myles Publisher, 1970).

25 Ibid., 226–27.

26 Personal correspondence. Creagh's *Histoire de l'anarchisme aux États-Unis* (Grenoble: La Pensée sauvage, 1981) is based on his exhaustive 1,164-page dissertation on American anarchism in the nineteenth century, *L'anarchisme aux États-Unis* (Paris: Didier Erudition, 1986).

27 http://recollectionbooks.com/siml/library/CS/Spain/cntZaragozaResolution1936.htm.

28 See Allan Antliff, *Anarchist Modernism: Art, Politics, and the First American Avant-Garde* (Chicago: University of Chicago Press, 2001), and *Anarchy and Art: From the Paris Commune to the Fall of the Berlin Wall* (Vancouver: Arsenal Pulp Press, 2007).

29 See Ronald Creagh. *Utopies Américaines: Expériences Libertaires du XXIXe Siècle à Nos Jours*, especially chap. 8, "Au-delà de l'Imaginaire: Mille Utopies," 253–89.

30 Bob Black makes a similar case in his critique of Bookchin in *Anarchy after Leftism* (Columbia, MO: C.A.L. Press, 1997), 46–49.

31 George Woodcock, *Anarchism: A History of Libertarian Ideas and Movements* (New York: World Publishing Co., 1962), 309.

32 Ibid., 310. Bookchin may have gotten the idea that propaganda of the deed is linked to individualism in part from Woodcock, who incorrectly describes it as "carrying individualism to a Stirnerite extreme" (307). However, Woodcock himself contradicts this diagnosis by saying that the terrorists acted on behalf of "justice" (which is anathema from a Stirnerite perspective) and he quotes statements of their own that show a commitment to social anarchism. Tuchman adds to the confusion by stating that Ravachol was "almost" an "ego anarchist" but "not quite," in view of his "streak of genuine pity and fellow-feeing for the oppressed." Barbara W. Tuchman, "Anarchism in France," in Irving L. Horowitz, *The Anarchists* (New York: Dell Publishing, 1964), 446.

33 Woodcock, *Anarchism*, 311.

34 Quoted in Marshall, *Demanding the Impossible*, 438.

35 Peter Marshall, personal correspondence.

36 There is some ambiguity in Bookchin's argument here. At some points, as here, he claims that the decline of social anarchism is followed by the rise of individualist or lifestyle anarchism. However, at other times he argues that individualist or lifestyle anarchism is dangerous because it contributes to the decline of social anarchism, which would mean that the rise of the former would precede rather than follow the decline of the latter.

37 For a meticulously detailed and quite fascinating study of an immigrant anarchist community, including discussion of the effects of assimilation, see Tom Goyens, *Beer and Revolution: The German Anarchist Movement in New York City, 1880–1914* (Champaign: University of Illinois Press, 2006).

38 Bookchin goes to great lengths lamenting the pernicious influence of postmodern thinkers on contemporary anarchism, and above all that of Nietzsche. For reasons of space, the details of his serious misunderstanding of Nietzsche will not be discussed here. Nietzsche's significance for anarchism is explored at length in John Moore with Spencer Sunshine, eds, *I Am Not a Man, I Am Dynamite: Friedrich Nietzsche and the Anarchist Tradition* (Brooklyn: Autonomedia, 2004) and outlined in Spencer Sunshine, "Nietzsche and the Anarchists," *Fifth Estate* 367 (Winter 2004–5): 36–37. Bookchin's shocking obliviousness to the nature of postmodernist thought is indicated by his belief that it has an "aversion to theory." In fact, postmodernists are quite preoccupied with theory and especially with what they typically refer to as "French theory."

39 Bookchin once had a much more positive, if deeply self-contradictory, view of affinity groups. In *Post-Scarcity Anarchism* he says that they constituted a "new type of extended family," they "allow for the greatest degree of intimacy," and they are

"intensely experimental and variegated in lifestyles." Nevertheless, he contends in the same work that if they succeed in their revolutionary goals they will "finally disappear into the organic social forms created by the revolution." "A Note on Affinity Groups" in *Post-Scarcity Anarchism*, 221–22. He does not explain how "the greatest degree of intimacy" can be attained in the various social forms he proposes for the future, specifically "factory committees," "workers' assemblies," "the neighborhood assembly," and "neighborhood committees, councils and boards." The idea of replacing one's extended family with a factory committee seems a bit disquieting. "The Forms of Freedom," in *Post-Scarcity Anarchism*, 168.

40 Clark and Martin, *Anarchy, Geography, Modernity*, 168.

41 Susan Brown, *The Politics of Individualism* (Montreal: Black Rose Books, 1993), 140.

42 Problems with libertarian municipalism will be discussed in detail in chap. 10. At this point, I would only note that both Bookchin and Biehl seriously neglect problems with majority rule in their most detailed discussions of the program of libertarian municipalism, for example Bookchin's "From Here to There," in *Remaking Society* (Montreal: Black Rose Books, 1989), 159–204, and Biehl's, *The Politics of Social Ecology: Libertarian Municipalism* (Montreal: Black Rose Books, 1999). Their approach in such discussions is usually to gloss rather quickly over the problems with majoritarianism, to hastily dismiss opposing views as unworkable, and to invoke a future civic ethos as the ultimate solution to all problems. Thus, in "From Here to There," Bookchin expresses his hopes that the citizens of the libertarian municipality will, like the ancient Greeks, "learn civic responsibility, to reason out one's views with scrupulous care, to confront opposing arguments with clarity, and, hopefully, to advance tested principles that exhibited high ethical standards" (179). Biehl explains vaguely that the "paideia" that Bookchin depends on will be created "in the course of democratic political participation," "in the very process of decision-making," and in "the school of politics" (89). Not only is their version of the anarchist ideal of "communal individuality" rather limited in scope, the expectation that liberatory self-transformation can be effected overwhelmingly by one (currently nonexistent) institution seems wildly unrealistic. In short, there is far too much "There" and not nearly enough "Here" in their analysis.

43 Murray Bookchin, *The Rise of Urbanization and the Decline of Citizenship* (San Francisco: Sierra Club Books, 1987), 282.

44 Murray Bookchin, *Remaking Society* (Montreal: Black Rose Books, 1989), 183.

45 This issue will be discussed in more detail in chap. 10.

46 Some of Dupuis-Déri's extensive research is found in *Les Black Blocs: La liberté et l'égalité se manifestent* (Lyon: Atelier de Création Libertaire, 2005).

47 Notes from Nowhere, ed., *We Are Everywhere: The Irresistible Rise of Global Anticapitalism* (London: Verso, 2003).

48 Francis Dupuis-Déri, "L'altermondialisation à l'ombre du drapeau noir: L'anarchie en héritage" in Eric Agrikoliansky, Olivier Fillieule, and Nonna Mayer, eds, *L'altermondialisme en France: La longue histoire d'une nouvelle cause* (Paris, Flammarion, 2005). My translation.

49 Francis Dupuis-Déri, "Manifestations altermondialisation et 'groupes d'affinité': Anarchisme et psychologie des foules rationnelles." Presented at a conference on "Les mobilisations altermondialistes," December 3–5, 2003; http://www.afsp.msh-paris.fr/activite/groupe/germm/collgermmo3txt/germmo3dupuis.pdf, 3. My translation.

50 Dupuis-Déri, "L'altermondialisation."

51 Ibid.

52 Dupuis-Déri, "Manifestations," 6. The idea expressed here that democracy is necessarily a form of tyranny is an example of the hyperbole used by some advocates of consensus, and is in a way the mirror image of Bookchin's view that consensus is never more than "the tyranny of structurelessness."

53 Dupuis-Déri, "L'altermondialisation."

54 Ibid.

8   Disaster Anarchism: Hurricane Katrina and the Shock of Recognition

1   Naomi Klein, *The Shock Doctrine: The Rise of Disaster Capitalism* (New York: Picador Press, 2008).

2   Elisée Reclus, *A Voyage to New Orleans: Anarchist Impressions of the Old South*, translated and edited by John Clark and Camille Martin (Thetford, VT: Glad Day Books, 2004), 49–50.

3   Ibid., 50.

4   According to an often-cited statistic, the loss of 2.7 miles of coastal wetlands results in about a one-foot (30.5 cm.) increase in storm surge.

5   Elisée Reclus, "The History of Cities," in *Anarchy, Geography, Modernity: Selected Writings of Elisée Reclus*, eds. John Clark and Camille Martin (Oakland: PM Press, 2013), 175–76.

6   Craig Colten, *An Unnatural Metropolis: Wresting New Orleans from Nature* (Baton Rouge: Louisiana State University Press, 2005).

7   John McPhee, *The Control of Nature* (New York: Farrar Straus Giroux, 1989), 58–64; Christopher Hallowell, *Holding Back the Sea: The Struggle for America's Natural Legacy on the Gulf Coast* (New York: HarperCollins, 2001), 163–79. See also Richard Campanella's indispensable work, *Time and Place in New Orleans: Past Geographies in the Present Day* (Gretna, LA: Pelican Publishing, 2002), especially 38–61 and 78–80.

8   After this was written several more tropical storms and one major hurricane occurred in the same season. The year saw the most storm activity in 150 years.

9   Reclus, "The Feeling for Nature in Modern Society," in Clark and Martin, *Anarchy, Geography, Modernity*, 127.

10   Ibid., 125–26.

11   Reclus, *Voyage to New Orleans*, 53.

12   Ibid., 55.

13   Ibid., 55–56.

14   Ibid., 59.

15   Elisée Reclus, *L'Homme et la Terre*, 6 vols. (Paris: Librairie Universelle, 1905–8).

16   See Clark and Martin, "The Critique of Domination," in *Anarchy, Geography, Modernity*, 87–112.

17   Clark and Martin, "The Modern State," in *Anarchy, Geography, Modernity*, 210.

18   Large private bureaucracies—the Charity Establishment—seemed no more competent than those of the state. The Red Cross, which had raised almost a billion dollars in the early weeks after the disaster, was conspicuous by its absence in the areas of greatest need, including the city of New Orleans.

19   Ibid., 212.

20   Reclus, *L'Homme et la Terre*, 1:145.

21   Elisée Reclus, Letter to Reclus's sister Louise (n.d., 1859), in *Correspondance*, vol. 1 (Paris: Librairie Schleicher Frères, 1911), 206.

22   Elisée Reclus, Letter to Clara Koettlitz (April 12, 1895) in *Correspondance*, vol. 3 (Paris: Alfred Costes, 1925), 182.

23   "Quelques mots d'histoire, Suivi de Préface à la Conquête du pain de Pierre Kropotkine" [cited May 31, 2003] at http://fraternitelibertaire.free.fr/reserve/quelques_mots_dhistoire.doc.

24   Alex Martin, "On a Street Named Desire," *Newsday*, September 26, 2005.

25   Ibid.

26   Ivor van Heerden and Mike Bryan, *The Storm: What Went Wrong and Why During Hurricane Katrina—The Inside Story from One Louisiana Scientist* (New York: Viking, 2006), 200.

27   Bill Walsh, "Corps Chief Admits to 'Design Failure,'" *Times-Picayune*, April 6, 2006.

28   van Heerden and Mike Bryan, *The Storm*.

29 Mike Tidwell, *Bayou Farewell: The Rich Life and Tragic Death of Louisiana's Cajun Coast* (New York: Vintage Books, 2003).

30 Mike Tidwell, "Goodbye New Orleans," *AlterNet*, December 9, 2005, http://www.alternet. org/ katrina/29274/comments/?page=1.

31 The essential work on the story of the Common Ground Collective is cofounder scott crow's *Black Flags and Windmills: Hope, Anarchy, and the Common Ground Collective*, 2nd ed. (Oakland: PM Press, 2014). Few works express so eloquently the spirit of communitarian anarchism that is defended here.

32 Since this was written, the total number of Common Ground volunteers has reached 35,000 and its work on some projects continues. For an update, see the Common Ground website at http://www.commongroundrelief.org.

33 http://www.flickr.com/photos/postkatrinaportraits/show/. A collection was also published as a large format art book, *The Post-Katrina Portraits, Written and Narrated by Hundreds, Drawn by Francesco di Santis* (New Orleans: Francesco di Santis and Loulou Latta, 2007). The work of post-Katrina volunteers, including many anarchists, is also documented extensively in many recent films, including Danish director Rasmus Holm's *Welcome to New Orleans*, which can be found at https://www.youtube.com/watch?v=V_lSdR1KZg and Farrah Hoffmire's *Falling Together in New Orleans: A Series of Vignettes* (www.organicprocess. com).

34 http://postkatrinaportraits.org/. The quotes that follow are from this site.

9 The Common Good: Sarvodaya and the Gandhian Legacy

1 *Frontline* 16, no. 11 (May 22–June 4, 1999), http://web.cecs.pdx.edu/~sheard/course/Design&Society/Readings/Narmada/greatercommongood.pdf; and in *The Cost of Living* (New York: Modern Library, 1999), 1–90.

2 In defense of the Flat World Theory, Thomas Friedman cites Bill Gates, who opines that while thirty years ago, if one could choose to be born either "a genius on the outskirts of Bombay" or "an average person in Poughkeepsie" one would obviously have bet on Poughkeepsie for a better life, but now, "as the world has gone flat, and so many people can plug and play from anywhere, natural talent has started to trump geography." *The World Is Flat: A Brief History of the Twenty-First Century* (New York: Farrar, Strauss, and Giroux, 2006), 226. Gates should have recommended to his genius to be sure to be born in a gated community in Mumbai and not randomly among the masses.

3 Mohandas Gandhi, "The Definition of Swadeshi" in *The Gospel of Swadeshi* at https://www.mkgandhi.org/indiadreams/chap31.htm.

4 Members of the *panchayat* or village council.

5 Pranaw Kr. Jha, "Chaupal as Multidimensional Public Space for Civil Society in India" at www.ignca.nic.in/kmsh0006.htm.

6 Ibid.

7 Ibid.

8 Thomas Vettickal, *Gandhian Sarvodaya: Realizing a Realistic Utopia* (New Delhi: Gyan Publishing House, 2002), 17.

9 Geoffrey Ostergaard and Melville Currell, *The Gentle Anarchists: A Study of the Sarvodaya Movement for Non-violent Revolution in India* (Oxford: Clarendon Press, 1971), 32.

10 Ibid., 33–39.

11 Tandon, *Selections from Vinoba*, 168.

12 M.K. Gandhi, *Village Swaraj* (Ahmedabad: Navajivan Publishing House, 1962), 4.

13 Ostergaard and Currell, *The Gentle Anarchists*, 30.

14 Gandhi, *Village Swaraj*, 52.

15 M.K. Gandhi, *My Non-violence* (Ahmedabad: Navajivan, 1960), chap. 55, https://www.gandhiashramsevagram.org/my-nonviolence/chapter-55-an-interesting-discourse-1.php.

16 Gandhi, *My Non-violence*, chap. 158, https://www.gandhiashramsevagram.org/
    my-nonviolence/chapter-158-his-last-will-and-testament.php.

17 Tandon, *Selections from Vinoba*, 160.

18 Ibid., 108.

19 Ibid.

20 Ibid., 108–9.

21 Ibid., 161.

22 Ibid., 163.

23 Ibid., 169.

24 Étienne de La Boétie, *The Politics of Obedience: The Discourse of Voluntary Servitude*
    (New York: Free Life Editions, 1975); http://mises.org/rothbard/boetie.pdf.

25 Gandhi, *Village Swaraj*, 39.

26 Gandhi, *Collected Works*, 21:133 at http://www.gandhiserve.org/cwmg/VOL021.PDF.

27 Gandhi, *Village Swaraj*, 32.

28 Ibid., 31.

29 Ibid., 31–32.

30 Ibid., 72.

31 Vettickal, *Gandhian Sarvodaya*, 30.

32 Tandon, *Selections from Vinoba*, 179.

33 This is implicitly a criticism of libertarian municipalism that is presented in the final
    chapter. Though Sarvodaya never carried through on the development of these tran-
    sitional institutions, it makes a great contribution in sketching their nature and in
    demonstrating their partial realization in the practice of the movement.

34 Vettickal, *Gandhian Sarvodaya*, 143.

35 Ibid., 151.

36 Ibid., 159.

37 Ostergaard and Currell, *The Gentle Anarchists*, 13.

38 Ibid., 59.

39 Vandana Shiva, *Earth Democracy: Justice, Sustainability, and Peace* (Cambridge, MA:
    South End Press, 2005). On the politics that follows from such a view, see Ariel Salleh,
    ed., *Eco-Sufficiency & Global Justice: Women Write Political Ecology* (London: Pluto Press,
    2009).

40 Gandhi, *Village Swaraj*, 12.

41 Ibid., 13.

42 Ibid., 12–13.

43 Ostergaard and Currell, *The Gentle Anarchists*, 13.

44 Ibid., 13–14.

45 Gandhi, *Harijan* (March 31, 1946); quoted at http://www.mkgandhi-sarvodaya.org/
    sfgandhi/sixth.htm.

46 Ibid.

47 Ibid.

48 Gandhi, *Village Swaraj*, 52.

49 Ostergaard and Currell, *The Gentle Anarchists*, 28.

50 Ibid., 17.

51 Gandhi, *Harijan* (March 23, 1936); quoted at http://www.mkgandhi.org/journalist/
    capstrikes.htm.

52 Additional information on this community-based, grassroots effort at self-help can
    be found at the Sarvodaya website: http://www.sarvodaya.org/.

53 The Mondragon cooperatives now have 83,000 workers, 9,000 students, and $45
    billion in assets. For further details, see the Mondragon official website at https://www.
    mondragon-corporation.com/en/about-us.

54 Joel Kovel, *History and Spirit: An Inquiry into the Philosophy of Liberation* (Boston: Beacon
    Press, 1991).

55 Ibid., 1.

56 Ibid., 192.

57 A.T. Ariyaratne, *Sarvodaya Peace Meditation Program Introduction and Guide for Participants* (Ratmalana: Sarvodaya Vishva Lekha Press, 2004). This is a small pamphlet distributed at meditations.

58 Joanna Macy, "For the Awakening of All: The Sarvodaya Shramadana Movement in Sri Lanka" in *Karuna: A Journal of Buddhist Meditation* (Summer/Fall 1988), reprinted at http://www.buddhanet.net/ftp03.htm. A revised and expanded version appears in *The Path of Compassion* (Berkeley: Parallax Press, 1988).

59 Quoted in Dale Cannon, "The Sarvodaya Movement in Sri Lanka," chap. 11.1 of *Six Ways of Being Religious*, https://human.libretexts.org/@go/page/37036.

60 Lewis Mumford, *Technics and Human Development*, vol. 1, *The Myth of the Machine* (New York: Harcourt, Brace, Jovanovich, 1967), 256–62.

61 Godfrey Gunatilleke of the Marga Institute, Sri Lanka, quoted at http://phoenix.akasha. de/~sarvdaya/pamphlet1/offer.html. It is noteworthy that after many years of depending almost entirely on its own resources, Sarvodaya Shramadana began to receive significant outside aid by the 1980s. However, beginning in the early 1990s there was a general trend for such international developmental aid to dry up. Unlike many more conventional organizations, Sarvodaya was not devastated by this reversal. Since it had retained its fundamental emphasis on self-reliance and base organization, it was able to adapt to these conditions and continue to expand its programs.

62 Sadeeva Ariyaratne is a Sarvodaya Shramadana activist, the daughter of Dr. Ariyaratne. "Highlights of Sarvodaya Peace Initiatives and the Deshodaya Movement for Good Governance," at http://www.sarvodaya.org/.

63 Samudhu Weerawarne, "Dr. A.T. Ariyaratne at Close Quarters" from *LMD-Sri Lanka's Business and Leisure Magazine* 6, no. 7 (February 2000): 28.

64 Common Ground, the large anarchist-inspired recovery organization, adopted EM for its extensive mold remediation program in post-Katrina New Orleans and helped educate the community about the many uses of this inexpensive, noncommercial, ecologically sound, nontoxic solution to many practical problems.

65 Ibid.

66 Richard S. Brooks, "In the Footsteps of Gandhi and Buddha, 11,000 Villages Grow," at http://www.sarvodaya.org/.

67 Ibid.

68 A.K. Ariyaratne, "Here on Earth," interview on Wisconsin Public Radio, May 22, 2004.

69 Sadeeva Ariyaratne, "Highlights."

10 Beyond the Limits of the City: A Communitarian Anarchist Critique of Libertarian Municipalism

1 For example, Dana Ward, in his now-defunct online "Anarchy Archives," included Bookchin in the "Cynosure," his list of the all-time "Top Nine" in anarchist theory (though one may suspect that Bookchin and Chomsky got extra points for being Americans).

2 The first part of this thesis will be defended in great detail in a forthcoming work on dialectical social ecology.

3 See John P. Clark, *The Philosophical Anarchism of William Godwin* (Princeton, NJ: Princeton University Press, 1977), 192–93, 243–47.

4 See John P. Clark and Camille Martin, eds., *Anarchy, Geography, Modernity: Selected Writings of Elisée Reclus* (Oakland: PM Press, 2013).

5 See Murray Bookchin, "From Here to There," in *Remaking Society* (Montreal: Black Rose Books, 1989), 159–207, and "The New Municipal Agenda," in *The Rise of Urbanization and the Decline of Citizenship* (San Francisco: Sierra Club Books, 1987), 225–88.

6   See Benjamin Barber, *Strong Democracy: Participatory Politics for a New Age* (Berkeley: University of California Press, 1984).

7   Since politics "uses the rest of the sciences" and "legislates as to what we are to do and what we are to abstain from, the end of this science must include those of the others, so that this end must be the good for man. For even if the end is the same for a single man and for a state, that of the state seems at all events something greater and more complete whether to attain or to preserve; though it is worthwhile to attain the end merely for one man, it is finer and more godlike to attain it for a nation or for city-states." Aristotle, *Nicomachean Ethics* (Ross trans.), Book I, http://classics.mit.edu/ Aristotle/nicomachaen.1.i.html.

8   Murray Bookchin, *Post-Scarcity Anarchism* (Berkeley: Ramparts Press, 1971), 124.

9   This idea, like many of Bookchin's concepts, was expressed almost a century earlier by the great French anarchist social geographer Elisée Reclus. Reclus begins his 3,500-page magnum opus of social thought, *L'Homme et la Terre*, with the statement, "l'Homme est la Nature prenant conscience d'elle-même," or "Humanity is Nature becoming self-conscious." Bookchin was not at all familiar with Reclus's work, so the parallels arise only indirectly, either through Reclus's influence on other figures with whom Bookchin was more familiar, or through the inevitable consonance between a project for an anarchist social geography and a project for an anarchist social ecology. It might be noted that Reclus would not have used Bookchin's similar but more anthropo-centric formulation in which nature's role in the human-nature relationship is depicted through the use of the passive voice. For Bookchin, humanity is nature "rendered" self-conscious, while for Reclus nature "takes consciousness" of "herself." In addition there is an ambiguity in Bookchin's formulation about whether the "self-conscious-ness" is that of nature or only a certain (human) dimension of nature, while Reclus clearly depicts humanity as a means through which nature comes to self-knowledge. For extensive translation of Reclus's most important work and commentary on its significance, especially in relation to social ecology, see Clark and Martin, *Anarchy, Geography, Modernity*.

10   Bookchin, *Post-Scarcity Anarchism*, 169.

11   Bookchin, *Toward an Ecological Society*, (Montreal: Black Rose Books, 1980), 183–86. Though this will no doubt become evident, the subtext of the present discussion is that Bookchin's later work betrayed this vision in many ways, while the present work seeks to carry it on and help fulfill its promise.

12   Bookchin, *Rise of Urbanization*, 55.

13   Ariel Salleh, *Ecofeminism as Politics: Nature, Marx and the Postmodern* (London: Zed Books, 1997), x. Vandana Shiva has developed this concept in great detail in her book *Earth Democracy: Justice, Sustainability, and Peace* (Cambridge, MA: South End Press, 2005).

14   Bookchin, "Comments on the International Social Ecology Network Gathering and the 'Deep Social Ecology' of John Clark," *Democracy and Nature* 9 (1997): 167. Bookchin wrote this text in response to an early draft of the present analysis presented at an International Social Ecology Conference in Dunoon, Scotland. Extensive revisions were made, so I quote Bookchin's comments only on those parts that remain unchanged. The term "deep social ecology," which I have not used, comes from ecophilosopher David Rothenberg.

15   See John Clark, "Bad I.O.U.: Badiou's Fidelity to the Event," *Logos* 10 (2011) at http:// logosjournal.com/2011/summer_clark/.

16   Bookchin, "Comments," 166.

17   Ibid.

18   Probably the most radical democratic advance was the Democratic-Republican Societies of the 1790s, which encompassed only a small minority of the population, and had a very limited influence on the course of American social history. See John

P. Clark, "The French Revolution and American Radical Democracy," in *Revolution, Violence, and Equality*, eds. Y. Hudson and C. Peden (Lewiston, NY: Edwin Mellen Press, 1990), 79–118.

19   Murray Bookchin, "Libertarian Municipalism: An Overview," *Green Perspectives* 24 (1991): 4. Note that in this statement Bookchin admits the possibility of "citizenship" in a region.

20   Murray Bookchin, *The Last Chance: An Appeal for Social and Ecological Sanity* (Burlington, VT: Comment, 1983), 48.

21   Ibid.

22   Bookchin, *Remaking Society*, 173.

23   Murray Bookchin, *The Modern Crisis* (Philadelphia: New Society, 1986), 150–51.

24   Ibid., 152.

25   Bookchin, *Rise of Urbanization*, 249.

26   Ibid., 282.

27   See Wilhelm Reich's classic *The Mass Psychology of Fascism* (New York: Simon and Schuster, 1970), and Joel Kovel's *The Age of Desire* (New York: Pantheon Books, 1981), which also deserves recognition as a classic. Kovel's analysis is an unsurpassed account of the complex dialectic between individual selfhood, the family, productionist and consumptionist economic institutions, the state, and the technological system.

28   Bookchin, *Remaking Society*, 183; emphasis added.

29   Bookchin, *Toward an Ecological Society*, 137.

30   Remembering that from a dialectical perspective, wholes are always only relative wholes. A dialectical holism is a holism/anti-holism. "The true is the whole," but the true is never the whole truth.

31   Bookchin, "Comments," 158.

32   Bookchin, *Rise of Urbanization*, 33. Actually, this distinction is implicit in much of previous anarchist theory, and Bookchin's own version of it is heavily influenced by Arendt's analysis in *The Human Condition* (Chicago: University of Chicago Press, 1958). See especially Part 2, "The Public and the Private Realm," 22–78.

33   Bookchin, "Comments," 158.

34   Ibid.

35   Ibid.

36   Ibid., emphasis in original.

37   Though there would, of course, be rare exceptions, as when one "disports oneself" in extraterritorial waters.

38   Bookchin, "Comments," 158.

39   Adolf G. Gundersen, *The Environmental Promise of Democratic Deliberation* (Madison: University of Wisconsin Press, 1995), 4.

40   Bookchin, *Rise of Urbanization*, 39; emphasis added.

41   This point is developed at some length in my article "Domesticating the Dialectic: A Critique of Bookchin's Neo-Aristotelianism," *Capitalism Nature Socialism* 19, no. 1 (March 2008): 51–68.

42   From a dialectical perspective, we see that the social is not only *always already* the political, but also *always not yet* the political, which is, indeed, the fate of the political itself.

43   Bookchin, *Toward an Ecological Society*, 119.

44   Bookchin, *Rise of Urbanization*, 259.

45   Ibid., 265.

46   Murray Bookchin, "Libertarian Municipalism: The New Municipal Agenda," *Anarchy Archives* at http://dwardmac.pitzer.edu/anarchist_archives/bookchin/libmuni.html.

47   Murray Bookchin and Janet Biehl, "A Critique of the Draft Program of the Left Green Network," *Green Perspectives* 23 (1991): 2. The Left Green Network was a small coalition of ecoanarchists and ecosocialists within the U.S. green movement. Bookchin became

disillusioned with the Network when it failed to adopt libertarian municipalism as its political position.

48 Bookchin, "Comments," 174.

49 Ibid., 175; emphasis in original.

50 Bookchin, "Comments," 175.

51 See *Living My Life*, vol. 1 (New York: Dover Books, 1970), 51–53.

52 Bookchin, *Rise of Urbanization*, 276.

53 Bookchin, "Libertarian Municipalism," 4.

54 At times he has harshly criticized others who support small businesses as part of a decentralized, localist, and regionalist economy, arguing that they are selling out to capitalism.

55 Bookchin, *Rise of Urbanization*, 275.

56 Ibid.

57 Ibid., 276. Taken together, Bookchin's suggestions are almost identical to the goals of the Solidarity Economy Group of Occupy New Orleans, which was the major focus of my own work with the Occupy movement.

58 Bookchin, *Remaking Society*, 175.

59 This was the position taken by the Sarvodaya movement, as discussed in the previous chapter. The assembly is the most important organ of local collective political decision-making, but many other institutions are equally crucial to the community's free self-determination. Only a very small part of the community's free self-activity can possibly take place in an assembly.

60 Bookchin, *Remaking Society*, 175.

61 Any serious libertarian political theory needs to include a developed theory of law or a theory of whatever is proposed as a substitute for law. The absence of such a theory in libertarian municipalism casts doubt on the seriousness of its claims to being a practicable, real-world politics rather than a form of political sectarianism.

62 Despite the often considerable Aristotelian influence on Bookchin, he unwisely narrows the Aristotelian definition of citizenship. Aristotle more realistically defined the citizen as one "who enjoys the right of sharing in deliberative or judicial office," recognizing that both legislation and the interpretation and administration of law were important and necessary aspects of political life; *The Politics of Aristotle* (London: Oxford University Press, 1958), 95.

63 See John Burnheim, *Is Democracy Possible? The Alternative to Electoral Politics* (Berkeley: University of California Press, 1985).

64 Bookchin, "Comments," 183; emphasis in original.

65 Rancière, *Hatred of Democracy*, 41.

66 Ibid., 40.

67 Ibid., 49.

68 Ibid., 42.

69 Admittedly, this is very limited experiment. The Occupy movement is not the free community, and membership in working groups is not decided by lot but is open to all volunteers. Yet important experience with participatory forms of organization, and with confronting issues such as balancing the responsibilities of assemblies and committees, is occurring.

70 Maple Razsa and Andrej Kurnik, "The Occupy Movement in Žižek's Hometown: Direct Democracy and a Politics of Becoming," *American Ethnologist* 39, no. 2 (May 2012): 238–58.

71 Zibechi, *Dispersing Power*, 13.

72 Ibid.

73 Ibid., 13.

74 Ibid., 55.

75 Ibid., 181.

76 It is not only the size of the modern urban sprawl that brings into question Bookchin's municipalist outlook, but the qualitative changes that have taken place. Mumford points out in *The City in History* that what has emerged "is not in fact a new sort of city, but an anti-city" that "annihilates the city whenever it collides with it"; *The City in History* (New York: Harcourt, Brace & World, 1961), 505. Bookchin approaches this change from a moralistic standpoint, seeing it as an evil to be denounced, but he does not take it seriously as an object of analysis and a challenge to concepts of practice tied to previous historical epochs. Luccarelli, in *Lewis Mumford and the Ecological Region* (New York: Guilford Press, 1995), points out that Mumford's idea of the "anti-city" prefigured recent analyses of a "technurbia" that has emerged out of social transformations in a post-Fordist regime that is "driven by telecommunications and computer-assisted design," that produces "forces that tend to disperse and decentralize production," and that results in a "diffused city" (191) that is quite unlike the traditional city that Bookchin takes as his point of reference.

77 Zibechi, *Dispersing Power*, 20.

78 Bookchin, *Rise of Urbanization*, 246

79 Ibid., 102.

80 Murray Bookchin, *Defending the Earth: A Dialogue between Murray Bookchin and Dave Foreman* (New York: South End Press, 1991), 79.

81 On this subject see Mike Davis's essential work, *Planet of Slums* (London: Verso, 2006).

82 Pierre Clastres, "In Flux," interview by Félix Guattari, in *Chaosophy: Texts and Interviews 1972–1977* (Los Angeles: Semiotext(e), 2009), 86.

83 Zibechi, *Dispersing Power*, 67.

84 Salleh, "Second Thoughts on *Rethinking Ecofeminist Politics*: A Dialectical Critique," *Interdisciplinary Studies in Literature and Environment* 1 (Fall 1993): 97.

85 Bookchin, *Modern Crisis*, 91.

86 Bookchin, *Rise of Urbanization*, 263.

87 Bookchin, *Remaking Society*, 194.

88 Bookchin, *Modern Crisis*, 93.

89 Ibid., 92.

90 Bookchin and Biehl, "Critique of the Draft Program," 3; emphasis in original.

91 Ibid., 4.

92 Ibid.

93 Bookchin, *Modern Crisis*, 160.

94 Bookchin, *Rise of Urbanization*, 275.

95 Peter Marshall, *Demanding the Impossible: A History of Anarchism* (London: HarperCollins, 1992), 462–63. Details can be found in Gaston Laval's *Collectives in the Spanish Revolution* (London: Freedom Press, 1975) and Sam Dolgoff's *The Anarchist Collectives* (New York: Free Life Editions, 1974). Anarchist militias sometimes forced all inhabitants of a village into the collective. Often, when the collectives were reorganized on a voluntary basis, the majority rejoined the collective, but a minority opted for individual enterprises. See Ronald Fraser, *Blood of Spain: An Oral History of the Spanish Civil War* (New York: Pantheon Books, 1979), which contains many narratives by former members of the collectives.

96 It might be expected that as communal individuality develops, fewer and fewer members of the community would find the "individualist" path as fulfilling as participatory collective endeavors. Yet this would be an experimental question, not a matter of dogma. Furthermore, as a community developed toward a system of distribution according to need, the logistics of maintaining an individualist sector within or in close relationship with the community might become very complicated.

97 Bookchin, "Comments," 186.

98 However, when the cooperative economic sector becomes very large, most if not all exchange could then take place within its bounds. Of course, if public support for the

solidarity economy becomes overwhelming, then a more immediate, society-wide revolutionary structural change can be effected.

99   Murray Bookchin, "The Meaning of Confederalism," *Green Perspectives* 20 (1990): 4.

100   Ibid.

101   Ibid.

102   Bookchin, "Libertarian Municipalism," 3; emphasis added.

103   Bookchin, *Rise of Urbanization*, 246.

104   Bookchin, *Remaking Society*, 168.

105   Ibid., 195.

106   Bookchin, *Ecology of Freedom*, 344.

107   Ibid.

108   Even when one adopts a community as one own, when one makes it one's home, or even one's second home, one does so because one is drawn to it, because one falls in love with it, not because one "chooses to like it."

109   Bookchin, *Remaking Society*, 195.

110   Bookchin, *Rise of Urbanization*, 253.

111   Bookchin, *Remaking Society*, 183.

Bibliography

Ackerman, Bruce. *Social Justice in the Liberal State*. New Haven, CT: Yale University Press, 1980.

Adorno, Theodor W. *Negative Dialectics*. New York: Seabury Press, 1973.

Agamben, Giorgio. *What Is an Apparatus? And Other Essays*. Stanford, CA: Stanford University Press, 2009.

Althusser, Louis. "Contradiction and Overdetermination." In *For Marx*. London: Penguin, 1969; http://www.marxists.org/reference/archive/althusser/1962/overdetermination.htm.

Anarchist FAQ Editorial Collective. *Anarchist FAQ*; http://theanarchistlibrary.org/library/the-anarchist-faq-editorial-collective-an-anarchist-faq.

Antliff, Allan. *Anarchist Modernism: Art, Politics, and the First American Avant-Garde*. Chicago: University of Chicago Press, 2001.

———. *Anarchy and Art: From the Paris Commune to the Fall of the Berlin Wall*. Vancouver: Arsenal Pulp Press, 2007.

Arendt, Hannah. *The Human Condition*. Chicago: University of Chicago Press, 1958.

Aristotle. *Nicomachean Ethics*, translated by W.D. Ross; http://classics.mit.edu/ Aristotle/nicomachaen.1.i.html.

———. *The Politics of Aristotle*. London, Oxford: Oxford University Press, 1958.

Ariyaratne, A.K. Interview on Wisconsin Public Radio. "Here on Earth," May 22, 2004.

———. *Sarvodaya Peace Meditation Program Introduction and Guide for Participants*. Ratmalana: Sarvodaya Vishva Lekha Press, 2004.

Ariyaratne, Sadeeva. "Highlights of Sarvodaya Peace Initiatives and the Deshodaya Movement for Good Governance"; http://www.sarvodaya.org/.

Artaud, Antonin. *The Theater and Its Double*. New York: Grove Press, 1958.

Bakunin, Michael. *God and the State*; https://theanarchistlibrary.org/library/michail-bakunin-god-and-the-state.pdf.

———. *Michael Bakunin: Selected Works*, edited by Arthur Lehning. New York: Grove Press, 1973.

———. *Oeuvres*. 6 vols. Paris: Stock, 1895.

———. "The Paris Commune and the Idea of the State"; https://www.marxists.org/reference/archive/bakunin/works/1871/paris-commune.htm.

———. *The Political Philosophy of Bakunin*, edited by G.P. Maximov. New York: Free Press, 1964.

Barber, Benjamin. *Strong Democracy: Participatory Politics for a New Age*. Berkeley: University of California Press, 1984.

Beecher, Jonathan, and Richard Bienvenu. *The Utopian Vision of Charles Fourier: Selected Texts on Work, Love and Passionate Attraction*. Columbia: University of Missouri Press, 1983.

Bell, Daniel. *The End of Ideology*. Glencoe, IL: Free Press, 1960.

Benjamin, Walter. *The Arcades Project*. Cambridge, MA: Harvard University Press.

Berlin, Isaiah. *Four Essays on Liberty*. London and Oxford: Oxford University Press, 1969.

Berneri, Marie Louise. *Journey through Utopia: A Critical Examination of Imagined Worlds in Western Literature*. Oakland: PM Press, 2019 (1970).

Biehl, Janet, and Murray Bookchin. "A Critique of the Draft Program of the Left Green Network" in *Green Perspectives* 23 (1991): 1–8.

———. *The Politics of Social Ecology: Libertarian Municipalism*. (Montreal: Black Rose Books, 1999).

Black, Bob. *Anarchy after Leftism*. Columbia, MO: C.A.L. Press, 1997.

Blake, William. *The Complete Poetry and Prose of William Blake*. Garden City, NY: Doubleday, 1982.

Bloch, Ernst. *The Principle of Hope*, 3 vols. Cambridge, MA: MIT Press, 1986.

Bookchin, Murray. "Comments on the International Social Ecology Network Gathering and the 'Deep Social Ecology' of John Clark" in *Democracy and Nature* 9 (1997): 154–97.

———. *The Last Chance: An Appeal for Social and Ecological Sanity*. Burlington, VT: Comment, 1983.

———. "Libertarian Municipalism: The New Municipal Agenda," http://www.social-ecology. org/wp/wp-content/uploads/2009/12/Libertarian-Municipalism-The-New-Municipal-Agenda.pdf.

———. "Libertarian Municipalism: An Overview." *Green Perspectives* 24 (1991): 1–6.

———. *The Limits of the City*. New York: Harper Colophon Books, 1974.

———. "The Meaning of Confederalism." *Green Perspectives* 20 (1990): 1–7.

———. *The Modern Crisis*. Philadelphia: New Society, 1986.

———. *Post-Scarcity Anarchism*. Berkeley, CA: Ramparts Press, 1971.

———. *Remaking Society*. Montreal: Black Rose Books, 1989.

———. *The Rise of Urbanization and the Decline of Citizenship*. San Francisco: Sierra Club Books, 1987.

———. *Social Anarchism or Lifestyle Anarchism: An Unbridgeable Chasm*. San Francisco: AK Press, 1995.

———. *Toward an Ecological Society*. Montreal: Black Rose Books, 1980.

———. *Urbanization without Cities: The Rise and Decline of Citizenship*. (Montreal: Black Rose Books, 1996).

Bookchin, Murray, and Dave Foreman. *Defending the Earth: A Dialogue between Murray Bookchin and Dave Foreman*. Boston: South End Press, 1991.

Brooks, Richard S. "In the Footsteps of Gandhi and Buddha, 11,000 Villages Grow," http://www.sarvodaya.org/.

Brown, Susan. *The Politics of Individualism*. Montreal: Black Rose Books, 1993.

Buber, Martin. *Paths in Utopia*. Boston: Beacon Press, 1958.

Burnheim, John. *Is Democracy Possible? The Alternative to Electoral Politics*. Berkeley: University of California Press, 1985.

Call, Lewis. "Postmodern Anarchism in the Novels of Ursula K. Le Guin." *SubStance* 36, no. 2 (2007): 87–105.

Campanella, Richard. *Time and Place in New Orleans: Past Geographies in the Present Day*. Gretna, LA: Pelican Publishing, 2002.

Castoriadis, Cornelius. *The Imaginary Institution of Society*. Cambridge, MA: MIT Press, 1987.

Clark, John P. *The Anarchist Moment: Reflections on Culture, Nature and Power*. Montreal: Black Rose Books, 1984.

———. "Bad I.O.U.: Badiou's Fidelity to the Event." *Logos* 10 (2011); http:// logosjournal. com/2011/summer_clark/.

———. "Capabilities Theory and the Limits of Liberal Justice: On Nussbaum's *Frontiers of Justice*." *Human Rights Review* 10.4 (2009): 583–604; https://www.academia. edu/2540622/_Capabilities_Theory_and_the_Limits_of_Liberal_Justice._A_review_Article_on_Martha_Nussbaum_s_Frontiers_of_Justice._

———. "Cornelius Castoriadis: Thinking about Political Theory." *Capitalism Nature Socialism* 49 (2002): 67–74.

———. "The Dialectical Social Geography of Elisée Reclus"; https://theanarchistlibrary.org/library/john-clark-the-dialectical-social-geography-of-elisee-reclus.

———. "Domesticating the Dialectic: A Critique of Bookchin's Neo-Aristotelianism." *Capitalism Nature Socialism* 19, no. 1 (March 2008): 51–68.

———. "The French Revolution and American Radical Democracy." In *Revolution, Violence, and Equality*, edited by Y. Hudson and C. Peden, 79–118. Lewiston, NY: Edwin Mellen Press, 1990.

———. "The Indigenous Struggle against Violence and Oppression: Resistance to State and Corporate Domination, Colonialism and Neo-colonialism in West Papua." In *World Peace: Problems of Global Understanding and Prospect of Harmony*, edited by Santi Nath Chattopadhyay. Kolkata, India: Punthi Pustak, 2005.

———. *The Philosophical Anarchism of William Godwin*. Princeton, NJ: Princeton University Press, 1977.

Clark, John P., and Camille Martin. *Anarchy, Geography, Modernity: Selected Writings of Elisée Reclus*. Oakland: PM Press, 2013.

Clastres, Pierre, et al. "In Flux." Interview in Félix Guattari, *Chaosophy: Texts and Interviews 1972–1977*, 69–89. Los Angeles: Semiotext(e), 2009.

———. *Society against the State*. New York: Zone Books, 1987.

Codrescu, Andrei. *The Disappearance of the Outside: A Manifesto of Escape*. Reading, MA: Addison-Wesley, 1990.

Cohn, Norman. *The Pursuit of the Millennium*. New York: Oxford, 1970.

Colectivo Situaciones. "Epilogue: Notes about the Notion of 'Community.'" Epilogue for *Dispersing Power: Social Movements as Anti-state Forces* by Raúl Zibechi, 135–42. Oakland: AK Press, 2010.

Colten, Craig. *An Unnatural Metropolis: Wresting New Orleans from Nature*. Baton Rouge: Louisiana State University Press, 2005.

Common Ground Relief; official website at http://www.commongroundrelief.org.

Coupat, Julien. "Interview with Julien Coupat." *Le Monde* (May 5, 2009); translation http://tarnac9.wordpress.com/2009/05/28/ interview-with-julien-coupat/.

Creagh, Ronald. *Histoire de l'anarchisme aux États-Unis*. Grenoble, France: La Pensée sauvage, 1981.

———. *L'anarchisme aux États-Unis*. Paris: Didier Erudition, 1986.

———. *Utopies Américaines: Expériences Libertaires du XXIXe Siècle à Nos Jours*. Marseille: Agone, 2009.

crow, scott. *Black Flags and Windmills: Hope, Anarchy, and the Common Ground Collective*, 2nd ed. Oakland: PM Press, 2014.

Dagger, Richard. "Autonomy, Domination, and the Republican Challenge to Liberalism." In *Autonomy and the Challenges to Liberalism: New Essays*, edited by John Christman and Joel Anderson, 177–203. Cambridge: Cambridge University Press, 2005.

———. *Civic Virtues: Rights, Citizenship, and Republican Liberalism*. New York and Oxford: Oxford University Press, 1997.

Dalbiez, Roland. *Psychoanalytic Theory and the Doctrine of Freud*. London: Longmans Green & Co., 1941, Vol. 1; 1948, Vol. 2.

Davis, Mike. *Planet of Slums*. London: Verso, 2006.

Davis, Uri. "Martin Buber's Paths in Utopia: The Kibbutz: An Experiment that Didn't Fail?" *Peace News* 2446 (March–June 2002).

Debord, Guy. *The Society of the Spectacle*. Detroit: Black and Red, 1970.

———. *Comments on the Society of the Spectacle*. London: Verso Books, 1990; http://www.notbored.org/commentaires.html.

de La Boétie, Étienne. *The Politics of Obedience: The Discourse of Voluntary Servitude*. New York: Free Life Editions, 1975; http://mises.org/rothbard/boetie.pdf.

Dewey, John. *Liberalism and Social Action*. New York: G.P. Putnam's Sons, 1963.

di Santis, Francesco. *The Post-Katrina Portrait Project* at http://www.flickr.com/photos/postkatrinaportraits/.

———. *The Post-Katrina Portraits, Written and Narrated by Hundreds, Drawn by Francesco di Santis.* New Orleans: Francesco di Santis and Loulou Latta, 2007.

Dolgoff, Sam. *The Anarchist Collectives.* New York: Free Life Editions, 1974.

Dupuis-Déri, Francis. "L'altermondialisation à l'ombre du drapeau noir: L'anarchie en héritage." In *L'altermondialisme en France: La longue histoire d'une nouvelle cause,* edited by Eric Agrikoliansky, Olivier Fillieule, and Nonna Mayer. Paris: Flammarion, 2005.

———. *Les Black Blocs: La liberté et l'égalité se manifestent.* Lyon: Atelier de Création Libertaire, 2005.

———. "Manifestations, altermondialisation et 'groupes d'affinité'. Anarchisme et psychologie des foules rationnelles," presented at the international conference on "Les mobilisations altermondialistes," December 3–5, 2003; http://www.afsp.msh-paris.fr/activite/groupe/germm/collgermm03txt/germm03dupuis.pdf.

Durkheim, Emile. *Selected Writings,* edited by Anthony Giddens. Cambridge, MA: Cambridge University Press, 1972.

Ehrlich, Howard J. *Reinventing Anarchy, Again.* San Francisco: AK Press, 1996.

Ellul, Jacques. *The Technological Society.* New York: Vintage Books, 1964.

Epstein, Barbara. "Anarchism and the Anti-Globalization Movement." *Monthly Review* 53, no. 4 (September 2001): 1–14.

Fifteenth Street Manifesto Group, *Manifesto for a Left Turn: An Open Letter to U.S. Radicals.* New York: Fifteenth Street Manifesto Group, 2008; https://www.asanet.org/sites/default/files/savvy/sectionmarxist/assets/pdf/ManifestoforaLeftTurn-oct.'08.pdf.

Fraser, Ronald. *Blood of Spain: An Oral History of the Spanish Civil War.* New York: Pantheon Books, 1979.

Friedman, Thomas. *The World Is Flat: A Brief History of the Twenty-First Century.* New York: Farrar, Strauss, and Giroux, 2006.

Fukuyama, Francis. "The End of History." *National Interest* 16 (1989): 3–18.

Gandhi, M.K. *Collected Works;* http://www.gandhiserve.org/e/cwmg/cwmg.htm/.

———. "The Definition of Swadeshi" in *The Gospel of Swadeshi;* http://www.mkgandhi.org/gospel/chap01.htm.

———. *Journalist Gandhi: Selected Writings of Gandhi* at http://www.mkgandhi.org/journalist/.

———. "Last Will and Testament"; http://www.gandhimanibhavan.org/eduresources/article15.htm.

———. *Selections from Gandhi* at http://www.mkgandhi-sarvodaya.org/sfgandhi/.

———. *Village Swaraj.* Ahmedabad: Navajivan Publishing House, 1962.

Godwin, William. *Enquiry Concerning Political Justice.* Philadelphia: Bioren and Madan, 1796; http://etext.virginia.edu/toc/modeng/public/GodJust.html.

Goldman, Emma. *Living My Life.* 2 vols. New York: Dover Books, 1970.

———. *Red Emma Speaks: Selected Writings & Speeches by Emma Goldman,* edited by Alix Kates Shulman. New York: Vintage Books, 1972.

Gowder, Paul. "The Liberal Critique of Domination" (presented at 2012 Western Political Science Association conference); http://wpsa.research.pdx.edu/meet/2012/gowder.pdf.

Goyens, Tom. *Beer and Revolution: The German Anarchist Movement in New York City, 1880–1914.* Urbana and Chicago: University of Illinois Press, 2007.

Graeber, David. *Fragments of an Anarchist Anthropology.* Chicago: Prickly Paradigm Press, 2004.

Graham, Robert, ed. *Anarchism: A Documentary History of Libertarian Ideas,* Vol. 1: *From Anarchy to Anarchism* (300CE–1939). (Montreal: Black Rose Books, 2005).

Green, T.H. *Lectures on the Principles of Political Obligation.* Ann Arbor: University of Michigan Press, 1967.

———. *Works of Thomas Hill Green,* 3 vols. London: Longmans, Green, and Co., 1889.

Gundersen, Adolf G. *The Environmental Promise of Democratic Deliberation.* Madison: University of Wisconsin Press, 1995.

Hallowell, Christopher. *Holding Back the Sea: The Struggle for America's Natural Legacy on the Gulf Coast.* New York: HarperCollins, 2001.

Havel, Vaclav. "Between Ideals and Utopias: A Conversation with Vaclav Havel." *East European Reporter* 2, no. 3 (1987): 13–17.

Hegel, G.W.F. "The Earliest System-Programme of German Idealism." In *The Hegel Reader*, edited by Stephen Houlgate, translated by H.S. Harris, 28–29. Malden, MA: Blackwell Publishing, 1998.

———. *Early Theological Writings*, translated by T.M. Knox. Chicago: University of Chicago Press, 1948.

———. *The Phenomenology of Spirit.* Oxford: Oxford University Press, 1977.

———. *The Philosophy of History.* Kitchener, Canada: Batoche Books, 1900; http://www.marxists.org/reference/archive/hegel/works/hi/history3.htm.

———. *Philosophy of Right*, translated by T.M. Knox. London: Clarendon Press, 1952.

———. *Science of Logic*, translated by A.V. Miller. New York: Prometheus Books, 1969.

Hobhouse, L.T. *Liberalism.* New York: Oxford University Press, 1911.

Hoffmire, Farrah. *Falling Together in New Orleans: A Series of Vignettes*; http://www.organicprocess.com.

Holm, Rasmus. *Welcome to New Orleans* at https://www.youtube.com/watch?v=V_lSdR1KZg.

Honohan, Iseult. *Civic Republicanism.* Abingdon, UK: Routledge, 2002.

Horowitz, Irving L. *The Anarchists.* New York: Dell Publishing, 1964.

Hyde, Lewis. *The Gift: Imagination and the Erotic Life of Property.* New York: Vintage Books, 1983.

Invisible Committee, *The Coming Insurrection.* Los Angeles: Semiotext(e), 2009.

Inwood, M.J. *Hegel.* London: Routledge and Kegan Paul, 1983.

Jha, Pranaw Kr. "Chaupal as Multidimensional Public Space for Civil Society in India"; http://www.ignca.nic.in/kmsh0006.htm.

Jones, Arthur. "Small Communities Bear Big Gifts, Study Shows." *National Catholic Reporter*, May 28, 1999; http://annhernandez.com/?page_id=907.

Jun, Nathan. *Anarchism and Political Modernity.* New York: Continuum Books, 2012.

———. "Deleuze, Derrida, and Anarchism." *Anarchist Studies* 15, no. 2 (Fall 2007): 132–56.

Kant, Immanuel. *Foundations of the Metaphysics of Morals.* Indianapolis: Library of Liberal Arts, 1959.

Karatani, Kojin. *Transcritique: On Kant and Marx.* Cambridge, MA: MIT Press, 2005.

Klein, Naomi. *The Shock Doctrine: The Rise of Disaster Capitalism.* New York: Picador Press, 2008.

Kolb, David. *The Critique of Pure Modernity: Hegel, Heidegger, and After.* Chicago: University of Chicago Press, 1986.

Kovel, Joel. *The Age of Desire: Reflections of a Radical Psychoanalyst.* New York: Pantheon Books, 1981.

———. *History and Spirit: An Inquiry into the Philosophy of Liberation.* Boston: Beacon Press, 1991.

———. *White Racism: A Psychohistory.* New York: Columbia University Press, 1984.

Kropotkin, Peter. "Anarchist Communism: Its Basis and Principles"; https://theanarchistlibrary.org/library/petr-kropotkin-anarchist-communism-its-basis-and-principles.

———. "Anarchism: Its Philosophy and Ideal"; https://theanarchistlibrary.org/library/petr-kropotkin-anarchism-its-philosophy-and-ideal.

Landauer, Gustav. *Aufruf zum Sozialismus*; http://www.anarchismus.at/txt2/landauer3.htm.

———. *For Socialism.* St. Louis: Telos Press, 1978.

———. *Revolution and Other Writings: A Political Reader*, edited and translated by Gabriel Kuhn. Oakland: PM Press, 2010.

Laval, Gaston. *Collectives in the Spanish Revolution.* London: Freedom Press, 1975.

Lee, Bernard J., et al. *The Catholic Experience of Small Christian Communities.* New York: Paulist Press, 2000.

Lefebvre, Henri. *The Production of Space*. Oxford and Malden, MA: Blackwell Publishers, 1991.

Le Guin, Ursula K. *Always Coming Home*. New York: Harper and Row, 1985.

———. *The Dispossessed*. New York: Harper and Row, 1974.

———. *The Left Hand of Darkness*. New York: Berkeley Publishing Group, 1969.

Lewis, Beverly. (Writer and director), "American Utopia." Firefly Productions and Louisiana Public Broadcasting, 1994.

Liebling, A.J. "The Wayward Press." *The New Yorker* (May 14, 1960).

Linebaugh, Peter. *The Magna Carta Manifesto*. Berkeley: University of California Press, 2008.

Lovett, Frank. *A General Theory of Domination and Justice*. Oxford: Oxford University Press, 2010.

———. "Reconstructing Republican Freedom: A Critique of the Neo-Republican Concept of Freedom as Non-domination." Forthcoming in *Philosophy and Social Criticism*.

———. "Republicanism" in *Stanford Encyclopedia of Philosophy* (article revised May 18, 2010) at http://plato.stanford.edu/entries/republicanism/.

Luccarelli, Mark. *Lewis Mumford and the Ecological Region*. New York: Guilford Press, 1995.

MacEoin, Gary. "Communities Offer Hope for Church, Society," *National Catholic Reporter* (September 20, 2002); http://natcath.org/NCR_Online/archives2/2002c/092002/092002z.htm.

Macy, Joanna. "For the Awakening of All: The Sarvodaya Shramadana Movement in Sri Lanka" in *Karuna: A Journal of Buddhist Meditation* (Summer/Fall 1988), http://www.buddhanet.net/ftp03.htm.

———. *The Path of Compassion*. Berkeley: Parallax Press, 1988.

Mannheim, Karl. *Ideology and Utopia*. New York: Harcourt, Brace and World, 1936.

Marcuse, Herbert. *Eros and Civilization: A Philosophical Inquiry into Freud*. Boston: Beacon Press, 1966.

———. *One-Dimensional Man: Studies in the Ideology of Advanced Industrial Society*. Boston: Beacon Press, 1964.

Marshall, Peter. *Demanding the Impossible: A History of Anarchism*. London: HarperCollins, 1992.

———. *William Godwin*. New Haven, CT: Yale University Press, 1984.

Martin, Alex. "On a Street Named Desire" in *Newsday*, September 26, 2005, http://www.michaelmoore.com/words/katrina-updates/on-a-street-named-desire.

Martin, James J. *Men against the State*. DeKalb, IL: Adrian Allen Associates, 1953; Colorado Springs, CO: Ralph Myles Publisher, 1970.

Marx, Karl. *Capital: A Critique of Political Economy*, Vol. 1; http://www. marxists.org/archive/marx/works/1867-c1/.

———. "Critique of the Gotha Program"; http://www.marxists.org/archive/marx/ works/1875/gotha/ch04.htm.

———. *The Poverty of Philosophy*. Moscow: Progress Publishers, 1955; http://www.marxists.org/archive/marx/works/1847/poverty-philosophy/ch02.htm.

Marx, Karl, and Friedrich Engels. *Die deutsche Ideologie*. Moscow: Marx-Engels-Lenin Institute, 1932; http://mlwerke.de/me/me03/me03_017.htm.

May, Todd. *The Political Philosophy of Poststructuralist Anarchism*. University Park: Pennsylvania State University Press, 1994.

McPhee, John. *The Control of Nature*. New York: Farrar Straus Giroux, 1989.

Michels, Robert. *Political Parties: A Sociological Study of the Oligarchical Tendencies of Modern Democracy*. New York: Hearst's International Library, 1915.

Mondragon Corporation official website; http://www.mcc.es/ENG.aspx. In *I Am Not a Man, I Am Dynamite: Friedrich Nietzsche and the Anarchist Tradition*, edited by Moore, John and Sunshine, Spencer. Brooklyn: Autonomedia, 2004.

Mumford, Lewis. "Authoritarian and Democratic Technics." *Technology and Culture* 5, no. 1 (Winter 1964): 1–8.

———. *The City in History*. New York: Harcourt, Brace & World, 1961.

———. *The Pentagon of Power*. San Diego, New York, and London: Harcourt Brace Jovanovich, 1970.

———. *Technics and Human Development*. New York: Harcourt Brace Jovanovich, 1967.

Newland, Sherwin B. *The Wisdom of the Body*. New York: Alfred A. Knopf, 1997.

Nichols, Robert. *Daily Lives in Nghsi-Altai*, 4 vols. New York: New Directions Books, 1977–79.

———. *Red Shift*. Thetford, VT: Penny Each Press, 1977.

———. *Travels in Altai*. Enfield, NH: Glad Day Books, 1999.

Notes from Nowhere, ed. *We Are Everywhere: The Irresistible Rise of Global Anticapitalism*. London: Verso, 2003.

Nussbaum, Martha. "Capabilities as Fundamental Entitlements: Sen and Social Justice." *Feminist Economics* 9 (July 2003): 33–59.

———. *Women and Human Development: The Capabilities Approach*. Cambridge: Cambridge University Press, 2000.

Ostergaard, Geoffrey, and Melville Currell. *The Gentle Anarchists: A Study of the Sarvodaya Movement for Non-violent Revolution in India*. Oxford: Clarendon Press, 1971.

Ostrom, Elinor, and Harini Nagendra. "Insights on Linking Forests, Trees, and People from the Air, on the Ground, and in the Laboratory." *Proceedings of the National Academy of Sciences* 103, no. 51 (December 19, 2006): 19224–31.

Pascal, René. *Pensées*. New York: Dutton, 1958; http://www.gutenberg.org/files/18269/18269-h/18269-h.htm.

Pelczynski, Z.A. "Political Community and Individual Freedom in Hegel's Philosophy of State"; http://www.works/ot/pelczyns.htm.

Pettit, Philip. "Keeping Republican Freedom Simple: On a Difference with Quentin Skinner." *Political Theory* 30, no. 3 (June 2002): 339–56.

———. *Republicanism: A Theory of Freedom and Government*. Oxford: Oxford University Press, 1997.

Pippin, Robert. *Hegel's Practical Philosophy*. Cambridge, MA: Cambridge University Press, 2008.

Plato. *The Republic of Plato*, edited and translated by Alan Bloom. New York and London: Basic Books, 1968.

Plotkin, Mark J. *Tales of a Shaman's Apprentice: An Ethnobotanist Searches for New Medicines in the Amazon Rainforest*. New York: Viking Press, 1993.

Rancière, Jacques. *Hatred of Democracy*. London: Verso, 2006.

Razsa, Maple, and Andrej Kurnik. "The Occupy Movement in Žižek's Hometown: Direct Democracy and a Politics of Becoming." *American Ethnologist* 39, no. 2 (May 2012): 238–58.

Reclus, Elisée. *Correspondance*, 3 vols. Paris: Alfred Costes, 1925.

———. *L'Homme et la Terre*, 6 vols. Paris: Librairie Universelle, 1905–8.

———. *A Voyage to New Orleans: Anarchist Impressions of the Old South*, translated and edited by John Clark and Camille Martin. Thetford, VT: Glad Day Books, 2004.

Redding, Paul. *Hegel's Hermeneutics*. Ithaca, NY: Cornell University Press, 1996.

Reich, Wilhelm. *The Mass Psychology of Fascism*. New York: Simon and Schuster, 1970.

Ricoeur, Paul. *Lectures on Ideology and Utopia*. New York: Columbia University Press, 1986.

Ritter, Alan. *Anarchism: A Theoretical Analysis*. Cambridge: Cambridge University Press, 1980.

Rosemont, Franklin. *Revolution in the Service of the Marvelous*. Chicago: Charles H. Kerr Publishing, 2004.

Rousseau, Jean-Jacques. *The Social Contract*; http://www.marxists.org/ reference/subject/economics/rousseau/social-contract/.

Roy, Arundhati. *The Cost of Living*. New York: Modern Library, 1999.

———. "The Greater Common Good." *Frontline* 16, no. 11 (May 22–June 4, 1999); http://www.hindu.com/fline/fl1611/16110040.htm.

Salleh, Ariel, ed. *Eco-Sufficiency & Global Justice: Women Write Political Ecology*. London: Pluto Press, 2009.

————. *Ecofeminism as Politics: Nature, Marx and the Postmodern.* London: Zed Books, 1997.

————. "Second Thoughts on Rethinking Ecofeminist Politics: A Dialectical Critique." *Interdisciplinary Studies in Literature and Environment* 1 (Fall 1993): 97.

Sarvodaya Shramdana Movement official website; http://www.sarvodaya.org/.

Sen, Amartya. *Development as Freedom.* New York: Knopf, 1999.

Shiva, Vandana. *Earth Democracy: Justice, Sustainability, and Peace.* Cambridge, MA: South End Press, 2005.

Simmel, Georg. "Group Expansion and the Development of Individuality." In *Georg Simmel on Individuality and Social Form,* edited by Donald N. Levine. Chicago: University of Chicago Press, 1971.

Skinner, Quentin. *Liberty before Liberalism.* Cambridge, MA: Cambridge University Press, 1998.

————. "A Third Concept of Liberty." *Proceedings of the British Academy* 117 (2002): 237–68.

Snyder, Gary. *Practice of the Wild.* San Francisco: North Point Press, 1990.

Solnit, Rebecca. *A Paradise Built in Hell: The Extraordinary Communities That Arise in Disaster.* New York: Viking, 2009.

Starhawk, "Affinity Groups"; http://www.starhawk.org/activism/affinitygroups.html.

————. *The Fifth Sacred Thing.* New York: Bantam Books, 1993.

Sunshine, Spencer. "Nietzsche and the Anarchists." *Fifth Estate* 367 (Winter 2004–5): 36–37.

Thalberg, Irving. "Visceral Racism." *The Monist* 56 (1972): 43–63.

Thoreau, Henry David. "Walking"; http://thoreau.eserver.org/walking2.html.

Tidwell, Mike. *Bayou Farewell: The Rich Life and Tragic Death of Louisiana's Cajun Coast.* New York: Vintage Books, 2003.

Tomasello, Michael. *Why We Cooperate.* Cambridge, MA: MIT Press, 2009.

Van Heerden, Ivor, and Mike Bryan. *The Storm: What Went Wrong and Why during Hurricane Katrina—The Inside Story from One Louisiana Scientist.* New York: Viking, 2006.

Vettickal, Thomas. *Gandhian Sarvodaya: Realizing a Realistic Utopia.* New Delhi: Gyan Publishing House, 2002.

Walzer, Michael. *Spheres of Justice: A Defense of Pluralism and Equality.* New York: Basic Books, 1983.

Watson, David. *Against the Megamachine: Essays on Empire and Its Enemies.* Brooklyn: Autonomedia, 1998.

————. *Beyond Bookchin: Preface to a Future Social Ecology.* Brooklyn: Autonomedia, 1996.

Weber, Max. *The Theory of Social and Economic Organization,* ed. Talcott Parsons. New York: Free Press, 1964.

Weerawarne, Samudhu. "Dr. A. T. Ariyaratne at Close Quarters." *LMD-Sri Lanka's Business and Leisure Magazine* 6, no. 7 (February 2000).

Williams, Robert R. *Hegel's Ethics of Recognition.* Berkeley: University of California Press, 1997.

Winner, Langdon. *Autonomous Technology.* Cambridge, MA: MIT Press, 1977.

Woodcock, George. *Anarchism: A History of Libertarian Ideas and Movements.* New York: World Publishing, 1962.

Zibechi, Raúl. *Dispersing Power: Social Movements as Anti-state Forces* (Oakland: AK Press, 2010).

Žižek, Slavoj. "Hegel and Shitting: The Idea's Constipation." In *Hegel and the Infinite: Religion, Politics, and Dialectic,* edited by Slavoj Žižek, Clayton Crockett, and Creston Davis, 221–31. New York: Columbia University Press, 2011.

————. *How to Read Lacan.* New York: Norton, 2006.

————. *In Defense of Lost Causes.* London: Verso, 2008.

————. *Less Than Nothing: Hegel and the Shadow of Dialectical Materialism.* London: Verso, 2012.

————. *The Ticklish Subject.* London: Verso, 1999.

Index

"Passim" (literally "scattered") indicates intermittent discussion of a topic over a cluster of pages.

About the Author

John P. Clark is a philosopher, activist, and educator. His books include *The Anarchist Moment*; *Anarchy, Geography, Modernity*; and *Between Earth and Empire*, and, as Max Cafard, *The Surregionalist Manifesto and Other Writings*, *Surregional Explorations*, and *Lightning Storm Mind*. He is director of La Terre Institute for Community and Ecology.

ABOUT PM PRESS

PM Press is an independent, radical publisher of books and media to educate, entertain, and inspire. Founded in 2007 by a small group of people with decades of publishing, media, and organizing experience, PM Press amplifies the voices of radical authors, artists, and activists. Our aim is to deliver bold political ideas and vital stories to all walks of life and arm the dreamers to demand the impossible. We have sold millions of copies of our books, most often one at a time, face to face. We're old enough to know what we're doing and young enough to know what's at stake. Join us to create a better world.

PM Press
PO Box 23912
Oakland, CA 94623
www.pmpress.org

PM Press in Europe
europe@pmpress.org
www.pmpress.org.uk

FRIENDS OF PM PRESS

These are indisputably momentous times—the financial system is melting down globally and the Empire is stumbling. Now more than ever there is a vital need for radical ideas.

In the many years since its founding—and on a mere shoestring—PM Press has risen to the formidable challenge of publishing and distributing knowledge and entertainment for the struggles ahead. With hundreds of releases to date, we have published an impressive and stimulating array of literature, art, music, politics, and culture. Using every available medium, we've succeeded in connecting those hungry for ideas and information to those putting them into practice.

Friends of PM allows you to directly help impact, amplify, and revitalize the discourse and actions of radical writers, filmmakers, and artists. It provides us with a stable foundation from which we can build upon our early successes and provides a much-needed subsidy for the materials that can't necessarily pay their own way. You can help make that happen—and receive every new title automatically delivered to your door once a month—by joining as a Friend of PM Press. And, we'll throw in a free T-shirt when you sign up.

Here are your options:

- **$30 a month** Get all books and pamphlets plus 50% discount on all webstore purchases

- **$40 a month** Get all PM Press releases (including CDs and DVDs) plus 50% discount on all webstore purchases

- **$100 a month** Superstar—Everything plus PM merchandise, free downloads, and 50% discount on all webstore purchases

For those who can't afford $30 or more a month, we have **Sustainer Rates** at $15, $10, and $5. Sustainers get a free PM Press T-shirt and a 50% discount on all purchases from our website.

Your Visa or Mastercard will be billed once a month, until you tell us to stop. Or until our efforts succeed in bringing the revolution around. Or the financial meltdown of Capital makes plastic redundant. Whichever comes first.

Anarchy, Geography, Modernity: Selected Writings of Elisée Reclus

Edited and translated by John P. Clark and Camille Martin

ISBN: 978-1-60486-429-8

$22.95   304 pages

Anarchy, Geography, Modernity is the first comprehensive introduction to the thought of Elisée Reclus, the great anarchist geographer and political theorist. It shows him to be an extraordinary figure for his age. Not only an anarchist but also a radical feminist, anti-racist, ecologist, animal rights advocate, cultural radical, nudist, and vegetarian. Not only a major social thinker but also a dedicated revolutionary.

The work analyzes Reclus' greatest achievement, a sweeping historical and theoretical synthesis recounting the story of the earth and humanity as an epochal struggle between freedom and domination. It presents his groundbreaking critique of all forms of domination: not only capitalism, the state, and authoritarian religion, but also patriarchy, racism, technological domination, and the domination of nature. His crucial insights on the interrelation between personal and small-group transformation, broader cultural change, and large-scale social organization are explored. Reclus' ideas are presented both through detailed exposition and analysis, and in extensive translations of key texts, most appearing in English for the first time.

"For far too long Elisée Reclus has stood in the shadow of Godwin, Proudhon, Bakunin, Kropotkin, and Emma Goldman. Now John Clark has pulled Reclus forward to stand shoulder to shoulder with Anarchism's cynosures. Reclus' light brought into anarchism's compass not only a focus on ecology, but a struggle against both patriarchy and racism, contributions which can now be fully appreciated thanks to John Clark's exegesis and [his and Camille Martin's] translations of works previously unavailable in English. No serious reader can afford to neglect this book."
—Dana Ward, Pitzer College

"Finally! A century after his death, the great French geographer and anarchist Elisée Reclus has been honored by a vibrant selection of his writings expertly translated into English."
—Kent Mathewson, Louisiana State University

Mutual Aid: An Illuminated Factor of Evolution

Peter Kropotkin
Illustrated by N.O. Bonzo with an
Introduction by David Graeber & Andrej
Grubačić, Foreword by Ruth Kinna,
Postscript by GATS, and an Afterword
by Allan Antliff

ISBN: 978-1-62963-874-4
$20.00   336 pages

One hundred years after his death, Peter Kropotkin is still one of the most inspirational figures of the anarchist movement. It is often forgotten that Kropotkin was also a world-renowned geographer whose seminal critique of the hypothesis of competition promoted by social Darwinism helped revolutionize modern evolutionary theory. An admirer of Darwin, he used his observations of life in Siberia as the basis for his 1902 collection of essays *Mutual Aid: A Factor of Evolution*. Kropotkin demonstrated that mutually beneficial cooperation and reciprocity—in both individuals and as a species—plays a far more important role in the animal kingdom and human societies than does individualized competitive struggle. Kropotkin carefully crafted his theory making the science accessible. His account of nature rejected Rousseau's romantic depictions and ethical socialist ideas that cooperation was motivated by the notion of "universal love." His understanding of the dynamics of social evolution shows us the power of cooperation—whether it is bison defending themselves against a predator or workers unionizing against their boss. His message is clear: solidarity is strength!

Every page of this new edition of *Mutual Aid* has been beautifully illustrated by one of anarchism's most celebrated current artists, N.O. Bonzo. The reader will also enjoy original artwork by GATS and insightful commentary by David Graeber, Ruth Kinna, Andrej Grubačić, and Allan Antliff.

"N.O. Bonzo has created a rare document, updating Kropotkin's anarchist classic Mutual Aid, *by intertwining compelling imagery with an updated text. Filled with illustrious examples, their art gives the words and histories, past and present, resonance for new generations to seed flowers of cooperation to push through the concrete of resistance to show liberatory possibilities for collective futures."*
—scott crow, author of *Black Flags and Windmills* and *Setting Sights*

Revolution and Other Writings: A Political Reader

Gustav Landauer

Edited and translated by Gabriel Kuhn

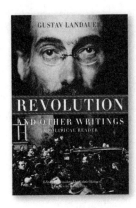

ISBN: 978-1-60486-054-2

$26.95   360 pages

"*Landauer is the most important agitator of the radical and revolutionary movement in the entire country.*" This is how Gustav Landauer is described in a German police file from 1893. Twenty-six years later, Landauer would die at the hands of reactionary soldiers who overthrew the Bavarian Council Republic, a three-week attempt to realize libertarian socialism amidst the turmoil of post-World War I Germany. It was the last chapter in the life of an activist, writer, and mystic who Paul Avrich calls "the most influential German anarchist intellectual of the twentieth century."

This is the first comprehensive collection of Landauer writings in English. It includes one of his major works, *Revolution*, thirty additional essays and articles, and a selection of correspondence. The texts cover Landauer's entire political biography, from his early anarchism of the 1890s to his philosophical reflections at the turn of the century, the subsequent establishment of the Socialist Bund, his tireless agitation against the war, and the final days among the revolutionaries in Munich. Additional chapters collect Landauer's articles on radical politics in the US and Mexico, and illustrate the scope of his writing with texts on corporate capital, language, education, and Judaism. The book includes an extensive introduction, commentary, and bibliographical information, compiled by the editor and translator Gabriel Kuhn as well as a preface by Richard Day.

"*If there were any justice in this world—at least as far as historical memory goes—then Gustav Landauer would be remembered, right along with Bakunin and Kropotkin, as one of anarchism's most brilliant and original theorists. Instead, history has abetted the crime of his murderers, burying his work in silence. With this anthology, Gabriel Kuhn has single-handedly redressed one of the cruelest gaps in Anglo-American anarchist literature: the absence of almost any English translations of Landauer.*"
—Jesse Cohn, author of *Anarchism and the Crisis of Representation: Hermeneutics, Aesthetics, Politics*

"*Gustav Landauer was, without doubt, one of the brightest intellectual lights within the revolutionary circles of fin de siècle Europe. In this remarkable anthology, Gabriel Kuhn brings together an extensive and splendidly chosen collection of Landauer's most important writings, presenting them for the first time in English translation. With Landauer's ideas coming of age today perhaps more than ever before, Kuhn's work is a valuable and timely piece of scholarship, and one which should be required reading for anyone with an interest in radical social change.*"
—James Horrox, author of *A Living Revolution: Anarchism in the Kibbutz Movement*

Between Earth and Empire: From the Necrocene to the Beloved Community

John P. Clark
with a Foreword by Peter Marshall

ISBN: 978-1-62963-648-1
$22.95   352 pages

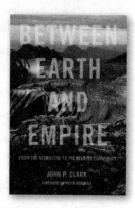

Between Earth and Empire focuses on the crucial position of humanity at the present moment in Earth History. We have left the Cenozoic, the "new period of life," and are now in the midst of the Necrocene, a period of mass extinction and reversal of the course of evolution of life on Earth. We are now nearing the end of the long history of Empire and domination, faced with the alternatives of either continuing the path of social and ecological disintegration or initiating a new era of social and ecological regeneration.

The book shows that conventional approaches to global crisis on both the right and the left have succumbed to processes of denial and disavowal, either rejecting the reality of crisis entirely or substituting ineffectual but comforting gestures and images for deep, systemic social transformation. It is argued that an effective response to global crisis requires attention to all major spheres of social determination, including the social institutional structure, the social ideology, the social imaginary, and the social ethos. Large-scale social and ecological regeneration must be rooted in communities of liberation and solidarity, in which personal and group transformation take place in all these spheres, so that a culture of awakening and care can emerge.

Between Earth and Empire explores examples of significant progress in this direction, including the Zapatista movement in Chiapas, the Democratic Autonomy Movement in Rojava, indigenous movements in defense of the commons, the solidarity economy movement, and efforts to create liberated base communities and affinity groups within anarchism and other radical social movements. In the end, the book presents a vision of hope for social and ecological regeneration through the rebirth of a libertarian and communitarian social imaginary, and the flourishing of a free cooperative community globally.

"Whether in Rojava where women are fighting for their people's survival, or in the loss and terror of New Orleans after the Katrina flood, Clark finds models of communality, care, and hope. Finely reasoned and integrative, tracing the dialectical play of institution and ethos, ideology and imaginary, this book will speak to philosophers and activists alike."
—Ariel Salleh, author of *Ecofeminism as Politics*

Autonomy Is in Our Hearts: Zapatista Autonomous Government through the Lens of the Tsotsil Language

Dylan Eldredge Fitzwater
with a Foreword by John P. Clark

ISBN: 978-1-62963-580-4
$19.95   224 pages

Following the Zapatista uprising on New Year's Day 1994, the EZLN communities of Chiapas began the slow process of creating a system of autonomous government that would bring their call for freedom, justice, and democracy from word to reality. *Autonomy Is in Our Hearts* analyzes this long and arduous process on its own terms, using the conceptual language of Tsotsil, a Mayan language indigenous to the highland Zapatista communities of Chiapas.

The words "Freedom," "Justice," and "Democracy" emblazoned on the Zapatista flags are only approximations of the aspirations articulated in the six indigenous languages spoken by the Zapatista communities. They are rough translations of concepts such as *ichbail ta muk'* or "mutual recognition and respect among equal persons or peoples," *a'mtel* or "collective work done for the good of a community" and *lekil kuxlejal* or "the life that is good for everyone." *Autonomy Is in Our Hearts* provides a fresh perspective on the Zapatistas and a deep engagement with the daily realities of Zapatista autonomous government. Simultaneously an exposition of Tsotsil philosophy and a detailed account of Zapatista governance structures, this book is an indispensable commentary on the Zapatista movement of today.

"This is a refreshing book. Written with the humility of the learner, or the absence of the arrogant knower, the Zapatista dictum to 'command obeying' becomes to 'know learning.'"
—Marisol de la Cadena, author of *Earth Beings: Ecologies of Practice across Andean Worlds*

"Autonomy Is in Our Hearts is perhaps the most important book you can read on the Zapatista movement in Chiapas today. It stands out from the rest of the Anglophone literature in that it demonstrates, with great sensitivity, how a dialectic between traditional culture and institutions and emerging revolutionary and regenerative forces can play a crucial role in liberatory social transformation. It shows us what we can learn from the indigenous people of Chiapas about a politics of community, care, and mutual aid, and—to use a word that they themselves use so much—about a politics of heart. A great strength of the work is that the author is a very good listener. He allows the people of Chiapas to tell their own story largely in their own words, and with their own distinctive voice."
—John P. Clark, from the Foreword

Black Flags and Windmills:
Hope, Anarchy, and the Common Ground Collective

scott crow with forewords
by Kathleen Cleaver and John P. Clark

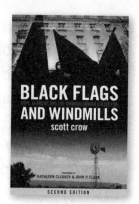

ISBN: 978-1-60486-453-3
$20.00   288 pages

When both levees and governments failed in New
Orleans after Hurricane Katrina, the anarchist-
inspired Common Ground Collective was created to fill the void. With the motto
of "Solidarity Not Charity," they worked to create power from below—building
autonomous projects, programs, and spaces of self-sufficiency like health clinics
and neighborhood assemblies, while also supporting communities defending
themselves from white militias and police brutality, illegal home demolitions, and
evictions.

Black Flags and Windmills—equal parts memoir, history, and organizing philosophy—
vividly intertwines Common Ground cofounder scott crow's experiences and ideas
with Katrina's reality, illustrating how people can build local grassroots power for
collective liberation. It is a story of resisting indifference, rebuilding hope amid
collapse, and struggling against the grain to create better worlds.

The expanded second edition includes up-to-date interviews and discussions
between crow and some of today's most articulate and influential activists and
organizers on topics ranging from grassroots disaster relief efforts (both economic
and environmental); dealing with infiltration, interrogation, and surveillance from
the State; and a new photo section that vividly portrays scott's experiences as an
anarchist, activist, and movement organizer in today's world.

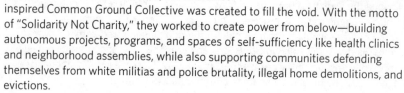

*"scott crow's trenchant memoir of grassroots organizing is an important contribution to
a history of movements that far too often goes untold."*
—Amy Goodman, host and executive producer of *Democracy Now!*

*"This revised and expanded edition weaves scott crow's frontline experiences with a
resilient, honest discussion of grassroots political movement-building."*
—Will Potter, author of *Green Is the New Red: An Insider's Account of a Social
Movement Under Siege*

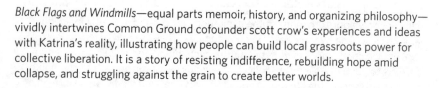

*"It is a brilliant, detailed, and humble book written with total frankness and at the same
time a revolutionary poet's passion. It makes the reader feel that we too, with our
emergency heart as our guide, can do anything; we only need to begin."*
—Marina Sitrin, author of *Horizontalism: Voices of Popular Power in Argentina*